MENTAL WELLNESS
IN AGING

MENTAL WELLNESS IN AGING

STRENGTHS-BASED APPROACHES

edited by

Judah L. Ronch, Ph.D.

and

Joseph A. Goldfield, M.S.W.

HEALTH
PROFESSIONS
PRESS

Baltimore • London • Winnipeg • Sydney

HEALTH
PROFESSIONS
PRESS

Health Professions Press, Inc.
Post Office Box 10624
Baltimore, MD 21285-0624

www.healthpropress.com

Typeset by Integrated Publishing Solutions, Grand Rapids, Michigan.
Manufactured in the United States of America by
Versa Press, Inc., East Peoria, Illinois.

This book is in no way meant to substitute for a physician's
advice or expert opinion; readers should consult a medical
practitioner if they are interested in more information.

Most individuals described herein are composites, pseudonyms,
or fictional and based on actual experiences. Individuals' names
have been changed and identifying details have been altered
to protect confidentiality.

Library of Congress Cataloging-in-Publication Data
Mental wellness in aging : strengths-based approaches /
edited by Judah L. Ronch and Joseph A. Goldfield.
    p.   cm.
  Includes bibliographical references and index.
  ISBN 1-878812-69-6
  1. Aged—Mental health.   I. Ronch, Judah L.
  II. Goldfield, Joseph. A.
  RC451.4.A5   M4627   2003
  362.2'084'6—dc21   2002038868

British Library of Cataloguing in Publication data
are available from the British Library.

CONTENTS

ABOUT THE EDITORS

Judah L. Ronch, Ph.D., is Executive Clinical Director and Founder of LifeSpan DevelopMental Systems, an organization that has established numerous creative, inter-disciplinary clinical and training programs to meet the mental health needs of older adults in various parts of the United States. Dr. Ronch consults with the New York State Depart-ment of Health on person-centered care for people with Alzheimer's disease; in nursing homes, assisted living, and adult care facilities. Prior to this position he served on the allied health services staff of the Department of Internal Medicine at Vassar Brothers Hospital in Poughkeepsie, New York, and as Director of the Four Winds Geriatric Service at the Four Winds Hospital in Katonah, New York. Dr. Ronch, Vice President of the Board of Directors of the Gerontological Institute, State University of New York in New Paltz, has served on numerous other boards and committees including the Dementia Advisory committee of the New York State Department of Health. Dr. Ronch is former director of the Brookdale Center on Aging at Hunter College of the City University of New York. He has written or contributed to numerous books devoted to issues of aging and strengths-based gerontological approaches, including *The Counseling Sourcebook* (edited with Van-Ornum & Stilwell, Crossroad Publishing Company, 1994) and *Alzheimer's Disease: A Prac-tical Guide for Those Who Help Others* (Crossroad-Continuum, 1989). In addition, he has published in various journals including *Counseling the Aging and Their Families, American Journal of Alzheimer's Disease, Nursing Home Economics,* and *American Journal of Alzheimer's Care and Research.*

Joseph A. Goldfield, M.S.W., received his master's of social work from the University of California at Berkeley. For the past 15 years he has been a nationally recognized lec-turer and teacher of strengths-based approaches to psychotherapy. He maintains a private practice in New York City, where he also provides consultation on strengths-based inter-ventions to agencies serving aging clients.

A faculty member of the Brookdale Center on Aging at Hunter College of the City University of New York, Mr. Goldfield also serves as an advisor to various behavioral managed care companies. As an experienced disaster/trauma counselor, Mr. Goldfield was extensively involved in the aftermath of the attacks on the World Trade Center on Sep-tember 11, 2001.

CONTRIBUTORS

Robert C. Atchley, Ph.D.
Chairman
Department of Gerontology
Naropa University
2130 Arapahoe Avenue
Boulder, Colorado 80302

Rona S. Bartelstone, M.S.W., LCSW, BCD, CMC
Chief Executive Officer and Founder
Rona Bartelstone Associates, Inc.
2699 Stirling Road
Suite C-304
Fort Lauderdale, Florida 33312

Anne Davis Basting, Ph.D.
Director
Time*Slips* Project
18 Rutland Road
Brooklyn, New York 11225

Marilyn J. Bonjean, Ed.D.
ICF Consultants, Inc.
1524 N. Farwell Avenue
Milwaukee, Wisconsin 53202

Gene Cohen, M.D., Ph.D.
Director
Center on Aging, Health,
   and Humanities
George Washington University
10225 Montgomery Avenue
Kensington, Maryland 20895

Alan Dienstag, Psy.D.
Clinical Psychologist
Private Practice
525 W. 238th Street, Apartment 4J
Bronx, New York 10463

Joseph B. Eron, Psy.D.
Catskill Family Institute
112 N. Front Street
Post Office Box 3901
Kingston, New York 12402

Sheldon L. Goldberg
President and Chief Executive Officer
Alzheimer's Association
919 North Michigan Avenue
Suite 1100
Chicago, Illinois 60611

Raymond Grimm, Ph.D.
Counselor and Coordinator
Senior Peer Counseling Program
Human Services Department
City of Fremont
Fremont, California 94537

Gary J. Kennedy, M.D.
Director
Division of Geriatric Psychiatry
Montefiore Medical Center
The University Hospital for the
   Albert Einstein College of Medicine
111 E. 210th Street
Bronx, New York 10467

Thomas W. Lund, Psy.D.
Catskill Family Institute
112 N. Front Street
Post Office Box 3901
Kingston, New York 12402

Scott D. Miller, Ph.D.
Co-director
Institute for the Study of Therapeutic
   Change
Post Office Box 578264
Chicago, Illinois 60657

Harry R. Moody, Ph.D.
Senior Associate
International Longevity Center—USA
60 E. 86th Street
New York, New York 10021

Lawrence Polivka, Ph.D.
Director and Associate Professor
Florida Policy Exchange Center on Aging
USF 30437
4202 E. Fowler Avenue
Tampa, Florida 33620

Jennifer R. Salmon, Ph.D.
Assistant Director
Florida Policy Exchange Center on Aging
University of South Florida
Tampa, Florida 33620

Jack Saul, Ph.D.
Director, International Trauma Studies
  Program
New York University
Clinical Assistant Professor, Department
  of Psychiatry
New York University School of Medicine
114 E. 32nd Street
New York, New York 10016

Raymond Vickers, M.D.
Retired Professor
Department of Family Practice
Brody School of Medicine
East Carolina University
200 Lee Street
Greenville, North Carolina 27858

Audrey Weiner, D.S.W.
President and Chief Executive Officer
The Jewish Home and Hospital
120 West 106th Street
New York, New York 10025

ACKNOWLEDGMENTS

As editors of this volume, we owe an unlimited amount of gratitude to our colleagues who accepted our invitation to participate in fulfilling our vision for this book. We knew that if our idea for this project was to be realized, we would have to ask a highly respected—and very busy—group of gifted professionals to believe that this warranted putting other responsibilities on hold to meet the timetable we set for them. They did so with generosity and grace, though this meant changing already overcommitted work and travel schedules. We appreciate their enthusiastic support for this endeavor and especially their enthusiasm as the work evolved.

The staff at Health Professions Press have been an absolute joy to work with. Director of Publications Mary Magnus embraced the project from our first conversation about it. She not only helped to frame the ideas we wanted the book to communicate but also provided insight about the book's content and kept us on track with production timelines. That this book has been published is in large part a tribute to her visionary understanding that mental health and quality aging come together synergistically when people's strengths are engaged.

Our thanks also go to Hope Brown and Leslie Eckard, production editors, for their careful attention to the many details involved at each production stage of the book, and to Anita McCabe for promoting this book as expertly as she has. We appreciate the work they did to finish the process of getting the book into the hands of readers.

We also want to thank all of the colleagues and students from whom we have each learned in our separate and collaborative journeys; they informed our work together on this project.

Each of us has the pleasure of acknowledging here the people whose support and confidence allowed our strengths to be applied to this book.

———

My thinking about strengths-based work with individuals and organizations was shaped in large part by many hours of discussions with Joe Eron and Tom Lund. I thank them for their collegiality and their ability to laugh at the absurdities of life that distract us from who we really are and what we are here for. I also want to thank my colleagues at the Marjorie Doyle Rockwell Center and the Eddy, a division of Northeast Health, and the New York State Department of Health,

Division of Community Based and Long-Term Care. During our collaboration that began in 1995, I have been given the unique opportunity to apply strengths-based approaches to the care of people with Alzheimer's and related dementias in the Electronic Dementia Guide for Excellence (EDGE), a project funded by a grant from the New York State Department of Health. Ann Marie Bradley, Liz Pohlmann, Nancy Cummings, Dave Howells, and Anne Gibson were especially instrumental during this project in helping me convert theory into practice.

None of this work would have been possible without the support and encouragement of my wife and colleague, Robin Doremus. Her insights about the best ways to care for older adults have informed my work through the years. I appreciate most of all the generosity, grace, and good humor with which she tolerated the many hours that I was shut away in my study doing yet another project that devoured more of my attention and our time together than was fair to her.

Judah L. Ronch

I thank my wife Pauline for her love, support, insight, and patience. Thanks also go to my longtime friend Daniel Halkin for his reliable wisdom and to Matthew Caron for his conceptual assistance and technical help. Finally, I thank my parents, Albert and Bina Goldfield, for the beautiful example of successful aging they have given me.

Joseph A. Goldfield

Foreword

Blurring the Lines, Expanding the Vision

At a recent family gathering, my mother, father, two brothers, and I were looking through some old photograph albums. Some of the pictures were nearly 100 years old; most were of our immediately family and more recent. We laughed out loud at some of the clothing and hairstyles we'd all worn—especially those broad-collar, floral-print, open-neck shirts; the super-wide bell-bottom jeans; and the Peter Frampton perms of the 1970s. There was a palpable silence when a turn of the pages brought pictures of family members and other relatives who were no longer with us. Our grandparents in particular had been an active and regular part of our early family life. Now, with the exception of the photos and our memories, they are all gone.

At some point, we began comparing pictures of our parents with those of our grandparents. By using the dates printed at the bottom of the pictures or written on the back, we were able to assemble a small number of images of our parents and grandparents at the same chronological age. We all agreed that our grandparents looked older.

Now, I must admit that as a child, my grandparents on both sides of the family seemed rather ancient to me. Everything about them—their lifestyle, energy level, manner of dress, home decor, even the reruns of the Lawrence Welk show we endured on family visits—screamed "old." There was never any question in my mind that they were from a different time and place. The photographs made clear that something had changed between the two generations. First of all, our parents simply seemed more hip (e.g., hairstyle and color, clothing). Moreover, in spite of each having dealt with serious and, in the case of our mother, life-threatening illnesses, our parents looked *physically* younger than their parents did at the same age.

I am sure that the differences in aging that my family observed are not unique to our family. From their active and engaged, postemployment lifestyle, involvement in current affairs, and adaptation to technological and social change, my parents, along with the current generation of retirees, are in fact blurring the once clear lines between youth and old age. In the process, the vision of possibilities for a vital and meaningful life as people grow older is expanding. Indeed, the 1990s witnessed a growing number of publications, web sites, and organizations dedicated to helping people age well.

Significant challenges lie ahead, not the least of which is overhauling a health care system organized around a view of aging that is more characteristic of our grandparents' than our parents' generation. In the electronic newsletter *Positive Aging*, editors Ken and Mary Gergen noted that although attitudes of the general public have become more focused on positive approaches to aging, "some 90% [of health care–related research] . . .

focuses on deficit and deterioration [and] consistently paints a picture of aging as inherent decline." The disparity in views between patients and health care providers is far from benign. Research shows, for example, that such differences affect evaluations of a person's quality of life that, in turn, may affect treatment decisions (e.g., the type or amount, whether to treat) (Addington-Hall & Kalra, 2001; Fagerberg, Kragstrup, Stovring, & Rasmussen, 1999; Fitzsimmons, George, Payne, & Johnson, 1999; Wilson, Dowling, Abdolell, & Tannock, 2000). Sadly, it seems much of the health care system would rather diagnose than inform, treat rather than empower, and dictate rather than collaborate.

The current health care system notwithstanding, there are reasons to be hopeful. First, numerous observers have pointed to the tectonic shift taking place in the demographics of the American population—a change that is already shaking up the politics of aging. In 1900, for example, there were 3 million Americans age 65 or older. By the year 2000, older people outnumbered children for the first time in history. And by the year 2030, one quarter of the total U.S. population (70 million) will be 65 years or older. Moreover, today's population of people older than 65 is the wealthiest ever to enter retirement. Given the customary power of money and numbers on the political process, one can argue that there is perhaps no better time than the present to be a member of the senior set.

A second reason to be hopeful is that there are signs that the health care system is becoming aware of and adjusting to the changing character of the aging population. For example, more research dollars than ever are being devoted to studies of health and wellness across the life span. One project, for example, studied how negative stereotypes about aging adversely affected the *physical* health and well-being of the elderly. Participants ages 62–82 showed significant increases in blood pressure when exposed to the negative descriptions of aging; those exposed to positive aging messages demonstrated significantly higher self-confidence and mathematical performance (Levy, Hausdorff, Hencke, & Wei, 2000).

On a positive note, available research evidence indicates that the field of mental health may harbor fewer ageist biases than the field of medicine in general. For example, a number of studies show that age in and of itself does not affect clinicians' diagnostic appraisals or decisions about the type or amount of treatment offered (including the use of psychotropic medication; Garb, 1998).

Nonetheless, a long tradition exists in the clinical literature of portraying clients of all ages rather negatively. Indeed, in the average case description, people seeking therapy often become something less than they were before they entered treatment. They cease knowing their own mind, are disconnected from their feelings, have distorted cognitions or unbalanced biochemistry, and, of course, do their devilish best to resist the therapist's efforts to help them. And herein lies perhaps the greatest danger.

Forty years of psychotherapy outcome research clearly shows that the single largest contributor to successful aging is the client. In other words, success is based on clients' strengths and resources, their world view and culture, the circumstances in which they live (including existing social support networks), and the fortuitous events that flow through their lives (Duncan & Miller, 2000; Miller, Duncan, & Hubble, 1997). Yet, as Speer (1970) pointed out, most existing therapeutic approaches to change are based on theories on deficit and dysfunction—on how people become ill rather than how they change. In a clinical marketplace that is increasingly sensitive to effectiveness, therapists can ill afford to be burdened by models that overlook or altogether vitiate the client's contribution to success—regardless of the age of those being served.

In *Mental Wellness in Aging: Strengths-Based Approaches*, Judah L. Ronch and Joseph A. Goldfield bring the concepts of positive aging to the field of mental health. The editors have assembled an impressive group of practitioners of strengths-based approaches to clinical work—a revolution rooted in the work of Alfred Adler, Abraham Maslow, and Milton Erickson and continued with Mihaly Csikszentmihalyi and Martin Seligman, among others. Thanks go to this volume's editors and its many contributors for broadening the vision of mental health services for the aging population. The content may not extend life, but it will most certainly aid clinicians in helping people be more alive—present, engaged, and self-directing—until the time of their departure.

Scott D. Miller, Ph.D.
Institute for the Study of Therapeutic Change
http://www.talkingcure.com
Chicago, Illinois

REFERENCES

Addington-Hall, J., & Kalra, L. (2001). Who should measure quality of life? *British Medical Journal, 322*(7299), 1417–1420.

Duncan, B.L., & Miller, S.D. (2000). *The heroic client.* San Francisco: Jossey-Bass.

Fagerberg, C.R., Kragstrup, J., Stovring, H., & Rasmussen, N.K. (1999). *Scandanavian Journal of Primary Health Care, 17*(3), 149–152.

Fitzsimmons, D., George, S., Payne, S., & Johnson, C.D. (1999). *Psycho-oncology, 8*(2), 135–143.

Garb, H.N. (1998). *Studying the clinician: Judgment research and psychological assessment.* Washington, DC: APA Press.

Gergen, K., & Gergen, M. (2001, December 28). Collaborative caring as a research goal. *Toward Positive Aging, 9,* 1. Retrieved Dec. 4, 2002, from http://www.healthandage.net/html/res/gergen/contenu/newsletter/issue9.htm.

Levy, B.R., Hausdorff, J.M., Hencke, R., & Wei, J.Y. (2000). Reducing cardiovascular stress with positive self-stereotypes of aging. *Journals of Gerontology: Series B: Psychological Sciences & Social Sciences, 55B*(4), 205–213.

Miller, S.D., Duncan, B.L., & Hubble, M.A. (1997). *Escape from Babel: Toward a unifying language for psychotherapy practice.* New York: Norton.

Speer, D.C. (1970). Family systems: Morphostasis and morphogenesis. Or "is homeostasis enough?" *Family Process, 9,* 259–278.

Wilson, K.A., Dowling, A.J., Abdolell, M., & Tannock, I.F. (2000). Perception of quality of life by patients, partners, and treating physicians. *Quality of Life Research: An International Journal of Quality of Life Aspects of Treatment, Care, & Rehabilitation, 9*(9), 1041–1052.

*To our families, who, through the generations,
demonstrated great strengths under extraordinary circumstances.
Their endurance and tenacity have inspired
our pursuit of wellness and hopes of longevity.*

INTRODUCTION

The *New York Times* headline read, "Decades After Midlife Mark a Frontier for Mental Health" (March 16, 1998). The accompanying article described how a "growing cadre" of professionals is challenging the idea that mental health care is wasted on the old. This challenge is timely, given the surge in life expectancy and the demand by the burgeoning cohorts of aging and "young old" baby boomers that they have access to the highest possible quality of life. For these "couch-broken" generations, as well as those influential and educated, wellness-oriented elders-to-be who have learned to take command of their own destinies, psychotherapy is an accepted part of the concept of taking care of oneself.

The *Times* article went on to warn of a coming crisis in which there will be too few properly prepared therapists for older people. Those who do provide therapy for older individuals can count on being inundated as projected increases in life expectancy create a wave of demand. The generation at risk is composed of the very same savvy consumerist "boomers" who can be expected to demand expert, specialized services before enough are available. The size of population needing these services is sobering and clearly documents the need. For example, life expectancy has grown three decades since 1900, from the mid-40s to 76.1 years. The number of people older than age 65 was estimated to be in excess of 34 million in 2000 and was projected to rise to 70 million (or 20% of the population) by 2030, with the largest increase occurring among those older than 85 (Administration on Aging, 2000).

Demographics are not the only trend driving this heightened opportunity/need. The availability of more effective treatments in medical and health care, psychotherapy, and pharmacology have created heightened optimism among the older population and pioneering geriatric specialists who have been treating them through the years.

Mental health providers will need to expand their horizons and continue their own professional development in ways that are intellectually well-grounded and reflect contemporary realities of how services are provided to the public. This includes the need to provide mental health services in the form of psychotherapy or counseling to people who seek help not because they are "sick" but because they wish to be stronger and enjoy a better quality of life into very old age. Future cohorts of older adults will assert their ability to be partners in the process of care, not passive patients, and will bring considerable talents, strengths, and life skills to the process. They will also be sensitive to the element of time as a factor, perhaps because their health benefits will be rationed or managed, or because they, like most busy boomers, prefer to solve problems as expeditiously as possible and get on with living.

The approaches represented in this volume reflect the idea that strengths-based, time-sensitive (not necessarily the "brief therapies" per se) mental health and wellness care are powerful resources and are perhaps the most appropriate modalities to meet the challenges of the 21st century's so-called "Age Wave" (Dychtwald, 1989). We see a trend toward increasing numbers of aging people who will assert their wish to be in control as much as possible of their "successful aging" (Rowe & Kahn, 1998).

This is a book of practical approaches based on contemporary thinking and techniques to help people engage and strengthen their own abilities to promote successful lives as they grow older. Our scope reflects both wellness-related behaviors for the lay reader to use to promote mental wellness as aging progresses and counseling and psychotherapy modalities that use personal strengths as the cornerstone for improvement.

The chapters are written by recognized experts in this field. Their unique collaboration has yielded a series of discussions about successful aging, not a controversy surrounding the *best* path to take (see Hubble, Duncan, & Miller, 1999). We recognize that people are different and that better ways to achieve mental wellness in aging are still to be discovered, both in and outside of the consultation room. This volume is a gathering of ideas that reflect, and hopefully accelerate, the historical transition in the field of geriatric mental health away from nihilism toward positivism. These strengths-based approaches veer from an exclusive focus on coping with deterioration toward the view that older people are not only "educable" but also (to turn Freud's old view around) have the potential to utilize their unique lifelong assets to benefit their aging.

THE FUTURE OF AGING AND MENTAL HEALTH ISSUES

The Surgeon General's Report on Mental Health (U.S. Department of Health and Human Services, 1999) attested to the societal challenge of meeting the demands of the enormous number of aging people who constitute the Age Wave. The size of this group is not the only challenge; it also will be larger and more diverse than any previous generation in our history. Some of the details are compelling and set a frame for future service design.

The population of older adults is expected to double in number and reach 70 million by 2030 and will represent the most heterogeneous group in history in terms of generational cohorts, gender balance, ethnic mix, income levels, living arrangements, and quality of physical and mental health. The growth in demand for mental health services will result not only from the sheer numbers of aging people but also from the impact of diverse experiences that created the enormous heterogeneity of this group. These cohorts will challenge any lingering assumptions mental health and other service providers may have that aging is a singular experience rooted only in chronological events. To put it simply, models of intervention that are based solely on chronological age of the recipients will become obsolete. A number of dimensions mentioned in the Surgeon General's Report are worth considering in order to fully understand what the aging population and mental health providers will be facing.

Stressors and Adaptations

Aging exposes people to a combination of stressors that is unique in both its nature and variety. Normal aging brings unplanned changes, declines, and losses that are potentially problematic for even the most well-adjusted individuals. What were once minor changes that people easily compensated for are more likely to become major, either because new barriers and challenges arise to the marshalling of resources people have used all their lives to function independently or because challenges increase exponentially and at an accelerating pace. Two of the most stressful unplanned events are declines in health and loss of loved ones. In addition, stresses may result from loss of community, relationships, or environmental resources. Most older people are able to adapt to these changes by using their traditional coping mechanisms or, if necessary, by adapting them. But there are those for whom these and similar stressors create major threats to well-being, especially when the belief that the experience of aging per se is the reason they cannot access their lifelong resources for achieving mental wellness. How will the next generations of aging people cope with stresses they didn't create (e.g., working too much) and those over which they have no control?

SERVICE DELIVERY ISSUES

Older adults typically underutilize mental health services. Reasons for this include denial of problems because of feared social stigma or the generational psyche (Ronch & Maizler, 1977) that casts a shaming and critical eye on the "mentally ill" as weak, crazy, or morally inferior; failure of professionals to identify the signs and symptoms of emotional and psychological problems; and barriers to access such as cost, location, and gerontophobic, ageist attitudes among providers. Systems currently in place function suboptimally due to a lack of collaboration between agencies and systems, funding and reimbursement problems, health care models oriented to acute medical illnesses of younger people, the role of managed care, and a shortage of trained providers in the medical and mental health arenas. How will the future generations deal with any barriers that block their access to services they have come to depend on for optimum wellness?

AGING AND MENTAL HEALTH

Contrary to myth, aging is not inevitably accompanied by deteriorating cognitive and emotional status. Nevertheless, conservative estimates indicate that nearly 20% of people 55 years and older experience mental disorders that are not part of normal aging. The most prevalent are anxiety disorders, severe cognitive impairment (e.g., Alzheimer's disease), and mood disorders (chiefly depression). Suicide is at an especially high rate among the aging, especially among Caucasian males. Although schizophrenia and personality disorders are less common, prevalence data should be considered in light of the underreporting and diagnostic inaccuracies common with this population. In terms of emotional or cognitive problems, most individuals experience them for the first time after age 55; however, not all of these disorders occur for the first time in later life. Onset is possible at all ages, from adolescence throughout the adult years, and severity and chronicity are highly variable as well.

The major issue with which future cohorts of aging people will have to contend is the lack of enough adequately trained professionals who possess the expertise and experience needed to understand the biopsychosocial origins and unique treatment requirements of mental health problems in these cohorts. How will the future aging population tolerate the lack of a well-trained and gerontologically enlightened health care provider network?

BARRIERS AND STIGMA

The underutilization of mental health services is probably a result of interacting biases. Mental health providers may avoid the aging client partially because of ageist myths, gerontophobia, and lack of expertise, while many of the aging avoid acknowledging their mental health problems because of the negative stigma associated with these difficulties that pervade the culture. The stigma of mental difficulties reflects and is reflected in social attitudes and the way society relegates these problems to subordinate status in health coverage, a powerful synergy for mutual disincentive on the part of providers and prospective consumers. Additional contributions to the erection and maintenance of barriers to appropriate service include fragmented and less-than-adequate funding and reimbursement for needed services; inadequate coordination and competing priorities between primary care, mental health, and aging service providers; gaps in service that reflect a view of people as disparate diagnoses or unrelated needs; an alarming shortage of properly trained professional and paraprofessional staff; and the lack of an adequately powerful consumer voice. How will these barriers be addressed and removed in the future when a consumerist, activist cohort comes of age and resists ageist stigmatization?

RELIANCE ON MANAGED CARE

At present, managed care is the most prevalent payer model in the health care arena. Called "managed cost" by some of its critics, it has of late been particularly troubled by managed Medicare debacles and a failure to deliver on preventive services that address the unique, interrelated health care (physical and mental) needs of the aging. Limits on mental health benefits combine with an inadequate network of expert providers to limit access for those aging people in need of state-of-the-art care. As these models confront their economic and conceptual limits, the number of aging people continues to grow with increasing rapidity. The result is increasing pressure on our current system of care that appears to be unprepared to answer the call for the health and wellness oriented system that would likely be the most beneficial and least costly in the long run. How will the business of health care in the United States respond to the converging gerontological challenges of a provider shortage and the conceptual and economic obsolescence of its models that it appears to be facing as the Age Wave hits?

PRIMARY AND LONG-TERM CARE

In the acute care arena, older people turn first to their primary care providers when they have a mental health problem. More than 50% of those who receive mental health care receive it from primary care physicians, probably because it carries fewer stigmas than going to a mental health provider, insurance plans encourage use of the primary care provider, and they are usually more accessible. But many primary care providers are not adequately trained in mental health problems of the aging and tend to use psychotropic drugs as the first or only line of treatment. Pressures from managed care economics also result in briefer physician visits, often averaging 8 minutes in duration. Finally, many primary care physicians have negative attitudes toward aging people that undermine physicians' effectiveness. More desirable collaborative service models that coordinate mental and physical health services in primary care are in the initial stages of investigation.

Long-term care settings such as nursing homes are characterized by high incidence of cognitive impairments and dementias (notably Alzheimer's and related disorders) and emotional disorders (especially depression) among their residents. Elderly nursing home residents are also prone to health conditions and medication side effects that cause cognitive and emotional symptoms. These older residents of care facilities confront significant barriers to adequate care as well, such as a shortage of qualified mental health professionals, lack of adequate knowledge and ongoing training for nursing home staff about mental health issues, lack of adequate Medicare and Medicaid coverage for the needed services, and problems in attracting the services of qualified mental health professionals due to inadequate reimbursement policies. How will these problems be addressed as aging cohorts arrive at their physicians' offices armed with scads of information gathered on the Internet about mental health issues of concern to them, and how will long-term care facilities respond to the boomer children of their residents who are similarly informed and unwilling to settle for a shortage of expert providers to meet the entire range of their loved ones' needs?

WE ARE ALL AGING PEOPLE

The issues identified in the Surgeon General's Report will play out in a society increasingly made up of professional and volunteer helpers, policy makers, and researchers who are growing older at the same time. The "us versus them" issues will become "we are them" such that aging will become a matter of personal interest for client and helper alike. We envision an increasing movement toward an *entente* of sorts between aging health care providers and their aging clients that we hope will create in providers a new sensitivity about the experience of aging, especially about the impact it has on one's sense of self. If this *entente,* or increased mutual appreciation of the aging experience in the context of being a helper, does emerge, it will be because each constituency will become aware of their common preference for an active later life. This awareness of how crucial it is to preserve access to all personal and societal resources that are needed to support positive aging will, we believe, join the client and helper around a common belief about what aging could optimally be like for them.

This book is, in one sense, a beginning step to bring about the *entente.* We envisioned that our readers might either come to this volume with experience in helping others but with relatively little background in aging, or as experienced providers of services to aging people who are unhappy with traditional deficit-based approaches and have not had much exposure to the clinical literature of strengths-based therapies. We hope to reach students or practitioners new to the field of aging services. We also hope that we have provided a basis for lay readers to engage their own strengths in guiding their search for resources that enhance the quality of the aging experience. It is important to us to present some valuable information people might use to enhance their own strengths as they age, especially as self-advocates, as they seek out or utilize the services of helpers. In addition, this material was included so that people might increase their knowledge about aging and thus realize benefits through their own intervention. They might thus become their own helpers and not need to utilize formal professional services or intervene for themselves in tandem with utilizing the services of others. The information presented in this book from experts is intended to make readers better informed consumers who hold fast their strengths while seeking services and who resist surrendering their traditional coping abilities as the price of receiving help.

Obtaining quality medical care, counseling, and psychotherapy; utilizing available community services; and coping with illness are all challenges to one's sense of mastery and quality of life. We hope that the contributions in this volume help inform individuals' choices, stimulate their creativity and enable them to mobilize their own individual strengths and those of their families, friends, and neighbors. These chapters are not a substitute for expertise in any field of health care, but rather a way to identify the nature of an approach to caring for aging people that might suit various preferences.

MENTAL WELLNESS

We use the term "mental wellness" to reflect our belief that health and illness are not dichotomously arranged in nature or in life and because people can, at times, in collaboration with knowledgeable helpers, move along the continuum toward optimal wellness at each stage of life by dint of their own efforts. People have more options than to be sick or healthy; they do not have to be sick in order to take advantage of the means to improve wellness. This is an especially important outlook for aging as a process—people can have an array of illnesses as they age and yet enjoy wellness and a good quality of life.

We also think that the old Cartesian mind–body separation is fading from view and that a growing body of evidence in the scientific and lay literatures is correct when it indicates that somato-psychic and psycho-somatic phenomena are mutually influencing and "influenceable." Damasio's (1999) writing on the neurological basis of the unity of mind and body, and the postmodern view of illness and the central role of individual experiences of disease on prognoses (Morris, 1998), suggested that mental and physical domains are inseparable and profit from approaches informed by these synergistic views. Feinberg's (2001) work added another level of richness to the analysis of how "the self" as a unifying, perpetually created, process of the brain, is a lifelong process. He shed important light on the intricate, fluid, lifelong nature in which the holistic nature of mind–body unity are played out in ways seen throughout the human lifespan.

Although we have framed the issue as mental wellness, we are not ignorant of the many infirmities and illnesses that befall people as they age. Our use of the term *wellness* is not intended to deny the existence of the maladies, frailties, and dependencies that occur in later life. We intend only to bring attention to the entire continuum of experience that is aging and the need to recognize the assets older people bring to the experience of their illness or dependency.

Though the terms *wellness* or *strengths* may not appear per se in every chapter, they are included as organizing constructs and philosophical approaches to the subject matter. The absence of illness paradigms or terminology is one aspect of this approach; another is that the authors view aging as a process and an era of development and as the purview both aging people and their helpers, paid and unpaid. The wellness orientation and its theoretical complement, strengths-based appraisal, assessment, and intervention (Butler, Lewis, & Sunderland, 1998; Cohen, 1993; Cohen, Kennedy, & Eisdorfer, 1984; George & Clipp, 1991; Kivnick, 1993; Kivnick & Murray, 2001; Lustbader, 1991; Rowe & Kahn, 1997; Sacks, 1985; Sherman, 1993) are reflected in the use of terms, including *skill, resiliency, autonomy, collaboration* and *historical preferences*. It is noteworthy, and perhaps a reflection of how far we have come in the development of approaches that are applicable across the entire lifespan, that the terms *wellness* and *strength* can be used in discussions about aging without fanfare as they would be for any other age group.

As pundits ponder the future of aging and of those who will age, the impact of scientific progress on aging as a future achievement—and indeed, the very nature of what it will mean to age—is open to revision. That alone will require us to re-think the essence of the relationship between the helping professions and the aging people they serve. Featherstone (1995) predicted that technology (especially nanotechnology) will prevent the physical decline that has for so long characterized the narratives of old age and thereby expand the opportunities to constantly redefine the self. This, he proposed, will bring about the ability to give meaning in old age through freely chosen self-narratives, rather than through the experience of disability and dependency. If Featherstone is correct, how might that change each of our future plans about our own aging and our future careers as practitioners? The concept of helping aging people may have to undergo radical transformation, even a questioning of whether achieving mental wellness in later life will require therapy and therapists at all?

STRENGTHS-BASED APPROACHES

The strengths-based approaches we have chosen have a number of aspects in common, and we hope the reader will appreciate both the historical evolution and richly diverse applications of theory and practice that have evolved. Though there are real differences evident in the chapters, they share a core of assumptions that are particularly beneficial in work with aging people. These include the following:

1. *Client resources*: All of these approaches assume that clients enter therapy with many skills, capacities, and resources (personal and environmental). The primary therapeutic endeavor is to elicit and channel appropriate and relevant client skills toward the achievement of the client's goals. This is in contrast to many pathology-based approaches, which emphasize the necessity of clients having to learn new skills and a new vocabulary in order to resolve their problems.

2. *Collaborative client–helper relationships*: In pathology or deficit-based approaches, the relationship between client and helper tends to be hierarchical, with the therapist or other clinician acting as a benevolent expert who has the responsibility of teaching the client new skills and that the helper alone knows what is best for him or her. In contrast, strengths-based approaches emphasize collaborative client–helper relationships in which the client and helper together seek to discover which client capacities will prove useful for developing solutions in line with the goals and outcomes that are important to the client.

3. *Causality and time effectiveness*: Whereas deficit or pathology models tend to spend a great deal of time in attempting to understand how unhealthy tendencies develop or maintain themselves, the strengths-based models discussed in this volume give more attention to building on healthy tendencies that already exist within a client's life. This process allows therapy to be efficient in terms of time as well as of other resources.

4. *Anti-ageist perspective*: The aspects just outlined are of special benefit to therapists working with older clients because these processes prevent therapists from limiting the scope of their thinking and actions (in assessing or intervening) in terms of generalizations based on age or diagnostic categories. Therapists are instead able to notice subtle possibilities and abilities in their clients that otherwise might have been missed. The principles of these strengths-based approaches also benefit older clients because these individuals are not forced to take on new roles based on societal myths about the deficits presumed to be intrinsic to aging in order to resolve their problems.

A FINAL NOTE

This book came about in response to a question one of us asked the other over a cup of coffee. We couldn't recall having seen a book that looked at strengths-based approaches in helping aging adults and their therapists who were coping with issues of living well as they aged in spite of the myriad problems that attend growing older in this society. Thus we decided to try to put one together that would elicit some creative conversations. We hope it will not be the last word on the subject.

We look forward to continuing the dialogue with you. If you have any thoughts or experiences using these or similar approaches in clinical practice, or would be interested in an interchange with the editors or chapter authors, please contact us at jronch@aol.com or JoeGoldfieldCSWR@aol.com.

REFERENCES

Administration on Aging. (2000). *Profile of older Americans.* Retrieved from http:// www.aoa.gov/aoa/stats/ profile

Butler, R., Lewis, M., & Sunderland, T. (1998). *Aging and mental health: Positive psychosocial and biomedical approaches.* Needham, MA: Allyn & Bacon.

Cohen, D., Kennedy, G., & Eisdorfer, C. (1984). Phases of change in the patient with Alzheimer's dementia: A conceptual dimension for defining health-care management. *Journal of the American Geriatrics Society, 32*(1), 11–15.

Cohen, G. (1993). Comprehensive assessment: Capturing strengths, not just weaknesses. In M. Smyer, (Ed.), *Mental health and aging* (pp. 93–102). New York: Springer Publishing Co.

Damasio, A. (1999). *The feeling of what happens: Body and emotion in the making of consciousness.* New York: Harcourt Brace and Company.

Dychtwald, K. (1989). *Age wave.* Los Angeles: Tarcher.

Featherstone, M. (1995). Post bodies, aging and virtual reality. In M. Featherstone & A. Wernick (Eds.), *Images of aging (pp. 227–244).* London: Routledge.

Feinberg, T. (2001). *Altered egos: How the brain creates the self.* New York: Oxford University Press.

George, L., & Klipp, E. (Eds.). (1991). Aging well [Entire issue]. *Generations, XV(1).*

Hubble, M., Duncan, B., & Miller, S. (1999). *The heart and soul of change: What works in therapy.* Washington, DC: American Psychological Association.

Kivnick, H., (1993). Everyday mental health: A guide to assessing strengths. In M. Smyer (Ed.), *Mental health and aging* (pp. 19–36). New York: Springer Publishing Co.

Kivnick, H., & Murray, S. (2001). Life strengths interview guide: Assessing elder clients' strengths. *Journal of Gerontological Social Work,* (34)4.

Lustbader, W. (1991). *Counting on kindness.* New York: The Free Press.

Morris, D. (1998). *Illness and culture in the postmodern age.* Berkeley: University of California Press.

Ronch, J., & Maizler, J. (1977). Individual psychotherapy with the institutionalized aged. *American Journal of Orthopsychiatry, 47(2).*

Rowe, J.W., & Kahn, R. (1998). *Successful aging.* New York: Pantheon Books.

Sacks, O. (1985). *The man who mistook his wife for a hat.* New York: Summit Books.

Sherman, E. (1993). Mental health and successful adaptation in late life. In M. Smyer. (Ed.), *Mental health and aging (pp. 85–92).* New York: Springer Publishing Co.

United States Department of Health and Human Services. (1999). *Mental Health: A report of the Surgeon General.* Rockville, MD: US Department of Health and Human Services, Substance Abuse and Mental Health Administration, Center for Mental Health Services, National Institutes of Health, National Institute of Mental Health.

SECTION I

Engaging People's
Strengths for Successful Aging

AGING IN THE NEW MILLENNIUM

What the Future Holds for Us

Audrey Weiner and Sheldon L. Goldberg

IN THE PREFACE to *Creative Mental Health Services for the Elderly*, Jack Weinberg, M.D., then president of the American Psychiatric Association, wrote

> Each period in the lifespan of man forces on him a different reality, based on the altered physiology and the extent of the richness of the human experience. Old age can become an expression of the summation of the human experience, and therein 'lies the rub.' It can be rich, varied, colorful, and enriching, conversely it may be impoverished or empty and only serve to emphasize the futility of life and its meaning to many of the old. (1977, p. xviii)

As we look toward the forces that are shaping aging in the 21st century, this statement holds particular weight.

POPULATION

In terms of caring for older adults, gerontologists, geriatricians, mental health clinicians, services providers, and individuals should first view the future of elder care through a demographic lens. In the year 2000, an estimated 35 million people in the United States were 65 years old or older, accounting for 1 in 8 (12.5%) of the total population (Hobbs & Damon, 2001). The U.S. Census Bureau (2000) determined that at least one person who was 65 years old or older resided in approximately 23% of all U.S. households. By the year 2010, the projected population of people 65 years old or older is estimated to rise to 39 million, with 17% of the population being 85 years old or older (Hobbs & Damon, 2001).

During the 20th century, an increased life expectancy dramatically influenced the United States' economic, political, and social landscape, re-shaping approaches to aging and caring for older adults. Medical advances, as well as innovations and information about safety measures in society and the workplace, fostered longevity. Unlike people in preceding decades, people in the 20th century saw a decline of death rates among children and the middle-age population. Consequently, the increase in life expectancy allowed the population to mature in larger numbers. African Americans, however, continued to have a lower life expectancy rate than the overall population (National Vital Statistics System, 1997); and Asian Americans and Pacific Islanders had higher rates of many chronic diseases and illness, including hypertension and heart disease.

Indeed, we are facing not just a period of time in which older people will increase as a share of the population, but a permanent shift to a society with a large number of older adults (Moon, 1991). Ken Dychtwald focused the lens of aging: "The elderly are not 'them'—they are 'us' a few decades into the future" (1999, p. xv). This chapter explores our readiness to respond to the important mental health—or rather, mental wellness—issues that confront our older population.

POPULATION DIVERSITY

The power of the demographic imperative goes beyond the sheer number of older adults; the increasing diversity of the older adult population is an important consideration for understanding, developing, and providing services—especially those addressing mental wellness. Within this group of individuals are those whose ethnic origins span the world, including African, Asian, Hispanic American, American Indian, Native Alaskan, Native Hawaiian, Pacific Islanders, and Soviet Union émigrés, among countless others. In 1990, for example, 5.1% of the Hispanic population was age 65 years or older. By the year 2020, this number is expected to reach 14.1% (U.S. Census Bureau, 2000). Some regions of the United States, such as California, have seen a dramatic upsurge in the number of older, minority adults (U.S. Census Bureau, 2000). The U.S. Census Bureau (2000) predicted that the older adult minority population would triple by 2030, when about one fourth of all U.S. older adults would belong to a minority racial ethnic group.

THE POWER OF THE demographic imperative goes beyond the sheer number of older adults; the increasing diversity of the older adult population is an important consideration for understanding, developing, and providing services—especially those addressing mental wellness.

When considering appropriate service and delivery planning needed to care for an increasingly diverse older adult population, caregiving professionals will experience the implications of the 2000 U.S. census data. "Transmigration, like all catastrophes, produces new traumatic world images and seems to demand the sudden assumption of new and often transitory identities" (Erikson, 1964). For the many older adults who were not born in the United States, but who immigrated from other countries, the loss of self-esteem, identity, friends, security, confidence, culture, and so forth as well as societal, economic, and family status is often emotionally overwhelming. The need for culturally appropriate and relevant services becomes evident for émigrés and all other elders.

SOVIET ÉMIGRÉS Working with older adult émigrés from the Soviet Union in the early 1990s in New York City, author Audrey Weiner understood the need for culturally appropriate and relevant services. The émigrés' experience provided a backdrop for the concept of cultural competency. Within this group, Weiner found that the population of adults older than 55 years faced the greatest difficulty in adjusting to life in the United States. Many émigrés reacted to the emotional impact of changes in their lives by withdrawing and isolating themselves from family, friends, and the potential that the new culture offered. This tendency to remove themselves from their new world not only limited the individuals' access to assistance but also fostered in them an escalating sense of despair that often resulted in severe depression, familial conflict, alcoholism, and greater physical deterioration. The suicide rate was quite high among older adult, first-year Soviet émigrés (Katsnelson, 1991).

KEY FACTORS FOR MINORITY WITHDRAWAL Key factors appear to have affected older adult émigrés' patterns of withdrawal. These factors offer a valuable lens through which to examine what might determine other emigrant and ethnic minority older adults' degree of withdrawal from or engagement in their new culture:

- Language barrier
- Anxiety and depression caused by the immigration experience
- Greater emotional investment in the culture and society of the home country
- Less receptivity to the American culture
- Lack of connection with mainstream community institutions
- Limited physical mobility
- Poor physical health
- Low priority within resettlement service (Providers tried to attend to the needs of employable younger adults, children, parents of younger children, adolescents, and refugees with acute medical and psychological problems.)

In addition to these factors, many older adults came to the United States in order to remain close to their grown children who, in turn, often had families of their own. The realities and priorities of resettlement for the grown children of the émigrés often left little time for them to spend with their older parents to help them to adapt to their new environment.

CULTURAL INFLUENCES

Certain experiences of other ethnic and racial minority groups have mental health implications, as well. For example, many older African American women are vulnerable to social isolation and economic hardship. Compared with their Caucasian contemporaries, older African American women are more than one and one half times more likely to live below the poverty level and less likely to be married (Administration on Aging, 2001). Poverty and widowhood place these women at risk of developing mental health problems.

It is incumbent upon service providers to be culturally competent when dealing with all of the racially and ethnically diverse cohorts of older adults (see Bonder, Martin, & Miracle, 2001). Cultural competency describes a person's "professional work in a way that is congruent with the behavior and expectations that members of distinctive cultures recognize as appropriate" within that community (Green, 1982). The Administration on Aging (2001) not only highlighted cultural appropriateness when defining cultural competence, but also broadened the concept to include cultural access and cultural acceptability. Barriers to gaining access to culturally competent services not only include those experienced by the Soviet émigrés but also include a distrust of the mainstream delivery system, a lack of appropriate information, and a low income and education level. Clearly, culturally appropriate materials, outreach, and education go far beyond translation (Center for Medicare Education, 2001). Because of the unprecedented growth in the older minority population, this mandate for cultural competence will only become more critical in ensuing decades (U.S. Census Bureau, 2000).

ECONOMIC CONDITIONS

The economic condition of the older adult population is a story of change and variation. When this book was written, it was assumed that personal savings, job-related pensions, and earned income from working for a long period of time would assume a larger role in guaranteeing economic security for all older Americans. In general, Social Security was expected to contribute a decreased share of the income needed for a secure retirement. Yet, these other sources are considerably less secure and reliable than Social Security and relying on them may pose a considerable economic challenge (Smeeding, 2001).

THE DISPARITY between older adults with more than an adequate income for basic concerns and those who must choose to stretch daily income to cover necessities such as utilities, food, and medication is growing.

Although many older adults are enjoying comfortable retirement years, many others are under a significant threat of economic deprivation. The disparity between older adults with more than an adequate income for basic concerns and those who must choose to stretch daily income to cover necessities such as utilities, food, and medication is growing. Minorities and older women living alone experience poverty rates in excess of 20% to 25% (Smeeding, 2001), whereas more than one in four African Americans have incomes that fall below the poverty line. Twelve percent of Asian Americans live below the poverty line compared with only 5% of older, non-Hispanic white Americans.

In the year 2000, the number of older adults who were lesbian, gay, bisexual, and/or transgender-oriented was estimated to be between 1.75 million and 3.5 million people (Administration on Aging, 2001). One key difference among lesbian, gay, bisexual, and transgender older adults, when compared with ethnic minorities, is the likelihood that they may face discriminations that affect their economic status based on their age as well as sexual orientation.

MEDICARE

In the book, *Aging and Mental Health: Positive Psychosocial and Biomedical Approaches*, Butler, Lewis, and Sunderland (1991) noted a striking series of developments that they predicted would ultimately have an impact on mental health care in the 21st century. These developments included the outbreak of the AIDS epidemic; the reduced possibility of nuclear extinction (perhaps overshadowed by the fear of terrorism and bio-terrorism following the September, 2001, terrorist attacks in the United States); the changes in health care reimbursement; the improved and expanded training for geriatricians and gerontologists; the broad developments in psychotherapy for older adults; the empowerment of patients in health care; and the sophistication of the consumer.

Although *DRGs* (diagnosis related groups) and the implications of that payer system reduced an individual's length of stay in the hospital, Medicare-managed care became a serious health care force in the 1990s. In 1999, the national Medicare-managed care penetration ranged from a high rank of 53% in California to a low rank of 0% in Alaska. In 2000, 17.2% of all Medicare beneficiaries in the U.S. were enrolled in a Medicare-managed care plan (AARP, 2000), despite the continuous withdrawal of commercial and Medicare-managed care products from counties from which no profit was derived. The roller coaster of enrollment and disenrollment had a negative influence on health care access and continuity. The challenge set forth in the 2000 U.S. presidential election by the strong 65 years old or older voting cohort reflected a desire to modify Medicare reimbursement to include pharmaceuticals. That change, if implemented, could have a significant impact on the successful treatment of illness for older adults.

SUCCESSFUL AGING

A dramatic reduction in the stigma associated with mental illness occurred during the end of the 20th century. Thanks in part to Tipper Gore's announcement about her own treatment for depression while her husband, Al Gore, served as U.S. Vice President and to advertisements about Prozac on television, people became more accepting of individuals who sought treatment for mental illnesses. Society began to have greater understanding of the mind—body connection.

When I Am an Old Woman I Shall Wear Purple, a book (Joseph, 1987) that takes its title from a famous line from a popular poem "Warning," focused on older adulthood as an opportunity for creativity and spirit, freed from significant responsibilities. It also suggests that such wisdom and inspiration should not have to wait for old age. Rowe and Kahn (1998) defined *successful aging* as the ability to maintain

- Low risk of disease and disease-related disability
- High mental and physical function
- Active engagement in life

Studies of centenarians, many of whom are healthy and independent (Brody, 2000), suggested that it is possible to live both well and long; 30% of longevity can be attributed to heredity. The remainder of a person's longevity and wellness is a direct result of his or her lifestyle, especially diet, exercise, smoking habits, and his or her use of preventive care including vaccines and early detection (Brody, 2000). This allows the individuals in the field of gerontology and caregivers to conceptualize wellness in older adulthood as a continuous rather than dichotomous variable over which the individual has a profound personal influence.

> THE GOALS OF longevity are now built on a *holistic framework;* the goal of individuals and professionals is to increase the *quality* of the years, not only the *quantity*.

The goals of longevity are now built on a *holistic framework;* the goal of individuals and professionals is to increase the *quality* of the years, not only the *quantity*. To best achieve this, the definition of wellness must be expanded to include the following dimensions:

- Physical
- Social
- Emotional
- Intellectual
- Avocational/vocational
- Spiritual
- Financial security

Key advances in the last generation of mental health practices recognized, defined, and valued these seven dimensions as independent and interdependent influences and predictors of well-being. With a growing arsenal of countermeasures to the physical ailments of aging, Johnson (2000) suggested that a quality older adulthood would depend on an individual's good mental health. For example, in a study of 169 centenarians, the only personality characteristic that the participants shared was the ability to manage stress well (Hilts, 1999). Rowe and Kahn (1998) also emphasized that "mental ability and social relationships" are essential factors to older adult mental and emotional fitness. Frequent emotional support was linked strongly to the likelihood of enhanced physical function over time. Hence, a dynamic and warm emotional lifestyle promotes optimal physical health.

AGE WAVE

Dychtwald (1999) suggested that as a cohort, baby boomers, or people who were between the ages of 37 and 50 years old by the year 2000, have radically transformed every stage of life that they have experienced. Whatever issues they have faced in their lives, including financial concerns, interpersonal concerns, or life transitions, have become the dominant social, political, and marketplace issues. As these boomers grow older, *age power* (Dychtwald, 1999) will rule the 21st century, and in many critical ways society is woefully unprepared.

The *Age Wave* is the aging of the baby boomer generation. Age Wavers, thus dubbed by Dychtwald (1999), have an optimistic vision of aging and are an empowered generation that is taking a leadership role in changing the way society ages. Age Wavers acknowledge the importance of environment in lifestyle and feel they can control many of the risk factors for illness and chronic disease. Researchers predict that many Age Wavers will remain active past the age of 65 as providers, volunteers, and caregivers. They are indeed the demographic, intellectual, and practical transition between today's older adults and those born after 1964.

The implication of the boomer generation and their reaching "golden pond" (i.e., age 65) is striking. Research indicates that boomers value youthfulness, independence, freedom, and self-expression (Schwartz & Rupert, 1996), and they will not grow older gracefully. They will want to look and act young and vibrant and will remain active much longer than preceding generations. Consistent with 20th-century trends, boomers will continue to spend a significant amount of money on spas, exercise, health food, vitamins, and cosmetic surgery (Grigsby, 1996).

ECONOMICS

The baby boom generation has been the most educated generation in American history, with more than half having attended college compared with about one out of five in previous generations (Schwartz & Rupert, 1996). The political fervor of the 1960s and early 1970s shaped their attitudes. As these boomers age, they will include the first generation of financially independent older women with their own pensions, savings, and Social Security. The women's movement and the expectation of equal opportunity in the workplace, as well as the economic demands

> As these boomers age, they will include the first generation of financially independent older women with their own pensions, savings, and Social Security.

for two-career households, resulted in individuals and couples who are "time strapped but affluent consumers" (Schwartz & Rupert, 1996).

TECHNOLOGY

For the Age Wavers, technology has implications far beyond Internet searches. The 20th century experienced the evolution of the computer from a defense/government/research box to an omnipresent Pentium chip. Such technological innovations as medical and safety monitoring, household appliance management, smart houses that monitor temperatures and turn appliances on and off via computer, financial management, and personal communications with friends and colleagues internationally have changed society's patterns of learning, interaction, and actual *instrumental activities of daily living* (IADLs). Technology's implications for baby boomers and in-person versus on-line contact and social isolation will merit evaluation.

As a logical outgrowth of the consumerism and empowerment trends, e-health consumers became a force at the beginning of the 21st century (O'Gara, 2001). In 2001, e-health consumers (i.e., people seeking health information and advice on-line) were estimated to have reached 74 million, with a mean age of 41 years old and an ethnic representation across all groups. Of these, 90% of individuals sought information about a physical illness and 26% about mental health. Sixteen percent sought information about sensitive topics that they believed were difficult to discuss in person.

HOW MENTAL HEALTH practitioners provide information and use telemedicine for diagnosis and monitoring while concurrently respecting confidentiality and maintaining standards of practice will be a challenge.

The authors of this chapter have every reason to believe that the number of e-health consumers will increase, and this will be especially relevant for the Age Wavers. How mental health practitioners will provide information and use telemedicine for diagnosis and monitoring (Roques & Hovanec, 2001) while concurrently respecting confidentiality and maintaining standards of practice will be a challenge.

CAREGIVING

Rother (1999) suggested that at the age of 65, people are at the peak of individual power. At this age, individuals are free from the responsibilities of child rearing and may continue to look forward to many good years. This is the first stage of retirement that often evolves into a second stage of retirement in which disabilities typically affect individuals' freedom. Although the first stage conceptually begins at 60 to 65 years old, the second stage is thought to begin at 75 to 80 (when disabilities typically affect individuals' freedom). This reflects a revised framework of the previously defined *young-old*, *middle-old*, and *oldest-old* cohorts.

Of great concern for the future generations of older adults is the challenge of caregiving. Caregivers come from all ethnic and racial backgrounds. According to the most recent National Long-Term Care Survey (Administration on Aging, 2001), more than 7 million people are unpaid caregivers—family members or friends who care for individuals who are ill or have disabilities and live at home. There are wide variations in the physical and emotional conditions of those who are receiving help, the kind of assistance they may require, and the level of caregiver satisfaction and stress. Carol Levine's work (2000) on caregiving described the impact on physical and mental wellness for caregivers and the current framework of the care provided.

As society looks toward the rest of the 21st century, it can anticipate that the ability for families and friends to provide caregiving will continue to grow more complex because of

- Long-distance caregiving
- Blended families
- Fewer children to provide care
- Continued increases in the numbers of working women
- Demands on older adults themselves in caring for their own children (for example, for grown children with mental illness, developmental disabilities, and long-term illnesses) and possibly grandchildren. Mental health practitioners must continue to respond to the concerns of these caregivers and develop options that recognize the precious nature of time.

HOUSING

America remains, in the early years of the 21st century, a country without a cogent social policy on housing, an essential ingredient for wellness. The increase in life expectancy has necessitated multiple options for living out one's life. In addition to the least desired nursing facility placement, varieties of living arrangements are available to older adults. Assisted living facilities, continuing care retirement communities, and programs to keep older adults at home independently for as long as possible flourished during the strong financial period of the 1990s.

These living arrangements developed from the demands and preferences of the *new aging consumer*. These consumers, who think of themselves as a youthful generation, are people who were 75 years old and older at the end of the 20th century, and their children were, typically, baby boomers. They are independent and want to remain so; they value both privacy and social engagement on their own terms. Successful providers will understand their expectations, concerns, wants, and desires, and respond in kind. Mental health practitioners will have a key role in communities, programs, and services grounded in a wellness model. These roles can range from the creation and conceptualization of programs that are holistic, senior-centered, and empowering to the direct provision of assessment, treatment, and referral services.

PERSONAL EMPOWERMENT

Personal empowerment, control, and decision making have important ramifications for care planning. Individuals have become active partners, rather than passive participants, in care. The kinds of services provided as well as the service array and the specific service providers will all be decisions made by this next generation of older adults. Palliative care, pain management, advanced directives, living wills, "Do Not Resuscitate" orders, and assisted suicide have become either standards of practice, law, and/or painful areas of serious debate.

In a poignant *New York Times Magazine* article entitled "Last Right: When a Friend Asked for Help (in committing suicide), I Couldn't Refuse. Her Choice Still Haunts Me" (Carmichael, 2001), a writer described the pain involved in helping an individual with an ongoing illness make a decision about assisted suicide. As the advances in medical science and technology continue, mental health practitioners need to join with traditional health care providers to assist in these intimate personal decisions. The mental health practitioner's role should be expanded to include the role of the *ethical counselor.*

Yet, even with these painful decisions, the challenges for caregiving, and the realities of chronic diseases, the authors remain very optimistic about their own aging. Indeed, it is our belief that overall, the face of aging in the new millennium will be positive. The baby boomer generation does not view the later years of life with a lens of loss (sickness, death, and incapacity) but as decades to gain and flourish. The public's improved attitude toward aging and retained sense of youth will keep this group more vital and active than society has ever seen before. Nonetheless, even in the framework of optimism, everyone must be mindful of Jack Weinberg's initial caution, because poverty, isolation, and poor physical health will remain issues for too many people in the 21st century.

More help and guidance will be available to older adults through various professions, especially those of mental health providers and advocates for social change. As our world and society evolves technologically, scientifically, and cybernetically, the aging population will embrace new methodologies and use them to lay the foundation for how we all will face aging. The revolution that the age 50 and older generation began in the 1960s is entering a new phase, and again, they will change the face of society, this time leading us into maturity.

REFERENCES

AARP. (2000). *Reforming the Health Care System: State Profiles 2000.* Washington, DC: AARP Public Policy Institute.

Bonder, B.R., Martin, L., & Miracle, A. (2001). Achieving cultural competence: The challenge for clients and health care workers in a multi-cultural society. *Generations, XXV, 1,* 35–43.

Brody, J.E. (2000, January 18). Personal health: Adding zeal to the golden years. *New York Times.* Retrieved January 18, 2000, from http://www.nytimes.com

Butler, R.N., Lewis, M.I., & Sunderland, T. (1991). *Aging and mental health: Positive psychosocial and biomedical approaches* (4th ed.). New York: Macmillan Publishing Company.

Carmichael, C. (2001, May 20). Last right: When a friend asked for help, I couldn't refuse. Her choice still haunts me. *New York Times Magazine, 98.*

Center for Medicare Education. (2001). Developing culturally appropriate Medicare education materials. *Issue Brief, 2*(4).

Dychtwald, K. (1999). *Age power: How the 21st century will be ruled by the new old.* New York: Jeremy P. Tarcher/Putnam.

Erikson, E.H. (1964). *Uprootedness in our time: Responsibility and identity.* New York: W.W. Norton.

Green, J.W. (1982). *Cultural awareness in the human services.* Englewood Cliffs, NJ: Prentice Hall.

Grigsby, J. (1996, November 29). Bridging the gap: Capitalizing on baby boomer buying power. *Business Press, 9*(31).

Hilts, P.J. (1999, June 1). Life at age 100 is surprisingly healthy. *New York Times.* Retrieved January 18, 2000, from http://www.nytimes.com.

Hobbs, F.B., & Damon, B.L. (2001, April). 65+ in the US. *US Bureau of Census Current Population Reports, Special Studies,* pp. 23–190.

Katsnelson, N. (1991). Bronx sub-committee examines mental health issues. *Resettlement Newsletter, 4.* New York: UJA-Federation Agency Professional Task Force on Immigrants and Refugees.

Johnson, C. (2000). Meditations on quality of life. *Scientific American Presents the Quest to Beat Aging, 11*(2), 94–97.

Joseph, J. (1987). Warning. In Sandra Martz (Ed.), *When I am an old woman, I shall wear purple.* Watsonville, CA: Papier-Mache Press.

Levine, C. (2000). *Always on call: When illness turns families into caregivers.* New York: United Hospital Fund.

Moon, M. (1991). Health issues in living longer and living better. *The Public Policy and Aging Report,* 11:3, National Academy on an Aging Society.

National Vital Statistics System (1997), Volume 47(28).

O'Gara, N. (2001, May 9). *Consumers and the Internet: Can care providers use the Internet to advance their business objectives?* A presentation to HANYs 2001 Continuing Care Symposium, Albany, NY.

Roques, C., & Hovanec, L. (2001). Tele-medicine and the reduction of psychiatric admissions for dementia patients—social work as the core discipline. *Journal of Social Work in Long-Term Care, 1*(1).

Rother, J. (1999, March 21). As interviewed by Robert Stock, *65: Not an aging, but an expanded state of mind.* Retrieved March 21, 1999, from http://www.nytimes.com.

Rowe, J., & Kahn, R. (1998). *Successful aging.* New York: Pantheon.

Schwartz, J., & Rupert, H. (1996, October 7). Boomer boom. *Ad Week—Western Edition, Supplement Superbrands,* 46:41.

Smeeding, T. (2001). Living longer, living better? Economic status in old age. *The Public Policy and Aging Report,* 11(3), National Academy on an Aging Society.

U.S. Census Bureau. (2000, January). Population projections of the US by age, sex, race. *Hispanic origin and nativity.* Washington, DC: Author.

Weinberg, J. (1977). Preface. In R. Glasscote, J. Gudeman, & D. Miles (Eds.), *Creative mental health services for the elderly.* Washington, DC: Joint Information Service of the American Psychiatric Association.

2

AUTONOMY AND CONSUMER EMPOWERMENT

Making Quality of Life the Organizing Principle for Long-Term Care Policy

Lawrence Polivka and Jennifer R. Salmon

MEMBERS OF THE HUGE BABY BOOM GENERATION became involved with the United States's long-term care system by helping their aging parents and grandparents receive the long-term care they needed. They learned that Medicaid was the primary payer for publicly supported long-term care, predominantly paying for nursing facility care, which by and large offered double-occupancy rooms in buildings resembling hospitals and lacked the homelike features supporting a frail elder's identity and quality of life. The baby boomers' mostly negative experiences with a system dominated by institutionalized care, along with a growing awareness of what they may face as older adults, is certain to make long-term care a highly visible public policy issue by 2010, when the first wave of the baby boom generation turns 65. As awareness of the 21st century's publicly supported long-term health care services increases, it is likely that public dissatisfaction with the policies, ethics, regulations, and moral obligations of the existing system will grow as well.

CONSUMER-DIRECTED CARE

Critics of the late–20th-century long-term care system advocated for qualitative changes in the methods and kinds of care provided to older adults, rather than incremental changes involving a "little more of this and a little less of that" (Angel & Angel, 1997; Institute of Medicine, 1986; Kane, Kane, & Ladd, 1998; Vladeck, 1995). Many supported a major qualitative change that would move control of long-term care resources from provider agencies to individual consumers who needed and used the available resources. This strategy was the foundation for a health care paradigm known as *consumer-directed care* (CDC), defined by the National Institute on Consumer-Directed Long-Term Care as

> A philosophy and orientation to the delivery of home and community-based services whereby informed consumers make choices about the services they receive. Consumer-direction ranges from the individual independently making all decisions and managing services directly, to an individual using a representative to manage needed services. Choice and control are both key elements of any consumer-directed system. (Wagner, Nadash, Friedman, Litvak, & Eckels, 1996, p. 1)

Although this approach to care originally pertained to programs that built on strengths of people with disabilities, such as the independent living movement, at the end of the 20th century this concept was also applied to elders, who represented 12% of the total population but 59% of the population with disabilities (Benjamin, 1996).

California, Oregon, Washington, and Michigan developed very large CDC programs for frail elders, and their evaluation findings indicate that they were exceptionally popular with recipients and caregivers. These programs were a cost-effective alternative to institutional care, traditional agency-directed home care, and community-based care for many frail older adults with serious impairment. The results from these programs provided clear evidence that CDC was not only an appropriate form of long-term care for many people with disabilities but also was a possible long-term care resource for frail older adults.

ETHICAL BASIS FOR CONSUMER EMPOWERMENT

In the development of long-term care policy and practice, policy makers do not adequately recognize or value autonomy as an achievable goal for frail older adults. To achieve short-term bureaucratic or fiscal goals, policy makers and providers compromise frail older adults' need and desire to remain as autonomous as their impairments allow through the provision of supportive, nurturing environments and services.

Consumer-directed care's philosophy recognizes the value of autonomy, in a strengths-based approach, as a moral obligation. CDC addresses this responsibility by nurturing the autonomy of people with disabilities, including frail older adults, and providing long-term care in the least restrictive manner compatible with the concerns and resources of the individual.

One way to develop a compelling ethical framework for long-term care is to redefine the relationship between personal autonomy and dependency and equally emphasize both. Policy makers must recognize the value of autonomy even for adults with the most severe impairments without losing sight of their physical and resource limitations. Autonomy is more than just having the power to keep others from intervening in an individual's life without fully informed and noncoerced consent (dubbed *negative autonomy* by Collopy, 1988). Autonomy is also the power of an individual, however dependent, to interact and to communicate freely with others, to give and to receive affection, and to initiate actions that are consistent with the person's sense of self. This *positive autonomy* is especially important in the development of an ethic for long-term care (Collopy, 1988). Positive autonomy preserves a person's sense of self and extends the boundaries of his or her own volitional capacities.

> CONSUMER-DIRECTED care's philosophy recognizes the value of autonomy, in a strengths-based approach, as a moral obligation.

The CDC philosophy supports the ethical principles of autonomy (self-rule), beneficence (doing only good), and justice (intergenerational fairness). Marshall Kapp (1999) noted

> The autonomy model respects individuals enough to allow and encourage them to make their own voluntary and knowing choices about . . . the financing and delivery arrangements of their home- and community-based [long-term care]. . . . [E]ffective promotion of the choice helps to achieve congruence with social and political values. Our society values choice as an end in itself, and therefore it is politically and philosophically important to facilitate such choice in public and private insurance programs. (1999, p. 28)

All generations of people consider the use of public funds to provide a person care in his or her own home or in a community-residential setting, such as an assisted living facility rather than in a nursing facility, a just use of public dollars. In fact, there is no evidence that an intergenerational conflict exists regarding the distribution of monies to include long-term care needs for older adults (National Council on the Aging, 2001).

There is evidence that strengths-enhancing policies benefit consumers by reducing their stress and increasing their satisfaction with care by empowering them with personal choice (Kapp, 1999), and by supporting the ethical concern for beneficence. Kapp argued that the regulatory and legal environment of long-term care increases anxiety in service providers and surrogates of disabled consumers, who will forego autonomy because "choices are thought to expose the provider, case manager, surrogate, or advocate to unacceptable legal risk, for

HEALTH CARE professionals and policy makers must consider positive autonomy when shaping policies and service strategies. They must view the world of long-term care from the frail elder's perspective and support the person's need to define and to make a world that is consistent with his or her own identity.

instance, even when those choices might have actually benefited the well-being of the patient/consumer" (p. 23). These stakeholders are concerned that allowing consumers to exercise choice may result in a negative event that puts them at legal risks.

To formulate an ethical standard for the care of people who are dependent, policy makers and caregivers need a concept of autonomy that is influenced by realities of the day-to-day life of long-term care recipients. Health care professionals and policy makers must consider positive autonomy when shaping policies and service strategies. They must view the world of long-term care from the frail elder's perspective and support the person's need to define and to make a world that is consistent with his or her own identity.

CASH AND COUNSELING

The Cash and Counseling program is the most common version of consumer-directed care, affording people a choice of a case-managed service benefit or a monthly cash allowance of a monetary value lower than the service benefit. The service benefit is a traditional agency-managed set of services that a consumer may or may not select and is under the direction of the agency case manager. To receive a monthly cash allowance, an individual would supply documentation showing how the allowance would be used effectively for his or her long-term care. The person, often in consultation with a family member, is then able to spend the allowance in ways he or she sees fit. As a *consumer,* the person may choose to purchase services from a home care agency or a referral service at current rates, or pay a friend or a relative to provide personal assistance services. He or she may also choose to make needed home modifications, move to an assisted living facility, or arrange other available housing opportunities.

The counseling component of this program provides consumers and their families with information and assistance to manage care. Counseling involves a case worker or social worker assessing a person's strengths and needs and providing advice about consumer information, financing, and information on housing alternatives, among other topics. Centers for independent living, area agencies on aging, other public or private organizations, or people who do not have a vested financial interest in the decisions made by the consumer may also provide counseling services. This cash and counseling version of the CDC paradigm could theoretically be incorporated into any state or federally funded long-term care program—including nursing facilities and assisted living facilities—that serves frail elders and people of all ages with a range of disabilities.

In addition to consumer satisfaction with the choice, control, and quality of care provided, there is considerable evidence that CDC programs are less expensive and more efficient than agency-based programs. The programs provide more hours of service at less cost than traditional agency-directed programs or nursing facilities. For example, California's CDC model in the late 1990s paid the state's minimum wage of $5.75 an hour for a maximum of 283 hours per month, totaling $1,627.25 (Doty, Benjamin, Matthias, & Franke, 1999). Medicaid, however, paid more than twice that amount for nursing facility care, while home care visits paid for by state and federal programs may cost as much as $25.00 per hour.

A consumer-directed care approach to long-term care provides frail elders, individuals with disabilities, their caregivers, as well as the state and federal government the following benefits:

> IN ADDITION TO consumer satisfaction with the choice, control, and quality of care provided, there is considerable evidence that CDC programs are less expensive and more efficient than agency-based programs.

- Maximum flexibility, autonomy, and decision-making power by offering access to information and professional advice and allowing individuals to decide how best to meet their long-term care needs

- Help from relatives, friends, or neighbors, using a simple and non-bureaucratic way to support informal caregivers

- Services that are less expensive and more appropriate to personal concerns and preferences

- Savings on the high unit costs of government-purchased services

- Lower costs per consumer by establishing the monthly cash allowance as a percentage of the case-managed service-benefit cost (other administrative savings may be achieved because of lower billings and claims handling costs)

- Long-term care services that are responsive to consumer concerns rather than government regulations and administrative decisions — giving consumers the flexibility and independence to spend their money as they best see fit, thereby improving the market for home- and community-based services

EXERCISING AUTONOMY

The importance of autonomy is evident from the findings of the Robert Wood Johnson Foundation's (RWJF) Independent Choices Project study of the values and the preferences of 294 randomly selected long-term care recipients in the Tampa Bay, Florida, area (Salmon, 2001; Salmon & Polivka, 2000). The participants in the study included home-care consumers, assisted living consumers, and nursing facility consumers. The study revealed that, generally, people within each consumer group highly valued the capacity to maintain control over their care and their lives. In addition, their sense of personal control over life, as measured by nine questions that address mastery (Ryff & Keyes, 1995), clearly contributed to their enhanced sense of psychological well-being and to consumer satisfaction. Statistically controlling for demographic and need characteristics, for consumers in all settings, personal control contributed the most to life satisfaction. It contributed more to life satisfaction than health, function, socioeconomic status, and having a caregiver available.

These consumers preferred to discuss housing, health, and financial issues with caregivers, but ultimately they wanted to make their own decisions. In fact, nursing facility respondents were more likely to want to exercise control over housing and finances than the consumers who resided in the assisted living and home care environments. For the home-care consumers in the study, one-third of them preferred CDC approaches and few preferred the traditional agency-directed model. Half of the home-care consumers expressed no preference for CDC or agency models or simply did not like any of the models presented.

These findings are compatible with those from studies conducted in Arkansas, Florida, and New Jersey, as part of another RWJF Independent Choices Project. For example, in a telephone survey of 491 Medicaid personal care consumers in Arkansas, one-third were interested in CDC and one-fourth were unsure (Simon-Rusinowitz et. al., 1997). Historically, interest in cash and counseling is high among younger people with disabilities, but these studies demonstrate there is a good deal of interest by frail elders as well (Simon-Rusinowitz et al., 1997).

The older adults' interest in a cash benefit may be related to the availability and interest of a family member. In Arkansas, 56% of surrogate decision-makers (who were generally family) were interested in the cash option when speaking for themselves (rather than answering for the frail elder) and the presence of an informal caregiver was associated with the frail elder's interest in the cash option (Simon-Rusinowitz et al., 1997). The authors suggested that the presence of a caregiver may give the frail elder the confidence to choose a cash option because the caregiver can serve as an emergency backup if the paid worker fails to come to work.

In a survey of 20 long-term care policy experts in aging and disability communities, Simon-Rusinowitz and colleagues found that although the experts were generally supportive of consumer-directed care they also expressed some reservations. These experts' main concerns included the potential for fraud and abuse, caregiver working conditions, potential incompatibility with managed care, and resistance from traditional providers (Simon-Rusinowitz, Bochniak, Mahoney, Marks, & Hecht, 2000).

IMPLEMENTATION OF CONSUMER-DIRECTED CARE

The ethical framework for caregivers as suggested by Simon-Rusinowitz and colleagues (2000) supports a policy designed to balance the protection of autonomy with the realities of dependency and interdependency in the provision of long-term care for frail older adults and individuals with disabilities.

The use of fiscal intermediaries, surrogate decision-makers, and care advocates who are responsible for quality assurance monitoring should help states keep fraud, abuse, and neglect to a minimum. In California, most consumers elect to have payroll and taxes done by accountants, reducing the amount of cash given directly to the consumer (Doty et al., 1999).

> THE USE OF FISCAL intermediaries, surrogate decision-makers, and care advocates who are responsible for quality assurance monitoring should help states keep fraud, abuse, and neglect to a minimum.

The vast majority of caregivers in all long-term care programs during the late 20th century were paid low wages and many of them did not have basic health care benefits. Family caregivers worked without any remuneration. CDC is designed to improve the lot of these caregivers by allowing them to be paid directly by the frail elder. Direct payments to the caregiver are generally higher than when the individual works through an agency. In addition, some caregivers may prefer lower wages if health care benefits are covered.

Although half of the consumers prefer consumer-directed care, half still prefer some form of agency-based services. This fact in itself may alleviate service providers' resistance to CDC since implementing CDC systemwide does not mean that agency-based services will end. In fact, these providers should incorporate many consumer-directed features into their agency-based programs and improve satisfaction with their services. For example, the current agency-directed approach does not allow the agency to hire the family caregiver. In the future, the agency-based programs could provide the fiscal and monitoring functions but still allow the consumer to select the caregiver.

Another form of agency-directed care is managed long-term care. Managed acute care connotes loss of consumer control over decisions and so managed care organizations (MCOs) could incorporate consumer-directed approaches to long-term care, as well. The fundamental difference is in payment; MCOs receive a capitated rate to provide long-term care services to frail elders. They may choose to provide a cash benefit to their members or to incorporate consumer choice into their services by doing a better job of matching services to clients and meeting their needs as defined by the client and not by the case manager.

As mentioned previously, CDC's ethical framework is designed to balance the protection of autonomy with the realities of dependency and interdependency in the provision of long-term care for frail elders and younger adults with disabilities. Health care professionals and policy makers have only begun to tap into the potential of programs designed to accommodate dependency by providing resources for the exercise of autonomy. Many people have waited for empirical research to demonstrate that these programs can be implemented with very frail older adults who also have cognitive impairments.

CONSUMER-DIRECTED CARE AND INDIVIDUALS WITH COGNITIVE IMPAIRMENTS

Policy makers and health care professionals have argued that CDC is not an appropriate model of long-term care for frail elders with cognitive impairments. Their concern is due to the potential conflict between a model of care designed to protect and nurture consumer autonomy and a segment of the population whose autonomy has been compromised by dementia. The challenge is to reconcile the moral and technical objectives of consumer direction (autonomy and cost-effectiveness) with the realities of cognitive impairment experienced by some frail elders. The capacity of consumer-directed care to meet the concerns of people with cognitive impairments is based on the following premises:

1. Autonomy is as important and as practical for people with cognitive impairments as it is for those without—as long as the former are capable of having and expressing their values, with assistance if necessary. The capacity to express values remains in the early to middle stages of dementia but is lost in late-stage dementia, along with any meaningful notion of personal autonomy. It is critical to help frail elders with cognitive impairments express their values and make decisions during these earlier stages of dementia.

2. People with cognitive impairments who are capable of expressing values can receive assistance from caregivers in carrying out activities consistent with their values.

3. Caregivers and frail elders act as a *collective consumer*, with the caregiver serving as a surrogate who provides reasonably defined substituted judgment for the care recipient who is cognitively impaired. From this perspective, CDC is designed also to empower the caregiver, who is most often a family member. In this strengths-based approach, the caregiver is acting in the presumed interest of the care recipient under monitoring by a care manager or advocate.

Research has demonstrated that early stages of Alzheimer's disease affect a person's ability to create new long-term memories based on recent events due to neuronal damage in the hippocampus. Interestingly, the disease does not impinge on the regions of the brain that affect the interaction of reasoning and decision-making with emotions and feelings, especially as they relate to personal and social values (Jaworska, 1999). As a result, it is possible for individuals with Alzheimer's disease to express values consistent with their past. In fact, those with mild to moderate impairment (scoring as low as 13 on the Folstein Mini-Mental Status Examination) were able to answer consistently, accurately, and reliably—over two points in time—questions about themselves, their preferences, and their involvement in everyday care (Feinberg,

> INTERESTINGLY, [Alzheimer's] disease does not impinge on the regions of the brain that affect the interaction of reasoning and decision-making with emotions and feelings, especially as they relate to personal and social values.

Whitlach, & Tucker, 2000). Four of five of these elders expressed that they valued remaining at home and not living in a nursing facility.

The frail elder does not need to be the person to carry out these values in order to feel autonomous; this can be the role of the caregiver. In fact, Jaworska noted that

> The essence of the capacity for autonomy consists in the ability to lay down the principles that will govern one's actions, and not in the ability to devise and carry out the means and plans for following these principles. . . the very ability to value, even if more instrumental abilities are absent, supplies the starting points for the exercise of autonomy, and thereby renders the person capable of autonomy. (1999, p. 19)

In another study, frail elders with cognitive impairments clearly did value family and friends over paid services for help with instrumental activities of daily living (IADLs) such as housekeeping, and ADLs such as personal care (Feinberg et al., 2000), so their ability to maintain some aspects of their autonomy should be supported.

Although autonomy is generally defined as *self-rule,* in the context of older adults with cognitive impairments, there is a *collective consumer*—the elder and his or her caregiver. In most ethical discourse, substituted judgment is the antithesis of autonomy, but in this case, it is not. Kapp noted, "We should favor the substituted judgment standard when individualized assessments indicate [that it is] an adequately reliable, honest record of the consumer's own pertinent wishes" (1999, p. 32). Both caregivers and frail elders with cognitive impairment expressed concern for the other's interests when making plans regarding the future; their position supports the ethical concern for justice between generations. Caregivers of frail elders with cognitive impairments should provide care or use services in ways that are congruent with the elders' preferences. For example, they could use paid services when the elder preferred that option and they could use family and friends when that was the elder's preference (Feinberg et al., 2000).

In summary, there is ethical and research support for consumer-directed care for frail elders with cognitive impairments such as Alzheimer's disease. Using a strengths-based approach that supports the existing capacity of a person to express values that the caregiver carries out is a reasonable compromise between independence and total dependency (Kapp, 1999).

OUTCOMES OF CONSUMER-DIRECTED CARE

In addition to the research on the desire for CDC in long-term care and on the capacity of individuals with cognitive impairments to express their values and preferences for CDC, there have been several statewide, regional, and national research studies demonstrating the effectiveness of CDC in terms of consumer satisfaction, cost/savings, and reductions in fraud and abuse. These studies provide convincing evidence of the efficacy of this approach to long-term care.

A regional study of 879 Medicaid home care beneficiaries in Maryland, Michigan, and Texas revealed that those clients who had more choices reported more satisfaction with their services than those without choices. Ninety percent of the clients who said they had a great deal of choice were very satisfied with their caregivers, whereas 60% who had very little choice were very satisfied. (Doty, Kasper, & Litvak, 1996; Taylor, 1991).

THE CALIFORNIA IN-HOME SUPPORTIVE SERVICES PROGRAM   The California In-Home Supportive Services (IHSS) program is the largest and oldest consumer-directed care program in the United States, serving more than 200,000 consumers annually, approximately half of whom are 65 years old and older. The IHSS program provides two models of long-term care. A *consumer-directed model* (CDM—the equivalent of CDC) permits consumers to hire and fire, schedule, train, and supervise their own personal assistance services providers, imposing little or no restrictions on the caregiver that a consumer may hire, such as friends, neighbors, family members, or agency-managed caregivers. A CDM typically places all of the responsibility for recruiting and selecting a caregiver on the consumer and any family or friends who are willing to assist in the decision. Alternatively, the *professional management model* (PMM—the equivalent of the traditional agency model) requires that the agency hires employees and assigns them to clients. Within the PMM, consumer choice of caregivers is generally restricted to veto power. The agency would honor a request for a new caregiver if it had a replacement available.

A telephone survey of 1,095 randomly selected IHSS consumers and 618 client-employed or agency caregivers revealed that the consumer-directed model outperformed the professional management model. Under the most rigorous comparisons, such as the severity of disability and availability of informal supports, the consumer-directed model of service provision consistently yielded superior results with respect to consumer satisfaction with services, empowerment, and quality of life (Benjamin, Matthias, Franke, & Mills, 1998).

The CDM consumers had more significant impairments and needed more assistance with ADLs and IADLs than the PMM consumers, but both were equally as likely to have cognitive impairments. The CDM consumers were significantly more likely to have service choice and to be satisfied with the technical quality of those services. They rated highly service impact and had higher levels of emotional, social, and physical well-being. There were no significant differences between the two programs in terms of client assertiveness, unmet needs, provider shortages, or general satisfaction (Benjamin et al., 1998; Doty et al., 1999). In addition, the PMM consumers did not have better safety outcomes. Although CDM consumers reported occurrences of abuse, neglect, and mistreatment, they reported such occurrences either less frequently or no more frequently than consumers in the professional management model. In fact, family caregivers are more likely to provide a higher quality of service than agency-employed caregivers (Doty et al., 1999). Family providers have a distinct advantage over non-family providers because they can legally perform paramedical or medically related tasks such as bowel and bladder care and administration of medications.

There were difficulties in recruiting providers, however, with one-quarter of CDM consumers reporting this problem. The professional-agency model may be the better choice for consumers with severe disabilities who cannot rely on informal helpers or who lack confidence in their own abilities to make alternative arrangements for backup help. At the same time, workers in both programs were equally satisfied with their jobs, even though the agency-employed caregivers earn 30% more per hour than the client-employed caregivers.

AUSTRIA'S LONG-TERM CARE ALLOWANCE   Austria implemented the Federal Long-Term Care Allowance Act in 1994, funded by the general tax revenues and payments from employers and employees. The program was designed to

1. Provide a uniform payment to help compensate for care-related expenses
2. Promote a *self-determination* lifestyle
3. Enable people with disabilities to remain in their own homes
4. Encourage families to provide care
5. Link previously existing provincial allowances

The program is available to citizens age 3 and older who have a permanent disability and who require 50 or more hours of care each month. Benefit levels ranged in 1994 from $250 to $2,500 per month. Consumers with cognitive impairments may select someone to manage their cash benefit (Keigher, 1997; Rubisch, Wotzel, & Phillip, 1995; Tilly, 1999). A survey of 3,120 beneficiaries, 75% of whom were over the age of 65 and many of whom were severely impaired, revealed that 81% of the respondents used their allowance to compensate family caregivers and 29% used their allowance to make home modifications. (Some beneficiaries used their allowance for both.) In addition, 71% of the individuals reported greater control over their caregiver arrangements and their ability to handle daily pressure.

GERMANY'S SOCIAL DEPENDENCY INSURANCE   Germany's Social Dependency Insurance (SDI) program is similar to Austria's allowance program. In 1995, insurance benefits became available to people with disabilities regardless of their age. The purpose of the program was to

1. Compensate consumers for the cost of care
2. Promote home care
3. Improve the lives of consumers and their caregivers

Beneficiaries can choose one of three options: cash benefits, agency services that have twice the monetary value of the cash benefits, or a combination of the two (*combination benefit*). They are paid based on three levels of dependency from needing help at least once a day with two or more ADLs to needing help 24 hours per day. Service benefits are available for those dependents in nursing facilities if home care or day care is not possible (Schneider, 1997).

In 1996, people with the lowest level of dependency in the cash benefit program received $250 per month, whereas the service benefit was $468 per month. This cash must be used to help meet the consumer's long-term care needs. In the SDI program's first year of operation, 84% of consumers with the lowest level of dependency chose the cash benefits, as did 67% of those consumers with the highest level of dependency. Consumers who choose cash also receive periodic counseling as well as visits from professionals who help assure quality and proper expenditure of the cash (Schneider, 1997).

In 1996, 10,400 SDI program consumers were surveyed about their use and satisfaction with the program. More than 75% of them were 65 years old or older. The study revealed that 72% of them felt that the program was necessary to maintain their independence. An overwhelming majority of consumers who responded reported high levels of satisfaction with being able to decide for themselves how to use their benefits. Of all respondents, 43% reported that their quality of care had improved under the program, and only 2% reported that quality had declined (Runde, Goese, Kerschke-Risch, Scholz, & Wiegel, 1996). Germans rated SDI an immense public policy success in terms of providing security and support to informal caregivers, balancing the long-term care system in favor of in-home care, improving quality of care, increasing the number of providers and consumer choice, and reducing dependence on social assistance even with a high use of SDI (Cuellar & Wiener, 2000). In addition to these benefits, expenditures were kept well below projections and within a politically acceptable range (Cuellar & Weiner, 2000). The German experience provided several lessons:

1. New long-term care programs can be implemented and stay within budget.
2. A national long-term care system can provide substantial fiscal relief to state and local governments that fund long-term care.
3. A new program that is clearly defined will justify additional taxes, especially when the new entitlement includes a cash alternative.
4. A large, western nation can provide a long-term care system that is balanced in favor of community-based rather than institutional benefits (Tilly, 1999).

OTHER CDC BENEFITS   Much smaller CDC demonstration projects were implemented in the Netherlands and France during the early 1990s. The Netherlands project had an experimental design that allowed random assignment of consumers to a CDC program and a regular agency-directed program. An evaluation of the project found that the CDC consumers were more satisfied in terms of worker efficiency and continuity of care than those in the agency-directed program, although the use of the CDC program decreased with advanced age. The research findings led to implementation of a permanent CDC program for people with disabilities (Tilly, 1999). On the whole, the findings from studies of these CDC programs, large and small, state and national, indicate considerable satisfaction with the kinds of choice and control this model provides and with the quality of care consumers are able to receive in CDC compared with the more traditional, agency-directed programs. Furthermore, there is considerable evidence that CDC programs are less expensive than agency-based programs and more efficient in that they provide more hours of service at less cost than the agency-directed programs.

CONCLUSIONS AND POLICY IMPLICATIONS

The philosophical and empirical cases for consumer empowerment through self-directed, long-term care may be summarized as follows:

1. Human identity in Western societies is substantially based on a strong sense of autonomy and personal agency. There is substantial evidence that the value of autonomy to identity, life satisfaction, and psychological well-being among Americans is growing. It will be even more important to the baby boom generation for whom sustaining a strengths-based approach, found by supporting autonomy, will be a major concern. Physical and cognitive impairments may limit an individual's capacity to act autonomously, but they do not diminish the significance of autonomy as a pillar of identity in organizing a principle sense of self.

2. The research done on the importance of choice and control (autonomy) to recipients of long-term care services indicated that a substantial percentage of individuals want greater control over delivery of care. The ability to exercise choice and control greatly affects the recipients' sense of psychological well-being and overall quality of life.

3. The value of autonomy has been largely ignored in the development of long-term care policy for the frail older adult, which is one of the major reasons the United States' publicly supported long-term care system is dominated by nursing facilities. This support of nursing facilities is a far more flagrant case of neglect of the frail older adult than would occur under any CDC program. CDC was designed to nurture the autonomy of the frail older adult and respond to his or her realities of dependency. Many non-affluent frail older adults who qualify for publicly supported long-term care services avoid them for fear of losing their autonomy and ending up in a nursing facility. Older adults also fear being caught in a bureaucratic environment that may erode their privacy and the intimate arrangements of their daily lives. This is why many frail older adults struggle with their impairments to the point that they have no choice but to surrender virtually all of their autonomy and enter a nursing facility.

4. Evaluation findings indicate that consumer-directed programs are exceptionally popular with consumers and caregivers and are a cost-

effective alternative to institutional care and agency-directed care for many seriously impaired older adults. These findings provide clear evidence that CDC is as appropriate a form of long-term care for many frail older adults as it has been for younger people with disabilities. As long as cognitively impaired people have the capacity to form and express values and have competent caregivers, they should be considered legitimate candidates for CDC.

5. Consumer-directed care is not for every frail older adult in need of long-term care services, but it should be an option for far more consumers who desire it. The available empirical findings suggested that CDC is the most flexible form of long-term care because it can be designed to permit the consumer to pay for individual caregivers, as well as community-residential care and, if necessary, nursing facility care. CDC could empower the consumer across the full spectrum of long-term care services by providing the financial means for consumers to choose the most appropriate care, rather than sending public dollars directly to home care agencies and nursing facilities without consumer involvement in the decision.

Long-term care providers should not be alarmed by the prospect of CDC programs. As the frail older adult population grows, these professionals will be pressed to meet the concerns of those who cannot benefit from a CDC approach to community-based long-term care. Furthermore, providers themselves may benefit from the development of CDC programs in that the programs' popularity with the general public could create a more favorable atmosphere for increased funding of home and community care, including agency-directed programs. Growth in funding for these programs has been slow or nonexistent in many states for several years (Ladd, Kane, & Kane, 1999) and CDC initiatives could help move home- and community-based care to the top of the policy agenda over the next decade.

The CDC approach to community-based long-term care will certainly require a change in the way agencies provide case management. As consumer strengths are supported, case managers will have to relinquish the kind of control characteristic of conventional case management strategies and take on the role of advisor, counselor, and advocate for the consumer. The increased satisfaction that these role changes are likely to bring the consumer and caregiver should be gratifying for the case manager as he or she witnesses lives enhanced by the exercise of autonomy under conditions of physical and mental impairment (see Chapter 4). Providers must be prepared to adapt to the emergence of CDC because, with the aging of the baby boom generation, the odds are it will become the preferred method for financing long-term care service.

CDC is not just a means of empowering the consumer; it is also a program to empower the collective caregiver—consumer unit and enhance the capacity of the informal system. CDC can provide high-quality care for much longer periods of time than many unsupported caregivers could sustain. A CDC design that incorporates family caregivers is likely to be more effective than a design that excludes family members and more compatible with a broad commitment to the value of public policies that support the family.

Finally, as state and the federal governments are now responding to the Supreme Court's 1999 decision (Olmstead v. L.C.; Rosenbaum, 2000), regarding the use of home- and community-based long-term care rather than institutional care, advocates should make every effort to convince the public and the policy makers that CDC is the best approach. The objective of health care professionals and caregivers should be to make CDC a principle vehicle for in-home care for frail older adults by persuading the federal government to implement powerful incentives to move states toward the CDC model. Advocates of the CDC program should work at state and federal levels of government to gain acceptance of CDC programs that include paying family caregivers an adequate amount so good care is sustained. More specifically, health care professionals should work to convince Congress and the Centers for Medicare and Medicaid Services (CMS) that states should be permitted to include CDC programs. These programs should be designed to pay family caregivers from the state's Medicaid plans, as either revisions to the state's personal care programs or as new programs.

REFERENCES

Angel, R.J., & Angel, J.L. (1997). *Who will care for us? Aging and long-term care in multicultural America.* New York: New York University Press.

Benjamin, A.E. (1996). Trends among younger persons with disability or chronic disease. In R.H. Binstock, L.E. Cluff, & O. Von Mering (Eds.), *The future of long-term care: Social and policy issues* (pp. 75–95). Baltimore: The Johns Hopkins University Press.

Benjamin, A.E., Matthias, R., Franke, T., & Mills, L. (1998). *Comparing client-directed and agency models for providing supportive services at home: Final report.* Los Angeles: University of California.

Collopy, B.J. (1988). Autonomy in long-term care: Some crucial distinctions. *Gerontologist, 28,* 10–17.

Cuellar, A., & Wiener, J. (2000). Can social insurance for long-term care work? The experience of Germany. *Health Affairs, 19*(3), 8–29.

Doty, P., Benjamin, A.E., Matthias, R.E., & Franke, T. M. (1999). *In-home supportive services for the elderly and disabled: A comparison of client-directed and professional management models of service delivery: Non-technical summary report.* Los Angeles: U.S. Department of Health and Human Services and the University of California.

Doty, P., Kasper, J., & Litvak (1996). Consumer-directed models of personal care: Lessons from Medicaid. *Milbank Quarterly, 74,* N3, 377–409.

Feinberg, L.F., Whitlach, C.J., & Tucker, S. (2000). *Making hard choices, respecting both voices: Final report.* San Francisco: Family Caregiver Alliance.

Institute of Medicine. (1986). *Improving the quality of care in nursing homes.* Washington, DC: National Academy Press.

Jaworska, A. (1999). Respecting the margins of agency: Alzheimer's patients and the capacity to value. *Philosophy & Public Affairs, 28,* N2, 105–138.

Kane, R.A., Kane, R.L., & Ladd, R.C. (1998). *The heart of long-term care.* New York: Oxford University Press.

Kapp, M. (1999). Health care in the marketplace: Implications for decisionally impaired consumers and their surrogates and advocates. *Southern Illinois University Law Journal, 24,* 1–51.

Keigher, S. (1997). Austria's new attendance allowance: A consumer choice model of care for the frail and disabled. *International Journal of Health Services, 27*(4), 753–765.

Ladd, R.C., Kane, R.L., & Kane, R.A. (1999, April). *State LTC Profiles Report, 1996.* Minneapolis: University of Minnesota, Division of Health Services Research and Policy, School of Public Health.

National Council on the Aging. (July 22, 2001). Survey finds young adults favor preserving social security. Retrieved July 22, 2001 from http://www.ncoa.org/news/archives.

Rosenbaum, S. (2000, November). *In brief: Olmstead v. L.C. Implications for older persons with mental and physical disabilities.* Washington, DC: AARP Public Policy Institute.

Rubisch, M., Wotzel, W., & Phillip, S. (1995). *Provision for long-term care in Austria.* (P. Stallybrass, Trans.). Vienna, Austria: Federal Ministry of Labour and Social Affairs.

Runde, P., Goese, R., Kerschke-Risch, P., Scholz, U., & Wiegel, D. (1996). *Einstellungen und Verhalten zur Pflegersicherung und zur Hauslichen Plege.* (J.P. Hopperger, Trans.). Hamburg, Germany: Universitat Hamburg.

Ryff, C., & Keyes, C.L.M. (1995). The structure of psychological well-being revisited. *Journal of Personality and Social Psychology, 69,* 719–727.

Salmon, J.R. (2001). *The contribution of personal control and personal meaning to quality of life in home care, assisted living facility, and nursing facility settings.* Unpublished doctoral dissertation, University of South Florida, Tampa.

Salmon, J.R., & Polivka, L. (2000, Spring). Study shows link between control and consumer satisfaction. *Consumer Choice News,* p. 4+.

Schneider, U. (1997). *Germany's new long-term care policy: Profile and assessment of social dependency insurance. Policy paper #5.* AICGS Seminar Papers. Washington, DC: American Institute for Contemporary German Studies.

Simon-Rusinowitz, L., Bochniak, A.M., Mahoney, K.J., Marks, L.W., & Hecht, D. (2000, Fall). Implementation issues for consumer directed programs: A survey of policy experts. *Generations, 24*(3), 34–40.

Simon-Rusinowitz, L., Mahoney, K.J., Desmond, S.M., Shoop, D.M., Squillace, M.R., & Fay, R.A. (1997). Determining consumer preferences for a cash option: Arkansas survey results. *Health Care Financing Review, 19*(2), 73–96.

Taylor, H. (1991). *The importance of choice in Medicaid home care programs: Maryland, Michigan and Texas.* New York: The Commonwealth University.

Tilly, J. (1999). *Consumer-directed long-term care: Participants' experiences in five countries.* Washington, DC: American Association of Retired Persons.

Vladeck, B.C. (1995). Long-term care: The view from the Health Care Financing Administration. In J.M. Wiener, S.B. Clauser, & D.L. Kennell (Eds.), *Persons with disabilities: Issues in health care financing and service delivery.* Washington, DC: Brookings Institution.

Wagner, D., Nadash, P., Friedman, A., Litvak, S., & Eckels, K. (1996). *Principles of consumer-directed home and community-based services.* Washington, DC: National Council on the Aging.

3

STRENGTHS-BASED HEALTH CARE

Self-Advocacy and Wellness in Aging

Raymond Vickers

IN JONATHAN SWIFT'S CLASSIC NOVEL, *Gulliver's Travels* (1726), protagonist Gulliver traveled to the Kingdom of Luggnagg where he found that most of the inhabitants were rather like human beings in the 20th century. Luggnuggians hoped that they could live a healthy life with few signs of aging and ultimately die peacefully after four score or so happy years. Other inhabitants, the Struld-bruggs, developed all of the signs of aging but were incapable of dying. The Struldbruggs were destined to live on, year after year and century after century. Ultimately, they became horribly wasted and ugly; they were rejected socially and existed only on handouts.

Swift's skillful use of irony helped his audience confront their simultaneous longings for immortality and their fears of decrepit dependency and thereby come to terms with the unavoidable process of aging. In the 21st century, advances in public health and medicine have increased a person's chances of surviving into old age and have helped individuals avoid many of the disorders associated with aging that were considered unavoidable in Swift's time. This means that by achieving wellness, a person might add life to years, not merely years to life.

As the population ages and more and more people reach their centennial birthday, terms such as *age-appropriate behavior, average life expectancy,* and *65-plus* will have less and less meaning. To try to define norms against which older people can be compared is to belie their extreme variability. Perhaps appropriate investigations into health concerns are overlooked because of expectations regarding human characteristics that are based on prejudices that a person's behavior is part of the aging condition.

Abraham Maslow (1974) pointed out that instead of comparing human beings with the norm, the only worthwhile scale to measure human characteristics is one that sets its peak performance standards at the highest possible level of attainment. Maslow's approach has been gaining ground in medicine. Utilizing the best available evidence for effective health care, many preventive practices have been introduced that are designed to avoid, or at least modify by early detection, unwelcome changes in the body and mind. These evidence-based guidelines include many conditions seen in older age (see http://www.guidelines.gov; enter *prevention* as a search word).

THE FIRST, THE SURVIVOR strategy, is cautious, more trenchant, and is for times when the person wishes to invest "whatever it takes" to achieve maximal results, even if the strategy is less well established. The second, the strategy for the maximal achiever, or *power user*, was borrowed from computer mavens and describes a person who wants to know the shortest and/or best way to reach a goal of peak performance.

This chapter discusses what happens to people as they age by helping readers to understand the changes associated with aging and where older adults stand in regard to their own perceived peak performance. For each challenge, this chapter usually suggests a health-care strategy for each of the two types of responses. The first, the *survivor* strategy, is cautious, more trenchant, and is for times when the person wishes to invest "whatever it takes" to achieve maximal results, even if the strategy is less well established. The second, the strategy for the maximal achiever, or *power user*, was borrowed from computer mavens and describes a person who wants to know the shortest and/or best way to reach a goal of peak performance. Aging gracefully requires ongoing choices about which, if any, of these two tactics (survivor or power user) to take.

Maslow also taught that before individuals can begin to satisfy their *higher needs* of life/love, self-esteem, and actualization, they must satisfy certain *basic needs*. All living organisms have these same basic needs that must be met, usually on a daily basis, in order to make survival possible. These physiological needs are

- Sensory awareness
- Oxygen
- Movement
- Rest
- Nutrition
- Excretion
- Defense

The medical model approach to health care accepts these basic and biological needs as essential to a human's existence and, consequently, attaches a pathological connotation to all physical ailments that interfere with the ability to meet any of these essential needs. Medical treatment has the simple objective that a person should regain a "disease-free" existence, but that is not as desirable an objective as the *positive wellness* objective conceived by the World Health Organization (WHO). Some of the changes that concern people as they age are not pathological but anatomical, physiological, and psychological; they do not threaten an individual's survival but may interfere with getting his or her physiological concerns met and may damage the person's self-esteem. So, instead of approaching the assessments of the diseases of aging in the traditional medical way, by reviewing the body organs system by system and disease by disease, the remainder of this chapter goes directly into describing how best to meet these biological concerns to ensure a person's survival. This is explained in a way that allows a person to exercise choice and enhance the sense of power involved in the process of self-determination. The goal is to assist people with growing older by explaining and clarifying some of the less threatening but pesky baggage of the aging process. Thus, positive wellness includes the strategy of accepting the changes of aging while using various tactics of coping with or ameliorating their effects.

SENSORY AWARENESS

Each of our five senses operates continuously, but at any one time, people may ignore the messages that some of their senses are sending to their brain so as to concentrate on one or two of the particular messages.

SENSORIUM

Picture how a person at a cocktail party can ignore all but the sound of one conversation and suppress the rest of the chatter, or how a woman can use her tactile senses to fasten the clasp of a necklace while suppressing the reversed visual reflection seen in the mirror. This rapidly shifting perception that lets people concentrate on what most interests them in their surroundings is termed the *sensorium.* What is commonly called *consciousness* is the process that takes this sensorium awareness of the world and instantly checks it against relevant items from memory. Reality testing is another way of describing this process, wherein the person consistently compares new sensory input with remembered beliefs. People's orientation to their surroundings is one result of all of these comparisons—they know when it is, where they are, and where they are headed by integrating what they currently perceive with what they already know. If perception becomes too preoccupied to conduct reality testing, or if consciousness is not working, then a person may become disoriented. Older people become disoriented more easily than younger people, but if it occurs frequently, a person should assess what exactly is causing it, rather than simply assume that his or her

> OLDER PEOPLE BECOME disoriented more easily than younger people, but if it occurs frequently, a person should assess what exactly is causing it, rather than simply assume that his or her disorientation is due to senility.

disorientation is due to senility. To do this, a *survivor's strategy* would be to try a simple psychological screen such as the Mini-Mental State (Folstein, Folstein, & McHugh, 1975), whereas the *power user's strategy* would be to undergo cognitive testing and ask a neuropsychologist to pinpoint the problem.

Psychologists agree that psychological processes often influence an individual's interpretive skills and judgment. Anxiety, fear, paranoid feelings, depression, and psychosis all distort a person's ability to interpret what he or she sees, hears, and feels. In particular, the mechanism of denial is a very important psychological process that affects a person's judgment because it distorts self-reporting, for example, about the symptoms of aging.

When people have a severe disturbance of their sensorium, in that sensory messages and memory blend, they experience a state of confusion. Confusion may occur when a person first awakens, is at high altitude, experiences a high fever, or following a blow to the head. An individual may also experience confusion from the mental effects of medications, such as antihistamines, or recreational drugs, such as alcohol. People who are experiencing a state of confusion may not acknowledge that anything is wrong with their consciousness, and they may need firm advice to get medical attention. If the symptoms of confusion last for more than a few minutes, or if the level of consciousness becomes erratic, then it may indicate a medical emergency known as *delirium.* In its mildest form, delirium is sometimes unrecognized by those caring for sick older individuals who are taking medication. Inquiry into this condition may be disregarded because of commonly held expectations and prejudice that confused or forgetful behavior is part of the aging condition.

VISION

Most people rely on vision as their main source of sensory awareness, so any optic symptoms should be investigated immediately to determine whether they represent a threat to a person's vision. A physician will ask for a history, including the rate at which visual acuity has changed, and the positive or negative effects experienced from current medications, whether taken for the ocular symptoms or for unrelated symptoms. Many diseases in other parts of the body, such as diabetes or hypertension, also affect a person's eyesight. Knowing the family history of eye disease—for instance, glaucoma or retinitis pigmentosa—is helpful to an ophthalmologist to make an accurate assessment.

Although people unconsciously assess their own visual acuity continuously, they may either deny changes or attribute any deterioration they note to old age. Only 10% of people age 55–84 have significant visual impairment, but that proportion doubles in those over the age of 85. If a person can't correct visual acuity to 20/20 with glasses, then it may be time to see the optometrist for new lenses. The survivor who feels a frequent need to change glasses or who notices other persistent symptoms would probably seek an examination by an ophthalmologist—a medical specialist in diseases of the eye. A power user might schedule annual visits to an ophthalmologist whether eye symptoms are noted or not.

Because people first recognize objects by their shape, the border contrast between an object and its background is important. As people age, their pupils get smaller, admitting less light, and fine deposits in the lenses of the eyes cause increasing loss of focus. These symptoms, along with aging changes in the ocular nervous system, contribute to a person's difficulty with contrast discrimination. A frequent cause of falls in older adults is their failure to recognize the outlines of objects that are physical obstructions. Testing for visual acuity by reading letters on a card may not be sufficient to reveal contrast discrimination difficulties.

The strategy of the survivor who recognizes this difficulty in his or her eyes could be to clear away all underfoot clutter in the home and workplace, especially slippery mats, and to make sure the lamp cords are white or yellow, not brown. Good lighting is a worthwhile goal, and dangerous places, such as step edges on stairs, might be painted bright colors such as yellow. For anyone who has trouble with balance because of impaired contrast discrimination, creating a clear eye-level artificial *horizon* indoors with paint or wallpaper border is very useful. In addition to these things, the power user who is visually challenged might wear lightly tinted gray glasses outdoors or amber-tinted ones indoors to improve contrast.

The retina is located at the back of the eye and contains the rods that permit night vision and the cones that permit color recognition and send this visual information to the sensorium. The retina is prone to aging changes, one of which is the ability of the eye to adapt quickly to darkness. *Dark adaptation* is dependent on the human body's generation of a chemical known as visual purple — a derivative of vitamin A — that allows people to see better in the dark. The rate at which people can generate this visual purple is proportional to their age; the retinas of older adults require several minutes of adaptation to match what a youngster's retina can do in several seconds. On entering a darkened room, the survivor would allow time to pass, such as a second to elapse for every year of his or her age, to allow the visual purple to regenerate before trying to move about; a person who carries a small flashlight for use in the dark is certainly a power user.

By the time a person is in his or her fifties, the loss of muscular elasticity in the lens, which is located behind the pupil, reduces the lens's ability to stretch and contract to bring very close and very distant objects into focus. The distance of which objects can be sharply focused on the retina increases from a usual 10–16 inches to greater than an arm's-length away. This change in the eye is known as *presbyopia*. Survivors usually wear simple convex reading glasses or use magnifiers to restore their usual reading ability. The power user might also carry a small pocket magnifier as a backup.

Cataracts are a common cause of failing vision seen in aging. Cataracts cause lens opacity due to an accumulation of protein waste. In good light, a person with cataracts may believe his or her presbyopia may seem to be improving, but in twilight, when the pupil is dilated, the opacity can be pronounced and the glittering that cataracts cause makes vision a bewildering experience. People with cataracts say the glaring lights of oncoming traffic make the highway look like a Christmas tree. Perhaps the principal reason older survivors don't have more automobile accidents is because they tend to restrict their driving to daytime hours when the light is less troublesome. A survivor wishes to be told initially when a cataract is present even though nothing radical needs to be done at that stage; most survivors appreciate the time to accept the change and cope with its effects. When a cataract in the better eye begins to interfere with desirable functioning, the survivor usually becomes a power user because surgical extraction and replacement of the lens is the only effective treatment that is available.

Today's individuals with cataracts can anticipate surgical success rates better than 95% by techniques that are remarkably safe and that restore vision by replacement with synthetic intraocular lenses. The object of vision counseling of survivors with cataracts, then, is to reassure them that there is no need to have surgery until they develop problems. Anyone who experiences the replacement of an ochre-colored, cataract-clouded lens is rewarded with a restoration of the true colors of the world. The shining whiteness will return to the previously leaden clouds, traffic lights will beckon with an emerald green, and the pocket magnifier will be put away.

Chronic glaucoma is one disease of aging that would alone justify regular eye examinations because its threat to a person's vision can be almost entirely neutralized if detected in time. It is the most common cause of blindness in western nations. Chronic glaucoma is, however, quite symptom-free until irreversible changes have become established. It causes damage to segments of the retina responsible for peripheral vision, reducing the *useful field of view* (UFOV). Although a careful examination of the eye, using an ophthalmoscope, can detect ocular changes caused by mounting pressure inside the eyeball in an early stage of the disease, it is the measurement of the intraocular pressure by tonometry that is diagnostic. This quick and painless test should be done at least every 5 years after age 40, probably more often with males and with all African descendants. The more dramatic, but rare, acute (narrow-angle) glaucoma occasionally occurs in older adults. This form of glaucoma can also be detected by regular tonometry. It is easier to recognize because it produces obvious symptoms at an earlier stage—pain, blurred vision, and a red eye—at which point its occurrence constitutes an emergency, which requires immediate surgery in the survivor.

Treatment of chronic glaucoma in the survivor is usually by prescribed drugs and eye drops, but laser treatment and/or surgery is occasionally necessary later to ensure drainage of excess fluid. In striving for peak performance, power users with glaucoma will develop a compulsive routine of taking their eye drops on time, obsessively checking their latest eye pressures, and insisting that laser treatment or surgery not be delayed, thereby assuming a greater responsibility for the success of their treatment.

The two retinal diseases that cause the most cases of blindness in the United States and Canada affect the smallest blood vessels of the retina. The first is *diabetic retinopathy,* which occurs in the later stages of both Type I and Type II diabetes. In the initial background stage, capillaries disappear, causing only a minimal loss of visual acuity. Later, in the proliferate stage, fragile new blood vessels may hemorrhage, resulting in blocked vision and even causing sudden blindness from the detachment of the retina. The survivor recognizes that Medicare and other insurers will pay for an annual assessment of diabetic patients by an ophthalmologist to detect these eye changes at an early, treatable stage of the disease. The power user who experiences such changes may agree to undergo a procedure called *laser photocoagulation,* in which the ophthalmologist might be able to improve the prognosis; results are unpredictable.

The second disease, *macular degeneration,* causes a little-understood growth of blood vessels in the macula—the area of the retina where the fine focus of our eyes is concentrated and confined. Unlike glaucoma, which first damages peripheral vision, macular degeneration targets the bull's eye, or center, of the visual field and produces a reading disability much greater than its limited extent would seem to implicate. The loss can be detected by standard tests for acuity of vision, but a much more sensitive diagnostic test is the Amsler Grid Test in which the disease produces the distortion of a reticule printed on a small card. A power user who wants to detect the earliest stage of the disorder can carry a wallet card for a daily self-test but should understand that the medical community does not yet have any effective treatment at this stage. In the later (wet) stage, which seriously affects vision, a photocoagulation technique similar to the technique utilized for the treatment of diabetic retinopathy may be used, but it won't benefit everyone, and some people will philosophically accept the changes as permanent.

Because the remainder of the retina is intact, the person with permanent macular degeneration is a prime candidate for low vision aids—a whole armamentarium is now available for survivors who are prepared to work on acquiring the necessary techniques of using them to overcome some of their visual disability. Magnifiers, maybe simple lenses, portable scanners for video monitors, electronic telescopes, and large-print and audio books can also be used to help the survivor to see. The power user will look into information on ergonomic *smart houses* with tactile and high-tech robotic devices designed to reduce a person's dependence on a care provider.

Low-vision assessments are available at state Aid to the Blind offices. These state offices, along with Lighthouse International, a national center, can provide low-vision devices and offer training in low-vision assessments and counseling. Visual impairment in older adults has been estimated to cost this country 11 billion dollars a year; yet, more funding for research on prevention and better reimbursement for early detection and treatment are greatly needed. For more information on visual impairments, treatment, and services, see http://www. lighthouse.org.

HEARING

The sense of hearing is probably the first of the five senses to become activated within the womb. Because it may retain a more primary connection with the emotions than the other four senses, hearing is often considered our most primal sense. Aging adults might suppose that even a small change of hearing would be noticeable to them, but that is not the case. Many people lose a lot of their hearing before being aware of it. Published prevalence studies show that approximately 30% of community-dwelling older adults report impaired hearing, and women may have a lower prevalence than men (Moss & Parsons, 1986).

Not being able to hear a wristwatch ticking when pressed to one's ear is a sign of minimal hearing loss, as is the sense that people are speaking too softly. Paranoid suspicions that people are deliberately speaking in low tones is apparently common in people who are hearing impaired, and when someone indicates feeling this way, it may be an indication of hearing loss. Sometimes people with minimal hearing loss complain that others are talking too fast for them to clearly distinguish the words, or their family complains that they turn the television volume up too high. An older person who doesn't think the sound of a rock band or a cinema is too loud for comfort is already experiencing some deafness. The survivor experiencing such symptoms will arrange to get a hearing acuity test; a hand-held screening audiometer is available for this purpose in many physicians' offices. The power user, however, will obtain professional testing by an independent audiologist. To pass the test, he or she will need to discriminate more than 80% of a battery of words correctly. He or she will then be asked to indicate the thresholds at which pure tone sounds of increasing intensities and various pitches are first heard by each ear. The output is an audiogram, which is the diagnostic gold standard. The output is abnormal if the threshold for any frequency between 250 and 8,000 hertz is above 30 decibels. The audiogram may show one of the following losses: conduction loss, sensorineural loss, or mixed loss.

CONDUCTION LOSS   For older adults, the most common reason for conduction loss is obstructed airflow in the external canal by *cerumen* (wax) impaction. Wax is normally propelled through the ear canal by slight movements of the skin and expelled imperceptibly. In older people, especially some older men, growth changes in the shape of the earlobes, drying, and excessively hairy ears may combine to harden and impact the wax. The power user who has this trouble will instill a couple of drops of olive oil each week and use a cheap otoscope, such as those sold for children, to have someone take a peek in his or her ear occasionally to check for wax buildup. Although some wax is usually present, no intervention is called for as long as any of the eardrum is visible. If wax buildup fills the canal, then softening the wax and gently flushing (syringing) it out using a kit sold in drugstores solves the problem of removal. Liquids, however, should never be put in the ear if the eardrum has not been previously inspected for perforations by a competent examiner, whose help may also be needed to restore hearing loss from persistent wax impactions. Hairpins, cotton-tipped picks, or other ramrods should never be used in the ear because of the potential to damage the sensitive organs of the inner ear. Follow the old adage that says not to put anything smaller than an elbow in the ear canal!

SENSORINEURAL LOSS   The hearing organ, *cochlea,* contains fine hair cells that are tuned to the various sound frequencies and send messages to the sensorium via neural connections. Sensorineural deafness results when the hair cells are damaged, especially by aging. The most common loss of this type experienced by older people is known as *presbycusis.* It may begin as early as age 40, but because only the higher pitched sounds are lost at first, the change may go unnoticed. Usually, the first difficulty encountered with presbycusis is in discriminating the sounds of speech, particularly consonant sounds, which have a higher pitch than vowels. For example, during a card game, an older player may mistake a call for an "ace" and play "eight" instead. In addition, difficulty in hearing speech may partly be caused by the aging nervous system. This adds another problem called *recruitment,* in which sounds with increased volume are distorted so much they become intolerable, making discrimination in group conversations almost impossible. Paradoxically, people who experience hearing impairment complain about both loud and soft noises!

OTHER TYPES OF HEARING LOSS   Another type of hearing loss very similar to presbycusis is known as *noise-induced hearing loss,* which is caused by what used to be called *deafening noise.* Urban civilizations are becoming noisier, especially among the young people who prefer their cars and their music loud. Younger people initially experience reversible hearing loss, but older people with a lifetime of exposure to noisy environments may have irreversible changes. Some older people have conduction or mixed hearing loss that may date from middle ear infections in childhood or untreated otosclerosis in middle age. Also, certain drugs commonly prescribed for older adults, such as the diuretic furosemide and some antibiotics, cause neural damage that can affect hearing. Symptoms of *Ménière's disease* and *acoustic neuroma* both have sensorineural deafness with severe dizziness and tinnitus, a ringing in the ears.

HEARING ENHANCEMENT   Although modern digital hearing aids can be tailored to match precisely the losses shown on the audiogram and keep background noise amplification to a minimum, people with *central auditory perception defect* (CAPD), which is a type of sensorineural deafness, may not find hearing aids to be much help in improving sound discrimination. Hearing aids are not as widely utilized as they could be for technical as well as economic reasons: Good hearing aids are expensive, not covered by Medicare or insurance, and require more than a minimum of care to keep wax and moisture out of them. It is also important to recognize that depression is common in people who are deaf, and this, added to the self-consciousness often felt by people who wear hearing aids, may lead them to discard the devices as hopeless. The survivor will have a regular hearing assessment that should include regularly inspecting the hearing aid, training in its use, and accurately following up its utilization, including evaluating the mood and intelligence of the hearing aid user. Family support should be solicited, especially to discourage unrealistic expectations for total hearing restoration. The strategy of the hearing-challenged power user will be to keep abreast of the rapid advancements in digital hearing aid technology, especially the field of implanted cochlea receivers. Perhaps he or she could fill out a depression self-test questionnaire from time to time (see http://www.betterhearing.org/faq.htm).

SMELL AND TASTE

Doctors do not usually assess senses as part of a routine medical examination and must rely on a patient's awareness and report of the changes that occur in the areas of smell, taste, touch, vision, and hearing. The olfactory organ that processes smell is in the roof of the nose. This organ transmits nerve impulses to the sensorium through an extension of the brain that grows through perforations in the intervening bone. It is not known whether this seemingly vulnerable connection between the nasal cavity and the brain can introduce infections, but this route has been postulated for viruses causing dementia.

Humans, like animals, use smell to sniff out unseen dangers and delights, especially in food. However, people are able to adapt rapidly to smells after continued contact with odorous material. Also, *anosmia,* which is a diminished sense of smell, may contribute to the tolerance of some isolated older adults to domestic odors such as rotting food or pet excrement. The person who has total anosmia might fail to detect a gas leak, so they should live in an all-electric home.

Most of what people experience as taste is really also smell. But pure taste for sweetness, saltiness, sourness, and bitterness are recognized by taste buds in the mouth, mostly on the tongue. Chemical irritants are also recognized in different locations of the mouth and nose. For some people, certain irritants can be pleasantly stimulating, such as pepper, whereas others can be noxious, such as smoke. Taste buds are connected to the corresponding hippocampal gyrus of the brain through nerves in the sides of the face. If one of these nerves is injured, then a sufficient sense of taste is transmitted through the opposite side of the face. There is little loss of taste due to aging, but acuity can be compromised by chronic dry mouth, often a side effect of some medications, many of which blunt both the senses of taste and smell. Also, smoking and alcohol consumption cause *dysgeusia,* a distortion of taste (disgust) that soon returns to full function after quitting, allowing foods to taste as they should.

Taste and smell are factors that modify appetite, but establishing their role in influencing actual consumption is difficult. Older adults tolerate monotony in food more than younger adults. Appetite research gained popularity in the medical field at the beginning of the 21st century (Swartz, 2001), and the theories of its neurochemical basis are in constant flux. It would be valuable to have some sort of assessment of smell and taste as part of the evaluation of a person's nutritional status, but evaluation methods are in their infancy. A useful source for learning about smell and taste is the Monell Institute web site (see http://www.monell.org).

TOUCH AND PAIN

The fifth sense by which humans perceive their environment is the sense of touch, which includes the sensations of heat, cold, pain, and vibration. The awareness of pressure and of joint position that underlies posture and balance is also a part of the sense of touch. The peripheral neurons that carry these sensations to the sensorium decrease and change during the aging process, and the rate of impulse transmissions is reduced, so the reflexes and other responses to stimulation become delayed by a few milliseconds. The slowing observed in many older people, however, is not due to nerve degeneration but rather to muscle weakness, which can be corrected by training. Occasionally, these peripheral nerves also send false messages that are perceived as pains, cold patches, itching, and burning sensations; some of which may be caused by vitamin deficiency or diabetes in older people, but more often they have unknown causes.

PAIN   Pain, especially chronic pain, looms large in this sensory category. The most common disease affecting the pain fibers in the adult who is aging is *diabetic neuropathy,* which imitates and amplifies all the false messages described previously and may also cause *anesthesia,* or a lack of sensation. In the latter case, large, painless ulcers may develop in the feet, leading frequently to amputation of a limb or even to death. The treatment approach taken by an older diabetic survivor would include scheduling regular foot care with a podiatrist and maintaining well-controlled blood sugar in order to minimize these complications. The power user who develops anesthesia could additionally use an air-cushioned walker.

A greatly feared viral infection in older adults that causes pain by directly acting on the nerve fiber cells is *herpes zoster,* or shingles. It usually affects only one side of the torso in a band corresponding to a local nerve distribution. (It is hoped that this late-life complication of childhood chicken pox will disappear when today's immunized children grow into older adulthood.) A day or so after the pain of shingles begins, a rash appears, which later heals, often with a few scars. A less common kind of shingles affects the face and can cause scarring of the eye, which may lead to blindness. After the rash heals, the pain continues and may even get worse or persist for a lifetime. Tragically, some sufferers are reported to have resorted to suicide because of the severity or relentlessness of the pain.

Nerves are not the cause of most cases of pain encountered in aging, however, but rather, it is most often caused by other pain sources in the surrounding tissues. Chronic pain stimuli include *ischemia*—or the cutting off of the blood supply—various inflammations, and infections including AIDS, skeletal or joint problems, and cancer. Pain of this kind usually tends to get worse with time.

The treatment of severe, chronic pain presents a common problem in geriatrics. Aging itself may contribute to this condition by lowering the threshold at which a sensation is felt as pain. Serious pain requires analgesic drug treatment. The WHO, which is concerned with drug trafficking of analgesics, introduced a ladder of potency and, supposedly, addiction potential.

The lowest rung (Step I) of the Drug Ladder includes the nonsteroidal, anti-inflammatory drugs (NSAIDs) such as aspirin and ibuprofen, which are best for inflammation pain. Their main drawback is that they occasionally produce life-threatening bleeding in the bowel without warning. Also, prolonged use may cause kidney failure. Acetaminophen, also a Step I drug, does not cause hemorrhage but is not an anti-inflammatory medication; also, it cannot be used if liver failure is present. The drugs higher up on the steps of the Drug Ladder are mostly derivatives of the narcotic opium. The milder Step II narcotics, such as codeine, are often used in combination with Step I drugs to minimize the addictive risks of Step II drugs. The most common Step III drug is morphine, which also may be reinforced by Step I drugs.

Unfortunately, opium-derived narcotics produce severe constipation, increased somnolence, and other mental complications in the older adult population; direct injection of morphine derivatives into the spinal canal or painful joints lessens these side effects. Prolonged treatment of severe chronic pain with narcotics eventually leads to physical dependency, meaning individuals will have withdrawal effects if the dose is reduced. This is not the same as addiction, which usually involves loss of control and compulsive use patterns—rare in pain treatment. For some unaccountable reason, members of Congress are more compulsively obsessed in passing legislation to prevent older adults from receiving adequate narcotic medication than they are in stopping the tide of illegal narcotics that openly flows into this country to supply addicts. Fear of conflicting with draconian laws, which control narcotic prescriptions, often results in physicians failing to prescribe adequate pain medication to those who have no characteristics of addiction.

> FOR SOME UNACCOUNTABLE reason, members of Congress are more compulsively obsessed in passing legislation to prevent older adults from receiving adequate narcotic medication than they are in stopping the tide of illegal narcotics that openly flows into this country to supply addicts.

The survivor in severe pain will seek out a physician who refuses to be coerced by those who confuse dependency with addiction and thereby obstruct the primary duty of a physician to relieve pain. The power user with severe chronic pain will enroll in a modern specialty pain center that may be able to offer adequate medication by self-regulation as well as some of the newly developed technological solutions to pain, such as spinal tract incisions or ablation of the pituitary gland.

SUMMARY OF THE SENSES

In summary, the basic need for sensory awareness is a major function of the nervous system. Special sense organs connected to the sensorium by cranial and spinal nerves transmit the sensations of smell, vision, hearing, taste, touch, pain, and temperature. These sensations are responsible for providing the information that people need for orientation and for awareness of what is bad and good in their surroundings—a prerequisite for judgment and independence.

RESPIRATION

The purpose of breathing is to get oxygen (O_2) from the air into the lungs and to excrete the carbon dioxide (CO_2) that is formed as a waste material in the body's tissues. Part of the purpose of the circulatory system is to carry these two gases between the capillaries of the lung and those of the rest of the body. In the tissues, the purpose of the O_2 is to convert energy sources into simpler substances, including CO_2 and water. Together, all this activity is known as respiration. Because the brain is the largest continuous user of O_2, it might be said that the first priority of respiration is to keep the brain supplied with O_2. Although there are certain enzymes present in the other tissues that allow anaerobic respiration to continue for a while without O_2, the metabolic system in the brain is completely dependent on glucose and O_2 and cannot maintain consciousness without them. In fact, irreversible brain damage results after the O_2 supply to the brain fails for more than a few minutes.

Oxygen is carried in the blood mostly in the hemoglobin of the red blood cells (RBCs), whereas CO_2, though controlled by RBC enzymes, is mostly dissolved and carried in the plasma. A decrease in the O_2 concentration or an increase in the CO_2 acids in the brain will trigger an increase in the rate of blood flow through the heart until these imbalances are corrected. At the same time, the respiratory rate of the lungs is increased to bring in more O_2 and blow out more CO_2.

THE AGING LUNG

Many physical changes take place in aging and one apparently inevitable change compared with younger people is a reduced capacity to increase airflow through the lungs and to increase the heart rate. The result of reduced capacity is a *limited respiratory reserve capacity,* which becomes an important issue in lung disease. For example, unlike a younger person who might have *walking pneumonia* without knowing it, an older person who gets pneumonia may rapidly become critically ill with severe breathing problems. Another very common type of lung disease that compromises respiratory capacity is *chronic obstructive pulmonary disease* (COPD), including chronic bronchitis, emphysema, and asthma. In COPD, many alveoli, containing the capillaries of the lung, have ruptured and cannot support the exchange of O_2 and CO_2. Although the survivor with COPD will quit smoking, maintain his or her pulmonary reserve capacity by a supervised training program, and treat every flare up of infection seriously, only limited results can be expected. The power user will join a lung support group, get a disability sticker for the car, use a portable source of liquid oxygen, and qualify, perhaps, for a lung transplant.

Once the scourge of the slums, *pulmonary tuberculosis* (PTB) continues to lurk around, sometimes in nursing facilities and in Native American or immigrant communities, as a serious disease of almost exclusively older people. Older individuals may have remained undiagnosed because of misleading PTB skin tests or have gone untreated because of poor medical care. At the beginning of the 21st century, a new kind of drug-resistant PTB was appearing among younger people in AIDS-heroin communities and in prisons without careful surveillance. It seemed probable that this new PTB strain would eventually spread to the older adult population.

The survivor with a chronic cough will rule out PTB with a chest X-ray and a Double Mantoux TB skin test and, in the case of a positive skin test, will pursue a sputum culture for TB, with careful X-ray follow-up. The power user with a positive skin test might choose to undertake a year's course of treatment with regular liver testing.

Although *lung cancer* is not a prominent cause of respiratory failure except in its later stages, the converse, that chronic lung disease increases the incidence of cancer, is true. Lung cancer, also a consequence of years of smoking, may occur up to 15 years after quitting and, thus, is characteristically an older person's disease. Of those people who contract carcinoma of the lung, only one person in eight is still alive 5 years later. Because of this, the survivor might choose palliative care, and the power user may opt for the works: surgery, radiation, and chemotherapy.

Heart failure is the most common cause of medical hospitalization for older adults; it also affects the transport of O_2 and CO_2. It causes fluid to accumulate in the body as edema instead of circulating throughout the system. In addition, fluid accumulates in the lungs, causing congestion and possibly leading to asthma. The causes of heart failure include heart attacks, prolonged hypertension, and diseases of the heart valves. The average 2-year survival rate is only 50%, so the survivor who wants to beat these odds will have to be strict with any prescribed treatment regimen, especially the bans on smoking and the episodic consumption of salt. The power user will find the increasing availability of heart transplants a subject worth pursuing.

SUMMARY OF RESPIRATION

In summary, respiration is the process of life in the body's tissues and is the most important component in the brain. The purpose of the variable responses of the heart and circulation is the preservation of ideal O_2 and CO_2 exchanges in the brain.

MOVEMENT

Movement is a characteristic of all animals; it is achieved by muscle contraction but limited by ligaments and joint shape. These muscle contractions are controlled by nerve impulses that originate in the conscious cortex of the brain but are further modulated by unconscious controllers and stabilizers. After a period of rest and sleep, the body awakens to nervous activity at two levels. The first level is to restore and maintain unconscious muscle tone and postural reflexes so people can stand up, and the second level is to initiate the conscious muscle contractions that constitute purposive movement. Special messages inhibit any spinal reflexes that operate freely during sleep but would prevent voluntary movement when awake.

Several areas of these movements are of special interest to gerontologists because of the many changes in the skeleton and muscular mass during the aging process. Depending on genetic inheritance, levels of daily exercise and nutrition, and a history of trauma or disease or both, different individuals go into the later years with a wide range of muscular abilities. At one end of the spectrum are those laboring men and women who have spent most of their waking hours on their feet, flexing and lifting, and who have consumed a simple but adequate diet of unrefined home-cooked meals. If they have been lucky, and adversity has not distorted their body by injury or ailment, then their skeleton and muscles might be expected to remain relatively unchanged as they age. An intermediate group of men and women consists of those who have been more favored economically. This group may have spent many years in more sedentary living and may have eaten the richer foods that prosperity brings. Although this group may be avoiding the major causes of serious disability, they have followed the path of what Rowe has called "usual aging" (Rowe & Kahn, 1987). Finally, there are those individuals who are referred to as the "frail older adults," whose wracked bodies have the habitus that has become a caricature of the aged—bent, weak, and slowed by the ills that the world has bestowed on them.

Medical textbooks almost uniformly quote figures of a 10%–20% reduction in the ratio of lean muscle and bone mass to body weight in most aging individuals, but these changes are not inevitable. When they occur, they probably have a sedentary cause rather than an aging cause. At any age, loss of muscle and bone mineral begins only hours after people stop moving around. In fact, mobilization of calcium from the bones increases even during regular nightly sleep to be deposited again when a person gets up and about. The phrase "if you don't use it, you'll lose it" is never truer than with calcium in the skeletal system and muscle mass. For a survivor experiencing "usual aging" who is not involved in daily physical labor, a well-planned exercise program, together with a wise dietary intake, can help maintain the former lean body mass. Less certain is a person's ability to ensure a dense bony skeleton simply by an exercise program; thus, the power user will add a supplement program for calcium and vitamin D, as described later.

EXERCISE

The meat of the body, the muscle mass of skeletal muscles that work to move the limbs, consists of muscle cells gathered into bundles, each of which contracts in response to impulses from a single nerve branch. Many thousands of bundles within a muscle may receive a flood of impulses arriving continuously to keep up the *muscle tone.* The force and frequency with which muscles contract is known as *strength* and *power.* Each cell contains contractile proteins, and the type is determined by whether the muscle is used for repeated sharp contractions or for prolonged endurance. During aerobic exercise (the usual kind of activity), the overall strength and power is limited by the rate at which respiration can supply oxygen to the muscle. This is in turn controlled by the heart rate, the volume of each heartbeat, and the speed at which the oxygen can disassociate from the hemoglobin and enter the muscle. The only consistent difference in exercise capacity between females and males is in the rate of oxygen delivery, which is about 10% less in women than in men.

After age 60, muscle mass, strength, and power all fall. This is partly due to a steady fall in the maximum heart rate (which can be estimated as 220 minus current age). However, strength training can keep this loss to a minimum, and an older man in training is stronger than a sedentary man half his age. Endurance does not drop in those who keep up their training. In aerobic exercise, the energy comes from oxygen burning the fatty acids and glucose that have been released from storage deposits of fat and glycogen in the body. In the case of fatty acids, adequate oxygen must always be available. However, in order to provide reserve energy for a sudden demand for strength, such as climbing stairs, a so-called *phosphagen system* can release some energy anaerobically; that is, before enough oxygen arrives. In this case, a byproduct (lactic acid) is produced by the partially consumed glucose, and it is the accumulation of this acid that produces the fatigue and even pain of excessive exertion. This is not a big problem for many older people who rarely need to produce frequent bursts of energy. Instead, their problem often is in getting glucose into the muscle cell, a metabolic process performed by the hormone insulin. The glucose becomes dammed up and spills into the bloodstream. This process characterizes Type II diabetes or, more correctly, the metabolic syndrome known as insulin resistance, which is prevalent in older adults, especially obese older adults.

All movement exercises some muscles, but to undertake a program of regular exercise involving a major portion of the muscle mass is desirable for sedentary people as they age. After a few weeks of regular exercise, even an older person's blood pressure tends to decrease, and total cholesterol levels also tend to decrease. The good news is that the lipid fraction of the blood known as HDL-C, or *good cholesterol,* predictably increases significantly in proportion to the amount of time spent in moderate exertion. Other health benefits of regular exercise include preventing coronary artery disease and reducing the risk of a heart attack by 35%–70%.

Remaining sedentary and not starting an exercise program are hazardous to good health. Even when a cardiogram has shown heart damage, exercise has a place in rehabilitation and further prevention. Many people, especially older adults, worry about having a heart attack when working out, and although it is true that it can happen, it is rare. Perhaps because of heightened awareness, people are more likely to heed warning symptoms in time to avoid cardiovascular complications. No matter what horror stories people hear, a well-conceived, supervised exercise program is better for a person's health than a sedentary life.

Before beginning an exercise program, the sedentary survivor will take some simple precautions such as getting a physical examination and a treadmill cardiogram. The power user will not only request a treadmill-echo test if there is any abnormality in the cardiogram but also will realize that even an angiogram may not show a soft plaque that could rupture and precipitate a heart attack.

Gradually increasing endurance, preferably with a personal trainer, while avoiding exhaustion is an important aspect of rehabilitation. Diet, rest, and attention to fluid balance also are important. During exercise, the body loses up to 3% of weight in fluids through sweating. Because older adults have a blunted thirst sensation, it is important for them to drink enough fluids to replace any weight loss. It is unwise, however, to use the high-sodium athletic drinks for this purpose because they may worsen hypertension.

An exercise regimen should include a light warm-up stretch for 10 minutes, and a similar cool-down period. Survivors should need to perform at least 20 minutes of brisk-to-vigorous exercise three times a week; more would be better. If cardiac function is an issue, then the goal is to sustain a pulse of 65%–80% of maximum, as determined by an exercise test. A power user may be curious about the use of drugs to boost the results of exercise, but this topic continues to be controversial.

The only booster shown to be safe is the judicious use of caffeine, which enhances performance temporarily. Male sex hormones (androgens and preandrogens such as testosterone and dehydroepiandrosterone [DHEA]) have been used to increase muscle strength, but women naturally are hesitant about these because they produce facial hair and a deeper voice. The older power user may wish to consider taking testosterone by the skin patch method to increase general vigor but only under medical supervision.

AMBULATION

Ambulation, the act of walking, is the most important movement to the older person. It prevents complications, such as skin pressure sores, lung stasis, and kidney stones, which come from simply sitting and lying prone for long periods. As noted previously, the bone and muscle loss that occurs with immobility increases vulnerability to falls and fractures. People who stay off of their feet may find it difficult to get back on them again. If ambulation had been preserved, then many admissions to care facilities could have been avoided. The cost of care of a chair- or bedridden person is much higher than for a person who is mobile, in bboth dollars and human terms, which include losing independence and self-esteem and becoming a burden to caregivers.

PAIN THAT COMPROMISES AMBULATION   One group of common problems that causes pain in walking is foot complaints. A list of apparently minor but painful foot problems includes *ingrown toenails, plantar warts,* and *heel spurs* (e.g., plantar fasciitis). Self-help for these ailments may make matters worse, especially if the sufferer has diabetes or peripheral artery disease. The survivor who is over the age of 65 needs a check-up with a podiatrist at least annually. Advice on footwear purchases should be included because most foot problems are either caused or aggravated by wearing the wrong shoes.

Another ambulatory problem is leg pain. People who feel cramping pain in their calf when they walk are usually experiencing *blood vessel disease,* and if they feel a burning or shooting pain, it may be due to *diabetic neuropathy.* The most common diagnosis for the inability to walk is osteoarthritis of the knee or the hip. This condition, often arising from misalignment of the bones or an old injury long forgotten, may cause pain anywhere in either leg but usually over the affected joint. In the early stages, analgesic drugs are helpful, but joint injections may be necessary later on to preserve ambulation. Also, the question of replacement surgery will usually arise.

The strategy of the survivor at this stage would be to ensure a correct diagnosis by first considering alternative, nonoperative causes. A disabling sharp pain an inch or so below the inner side of the knee is probably due to *anserine bursitis,* a frequent but often missed diagnosis treatable by a simple injection. Pain within the knee might be due to a *meniscus* or a *ligament tear,* often diagnosable only by an MRI or arthroscopy. Often, in older people, pain in the knee is caused by *chondromalacia* of the patella, which is due to misalignment. When arthritis is present, it may not be the cause of the pain, but a trial of injections into the joint can be helpful in proving that it is. The power user will probably wish to truncate this lengthy period of trying alternatives. Therefore, the best alternative is to work closely with a conservative orthopedist and a radical physiotherapist to achieve the best results. The results of hip replacement are so good that it is usually justified.

Spinal stenosis is a narrowing of the spinal canal that causes pressure on the nerve roots that control urinary and bowel continence. It causes aching and pain in the buttocks and upper thighs, especially with prolonged standing. The most common variety of stenosis is in the lower end of the spine where the pressure is on a bundle of nerve roots named the *cauda equina* (horse's tail). Initial treatment for survivors is weight reduction and posture improvement. The power user may elect to have surgery (laminectomy) to preserve urinary and bowel control. This condition is not described in all medical texts, but basic information can be obtained on the Internet at http://www.nih.gov/niams/healthinfo/spinalstenosis/spinalsten.htm.

MUSCLE PAIN THAT MAY COMPROMISE MOVEMENT

The conditions discussed in this section are found in a majority of people seeking medical treatment for pain that inhibits movement and reduces activity. *Fibromyalgia,* for example, is characterized by tremendous fatigue and chronic pain felt "all over" but particularly in the upper and lower back and in the neck; sometimes the knee or elbow is involved. Tender nodules form in the muscle, which become trigger points for pain if pressure is applied. The cause of fibromyalgia is unknown but may be from a disturbance of the energy supply by the phosphagen system. Sleep disturbance is a standard symptom but whether this is a cause or an effect of this condition is a source of debate. A history of depression is common, and the tricyclic antidepressant drugs do relieve symptoms, but other types of more powerful antidepressants do not. Aerobic exercise helps, and the survivor may seek a fibromyalgia support group, often sponsored through community athletic programs or gyms (see http://www.fmnetnews.com/pages/basics.html).

A more serious muscular disease is *polymyalgia rheumatica* and a variant, *temporal arteritis*. Like fibromyalgia, polymyalgia causes chronic pain in the muscles of the shoulders and the back above the waist. Temporal arteritis also causes severe headaches. Unlike fibromyalgia, these conditions have no trigger points but are associated with a very painful stiffness, a sense of weakness, and hopelessness. The blood tests in both diseases show a sedimentation rate that is extremely abnormal, but the medical reason is unknown. These diseases are almost exclusively confined to older adults. Treatment by high doses of prednisone is dramatically effective, resolving all symptoms in a few days. Perhaps even more important for both the survivor and the power user, emergent prednisone treatment seems to prevent a tragic complication — sudden, permanent blindness; this justifies using a drug that has occasional dangerous side effects including bowel hemorrhage, diabetes, and mental disturbances.

As many as 20% of older adults suffer from chronic shoulder pain, making it a common complaint. The tendon of one of the muscles of the shoulder blade, the *supraspinatus,* becomes trapped between the top of the humerus (arm bone) and the bone lying above the shoulder, the *acromion,* often months after an injury. This may persist as a *chronic impingement syndrome.* Characteristically, this condition causes pain in the rotator cuff on the front and side of the shoulder. Lifting the arm worsens the pain, so people tend to avoid pain in the shoulder by not raising their arms, but this creates a new problem: a shoulder frozen by disuse. An untreated *frozen shoulder* can eventually lead to a ruptured tendon or capsule tear. Seventy percent of people with chronic impingement syndrome have *rotator cuff damage* and 2%–3% have a frozen shoulder.

Many therapies for shoulder pain are available, and the most widely used treatments are over-the-counter NSAIDs (e.g., ibuprofen) and steroid injections. The latter combined with forced manipulation of the shoulder is effective for some people. Most medical treatments, however, are disappointing. This has given rise to alternative treatments, including acupuncture and acupressure, transcutaneous nerve stimulation, and magnetic field generation—all of which are medically unproven and thus not yet covered by most insurance companies. If the ligaments are calcified, then the daring power user may wish to consider having the deposits crushed by extracorporeal shock wave therapy (ESWT), an experimental procedure that may help. Results of shoulder surgery are unpredictable, especially in chronic cases. The survivor has no clear course for this problem. Additional information can be found on this subject at http://www.scoi.com/cuffdise.htm.

Movement of the hand may be compromised by pain at any stage of life. *Carpal tunnel syndrome* is among the conditions that cause frequent office visits by older women. Essentially, the median nerve of one or both hands is nipped as it passes under the carpal ligament in front of the wrist, causing burning and sharp pain; hyper-flexing the wrist worsens it. The pain caused by this syndrome may be relieved momentarily by vigorously shaking the hand. The prevalence in older women may be attributable to muscle weakness. The survivor should at least initially seek relief through injections of steroids into the tunnel. More aggressive and potentially curative treatment involves surgically cutting the ligament, which would be a reasonable strategy for the power user.

NEUROMUSCULAR DISABILITIES COMPROMISING AMBULATION

The most common movement disorder in late life is *essential tremor,* which is not a serious disorder. It is frequently misdiagnosed as Parkinson's disease, which is rare. Primarily, essential tremor is a familial inherited disorder that produces a simple tremor in 50% of cases. It is most obvious in the hands but may cause shaking of the head and voice. For the person with the condition, the stress of knowing that someone is watching makes it worse, which causes observers to think that the person is nervous. A unique diagnostic feature seen in many people is that a small drink of alcohol abolishes the tremor for a few hours, whereas with Parkinsonism, alcohol either has no effect or makes it worse. Propranolol treatment, rather than alcohol, would be the preferred treatment for the power user to temporarily abolish the tremor. The survivor who might not wish to treat a nonthreatening symptom could be more comfortable seeking out one of a number of support groups (for more information, see http://www.west-net.org/essentialtremor.htm).

As mentioned previously, a more serious motor disorder is *Parkinson's disease.* In the early 21st century, about 1% of older men developed the disease; more than a million cases existed in the United States. Parkinson's disease is caused by a reduction in the formation of dopamine in the basal ganglia of the brain. Because dopamine helps to smooth and modulate muscle movement, the reduction in dopamine produces the characteristic symptoms of Parkinson's disease: a great slowing of limb movements; a fine—or later, coarse—tremor; rigidity or stiffness; and a tendency to fall. The muscles of the face may be expressionless and mask-like; however, behind this seeming facial impassivity, the individual often has an active mind that is distressed and depressed by the effects the disease has on him- or herself and others. Both the survivor and the power user will need several drugs that supplement and modulate dopamine and other neurohormones in the basal ganglia, particularly the substantia nigra. Initial therapy may be quite successful, but as the disease advances, resistance to drugs develops and symptoms return. A once-abandoned neurosurgical operation that eliminates the globus pallidus area has re-emerged during the 21st century in a hi-tech form. An older power user with Parkinson's disease might take a great interest in the operation, but at the present, surgery is reserved for cases of severe disability at an early age. All patients with Parkinsonism (i.e., those with Parkinson's disease), and those with other, similar conditions, should be in an exercise program to avoid excess disability. It is our impression that they benefit not only from aerobics and swimming but also from the accompanying social contacts. A good support group helps keep them up-to-date on the latest advances in this rapidly moving field; there are several national support groups, including the Parkinson's Disease Foundation (http://www.pdf.org.).

Stroke is the most common fatal disease in the industrialized world after coronary artery disease and cancer. Each year in the U.S., half a million people experience strokes. After a stroke, a third of those people die within days or a few weeks, a third recover completely over a period of months, and a remainder of people have permanent disability. Because a stroke causes tremendous personal, social, and economic losses, the threat of having one hangs over older adults like the sword of Damocles. Thirty billion dollars a year is the estimated cost of caring for people who experience strokes in the U.S., which includes the cost of medical care, rehabilitation, and custodial care, among other related expenses. *Hemiplegia,* a weakness and paralysis of muscles occuring in up to half of the body, is the most common disability resulting from stroke. Not only can the person no longer voluntarily send motor impulses from the brain to move his or her leg and/or arm, but also spinal reflexes, which are cut off from brain inhibition, contract the muscles continuously. The effort of coping with these useless, heavy, spring-like, and sometimes extremely painful appendages is difficult and tiring, which is why people rapidly become wheelchair dependent.

Psychological disorders, especially depression but also cognitive and behavioral changes caused by brain damage, can complicate care and lifestyles. A lot of support is needed for the individual who survives a stroke, and a neighborhood stroke group should be located. A very useful site for more information is http://www.stroke.org.

SUMMARY OF MOVEMENT

People tend to associate aging with disability, especially in ambulation. Movement and exercise are among the imperatives of the animal kingdom, however, and older adults should expect that fitness is a part of wellness. Older people sometimes contribute to their own problems by accepting disability as synonymous with aging. Both survivors and power users will take steps to maintain or improve their physical mobility, even in the face of limiting disabilities.

REST AND SLEEP

Sleep is an unconscious state from which a person can be awakened. Deep sleep allows the fatigable parts of the brain to recover and the muscles to rest. Rest without sleep is a parallel state in which relaxation of the postural and locomotion muscles of the trunk and limbs occurs; rest can occur whether waking or sleeping. Sleep is divided into two phases: *deep sleep* and *REM* (rapid eye movement) sleep. Deep sleep is characterized by the slow delta waves of resting brain activity seen in the EEG (electroencephalogram) and occupies 75% of sleeping time. Except for eye movements, muscular activity is virtually paralyzed in REM sleep because the brain is very active, and the EEG is the same as if the individual were awake. Sleep is a dynamic process, partly induced by a special neuropepsin; thus, individuals go to sleep gradually rather than *fall* asleep. When people go into normal sleep, they pass through a light sleep (phase I) and into various levels of deep sleep (stages II–IV) for about 90 minutes, or longer if people are young or very tired. Next, a period of REM sleep occurs for 10–30 minutes, followed by more delta wave sleep, then a longer period of REM sleep, and so on until awakening. People have dreams continuously during REM sleep, some of them quite irrational, and individuals often can recall the one they were having as they awaken. The dreams that occur during deep sleep are rarely recalled but then seem more rational. Older people often claim they do not dream; however, evidence shows that they do dream, even if they cannot recall their dreams.

SLEEP DISORDERS

People spend a third of their lives asleep, but each person's sleep needs are unique. If a person awakens spontaneously and feels refreshed, then he or she is getting restful sleep. Even if people sleep an average time period, the quality of sleep may be poor if REM sleep occupies more than a third of their sleep time. *Sleep deprivation* can occur if people don't allow enough resting time or if they have insomnia. Sleep deprivation leads to a sleep debt. If a person is lucky, then he or she may be able to catch up later. But, if the debt keeps rising, then they become less alert and may be inattentive, withdrawn, and irritable. This change in behavior was demonstrated in one experiment in a nursing facility in which a 4 A.M. wake-up time was extended by 2 hours. The outcome was a reduction in the number of prescriptions required for aggressive behavior during the day. Sleep deprivation impairs concentration and causes people to make uncharacteristic mistakes. For example, a sleep-deprived individual becomes as accident-prone as an intoxicated driver, even if he or she does not feel sleepy.

A widespread myth that older adults need less sleep arose from a mistaken interpretation of research (Feinberg, Koresco, & Heller, 1967). The study population of six women and nine men was divided into groups by age-decade. When the research revealed that the average duration of sleep decreased in the group, the conclusion drawn was that sleep demands declined with advancing age. Unfortunately, the groups were not controlled for causes of organic insomnia such as night pain, nocturia (nocturnal urination), and respiratory problems that frequently occur in the older cohorts. Other studies showed that those who do not develop organic causes for sleep loss displayed unchanging sleep needs as they age. Those individuals who complain they get less sleep than they feel they require have *insomnia,* which is a difficulty in falling asleep or intermittent sleep—or *terminal insomnia,* which is waking too early and being unable to fall back asleep.

> A WIDESPREAD MYTH that older adults need less sleep arose from a mistaken interpretation of research.

Difficulty in falling asleep is common when people are preoccupied or worried, which keeps their mind too active. This transient insomnia should disappear in a few days unless a person's problems are epochal in significance or he or she is constitutionally unable to make decisions to resolve them and is a chronic worrier. The use of hypnotic drugs to help a person get to sleep should be seen as a temporary and tranquilizing solution and not a desirable treatment. Benzodiazepines is the class of drugs often prescribed for this purpose and includes diazepam (Valium), temazepam (Restoril), alprazolam (Xanax), and triazolam

(Halcion). These drugs, however, interfere with REM sleep and contribute to poor sleep quality. They may also become addictive if used for more than a few days consecutively.

Intermittent insomnia is prevalent among elderly people. To understand its origins, a careful survey of an individual's particular lifestyle and sleeping habits must be conducted. Too little exercise is a common cause, but if an evening stroll is recommended, it should be completed more than 2 hours before trying to sleep. Arthritic or other pain, which may be worse after retiring for the night, can interfere with sleep and may require a short-acting analgesic at bedtime. Long-acting NSAIDs have been found to damage the quality of sleep, but narcotics increase its duration. Bladder problems are another common cause of frequent awakenings, as well as coughing from esophageal reflux. Eating a heavy meal late in the evening will interfere with natural sleep—sleeping directly after eating may actually cause sleep deprivation! Caffeine, of course, will prevent sleep if consumed fewer than 6 hours before sleep; theobromine, which is in tea and cocoa, is just as troublesome. Alcohol, which some mistakenly believe will help insomniacs, produces poor-quality sleep. Moreover, alcohol is a diuretic and increases urine output, which in turn causes frequent awakenings with bladder fullness.

Another fairly common condition that ruins the quality of sleep is *restless legs* (or Ekbom's) *syndrome* (RLS). It usually comes on at rest, sometimes in the evening, but more frequently during the sleeping hours when it may seriously disturb the sleep of the sufferer as well as the bedmate. Attacks begin as a strange feeling in the lower legs: The skin may become irritable, burning, or painful and the symptoms develop into a compulsion to agitate the legs. Pacing, stretching, or rubbing may be used for relief. The condition is inherited in at least 75% of cases, but the cause is not known. Caffeine has been shown to make it worse, and low iron stores typically accompany it. The most popular current treatment seems to be anti-Parkinsonism drugs, which increase dopamine. A helpful resource for information and support groups is The Restless Legs Syndrome Foundation (http://www.rls.org).

If insomnia cannot be attributed to any of these causes, then the survivor should begin a gentle afternoon walking program, eliminate alcohol and tobacco, and try some preventive strategies including making a list of things to remember in the morning, then forgetting about it; going to bed at the same time each night; keeping the air fresh and cool; reserving the room for sleeping and engaging in quiet activities rather than watching television; and getting up at the same time on work days or holidays. If awake, reading an engrossing book with the light on is better than smoldering under the sheets in the dark.

The power user will observe the presleep hygiene routines mentioned previously. A strategy to eliminate sleep deprivation involves getting up at the same time each morning but going to bed progressively—a half-hour—earlier each night until awakening refreshed becomes natural and regular. A nightcap or hypnotic should not be taken until two successive nights of major sleep loss have occurred, and then only as an expediency. Driving between the hours of midnight and 6 A.M. should be avoided as much as possible. If a person needs to drive during this time, then he or she should take a nap the previous day and have a companion in the car. For the 50% of retired people who do not have insomnia, a 1-hour siesta in the afternoon is an appropriately healthy reward for the years of toil that brought them to this more relaxed stage of life.

NUTRITION

"PEOPLE LIVE TO EAT AND EAT TO LIVE"

The imperative for people to eat accounts for much of their activity of daily life. Planning for the future was "saving against a rainy day" when an individual could no longer work and independently meet his or her needs. In the late 20th century, traditional dining changed. Not only the young, but also now their grandparents, often rely on fast food rather than cooking. At best, when grocery shopping or dining out, people make impulsive choices from a maze of advertised items that have neither the sanction of tradition nor the reassurance of nutritional benefit. At worst, isolated or depressed elders who have lost their zest for living may slip into a routine of monotonous and unwise food choices served in uninteresting ways. They are said to have food insecurity that can be evaluated by a questionnaire—the Mini Nutritional Assessment (MNA)—or blood tests, such as the prealbumin and transferrin levels.

So that readers can adopt a position of strength in choosing foods wisely, this discussion will begin with how the body processes food via calories, carbohydrates, proteins, and fat. It is also important to discuss the often-controversial role of vitamins and minerals. In addition, water consumption and hydration are other factors that can have a profound impact on the nutritional health and wellness of older adults.

CALORIE INTAKE

Locked in the molecules of our food is energy derived from the sun, and it is part of the task of nutrition and respiration to release it. Energy is measured in calories and is printed in the *nutrition facts* label on packaged foods. When consumers eat more calories than they need, the extra energy is stored as fat molecules. When they need more calories than they are assimilating, they tap into their stored energy reserves, breaking down those fat molecules, producing weight loss. Most people have a "usual weight," although it may fluctuate up or down a little from day to day; even after going on a binge or trying a diet for a while, individuals tend to return to this usual weight, and recent research has cast some light on how this regulation takes place.

Creatures experience the need to eat as appetite, which may be increased by the sight and smell of food. If ignored, this feeling intensifies to a gnawing sense of hunger. Satiation occurs for several hours after food is put in the stomach.

Although not enough is known about satiety, it seems that fat entering the small intestine and stimulating the release of cholecystokinin may trigger it. This may explain why *empty calories* such as sugar, which contain no fat, do not trigger satiety; on the contrary, they appear to be addictive.

It is less clear what the role of appetite and satiety is in the eating habits of healthy older people, but they are unaware that they frequently have some loss of taste and smell. Their interest in eating often revolves around the concept of meals as social events. Within family settings, older adults usually eat regularly. A diminishment of lipase secretion in the aging body may cause fats to be retained longer in the stomach and thus not initiate the satiety reflex. Deprived of satiety, sedentary older people who continue to eat their customary portions will steadily put on layers of fat as they grow older. The survivors who experience such weight gain with age may want to try calorie-controlled liquid diets, which can help disrupt unhelpful mealtime eating patterns.

In contrast to older people who seem to eat too much, some frail older adults have no interest in food; they are said to eat "like a bird." They may be suffering from the common condition of anorexia that often has its cause in some unrecognized disease process. There are also the "tea and toast" women whose diets contain an adequate number of empty calories from sugar and starch but lack protein and fat. Tea, which contains phytates, also prevents absorption of iron and calcium from the bowel, so sooner or later these women experience malnourishment, anemia, and osteoporosis.

Among individual deficiencies of each of the three major food groups, only protein deficiency is significant because fat and carbohydrates are nonessential. When all of these are low, however, a condition known as *protein-calorie malnutrition,* or starvation, exists. A person can survive with this type of malnutrition for a few months up to a few years; this is the condition seen in parts of the world with prolonged famine. The condition is rare in industrialized countries, except in people who are extremely impoverished or sick, in people who are isolated in their homes, and in people who are alcoholics. It is doubtful that this condition would ever be seen in survivors or power users.

CARBOHYDRATES

Carbohydrates contribute the largest number of calories to human diets. Until this century, the great majority of calories eaten in the world came from various grains. The basic molecules of carbohydrates are sugars—consisting of chains of carbon atoms combined with the elements of water. In turn, chains of sugars themselves, such as glucose, are often strung together as disaccharides, such as sucrose and lactose, and as polysaccharides, such as starch—the main product of grain. Following commercial expansion in the Caribbean and Hawaii in the last 100 years, sugar cane has gone from being a little-used, expensive curiosity to becoming refined sucrose, a staple part of the diet of most industrialized countries. In this country, older people consume about 50 pounds of sucrose annually, and it may constitute half of their caloric intake. Increasing amounts of sucrose are found in processed food, including the fructose used in soft drinks. Because of its addition to so many foods, the amount of sucrose a person consumes now is largely determined by the food industry.

Some experts assert that the preponderance of sugar in modern diets has given rise to a condition known as *reactive hypoglycemia.* Normally, it arises after an episode of simple sugar intake—the blood sugar (i.e., glucose) rises steeply for about an hour, then falls gradually. The fall is due to the release of the hormone insulin from the islet cells of the pancreas, causing an increase in the rate at which glucose is utilized by the muscles and liver. Gradually, the secretion of another islet cell hormone, glucagon, corrects the fall and allows the sugar to return to normal. Proponents of the reactive hypoglycemia theory believe this corrective mechanism does not work in many people, so that glucose continues to fall (hypoglycemia), producing weakness and mental confusion. In an effort to restore balance, the body secretes epinephrine to activate and release glucose from storage. Unfortunately, the presence of epinephrine produces alarming side effects, including a gnawing hunger in the pit of the stomach, a sense of anxiety, heart palpitations, tremors, sweating, and possibly headaches. This constellation of symptoms from which many claim to suffer is what proponents call reactive hypoglycemia.

Traditionalists, however, exhort that many people have low blood sugar levels without these symptoms. Moreover, people can have these symptoms without hypoglycemia because of some other causal condition. The survivor who suffers from these symptoms would avoid meals high in simple sugars, especially sucrose, and ensure that at least 60% of his or her daily calories come from complex carbohydrates such as grains.

A different condition that is often unrecognized but widely acknowledged as common in older adults is *lactose intolerance*—the inability to digest lactose. Lactase, an enzyme that is produced in the small bowel wall, is required to split the disaccharide lactose found in milk. Many Native Americans and some people of Mediterranean origin who have a deficiency of lactase have lactose intolerance from an early age; by mid-life, many other people have a degree of it. Without lactase, the undigested lactose passes into the large bowel intact. It then undergoes bacterial souring, which results in diarrhea, gas, and cramping pain. However, a person who consequently stops consuming dairy products also cuts the intake of vitamins A and D and calcium. Therefore, survivors with lactose intolerance will switch to yogurt and other lactose-free dairy foods for their calcium and to fat-soluble vitamin supplements. Power users will alternatively take a lactase tablet and go right on enjoying their ice cream.

A similar condition associated with a polysaccharide is *alpha-galactoside intolerance,* which is also very prevalent in old age due to the loss of the enzyme that can digest it. For people trying to increase their fiber intake by eating beans, broccoli, peppers, and similar vegetables, this condition is particularly distressing. The intact polysaccharide passes into the bowel, where it is fermented by colon bacteria, producing large quantities of gas together with cramping pains.

Although the survivor can avoid these foods, the flatulent power user can take a tablet of alpha-galactosidase (sold under the brand name Beano) for comfort and greater social acceptability.

Glucose is carried in the bloodstream, and a normal level is statistically correlated with a longer life expectancy. A mildly higher-than-normal level used to be known as "a touch of sugar" by the friendly family doctor who reassured the patient and told him or her to have it rechecked in a year. Today's scientifically correct physician would equate this approach with saying someone has "a touch of pregnancy." There are two types of the disease. Of these, Type I, or *insulin-dependent diabetes* (IDDM), is caused by a failure of the beta cells of the pancreas to secrete insulin. Often called *juvenile diabetes* because the onset is early in life, the disease has a definite genetic basis. It does not always manifest itself, however, until an adult health stress serves as a trigger. The basic problem is that without insulin, the blood sugar cannot be utilized for energy; it doesn't get consumed, so it rises continuously. Also, without insulin, fat cannot be mobilized effectively as an energy alternative; instead, it is broken down into products that cause a potentially fatal condition—ketoacidosis, characterized by a diabetic coma. The complications of Type I diabetes can resemble premature aging, but with good care, it can be controlled, allowing a typical life span.

Type II diabetes is non–insulin-dependant (NIDDM) and is also known as *metabolic syndrome.* With an onset that is often triggered by significant middle-age weight gain, this variety is characterized by a resistance of metabolic cells to respond to the hormone insulin rather than by its absence. Enzymes within the cells of the body need insulin if glucose is to enter or if fat is to be metabolized completely. The resistance to insulin seems initially to be caused by an excess of fat storage, but then the surplus glucose in turn results in greater fat storage—a vicious circle. All of the complications of IDDM also occur in this type, except for a different type of coma. Avoiding these complications requires the same blood sugar control as in juvenile diabetes.

Survivors with diabetes perform a routine procedure of finger stick tests to monitor and control their own blood glucose level. The technology of self-management is becoming even easier; individuals can now use noninvasive monitors. Treatment for IDDM and some Type II diabetes requires insulin injections. A variety of drugs are used alone or in combination to increase insulin. And some new drugs have a direct effect on the metabolic enzyme system. The three most powerful treatments for insulin resistance, however, are weight reduction, a high-fiber diet, and exercise, all of which naturally lower blood sugars and can often eliminate the need for drugs. A high-residue diet with a lot of fiber and exercise also reduces dependence on insulin.

For the power user, a program known as *intensive therapy,* consisting of continuous blood glucose monitoring and an insulin pump, offers the most complication-free treatment. For Type I diabetes, immunization shots and the possibility of islet cell or pancreatic transplants are on the experimental horizon as well.

PROTEINS

Some of the most important tasks of our metabolism are bodybuilding and repair, which require amino acids derived from protein. The parsimonious economy of the body recycles the products of protein breakdown so successfully that only about a half of our daily requirements need to be filled from the food we eat. For this needed intake, the recommended total daily allowance is about 0.9g protein intake for every kilogram of body weight, or a total of about 60–80g daily. Nine essential amino acids must be acquired through an individual's diet; a person's own body can produce another dozen. Older people have only 60% of the lean body mass that they had when they were young and, consequently, they have smaller total protein needs. Because older adults consume fewer total calories, however, protein should comprise a higher proportion of their diet than when they were younger to maintain good health.

The kidney sets a limit on the amount of excess protein nitrogen that can be excreted but few can reach the dubious distinction of England's King John, who, in 1216, literally ate himself to death from protein poisoning. The survivor will simply make it a habit to eat more vegetable than animal products. The power user should feel free to enjoy protein but should bear in mind that most proteins are wedded to fat, which should be restricted.

FATS

Although the main source of calories until a century ago was carbohydrates in the form of natural vegetable foods, more and more Americans are increasing their fat consumption to more than 50% of their energy intake—a level that only Inuits living above the Arctic Circle exceed. Fats contain 9 calories per gram, twice that of carbohydrates or protein, and are the body's main storage containers of energy reserves. Body fat provided both the fuel and the insulation needed by our Ice Age ancestors to survive the cold. We also rely on dietary fats for several vitamins and an essential fatty acid that cannot be made in the body. Aside from their physiological benefits, fats are responsible for the flavor and texture of most foods, and a totally fat-free diet would be inedible.

More than 90% of fat in food is triglyceride, a lipid in which a molecule of glycerol is combined with three fatty acids. The fatty acids of hard animal fats are saturated with hydrogen and are called *saturated fats;* most vegetable oils contain unsaturated fatty acids. To artificially produce the more expensive, harder fats such as margarine, manufacturers often hydrogenate cheaper vegetable oils, producing transhydrogenated fatty acids. All forms of saturated fats, except for stearic acid, increase the cholesterol levels in the blood; when unsaturated fats are substituted for saturated ones in the diet, total cholesterol falls. In addition to the widely known adverse affect of cholesterol on the heart and circulatory systems, saturated fats are suspected of increasing the incidence of cancer of the colon and the prostate.

Like protein, the body conserves and recycles fats so that food intake only needs to supply approximately half of the daily turnover. After being absorbed, fat is transported from the bowel into the blood. There, it is broken down by lipase and stored as triglyceride in special fat cells—the adipocytes. As these cells fill, they send a message to the brain by secreting leptin, the satiety hormone, which inhibits the production of an appetite-enhancing neuropeptide and reduces the desire for food intake.

Children store most of their fat evenly under the skin, where it acts as a heat insulator. In slim adults, fat is concentrated around the vital organs, where it helps to protect them from trauma. Overweight people deposit fat irregularly under the skin and in adipose tissue pads around their middle; this tends to produce an apple shape in men and a pear shape in women. Older people considered merely overweight (those whose weight exceeds ideal weight by 15% or less), especially those from overweight families, need not worry too much about fat. The belief that being overweight increases one's risk of heart attack has not been proven by scientific studies; a pleasantly plump person may be healthier than an anxiously underweight person. As more weight is gained, however, fat cells swell until, at the stage that a person is approximately 20% overweight, they begin to divide. This stage represents true obesity and, thereafter, weight reduction becomes harder to achieve; obesity *is* a risk factor for heart attacks.

The survivor who wishes to stay trim will strive to keep total fat in the diet to less than 30% of calories, with equal proportions of saturated, monounsaturated, and polyunsaturated fats. This will require reading the small print on food package labels to determine if there is any partially hydrogenated *trans*acid content. (Fat analysis is required to be on the package, but it is not always in the *Nutrition Facts* box; if it is hidden elsewhere and the type is too small to read, assume the packager is trying to hide something!) The overweight person who decides to take a power user approach will regard obesity as a cause of diabetes, hypertension, and sleep apnea, which will require interventions with a dietician, a behavioral psychologist, and possibly a surgeon to avoid it. Obesity is the easiest disease to diagnose and the hardest to treat.

CHOLESTEROL

Approximately 10% of the average lipid intake in a mixed diet takes the form of cholesterol, which is a normal constituent of animal fats. Strict vegans, who eat no animal products, consume no cholesterol because all plant foods are cholesterol-free. In fact, the body utilizes not much of the cholesterol eaten. Most is broken down, but in the process, it adds to the level of stored fat. Because of this, the survivor tries not to consume more than 300mg of cholesterol a day, not because it raises the blood cholesterol, but because it adds fat.

Almost all of our cells are capable of making cholesterol themselves, which they form from fats, especially saturated fats. Thus, one important step toward reducing blood cholesterol is in strictly limiting the amount of saturated fats.

Cholesterol is not soluble in blood and is carried by a number of lipoproteins of differing densities. When these are in a lipoprotein report prepared by a professional laboratory, they are labeled high-density (HDL), low-density (LDL), and very-low-density (VLDL) lipoproteins, as well as triglycerides and chylomicrons. Consumers should be wary of health fair and shopping mall tests of "total cholesterol," which are notoriously inaccurate. By and large, the LDL, VLDL, triglycerides, and chylomicrons are carrying fat and cholesterol to fat storage locations, so that high levels indicate the presence of high levels of excess fat in the metabolism. The HDL is responsible for returning cholesterol from storage to the liver to be metabolized, which is why it is called *good cholesterol*—it is reducing fat stores, including vessel deposits. The survivor will strive to consume more polyunsaturated fats in his or her effort to reduce total blood cholesterol levels, but exercising, consuming monounsaturated fats, and taking cholesterol-lowering drugs will fall into the purview of the power user, who will be striving more actively to reduce the level of LDL and triglycerides and increase the HDL.

Cholesterol blood levels were first associated publicly with heart disease after publication of the results of the Framingham study and then were confirmed by later studies (Gordon et al., 1977). Today, concern about the dangers of high cholesterol levels is widespread, yet more myths than facts abound. For one thing, the total blood cholesterol is affected by many factors, which include diet but also gender, race, genetic inheritance, and health status. Furthermore, cholesterol has only a loose association with heart disease. No statistically persuasive studies involving older participants linking blood cholesterol levels, LDL, or HDL with heart disease are available. The current view is that cholesterol-lowering drugs have a salutary effect at any blood lipid level if a person has any cardiovascular symptoms, but there is no need for asymptomatic people to take these very expensive drugs.

VITAMINS AND MINERALS

Vitamins and minerals may be found in animal, vegetable, or mineral sources and are known as micronutrients because the quantity needed by the body is very small, compared with regular food. They are essential for life, yet taking them as supplements is not a substitute for food as some people seem to believe. They must be taken with food to ensure proper absorption and metabolism. U.S. Recommended Dietary Allowances (USRDAs) needed for health have been published by the WHO and incorporated into the percentage of Daily Values (DVs) of the National Academy of Sciences (this information is required by law in "Nutrition Facts" printed on food packages). Figure 3.1 is the familiar food triangle adapted for people whose age is over 70. Each micronutrient is found in several kinds of food and will be considered next, food group by food group.

LEAFY VEGETABLES: 3–5 SERVINGS DAILY; FRUITS: 2–4 SERVINGS DAILY
Leafy vegetables and fruits have a skeleton of cellulose. In the bowel, cellulose helps to provide bulk, stimulating peristalsis. Diets high in cellulose are low in fat and help to reduce gallstones, constipation, diverticulosis, irritable bowel,

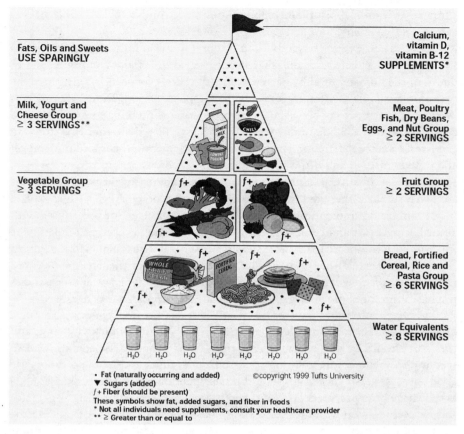

Figure 3.1. Modified food pyramid for older adults. (From Russell, R., Lichtenstein, A., & Rasmussen, H. [1999]. *Modified food pyramid for mature (70+) adults.* Medford, MA: Tufts University; reprinted by permission.)

and hemorrhoids. Recent results from the Nurses Health Study have suggested a protective relationship between consumption of fruit and vegetables—particularly cruciferous and green leafy vegetables, citrus fruit, and juice—and ischemic stroke risk (Bazzano et al., 2000). The survivor will eat two to four servings of vegetables and fruit a day. The micronutrients in these vegetable foods are discussed next.

Green vegetables, including spinach, watercress, and parsley, contain beta-carotene. In the body, beta-carotene is converted to retinol, which can prevent night blindness and also functions to stabilize mucous membranes. Deficiency is rare in the U.S. except among chronic alcoholics who may be both night-blind and sterile. Vitamin A is a concentrated ester of retinol that has the same functions as beta-carotene but is found only in animals (good sources are egg yolk and liver). Some is naturally present in the milk of pasture-fed cows and also is added in the dairy as a fortifier. However, unlike beta-carotene, there is no limit to the quantity that can be absorbed from the bowel, so if a tremendously rich source of vitamin A, such as cod liver oil or some megavitamin supplement, is taken too liberally, poisoning can result. The wise older survivor does not consume any vitamin A supplement but relies on natural sources, using a beta-carotene supplement if needed.

Vitamin K_1 is also fat-soluble and is found in green leafy vegetables such as spinach, cabbage, kale, and collard greens, as well as in cereals. Vitamin K_2 is produced in the human bowel by bacteria resident there. Not surprisingly, then, the best animal source of vitamin K_1/K_2 is liver, especially pork liver. Vitamin K is needed for the growth of bone and in the production of proteins essential to blood coagulation (K = Koagulation—German). All assimilated vitamin K is stored in the liver. Dietary deficiency, antibiotic bowel sterilization, chronic mineral oil abuse, liver disease, and drugs can produce a low store of vitamin K in the liver. In the medical treatment of unwanted thrombosis, coumarin anticoagulant drugs are given to block the vitamin K and delay clotting; other drugs such as aspirin have a similar but more unpredictable effect. Anticoagulant therapy is used with a fibrillating heart and seems to be a very effective way to prevent strokes. The survivor with this heart arrhythmia should be taking anticoagulants (often known as blood thinners), although he or she will recognize that this treatment is not without its own dangers attendant on the risk of bleeding. The power user assumes responsibility for home management of his or her *prothrombin-time* tests.

Cabbage, cauliflower, citrus fruits, and cereals (fortified) contain vitamin C *(ascorbic acid)*. For maximum content, the greens should be picked young, and the fruit should be picked when it is ripe. Grains that have been allowed to sprout also manufacture ascorbic acid, so bean sprouts and bamboo shoots are good sources. Fresh vegetables should be refrigerated intact and cooked as soon as they have been prepared. Ascorbic acid is destroyed by cooking in copper pans and by keeping food warm for some time; thus, health regulations requiring the use of hot food carts in hospitals unfortunately ensure that there is no vitamin C left when the individuals get the food! The body utilizes vitamin C to form capillaries and collagen; it is an antioxidant, or reducing, substance. Pronounced ascorbic acid deficiency no longer seems to exist in America, but it was prevalent 100 years ago when it was known as scurvy. Mild deficiency, however, does occur in older adult shut-ins and chronic alcoholics and may cause fatigue, follicular dermatitis, and swollen friable gums. Excessive doses of ascorbic acid have been responsible for attacks of sweating, heart irregularities, and oxalate kidney stones. Because many older people get less than the recommended allowance, the survivor should not rely on the warmed greens in the cafeteria but get his or her 50mg of ascorbic acid daily from fresh fruits and salads. In addition, the power user will wish to benefit from the antioxidant properties of increased ascorbic acid but take no more than a 250–500mg supplement a day.

The same plant sources (e.g., dark green leafy vegetables such as broccoli, asparagus, legumes, or fruits, especially oranges) that supply ascorbic acid supply folic acid (folacin). Folic acid is found in flour and is added to fortified breakfast cereals. In addition, yeast is a rich source, as are dairy products and liver. Folate is unstable to light and heat and stores poorly. It is preserved better when ascorbic acid is present, as in greens and oranges. As a single carbon acceptor, folate has a major role to play in the formation of DNA in the body, especially in the central nervous system and in red blood cells. It is needed when the mucosal cells of the gut are recovering from damage. Chronic deficiency is probably fairly common. The Third National Health and Nutrition Examination Survey reported an almost two-fold increase in the likelihood of myocardial infarction among people with a low folate and a total homocysteine concentration more than 15 μmol/L. Because excess folate does not seem to be harmful, many physicians recommend survivors receive a supplementation of 400mg folate daily. (For the power user recommendation on this, see the passage on cobalamin on page 67.)

Green vegetables are a good source of *iron,* which is also present in red meat. Not all of the iron in vegetables can be absorbed, however. Spinach, for instance, often coercively forced on children because of its high iron content, contains iron-chelate, which will not release its iron in the intestine and might even capture more for excretion. Apparently, the body of an adult has the wisdom not to absorb more iron than it needs. Studies on the older population in the U.S. have shown that high proportions do not quite achieve the recommended daily allowance. Iron is needed for hemoglobin, the oxygen-carrying pigment in red blood cells. Mild iron-deficiency anemia is quite common among older adults, especially poorer older adults, who do not consume much in the way of green vegetables or red meat. The body has adequate iron stores to tide it over for more than several months of an iron-deficient diet, especially if there is no blood loss. Ultimately, the stores run out and anemia gradually appears. The onset of anemia, especially suddenly, in a person with adequate iron intake may mean a loss of blood and requires a thorough work-up. All anemias are not due to iron deficiency, however, and in such cases iron is bad therapy because it might result in *hemochromotosis,* a fatal disease caused by too much iron stored in the internal organs.

LEGUMES AND NUTS: 1 – 3 SERVINGS DAILY; GRAIN (BREAD, CEREAL, RICE): 5 – 10 SERVINGS DAILY   Americans eat relatively fewer legumes, including beans and peas, than most people in the world do. Beans produce protein and oil but no carbohydrates. The United States is the world's largest producer of soybeans, but only 2% are used for human consumption. Tofu, a soy product, is sold as a health food. Unfortunately, unless it has been fermented the oriental way, soy contains too many harmful phytins to be recommended. A moderate amount of peanuts is eaten in the United States, half of which is peanut butter. They have more protein, vitamins, and minerals per pound than beef liver, more fat than heavy cream, and more calories than sugar. Interest in nuts has increased in the 21st century, and frequent nut consumption was associated with a reduced risk of both fatal coronary heart disease and nonfatal myocardial infarction. People with colon problems should have their nuts ground to avoid diverticulitis.

Legumes, grains, and nuts all have a matrix of soluble fiber that delays the emptying of the stomach, producing a sense of satiety. Oats and barley are very good sources of soluble fiber. Nut and grain bars are, therefore, a better snack than "lite, cholesterol-free" buttered popcorn that is smothered in arteriosclerosis-generating partially hydrogenated trans-oils! In the bowel, soluble fiber delays absorption of fat and sugars, thereby reducing the blood levels of insulin and

LDL cholesterol, and thus aiding in the prevention of diabetes and heart disease. Milling of grain separates the outer husk that contains dietary bran and the inner germ that provides proteins, vitamins, and polyunsaturated fats from the middle endosperm that contains the flour. Most of this valuable nutritive material is used for animal food, but bran and wheat germ can be bought in health food shops.

Whole grain flour, brown rice, couscous, and yellow cornmeal are not re-fined and retain their full content of nutrients. With less processing, they should be much cheaper than milled flour but are not because of issues of supply and demand. The power user will incorporate these nutritious supplements into his or her diet. The survivor will eat six or more legume, grain, or nut products a day and more fresh and homemade foods than processed ones.

Some of the B-complex vitamins, thiamine (vitamin B_1), riboflavin (vita-min B_2), and niacin (vitamin B_3), are very similar to each other in their function. They are all contained in the same foods—legumes, grains and nuts, and liver. Liver and dairy products will offset niacin deficiency because of their content of tryptophan, an amino acid from which the body can make niacin. Of the three, riboflavin and niacin are not destroyed by heat, but riboflavin is destroyed by sunlight. Thiamine is not damaged by light boiling but is destroyed by toasting and roasting. All are water-soluble, so they leach into cooking water and may be discarded but can be recovered if this water is made into stock. Thiamine, ribo-flavin, and niacin are all absorbed by similar mechanisms and are all needed for the final oxidation of carbohydrates and amino acids. They cannot be stored in the body, so we need a constant supply of them. Often, deficiencies of all three are combined, so it is difficult to make an accurate diagnosis. In addition, the initial symptoms of deficiency are often nonspecific and seen within other health problems. The common factor in each is changes in the digestive system that decrease the desire for food and create a vicious circle that prolongs deficiency. Deficiencies in thiamine, riboflavin, and niacin can all produce nausea and con-stipation, but niacin deficiency also results in bloody diarrhea. Nervous system problems from riboflavin deficiency include headache, depression, and forgetful-ness. In the early stages of thiamin deficiency, a painful neuritis occurs that is re-versible with treatment. Permanent nerve damage occurs in niacin deficiency, which can go on to produce dementia. Thiamine deficiency is known as *beri-beri* and causes nerve damage as well as heart failure because the heart muscle is weakened and cannot cope with the high blood flow. Deficiencies in all three cause cracking around the lips and burning of the mouth and eyes. Niacin defi-ciency causes the worst kind of dermatitis—*pellagra*—in which the skin is un-able to repair its wear and tear and becomes very rough and sore.

The remaining components of the B-complex vitamins, pyridoxine (vita-min B_6), pantothenic acid, and biotin, are all essential micronutrients found in the same foods as the B-complex vitamins described previously and are needed in the metabolism of amino acids. However, they are so widely distributed in na-ture that even though deficiency diseases can be described for each of them in children and laboratory animals, there are no corresponding diseases that affect older people. The survivor will know pantothenic acid does not prevent hair going gray, as some hucksters claim, and that well-nourished elders certainly do not require the pyridoxine, pantothenic acid, and biotin in expensive "geriatric supplements."

Flavonoids are found in a variety of foods, including onions, apples, and red wine. Although they are not vitamins in the traditional sense, the consumption of flavonoids does seem to be related to a resistance to coronary artery disease and stroke. The similar protection that comes from a limited amount of alcohol intake seems additional to that specific to red wine. So, the survivor who enjoys one to two alcoholic drinks a day, and the power user who chooses up to 10 ounces of red wine, can feel justified by the results of current research. This may not be true for people with hypertension.

MEAT, POULTRY, FISH, AND EGGS: 2–3 SERVINGS DAILY   As protein sources, meats are the favorites for most people. Unfortunately, they are inseparably bound to fat, which is usually saturated and contains a lot of cholesterol. The survivor makes careful choices of lean cuts of meat, trims off excess fat from beef, removes the skins from poultry, and cooks pork and mutton by fat-reducing methods that will reduce their content of lipids. The power user keeps all meat portions below the recommended DV of 4 ounces.

Eggs were the scapegoat when cholesterol was first discovered, and a lot of people stopped eating them. Most of the cholesterol in eggs is in the yolk, and only 15% of that remains cholesterol when it reaches the blood. The survivor, however, keeps daily cholesterol intake below 300mg, sets a limit of one egg yolk or its cooked equivalent a day, and consumes reduced-fat or skim milk to ensure getting the calcium and vitamins it contains without the extra fat. The power user is learning to appreciate cholesterol-free eggs.

The only essential micronutrient exclusively supplied by animal products is cobalamin (vitamin B_{12}), which contains the trace element cobalt. It is described chemically as a hydrogen acceptor—an essential component in the growth and function of blood cells and the nervous system. About a quarter of one sample of older adults were found to be mildly B_{12} deficient. A more marked, nutritional problem can occur in vegans, but the major cobalamin deficiency known as *pernicious anemia* is caused by an internal condition—the lack of the intrinsic absorption factor in the stomach. Combination with this factor is necessary if B_{12} is to be assimilated from the small intestine. Pernicious anemia consists of red blood cells that are immaturely large but few and fragile.

ABOUT A QUARTER OF one sample of older adults were found to be mildly B_{12} deficient.

Perhaps more important is a severe associated neurological disease that results in dementia and permanent damage to some of the tracts of the spinal column affecting sensation and potentially causing paralysis. Lack of folic acid produces similar symptoms, but if pernicious anemia is treated by folic acid alone, further damage occurs. Thus, both the survivor and the power user who are diagnosed as deficient in either vitamin will request treatment with both: the folate by mouth and the cobalamin by injection.

MILK, YOGURT, AND CHEESE: 3 SERVINGS DAILY   Although classed with the vitamins, *calciferol* (vitamin D) is really a hormone made from cholesterol in the skin, a process that is diminished in older adults. A form of the vitamin also can be found in egg yolks, liver, and fatty fish. Many drugs, alkalis, and laxatives can reduce bowel absorption so as many as 75% of older adults may get an inadequate intake. Another form, vitamin D$_2$, produced by irradiating plant ergosterol, is used to fortify milk products and some cereals. Introduced during the Great Depression, this fortification eliminated *rickets,* once a widespread deficiency disease of children. Rickets, which caused ugly and health-threatening skeletal deformities in children, and osteomalacia (its adult equivalent), are so rare now that their diagnosis is often missed when they do appear in impoverished people. However, rickets is now re-emerging in dark-skinned children who were breast-fed, drink milk substitutes, and stay indoors watching a lot of television.

Milk is often the main source of *calcium* for older people. Most of the calcium in the body at any one time is in the mineral content of bone, but some of it is exchanged continuously with the calcium in the blood. Rarely, raised blood calcium indicates a parathyroid tumor, causing multiple symptoms, perhaps resembling a neurotic disorder. Too little calcium in the serum would cause tetanic spasms in the muscles and is rare. Too little calcium in the bones is very common. It is known as *osteopenia,* defined as a bone-mass density more than one standard deviation below normal. One cause of this is *osteomalacia,* often due to vitamin D deficiency. But an even more common cause is *osteoporosis,* which affects 20 million Americans, of whom 80% of those affected are women. A high percentage of women suffer from osteoporosis because of postmenopausal estrogen withdrawal. Understandably, osteopenia leads to fractures and disablement at a national cost of $10 billion annually. Increasing calcium and vitamin D by a simple dietary supplement is not sufficient to correct osteoporosis, so the usual approach has been hormonal replacement therapy (HRT). This has the additional benefits of reducing postmenopausal symptoms, such as hot flashes, and providing possible protection against heart disease and dementia. However, there are also some drawbacks, including uterine bleeding, increased incidence of endometrial and, probably, breast cancer, and possible increased risk of heart attacks, strokes, and clotting disorders. For *prophylaxis,* all older adult men and women should take 1200mg calcium and 400mg calciferol a day and have a bone density test every 5 years. If osteoporosis occurs, then the survivor female should probably decline the HRT for safety and take raloxifene, etidronate, or calcitonin, all of which unfortunately are more costly and troublesome than HRT. An alternative medicine substitute is taking isoflavones, which are phytoestrogens derived from soybeans. These may also help to reduce postmenopausal symptoms, lower cholesterol, and have an anticancer action, but these benefits still need to be proved through further research. Osteoporotic men may be treated with these drugs, too. Previously, the female power user might have decided the added cardiac protection she got by taking HRT compensated for any increased risk it caused, and would take progesterone to reduce the risk of uterine cancer and have regular biopsies to monitor her endometrium, but this assumption is probably false.

Legumes, cereals, meat, and milk all contain *zinc*, so deficiency is rare. Zinc appears to be very important for aging people because it is needed for preserving the sense of taste, forming keratin in skin and nails, forming bone, healing wounds, responding to diabetes, and detoxifying of alcohol. It is found in the red blood cells where it forms enzymes that help transport CO_2 back to the lungs and in the digestive tract where it is incorporated in enzymes that digest protein. It may play a role in the defense against macular degeneration. An RDA has not been established, but while the jury is out, the survivor takes a supplement of 15mg to 50mg daily.

The element that gives salinity to the fluids that surrounds the cells, including those of the blood, is *sodium*. There are about 6–10 grams of sodium chloride in our daily diet. A lot of sodium is secreted in the digestive juices each day, but most is reabsorbed. In perfectly healthy people, absorbing increased sodium results in a rise of blood volume; then, the kidney excretes the excess sodium and water, and the blood volume returns to normal. If the body is dehydrated, then the adrenal gland secretes aldosterone that acts on the cells of the gut and kidney to force them to reabsorb even more sodium, along with chloride ions and water needed to maintain osmotic pressure. In older people, the kidney does not conserve salt too well, and dehydration may persist. However, in people with hypertension, excess salt intake results in increased blood pressure, so salt restriction is usually prescribed for them; normotensive individuals need not restrict salt. A lack of sodium in the diet causes hypotension and stimulates a salt craving comparable to that of animals that make long trips to their "salt licks." Salt is an important part of flavor, but many popular foods contain an excess of salt; well-known examples include commercial vegetable drinks, canned soups, and soy sauce. In the bowel, reabsorption of salt and water from the liquid contents of the upper colon results in the formed consistency of the stools passing on to the rectum; excessive reabsorption seen in a dehydrated individual results in hard stools. The survivor takes in adequate fluids and enjoys moderate salt flavor but removes the salt shaker from the table and learns to use potassium as a salt substitute if the blood pressure is raised. The power user limits salt to less than 5g a day.

In a very hot climate, unacclimatized people can only lose a maximum of 700ml sweat per hour, and this contains an excess of salt. If sweating cannot control their temperature, then these people should stay indoors to avoid heat cramps that may occur unless the sodium is replaced. Yet, acclimatized people can stay out in the heat, sweat 2L per hour, and lose very little salt. Thus, the acclimated survivor does not need to drink the sodium-heavy sports drinks, which are promoted to avoid heat cramps. The power user may use them to douse the coach.

Potassium does not figure in nutrition problems because it is imprisoned in the cells. The survivor taking diuretic drugs needs a dietary potassium supplement such as a banana a day. The power user taking diuretics expects his or her caregiver to check his or her serum potassium level once a quarter. In addition, the potassium level should be checked following any episode of severe diarrhea, which is the other common cause of potassium loss.

EXCRETION

Once the body has utilized food for its structural value and energy, it needs to excrete the residues. Excretion, then, is clearly one of the basic biological needs of humans. Several organs are primarily involved with this function: the lungs, the kidney, the urinary tract, the liver, and the bowel.

LUNGS Earlier in the chapter, it was noted that energy metabolism breaks food down in the tissue cells to CO_2 and water. CO_2 dissolves in the blood plasma and is carried to the capillaries in the lungs, where it diffuses rapidly into the alveoli and is excreted as part of the expired air. Some water is also excreted through the lungs.

Most lung diseases do not cause CO_2 retention because the gas diffuses so well. An exception is sleep-related respiratory disturbance (SRRD), which is a condition that is becoming widely recognized as a prevalent disease of aging. In it, disturbed sleep, usually not enough to fully arouse the sufferer, is so bad that a huge sleep deficit builds up, and daytime somnolence becomes a severe problem. If it is associated with loud snoring, then complete interruption of breathing (sleep apnea) may occur more than a dozen times an hour, each period lasting many seconds. The snoring signifies a collapse of the air passages. The circulation suffers from the lack of oxygen, and hypertension and heart failure can result. Sudden bursts of rapid heart rhythm and even death may ensue, and mental functioning can also suffer. The diagnosis is made in a sleep laboratory by means of polysomnogram (PSG). The survivor will be encouraged to use a low-pressure mask (C-PAP) to keep the airways patent; the power user may prefer to visit an ear, nose, and throat specialist and consider having the airways surgically modified.

KIDNEYS When the blood circulates through the kidneys, more than half of the plasma is excreted through the filtering capillaries (glomeruli), while the remainder, along with all the cells, remains in circulation. The 180L or so of that daily filtrate includes valuable water, salts, glucose, and amino acids—99% of which the body promptly recovers by absorption tubules deeper in the kidneys. The filtrate also contains waste materials such as the nitrogenous products of protein metabolism and cell breakdown; these are not reabsorbed. Drugs or any other chemicals that have been detoxified by the liver also remain in the excretory filtrate. After the reabsorption of essential products including water, the remaining volume of waste from the circulatory system has reduced to about 1.5L a day and takes the form of urine, which drains into the bladder.

An inability to excrete these unwanted substances is known as *renal failure* and results in their buildup in the blood. Examples are *uremia* (urea and creatinine buildup), *gout* (uric acid buildup), and *drug toxicity* (overdose). Diabetes and hypertension are the most common causes of renal failure in older people. A creatinine backup in the blood and a microscopic amount of albumin in the urine are usually the earliest stages of renal failure. In the past, a low-protein diet was prescribed to reduce the amount of nitrogen excreted; unfortunately, it does not slow the disease. Renal failure is progressive and ultimately leads to *end-stage renal disease* (ESRD) that can only be treated with dialysis and kidney transplantation. In the beginning of the 21st century, there were approximately 200,000 individuals receiving dialysis. At the time this book was published, it was a Medicare benefit, free of age restrictions. Most people on dialysis are hoping for a kidney transplant, but the rate of organ donations does not match the demand.

URINARY TRACT Another problem in the urinary system, which only affects men, is *benign prostate hypertrophy* (BPH). The prostate gland, an accessory sexual organ, surrounds the urethra, or lower urinary conduit between the bladder and the root of the penis. In most men, it enlarges with age, and can eventually obstruct the flow of urine. Enlargement of the prostate is so common that the symptoms of obstruction are well known to most older men: difficulty in starting urination, dribbling, failure to make a clean break, and the consequent soiling of undergarments. The bladder is frequently not emptied completely and becomes irritable, requiring more frequent emptying before it is full. Sleep becomes interrupted by frequent bathroom trips during the night. Although men joke about the condition, the reality is no joking matter; many fear the day when the flow suddenly becomes completely obstructed and requires a catheter or even surgery to open it up. Besides normal fear about surgery, most men's fears are based on rumors that associate prostate surgery with impotence and incontinence. The survivor will seek a urological examination early so that the facts can prevail more than the fears. Drug treatment to block the hormonal growth of the prostate often can help delay enlargement, especially if the BPH is detected early. Other drugs can relieve symptoms of urinary urgency and frequency by relaxing the muscles of the urethra and reducing the strength of bladder contractions. The power user will want surgery to fully resolve the condition but will seek out a surgeon who can assure him that the nerves controlling erection can be preserved.

LIVER The other organ responsible for excretion is the liver. As part of its metabolic function, the liver contains a host of enzymes that break down waste products and send them in soluble form to the kidney. Certain substances that would cause trouble if they were precipitated in the urinary tract, especially cholesterol and hemoglobin, are instead excreted into ducts in the liver as bile. Bile (gall) is emptied into the bowel after being concentrated in the gall bladder. Major failure of the liver to excrete bile results in a yellow-tinted skin (jaundice) due to a backup of bilirubin, which gets its pigment from hemoglobin. Liver failure can happen from poisoning, during an acute liver infection (hepatitis), or as a chronic end-stage disease (cirrhosis), which in turn may be caused by prior hepatitis or chronic alcoholism. At the stage of cirrhosis, death is probable without a liver transplant. Jaundice can also be caused by stones (calculi) that form in the bile ducts; if the stone entirely blocks one of the ducts, then cholecystitis, or inflammation of the gall bladder, will result, which usually requires a surgical procedure. The survivor will opt to have the gall bladder removed, which can be done laparoscopically today through a small abdominal incision. In the U.S., more than 600,000 gall bladders are removed annually, mostly in older people. The power user may elect to preserve the gall bladder and have the stones crushed by a noninvasive procedure called *lithotripsy.*

BOWEL It is perhaps strange that the bowel, which we would think of as characteristically representing excretion, is responsible for excreting so little. What is excreted is various food residues, especially nonabsorbable fiber, together with food the body does not absorb such as some fat. As mentioned previously, excretory substances such as bile also end up in the bowel and in some cells from wear, tear, and repair.

In Western societies, *constipation* can be listed as one of the scourges of old age. It is defined as a reduction in an individual's frequency of regular stool evacuations. Regularity is individualized and normality can range from as many as three bowel movements a day to as few as three per week. Constipation is not relegated to older individuals, either; a person's tendency toward constipation may have begun many years ago, when social pressure forced him or her to suppress the "call to stool" that indicates a full rectum. The result is sluggish bowel action, which is perpetuated by any lack of exercise, irregularity of dietary habits, or dehydration and may be dulled by the use of laxative drugs. The major contributory cause, however, is the removal of *insoluble fiber* by food processors. By changing the consistency of food, the processor not only makes eating it easier and faster, but also reduces its bulk in the bowel to the degree that typical stools cannot form; the rotting residue remaining in the colon becomes progressively more dehydrated, requiring straining to evacuate it. The power user eats plenty of whole grains and at least 30g of supplementary roughage such as cellulose or bran in the daily diet. If constipation persists, then he or she will drink more than 2L of water a day, get daily exercise, and observe regular bowel habits. The survivor who finds these remedies too taxing may have to resort to psyllium products for further bulking and a stool softener to reduce straining and smell.

PROTECTION

Both survivors and power users use preventive strategies for basic safety. Education and awareness are the most important preventive strategies. There are a host of common hazards and conditions of which older adults should be aware, including threats from the physical and chemical environment, bacteria, and plants. Because some threats are recurrent and predictable, the body has developed protection against them. Many protections against environmental dangers are inherited. The templates to other dangers such as childhood viral diseases are latent in the immune system, only waiting to be triggered by the corresponding antigen—thus, the reason for immunizations.

PHYSICAL INJURY

In terms of physical injury, older adults are particularly concerned with protecting themselves against falls. Falls and their complications are the sixth leading cause of death among people age 65 and over (Rabebaugh, Hadley, & Suzman, 1985); in fact, people in this age group are up to 150 times more likely than those in younger age groups to experience a fall (Tideiksaar, 2002). Women are especially prone to fall-related death. Up to a half of older people hospitalized for a fall will not live another year.

Fall prevention involves taking a wide variety of precautions, and it is never too early in life to begin some of these. Deteriorating eyesight, which can happen at any point in the lifespan, can be corrected. Poor physical conditions due to inactivity, obesity, or nutrition problems, especially calcium intake, are remediable. The walking surface of floors and steps, foot care and footwear, and lighting can be improved. Physicians who do not question their patients about fall risk and who always perform physicals on people who are recumbent may miss problems of balance and gait that should be investigated. A simple screening test for vulnerability is to have an individual stand on one leg for 15 seconds.

One side effect related to the commonality of falls in older people, whether the individual actually experiences this type of trauma, is fear of falling. This condition accounts for a great deal of isolation and potential depression of older people who are afraid they will fall. A survivor would likely report all falls and near falls to a physician and expect the cause to be diagnosed and corrected. A power user might take advantage of a radio response alarm, which provides great reassurance (see http://www.lifelinesys.com).

Another fairly successful prevention program is the campaign for use of seat belts to reduce brain injury in automobile collisions. In 1994, more than 30,000 people died from automobile accidents, mostly because of head trauma. The survivor recognizes that seat belt use can reduce much of this trauma (Rivera, Grossman, & Cummins, 1997); the power user's vehicle is equipped with numerous crash safety devices. Older people who have difficulty with buckling up often resist wearing seat belts. Much of the same can be said of older individuals' attitude toward wearing helmets when bicycling—it is not uncommon to see a child who is wearing a helmet riding with a grandparent who is not.

FIREARM SAFETY AND PREVENTION

More people die annually from firearm injuries than from automobile accidents. Older adult Caucasian American males have the highest suicide rate of any group in the world, with firearms being the preferred method of committing suicide. Thus, this is an important area for prevention strategies, and any diagnosis of depression or dementia should point to inquiries about guns.

DROWNING AND COLD EXPOSURE

For children, the primary prevention of deaths from drowning and cold exposure from immersion is educating them about the dangers and mandating swimming pool fences. Older individuals face different water dangers in that more older people than younger people use boats for fishing, sailing, and other uses. Older individuals tend not to use flotation vests, which contributes to a high mortality rate from capsized boats. In the 21st century, the use of life vests is at the same level of acceptance as the use of seat belts was in the 1990s.

INJURY FROM BURNS

Finally, in this battle with the physical world, older adults are at risk of being burned, scalded, or injured in a fire. Older people might have increased danger from fires and hot water because they generally have difficulty using an open flame; they tend to use old, unserviced appliances; they hoard flammable materials; they may not be able to see smoke or smell something burning; and they may have difficulty escaping in time because of general frailty.

In order to prevent injury or death from incendiary causes, the survivor practices proper installation and regular maintenance of heating and hot water systems and smoke alarms.

THERMAL INJURY

Large numbers of older people suffer from thermal injury. The primary thermostatic control mechanism is deep in the brain. Variations in the surrounding temperature result in prompt responses of the thermostat that cause sweating or shivering. If body heating is prolonged, especially in humid conditions, or if sustained cooling occurs, especially in older adults and alcoholics, then the body's control center may quit, and there is no limit to the rise or fall of temperature that follows. When this occurs, *heat stroke* or *hypothermia* sets in, and either one may be fatal.

It is a myth that taking extra salt will prevent heat stroke. Salt helps a person avoid heat exhaustion—a less serious condition of water and salt balance—but not heat stroke. Jogging in hot, humid weather is not a good way to lose weight; it is more likely to lead to a loss of consciousness due to heat stroke, especially in older adults! Obese older adults living in houses without air-conditioning are most vulnerable to heat stroke.

An even more prevalent risk related to body temperature control is hypothermia; 7,500 deaths from hypothermia are reported each decade in the U.S., half of them in older adults. The condition is probably unrecognized in many other cases, however, because mercury thermometers do not correctly show body temperatures under 94° F, and health workers caring for people who might have hypothermia are uninformed about the condition.

SKIN CONDITIONS

Actinic radiation from the sun is now well recognized as a cause of *skin cancer.* For a newly appearing cancer, the damage to the skin may have been done more than a half-century ago. Although any new reddish-brown or black blemish might indicate malignancy, it should be noted that not all melanomas are black and not all black moles are melanomas! The ABCD of skin cancer alarms is *Asymmetry, Border irregularity, Color variability,* and *Diameter* more than 6mm. The survivor will always wear a sunscreen with an SPF of 15 or higher, and the power user will waste no time in having a skilled dermatologist look at any growths that show these characteristics.

Another common condition, if not caused by sunlight, is certainly made worse by it, is *rosacea*. This can often be seen as a butterfly-shaped pink rash on the upper cheeks below the eyes. If not treated, this condition may become more disfiguring — readers may remember the bulbous nose of the comedian W.C. Fields, who suffered from this condition. Metronidazole, an antifungal treatment for vaginal infections, is prescribed for rosacea. Support groups are very helpful, particularly in sharing wisdom on how to avoid flare-ups (see http://www.rosacea.org/).

A very minor, but quite annoying, problem caused by the cold is *chilblains*. This severe, itchy, red swelling appears in cold weather, usually on the little toes but occasionally on the fingers and, rarely, on the nose. Older adults are very susceptible, so it is often blamed on poor circulation or poor calcium intake. It actually is due to a local area of blood vessels reacting abnormally to entering a warm room from the cold outdoors. Scratching makes it worse. The survivor wears warmer socks, and the power user keeps witch hazel nearby as an alternative medicine treatment, in addition to wearing warmer socks.

CHEMICAL INJURY

Certain chemical toxins are common enough to constitute a predictable threat to older individuals. At some point in their lives, individuals may be exposed to domestic poisoning due to carbon monoxide, a sometimes fatal gas produced by fires, badly vented stoves, and automobile exhausts, among other sources. The carbon monoxide death rate of 5,000 annually includes a large number of suicides, but accidental inhalation victims are also numerous and are often older adults. Prevention requires proper inspection of burners, supply pipes, monitors, and exhaust systems. The survivor will likely install the recommended number of smoke and carbon monoxide alarms, changing the batteries semi-annually, and contracting with a service company to regularly inspect gas and appliances that might burst into flames or leak gas. A new and clever idea that might be used by the power user is to have his or her sense of smell tested to find out whether he or she could detect the odor that is deliberately added by the gas company for recognition purposes.

POISONING

The consumption of alcohol causes no more harm to most elderly people than it did to them when they were younger. The survivor reads the labels of all drugs and notes if there is a warning not to combine them with drinking alcoholic beverages. The power user recognizes that regular drinking can worsen hypertension and that retirement offers the opportunity to become an alcoholic to both genders. Because the most widely used drug in the world is alcohol, it causes most of the cases of poisoning. The heavy drinker who develops tolerance to the drug is most likely to experience this type of direct poisoning. The associated symptoms of progressive intoxication — uninhibited behavior, slurred speech, increasingly unsteady walking, and coma—are familiar to most people. However, it is not intoxication but injuries and the inhalation of vomit that are the most common complications causing death; these can occur after only two or three drinks. In other poisonings related to alcohol, cheap methanol and ethylene glycol initially cause identical inebriation, but after a few hours, they cause a potentially fatal acidosis, and all victims require emergency room care.

Poisonous substances found in nature are often converted into useful drugs, but the basic toxicity of the parent substance is retained. This is true even with over-the-counter and herbal remedies. The nightshade plant (atropa) contains a very deadly substance, atropine, for which the Italians coined the word *bella-donna,* which means "pretty woman" because the plant extract was used by ladies to make their pupils dilated, dark, and desirable. Some belladonna users developed a flushed, dry skin and severe symptoms of mental illness, however. Today, many drugs provide the atropine-like effect in many cold and indigestion remedies, prescription drugs, and eye drops. Antihistamines and many psychiatric medications also have this toxic danger, especially to older people. People without cognitive impairment may develop sudden mania, or men with enlarged prostates may develop acutely obstructed bladders, especially when several similar drugs are combined. If atropine poisoning is suspected, a 911 call is justified because antidotes given promptly are able to forestall brain damage and prevent death. As a result, the older survivor will be skeptical about taking antihistamines for allergy or the common cold, especially if he has any symptoms of prostate obstruction. The power user with symptoms of bladder obstruction will have a sterilized catheter available and learn how to use it.

Salicylates make up another group of poisonous nonprescription drugs derived from nature. The bark of the willow tree (*Salix*) was used by Greek physicians for the pain and inflammation of arthritis, but natural salicylates, the active agents, have largely been replaced by a synthetic substitute developed in the 19th century—acetylsalicylic acid (ASA). Because so many older people take ASA for arthritis, many cases of poisoning occur. The symptoms of chronic salicylate toxicity include lethargy and confusion—symptoms not always unexpected in older adults. Tinnitus, or ringing in the ears, is typical of ASA overdose and may also occur after poisoning is established. *Hyperventilation* (deep and frequent breathing) due to acidosis follows the overdose, and an emergency call is overdue by then. Treatment is difficult, and the outlook is very uncertain. The consumption of an aspirin tablet a day for the prevention of stroke or heart attack is not an overdose, but a dozen a day may be. In addition, ASA is a NSAID drug and, therefore, may produce unpredictable hemorrhage.

The other over-the-counter analgesic that causes a fatal toxicity is the synthetic drug acetaminophen, often touted as *safer* than aspirin. Acetaminophen acts as an analgesic for pain but has no anti-inflammatory effects on swelling and inflammation. It is marketed as safe, not because of freedom from toxicity, but because it does not produce gastric irritation or gastrointestinal hemorrhage. In fact, many people have to take 500mg of acetaminophen every 4 hours—for a total of more than 3000mg a day—to get pain relief from the drug or its many combinations. Yet, if 4000mg a day is taken regularly by a healthy person, the toxic dose could be exceeded in a week or less. A person with alcoholic cirrhosis might go into liver coma in less than 24 hours with only a couple of tablets of this so-called safe drug.

The anti-inflammatory drugs belonging to the NSAID class (nonsteroidal anti-inflammatories), which include naproxen, piroxicam, diclofenac, the -profens, the -lacs, and several others, cost much more than ASA but were produced with the 20th century hope that they could treat pain and inflammation without causing stomach irritation or bowel hemorrhage, which ASA can do. Unfortunately, they only avoid some of the irritation; severe bleeding may still occur. In the 21st century, yet another class of analgesics, the COX-2 inhibitors, which are even more expensive, have been introduced. In these drugs, the danger of hemorrhage is considerably less but not absent.

A survivor would likely take up to 3000mg a day of acetaminophen for pain because he or she probably will not be stressing his or her life by taking more than three alcoholic drinks a day. The power user will try, but, if unsuccessful, will ask for a temporary narcotic for pain and also get a medical consultation regarding specific drugs for arthritis or indications for joint surgery as a more permanent cure.

Many prescription drugs taken by older adults can cause poisoning. The doctor or pharmacist should discuss the toxic dangers of each prescription when it is filled. The following discussion reviews only two because overdosage with them is quite common; yet the cause may be overlooked because of the vagueness of the symptoms. *Digoxin,* the most commonly prescribed heart medication, is taken by many individuals for years and causes toxicity in 10% of people at some time or another. The probable reason is that a correct dosage for someone 60 years old may be an overdose when that person is 70 years old, when the capacity of the individual's kidneys to excrete it is less. Survivors who take digoxin regularly should expect their physicians to reduce the dose or switch to a safer drug as they get older; in fact, 25% of people taking digoxin don't need it. The first symptom of digoxin toxicity is a loss of appetite, which often extends for months before its cause is recognized. Some readers might recall that during the 1960s, when there was a mad rush to take herbal cures, a slimming preparation was marketed that contained foxglove, the parent herb of digoxin. Its slimming action appeared to depend on causing an individual to experience toxic anorexia and nausea as a means of controlling food intake! After weeks of anorexia, a marked memory loss may develop. Later, nausea, vomiting, or diarrhea may occur, and an irregular or a slow heartbeat may begin. If this is not corrected, then sudden death can occur. The power user taking digoxin will stop the medication if anorexia or a pulse under 60 occurs, expect to get an occasional blood digoxin level, and perhaps request a *creatinine clearance test* to evaluate kidney excretion if any problems are suspected.

> MANY PRESCRIPTION drugs taken by older adults can cause poisoning. The doctor or pharmacist should discuss the toxic dangers of each prescription when it is filled.

Another type of heart drug commonly prescribed for long periods is a *diuretic* to remove the excess body water responsible for edema and hypertension. This causes a loss of sodium and often potassium ions. Although the drug rarely is toxic itself, it causes deafness in some, and the low potassium that typically results may cause extreme fatigue and an irregular heartbeat. Physicians commonly prescribe digoxin and a diuretic together; however, this combination may increase the danger of an arrhythmia. Survivors who take diuretics will expect to have their blood potassium levels monitored at least every 3 months, and the power user will take a potassium supplement, either in the form of a daily banana or a thrice-weekly supplement tablet.

INJURY AND ILLNESS BY PRIONS, VIRUSES, AND BACTERIA

Every phylum of plant and animal is likely to endanger us at times. The smallest known living infectious agent is the prion. Our bodies have no defenses against prions, and no antiseptic or treatment is known to kill them. The most recognized agent of this class is the notorious *bovine spongy encephalitis* (BSE) widely known as *mad cow disease.* When transmitted from animals to human beings, it may be latent for a long time, then emerge as brain degeneration and a dementia that is fatal in less than a year. A possible variant dementia of this type, which is transmitted from person to person rather than bovine to human, has been known for many years as *Kreutzfeldt-Jakob disease.* Because prions cannot be killed by ordinary sterilizing processes, a few cases of transmission via tissues such as corneal or blood vessel grafts have been documented.

Survivors would most likely avoid eating imported beef and perhaps even become a visiting vegetarian when traveling in Europe! Power users may be prepared to take some risk in the U.S. because strict controls have been established on imported beef suppliers. But, certainly anyone should obtain guarantees that any human tissue grafts implanted come from American sources with screened donors.

The organisms of the next level of the evolutionary ladder—the viruses—pose much greater risk to humans because they are so numerous. Fortunately, the immune system of the body is particularly well adapted to form a defense to foreign proteins and viruses, known as *antigens.* This means that most viruses get just one chance to infect us; after that, our lymphocyte cells recognize an antigen if it or others should return and are prepared to annihilate it before it does any damage.

The most frequently encountered viruses are those that infect the respiratory tubes. The average adult in a family has three to five such infections a year, which originate from the pool of viruses that exist in the schoolrooms that children and grandchildren attend. For instance, the *rhinovirus* and *coronavirus,* the agents that cause the common cold, are spread by contact through the nose-to-finger-to-finger-to-nose route; some viruses such as influenza travel as a cough aerosol in moist air, but most are spread as large droplets, such as those expelled with sneezing.

It is almost impossible for a doctor to tell exactly which virus is the cause of a particular upper respiratory infection unless throat washings are sent to the laboratory in which rapid tests can be performed. The results rarely arrive before the infection is over, however. Unfortunately, in older people, respiratory viruses interfere with the defenses against bacteria, so complications such as *sinusitis, bronchitis,* and *pneumonia* are more common in older adults, even when the viral infection has ended. Respiratory viruses do convey immunity, as described previously, so we get fewer of them as we grow older, but each type has so many strains that new ones come along each season. Survivors should try to avoid infection by staying away from crowded places during local epidemics and wash their hands frequently after contact with doorknobs and children. These individuals will also ensure that their intake of vitamins A and C, which boost the immune response, is adequate during the cold season. For those rhinoviruses that are new to them, survivors will rely on antiviral drugs for protection. Power users will obtain up to a week's protection during an influenza epidemic from *interferon alpha* taken intranasally. At the time this book was written, however, new antiviral drugs were under development, which were intended to treat the common cold.

The respiratory viruses that are most dangerous, especially for older adults, are the various strains of *influenza A* and *B.* In past epidemic years, there have been three to five times the rate of hospitalizations for pneumonia and up to 20,000 deaths, all attributable to complications of these viruses. Although the protection afforded by the flu vaccine does not always prevent infection, it reduces the severity of the attack and almost eliminates excess hospitalizations and deaths. Frequent variation exists in the virus DNA, so the vaccine only works for about 6 months and must be reformulated each year. The drug *amantidine* will give temporary protection against influenza virus *A* only, but other new drugs are now on the market that are also effective against the *B* type. The question of antibiotic use is controversial.

Overuse of antibiotics, especially for fattening livestock, has encouraged the development of bacterial resistance, and in the predictable future, humans probably will have many infections that are resistant to all known antibiotics. Antibiotics have no effect on virus infections, but they are appropriate if used to treat or prevent complications caused by bacteria. The survivor will take a flu vaccine every fall season, avoid unnecessary exposure, stay at home if infected, and forgo the added peace of mind a prophylactic antibiotic might bring. For those who refuse injections, an intranasal vaccine is available. The power user will request amantidine during epidemics of type *A* or take one of the newer neuraminidase inhibitor drugs the first day an influenza infection of either type is suspected.

The skin, of course, is our main protection against invasion by microorganisms and poisons. The skin is an organ—in fact, it is the largest one in the body; it is not quite impervious, and cracks in its surface make it much more vulnerable. The mucous membrane surfaces inside the mouth and throat are much more vulnerable to chemical absorption and infection than is the skin. The herpes family is a group of viruses that exploit this vulnerability. *Herpes simplex I,* the cold-sore virus (HSV-1), often appears first in childhood, either through the skin or a membrane; it will then take up residence in the body and never leave, although it remains dormant for long periods. Characteristically, it causes infectious cold sores in and around the lips and is spread by contact.

Herpes simplex II, genital herpes (HSV-2), is a sexually transmitted virus that usually causes blisters on and around the mouth and genitals and is similarly spread by contact. Approximately 25% of the baby boomers are taking the virus with them into their geriatric years. Because this first invasion never really ends, it means no immunity can develop. Once infected, a person will remain infectious even when there is no rash. Recurrent attacks occur, especially when the individual is stressed, but these are milder and people get used to them. In the case of HSV-2, older carriers may not feel concerned enough to warn their sexual partners who, understandably enough, often feel surprised and angry when they find they have been infected. Apart from having occasional discomfort from the rash and suffering social spurning from the reputation it bestows, a male or a postmenopausal female who has HSV-2 will suffer no health consequences as far as professionals know.

To try to avoid infection, the survivor will hope to remain monogamous or at least question a potential sex partner and insist on a condom anyway, in case of mistakes. Lesions can be kept under fairly good control by the drug *acyclovir,* but the person still remains infectious. Power users may not be able to escape HSV-1, but they should never put an ungloved finger in anyone's mouth. By avoiding promiscuity and by ensuring that new partners have never had genital herpes, they should be able to avert HSV-2.

IMMUNE DEFICIENCY

What would happen if we had no immune mechanisms to protect us against disease? As it happens, some infants are born with a rare primary immune deficiency and get repeated infections by the same organism. Also, after organ transplants, drugs are given to prevent rejection of the graft by suppressing part of the immune system, which also leads to an immune deficiency. More important, we are all familiar with viral *acquired immune deficiency syndrome* (AIDS), which is all too common in the world.

The *human immunodeficiency virus* that causes AIDS attacks the T-cells of the immune system to create a deficiency of immune response to any infection. Then, any organisms, even those that normally reside harmlessly on the surface of the body and could never get past the immune system of a healthy person, can exploit the opportunity and result in *opportunistic infections.*

It is often assumed that AIDS is a problem older people do not have to worry about. For instance, the presentation of a paper on HIV/AIDS among seniors drew only 8 out of 4,000 attendees at a recent American Society on Aging Conference. But, in the borough of Manhattan, New York, where AIDS is the fourth leading killer of women, 15% of AIDS individuals are over the age of 50.

In places with a high population of older adults, HIV is increasing; Palm Beach County, Florida, reports that 16% of new cases of AIDS are occurring in seniors. There are many reasons for this: Promiscuity is widespread in locales where women outnumber men; some older adult women think of condoms as birth control devices only and after menopause they may feel free to have unprotected sex; and some men need no persuading to dispense with condoms, blaming them for difficulties in performance that probably stem from age.

Older individuals may feel that AIDS is a disease of other populations and that they are not at risk. This is not the case, however. People who share diabetic syringes for economic reasons are also at risk of contracting AIDS. Some older caregivers have contracted HIV from disposing of body fluids of their terminally ill children. Many physicians are unaware of these mounting problems. They do not order the tests even when they encounter immunodeficiency, rationalizing that it also occurs in a mild form in the aged anyway. Physicians' older patients, who come from a more private generation, are too embarrassed to request testing, even when they know they have been exposed; thus, there is a great need for education and research in this area. The survivor regards abstinence and education about infections a personal commitment. The power user practices safe sex and is honest with his or her physician, but to keep current, often clicks on web sites to get more information (see http://www.hivmorethanfifty.org) or uses another source of information.

HEPATITIS

Of course, unsafe sex practices and shared needles also spread an even more common infection, *hepatitis B virus* (HBV), which is no longer viewed solely as a contaminant of blood transfusion. Adults who are infected by HBV usually overcome it, and in the United States, as opposed to many third world countries, carriers are rare except among certain high-risk groups such as drug abusers. The survivor who has had possible exposure to hepatitis B will request a *hepatitis B surface antigen test,* and if the exposure is likely to continue, as with health workers, a series of hepatitis B immunizations is mandatory.

A different pattern is seen in *hepatitis C virus* (HCV), which can also be a complication of pre-1992 blood transfusion and needle sharing, but is usually acquired by means we do not understand—but probably not from unprotected sex. Carriers of HCV are much more prevalent than those with HBV in the U.S. and an infection is much more likely to result in chronic hepatitis and a need for liver transplantation. Hepatitis C often first displays itself by signs of cirrhosis of the liver unless an abnormal liver function test is discovered earlier. No immunizations are available.

Treatment for HCV is with interferon alpha and ribavirin and is more effective if started early, resulting in prolonged remission in 30%–70% of cases. Months of treatment will take place before things are bad enough for a liver transplant; then, months of waiting occur before one is found. Although the HCV also infects the new liver, it usually remains benign. Not many members of the public donate their livers, so when an older individual needs a liver, ethical questions may arise regarding whether the transplant available should be reserved for younger recipients.

Today, vaccines can be prepared to help fight bacteria as well as viruses. Professionals in the health field can immunize people against at least 80% of the pneumococci that have caused pneumonia in the past. This can even partially protect people with AIDS against pneumococci, although they have immunodeficiency. It is a timely development because more and more non–penicillin-sensitive-pneumococci (NPSP) are appearing. The survivor will most likely be told that he or she needs one shot of pneumococcus vaccine for lifetime protection, whereas the power user will endure the localized pain and stiffness that accompanies revaccination and get one routinely (e.g., every 6 years) just to be sure.

One other bacterial disease that is rare today because of successful immunization is *tetanus*. Most of the deaths that occur annually are older adults who have never been immunized. An individual is usually offered a shot of tetanus antitoxin serum if he or she suffers a wound that might be contaminated by soil organisms, but this is a temporary *passive* immunization only (the type sought by the typical survivor). Unimmunized power users who want an active immunity must get three shots of tetanus antigen to arm the immune system, which will be virtually permanent. Having a *booster* every 5 years counteracts the tendency of the immune mechanism to allow a mild tetanus infection, but it is not necessary to prevent a fatal outcome. Curiously, the shot comes with a dose of *diphtheria* antigen; the reason is that we have eliminated diphtheria, and universal immunization is the method to keep it eliminated.

PLANT INVADERS

After the previous review of several protections we have against infectious agents, it may come as a surprise to find that many allergies exist as a result of recognizing plant proteins as foreign. There is no immunity available against diseases caused by plant invaders, although we seem to have good defenses to keep them at bay. Not many plants are saprophytes on the surface of our bodies, but when they gain access internally, it is a sign that our defenses are really down. Fungi are plants, and a number of them can grow in moist areas on the surface of the body or in the mucous membranes. For example, one of them, a yeast named *Candida,* is found in the throats of half the population. It also finds its way into the vagina, especially in older women with diabetes, where it causes soreness and discharge. In people who are immuno-compromised and those receiving antibiotics, it may opportunistically invade body tissues, converting its normally benign association with humans into a pathological one.

INJURY BY ANIMALS

Various protozoa live a fairly peaceful coexistence with man. The bowel contains a number of harmless amoebae, but one of them causes *amebiasis.* This parasite is often symptomless, but it can cause diarrhea and dysentery that is characterized by the absence of white blood cells. Amebiasis is diagnosed by microscopic examination of the stool for cysts or in warm fresh specimens for the actual amebae (trophozoites) moving about. Liver abscesses and a whole series of other complications can occur. After these begin, a serum test for antibodies at last becomes positive. The survivor refuses to eat raw, soil-grown vegetables when visiting tropical countries and sterilizes drinking water with iodine tablets. The power user is aggressive about ensuring hand washing by staff in restaurants. This protection against stool contamination is identical to that for hepatitis A, giardiasis, and other bowel parasites.

Of course, older people are not immune from bites by invertebrates. Mosquitoes carry diseases that infect all ages. Tick-borne fevers, especially *lyme disease* and *ehrlichiosis* are not peculiar to older adults, but their complications of heart arrhythmias and arthritis are likely to be confused with similar common complaints in older adult individuals. Prevention is much easier for people who search their anatomy for ticks after going out in the woods. The painful ulcers caused by the bite of the *loxosceles* (brown) spider are almost only seen on the exposed parts of those rural older adults still using outside latrines.

Older adults are second only to children in sharing in the half million or so reported dog bites a year. Educating people is the only prevention of other bites from animals such as snakes, poisonous spiders, and other reclusive predators. For example, snakebites need accurate identification of the culprit and immediate access to the appropriate immune serum. Before traveling to unfamiliar areas, the survivor should learn about any dangers not emphasized in the tourist brochures. The power user will have dog bites, which are surprisingly clean, sutured immediately without antibiotics and isolate the dog for a rabies watch; however, human, feline, and other bites will be left open and will need penicillin therapy.

SUMMARY

This chapter describes the seven categories of biological concerns that all animals—especially humans—have to satisfy to ensure survival. Any individual will have his or her own difficulties in ensuring wellness. Help from other people, from technology, and from drugs may at times be needed to overcome difficulties in meeting these concerns, even when emulating the survivor and power user. Survival does not result from a passive posture; one must seek the means to ensure it. The power user illustrates the benefit of developing an aggressive pursuit of wellness based on knowing which choices are available. Knowledge is power, and a greater degree of self-determination can only come about when each person can make his or her own choices on the basis of knowledge. By sharing this knowledge with the reader, I feel I can make my greatest contribution to his or her self-determination and ultimately to wellness itself.

REFERENCES

Bazzano, L., Ogden, L.G., Jiang, He, Vupputuri, S., Loria, C.M., Myers, L., Whelton, P.K. (2000). Dietary intake of folic acid and reduced risk of stroke in U.S. men and women: NHANES I: Epidemiologic follow-up study. American Heart Association, 75th Annual Meeting. *Circulation, 102*(10). Supp. II–861.

Bulot, J.J. (1991). *Identifying individuals at risk for malnutrition in community dwelling elders.* 1st Joint Conference of National Council on Aging and American Society on Aging. *Aging Today, 22*(3).

Feinberg, R.I., Koresco, R.L., & Heller, N. (1967). EEG sleep patterns as a function of normal and pathological aging in man. *Journal of Psychiatric Research, 5,* 107–144.

Folstein, M.F., Folstein, S.E. & McHugh, P.R. (1975). Mini-mental state. *Journal of Psychiatric Research, 12,*189–194.

Gordon, T., Castelli, W.P., Hjortland, M.C., Kannel, W.B., & Dawber, T.R. (1977). Diabetes, blood lipids and the role of obesity in coronary heart disease risk; the Framingham Study. *Annals of Internal Medicine, 87,* 393–397.

Maslow, A. (1974). *Toward a psychology of being* (2nd ed.). New York: Van Nostrand Reinhold.

Moss, A.J., Parsons, V.L. (1986). Current estimates from the National Health Inventory Survey, 1985. *Vital and Health Statistics, 10*(160), 1–51:1. Washington, DC:U.S. Government Printing Office.

Radebaugh, T.S., Hadley, E., & Suzman, R. (1985). *Clinics in geriatric medicine—falls in the elderly.* London: W.B. Saunders.

Rowe, J.W., & Kahn, R.L. (1987). Human aging: Usual and successful. *Science, 273,* 143–149.

Russell, R., Lichtenstein, A., & Rasmussen, H. (1999). *Modified food pyramid for mature (70+) adults.* Medford, MA: Tufts University.

Schwartz, M.W. (2001). Brain controlling food intake and body weight. *Experimental Biology and Medicine, 226,* 978–981.

Swift, J. (1726). *Gulliver's travels, The Luggnaggians commended* (Part III, Section X). Dublin, Ireland: Richard Sympson.

Tideiksaar, R. (2002). *Falls in older people: Prevention and management (3rd ed.)* (p. 3). Baltimore: Health Professions Press.

4

CARE MANAGEMENT

A Strengths-Based Approach
to Mental Wellness with Older Adults

Rona S. Bartelstone

WHEN WORKING WITH OLDER ADULTS, professionals in the social services and mental health fields commonly overlook some of the many aspects of living that are considered essential for younger populations. Until the late 20th century, health care providers viewed older adults as a group of people outside of the clinically focused mental health system. In fact, many people considered mental illness, especially depression, a natural part of the aging process.

The medical model on which Medicare, the United States' largest health insurance program for older adults, is based, minimizes access to mental health services. The Medicare program fails to recognize the need for types of care and support common to many chronic illnesses. Consequently, unless an individual has exacerbated symptoms, an acute episode, or a new diagnosis, Medicare does not provide care. Many adults with ongoing health concerns find that they must look to other, often inadequate, systems for assistance in managing chronic care needs. This is especially true for conditions that create functional limitations in, for example, mobility or activities of daily living.

The original design of the Medicare program, established in 1965, reflected the expectation that older adults would experience an acute illness, require short-term care, and then die in a relatively abbreviated time frame. With medical advances, improvements in food preparation and storage, and increased knowledge of healthy lifestyle practices, many individuals today live for extended periods of time with chronic health concerns.

This early expectation—that individuals would contract a major illness and die within a short time frame—has persisted in many of the stereotypes that society continues to embrace about later life. Indeed, federal policy continues to reinforce such stereotypes by clinging to limited acute care models of financing health care in later life. In an effort to counter the limited and ageist approach to later life, many human services professionals have been struggling to identify holistic perspectives, models, and techniques that have both scientific relevance and a more realistic view of older adulthood. One discipline that has emerged from this search is the field of *care management,* with the attendant focus on a full continuum of care that identifies and cultivates the strengths and capabilities of each older individual.

Professional health care providers using a care management process have learned that older adults can be successfully treated for depression and many other mental health diagnoses as well as for their physical concerns. Tice and Perkins (1999) wrote about the confluence of the case management and strengths-based models. "The strengths model recognizes that despite the difficult circumstances of advanced age, negative stereotypes and ageism, older adults have many personal strengths. The *aura* [emphasis added] of strengths encourages both workers and clients to expect positive outcomes, struggle for client empowerment, and achieve a mutually interactive service system between client, worker, and the client's support system" (p. 170).

HISTORICAL EVOLUTION OF CARE MANAGEMENT

Care management owes its foundation to the early social services organizations that functioned at the community level in an effort to assist individuals who were coping with issues of mass migration, urbanization, and industrialization at the end of the 19th and the beginning of the 20th century. The Settlement House movement, at the turn of the 20th century, was one of the first attempts at a comprehensive social services approach to deal with the complex medical, social, environmental, recreational, and emotional concerns of large and diversified populations. This movement was generally considered a successful model because of its closeness to the cultural norms of the communities being served. Many of the Settlement House workers were recruited from the indigenous community and trained by social workers to improve the conditions of their own immigrant communities who had migrated from Europe to the fast-growing industrial centers of the United States. This closeness to the community made it possible for the Settlement House workers to provide services that reflected the cultural, social, and faith traditions of the population. This approach might be considered a precursor to care management because of its concern with the comprehensive needs of the community and its identification with those needs.

As social insurances such as the worker's compensation programs of the 1940s and Medicare grew, concerns increased about the growing cost of health care. In health care settings, care management responded to this concern by evolving into the role of a gatekeeper because increasing access to health care meant greater public expense and the need to manage costs.

Care management in its broadest terms, however, is a holistic approach that empowers families to cope with the full range of biological, psychological, and social issues. Care management, specifically for older adults, evolved out of the proliferation of services under the Medicare- and Medicaid-funded programs that led to a fragmented service delivery system just at the time when the population was booming. This fragmentation was accompanied by negative stereotypes about aging, difficulty in gaining access to services, and the need for advocacy in order for older adults to utilize specific services. The care manager came to be seen as the single point of entry and the navigator through this service delivery system. Care management continues to gain acceptance by providers and consumers of services who are concerned with understanding the issues, controlling the course and location of care, and participating in the daily choices that provide for a quality of life. This acceptance has been paralleled by the growth of the consumer-directed movement in health and social services (see Chapter 2).

As part of the consumer empowerment movement in the mid-1970s, care management was first sanctioned in the federal funding of disability programs. Individuals with disabilities were becoming outspoken advocates for the maintenance of control over their own care, thereby enabling them to become more active participants in their recovery. This approach fostered the concept of the consumer as the "expert" concerning his or her own care within a holistic view of individual needs, lifestyles, and preferences.

For the people who have disabilities or chronic illnesses, care that requires assistance with activities of daily living, medication and dietary management, emotional support, and occupational or strength training is beyond the scope of institutional medicine. Therefore, it began to make sense to have a care team. The composition of the team varies based on the needs of each situation and might include nurses, social workers, therapists, counselors, dietitians, home care aides, and others. In this strategy, the physician is not the only person caring for the individual; there are often many others involved in the care process. Recognizing this need led to the evolution of a holistic, consumer-centered, and consumer-directed care movement, which is consistent with the strengths-based model.

Private care management emerged in the 1980s because of family mobility and the lack of eligibility for those middle and upper income individuals who did not qualify for publicly funded programs but still needed support to address their care concerns. Not only were families geographically separated, but also the traditional family caregivers—the women—increasingly worked outside of the home in the last quarter of the 20th century and were less available for such roles.

Private care management is also part of this consumer-centered and strengths-based perspective. It has the unique ability to engage with the entire family system, thereby fostering growth within each individual within that system. This more inclusive approach is usually not available under funded programs because the funds target the individual and not the family. Despite this last fact, interest and concern in fostering a consumer-centered model is growing because of the concerns about the cost of care for future generations of elders.

WHAT IS SUCCESSFUL CARE MANAGEMENT?

Successful care management relies on the ability of professional care managers to connect with their clients by recognizing each person's fundamental individuality, the richness of each person's experiences, and the accrued knowledge that has given the person strength. Counseling is a critical part of the successful care management role because each family and care team member needs to move toward the resolution of his or her unique issues in order to cope effectively with the present, concrete concerns. Saleebey (1997) described strengths-based caregiving as needing to view clients as having the inherent capability to transform their lives when they receive positive support. Similarly, Rose (2000) said, "authentically built relationships were premised on validation and active participation by clients in framing (producing or collaborating in producing) their own goals, direction, and meaning, and were inextricably connected to the macro or social-historical context" (p. 405).

THE ROLE OF PROFESSIONAL CAREGIVERS

Many professional health caregivers tend to view their clients who are older adults or who have a chronic illness as frail and in need of professional support in order to survive. These professionals may tend to forget that these adults have been coping, relating, surviving, and even succeeding for many years without professional help. Moreover, the counterpart to this stereotype of aging is a professional's stereotype about his or her own role in the therapeutic relationship. If a professional is working with an individual who is diagnosed as frail and incapacitated, then the professional caregiver often views his or her role as having to be strong and responsible for that individual. This kind of role places a heavy, unfair, and unrealistic burden on the caregiver. It also implies that the caregiver carries the responsibility for the health, welfare, and safety of the individual. This is not necessarily so, as many older adults do have inherent strengths and even extensive support systems. Instead, professional care managers could ask themselves this question: What is it about these older adults that helped them to get this far in life? Putting aside societal stereotypes and engaging with each situation as a unique set of circumstances are some of the first steps in successful care management. Focusing on the client's definition of need *and* his or her strengths will facilitate a stronger partnership with realistic goals.

Professional caregivers must acknowledge that every individual and every family or support system has demonstrated a capacity for learning, growing, and self-direction. Each individual has his or her own inherent talents, experiences, and resources that have enabled him or her to create a unique life story with all of its strengths and struggles. Rather than a professional viewing a person solely as a diagnosis to be cured or a problem to be solved, the professional must connect with a recognition and appreciation of the person's unique self. For it is within that definition of self that the care manager is able to discover the strengths on which the therapeutic relationship can be built to help an individual cope with the current adversity.

The process of a care manager connecting with a person's unique story must be described as a *collaborative partnership* between equals rather than as an "expert therapist" caring for a dependent or deficient client. By building on an individual's strengths, the care manager enables a *client-centered process* of problem solving and growth because collaboration elevates the client's responsibility for the outcome of the work that takes place.

> THE PROCESS OF A care manager connecting with a person's unique story must be described as a *collaborative partnership* between equals rather than as an "expert therapist" caring for a dependent or deficient client.

The collaboration model fosters a client's sense of control and feelings of mastery over his or her life. When care managers recognize that individuals are experts on themselves, and when they encourage these perspectives of the collaborative partnership, they reduce the tendency to try to "fix" the concerns of their clients (Tice & Perkins, 1999).

A model that focuses on identifying strengths of the individual and the individual's support system must also emphasize the power within that system to cope with life's changes. Despite having current frailties or illnesses, the individual and the existing system retain the knowledge of what has facilitated healing in the past. Eliciting and engaging successful coping mechanisms demonstrates to the individual that past knowledge can be tapped to exert a positive impact on the current circumstance.

Mrs. Martin

Mrs. Martin had been very social and outgoing in her younger years. She cherished her family and friendships and the mutual joy that these relationships brought. Unfortunately, she developed a disease that left her confined to a wheelchair. For a few years, her husband was able to care for her at home. The couple became increasingly isolated as Mr. Martin began to have trouble handling the wheelchair, and then had to give up driving because of poor vision. Mrs. Martin continued to invite friends over and stayed in touch with others by phone until Mr. Martin died.

After Mr. Martin's death, Mrs. Martin became increasingly isolated and depressed. She lived a long distance from family members, who were becoming increasingly concerned about her deepening depression. They engaged a care manager to visit with their mother and explore options for coping with her current situation. The care manager quickly learned that Mrs. Martin was an inherently strong-willed, outgoing person who thrived in social situations. Mrs. Martin clearly expressed her opposition to moving into an assisted living community because she felt it would mean a final separation from her prior life and her beloved husband.

The care manager also realized that Mrs. Martin had not allowed herself to grieve the loss of her husband. This inability to grieve appropriately for her husband was preventing Mrs. Martin from moving on with her life. Therefore, in addition to coordinating medical appointments, physical therapy appointments, and supervision of the home care workers, the care manager began to explore with Mrs. Martin the other losses she had experienced in her life. On a very personal level, Mrs. Martin had successfully adapted to the loss of considerable physical freedom because of disease. She had also survived the losses of both of her parents and in-laws, a sister, close friends, and many other important relationships.

Under the guidance of the care manager, Mrs. Martin revisited her most intimate and important relationships. She was reminded of the joys and sorrows, the funny situations, the lessons learned, and the shared legacy of a lifetime. She began to put each loss in perspective, coming to resolution about the strengths and weaknesses of each person and each relationship. Mrs. Martin finally began to speak of the loss of her husband and its devastating impact on her life. She was able to express not only her deep love but also her anger at him for leaving her "helpless." She recognized that her anger made her feel guilty, which interfered with being able to grieve his loss.

With this unfolding story and the insights it provided, Mrs. Martin's depression began to lift. She was able to consider new alternatives for the rest of her life. She knew with certainty that her outgoing personality would allow her to adjust to life in an assisted living community. She also came to realize that she could not accept and express her abilities until she let go of her anger and guilt about being abandoned by her husband. When Mrs. Martin finally moved to the assisted living community, she quickly became integrated into its social life and volunteer activities, giving her life meaning once again.

What this case demonstrates is the ability of an older adult who is frail to embrace her own self-knowledge. This knowledge and the ability to re-engage with it provides the energy and the power to facilitate a sense of control and mastery over a complex set of circumstances. The result is a new definition of successful aging and the commitment to achieve and maintain this empowering perspective, even in the face of overwhelming circumstances.

CONSUMER-DIRECTED AND CONSUMER-CENTERED CARE

The National Council on Aging (NCOA) has provided a definition of consumer-directed service that is an integral part of the client-centered care management process. According to the NCOA (National Institute on Consumer-Directed Long-

Term Services, 1996), a health care provider must adopt a philosophy and orientation to the delivery of supportive services whereby informed consumers participate in assessing their own concerns, determining how and by whom these concerns should be met, and monitoring the quality of services received. It may extend from an individual making all decisions and managing services directly, to using an advocate to manage needed services.

The dimensions of a consumer-directed model must include

- *The ability of the consumer to control and direct delivery of services.* This requires that the services be consistent with the consumer's lifestyle, preferences, and wishes, and reflect the individual's pre-consumer status.

- *The availability of a variety of service delivery options.* This necessitates the ability of the consumer to make choices over who will deliver the service, at what times, and in what manner.

- *The availability of appropriate information and support.* In other words, the consumer has the right to know under what conditions the services will be provided, if he or she is capable of understanding the information. This right to know also applies to information about the rationale for offering a particular service and the manner in which it is intended to aid the consumer.

- *The ability of the consumer to participate in the policy-making process.* Consumer input needs to be an integral part of quality assurance and policy making by the service provision entity and the funding source.

In addition, the core values of a consumer-directed model require that the worker make a commitment to

- *Assure that the client always comes first.* A service must first be *consumer-centric* before it can be *consumer centered.* In this philosophical approach, the needs of the consumer must have primacy over the needs of the agency providing the care. The ideal situation is one in which the consumer's best interest is consistent with the best interest of the provider and the community.

- *Partner with the client in achieving goals.* Neither the consumer nor the provider is a totally independent entity once they enter into an agreement to work together. In order for the other values to be upheld, this partnership must be an equitable one.

- *Strive for the least-restrictive plan of care.* This is an important concept from two perspectives. The first is the previously stated goal of being consistent with the consumer's lifestyle, which we can assume to favor the least-restrictive environment. The second is to make the most efficient use of resources, whether they are private or public.

- *Assure that other providers are specifically trained to meet the needs of the client.* This is mandatory when providing quality care services within the philosophical framework of the consumer-centered model. This must include sensitivity to the values, traditions, and beliefs of the care recipient.

- *Empower the client to act in his or her own best interest, enabling the client to take charge of his or her own care needs.* This can be a controversial statement if it is not made clear that the consumer must first be found to be cognitively capable of acting in his or her own best interest. This requires a staff who is able to tolerate dissension of the consumer in developing and implementing the plan of care. The more the provider is able to empower the consumer, the less the provider should be needed. The goal is to work the provider out of being responsible for the consumer so that, after a time, the individual or family can self-direct his or her own care.

In sum, the consumer-directed model is consistent with a commonly accepted description of the strengths perspective that is, according to Perkins and Tice (1999), "not a theory or a paradigm, but rather a collation of ideas and techniques that seeks to develop in clients their abilities and capabilities following the assumption that the client already had a number of competencies and resources that can work to improve their situation" (p. 170).

Successful Aging, by Rowe and Kahn (1998), is perhaps one of the best resources for exploring the factors that lead to capacity and vitality in later life. The MacArthur Foundation Study on which the book is based attempted to explode many of the myths of aging and has demonstrated that lifestyle is as important a determinant as is heredity.

Rowe and Kahn proposed a three-pronged definition of successful aging to include "1) avoiding disease and disability; 2) maintaining high cognitive and physical function; and 3) active engagement with life" (1998, pp. 38–39). I would suggest a fourth component that takes the concept of active engagement one step further. The feature that underlies the ability to remain actively engaged is the promotion of an attitude toward one's role in life that allows for the intrusion of life's tragedies without destroying the spirit of the individual, such as when it is no longer possible to avoid disease and disability. This is part of a more existential or "spiritual eldering" belief system about the nature of human beings and our ability to continue to find freedom and to take responsibility for joy and creativity even in the darkest circumstances of our lives. Examples of this might include the poetry and music that emerged from the Holocaust or the "gum boot" dances of South African mine workers. Others find mastery over adverse circumstances by controlling those aspects of life that provide fulfillment and meaning to them.

Dr. Mendez

A dramatic example of overcoming adversity is the story of Elena Mendez, M.D., a woman in her 80s who had been bedridden for more than 20 years due to multiple sclerosis. The disease had progressively limited her activity over the course of 40 years. Despite her confinement, Dr. Mendez was the creator and ongoing editor of a newsletter that offered resources, information, and inspiration to others who were similarly homebound. As the founder of the newsletter, Dr. Mendez raised funds to pay for the publication, wrote a regular column, and solicited articles from around the country that related to the broad range of needs and interests of the homebound individual.

Beyond working on her publication, Dr. Mendez had a wide circle of friends who visited with her on a regular basis for a range of discussion groups, socialization, and future planning. Dr. Mendez was able to attract and maintain these relationships from her bed because of the power and strength of her positive attitude, her free spirit, and her open perspective on life. Her attitude was that there was still so much of interest, so much to contribute, and so much to learn. This openness gave Dr. Mendez control and mastery over those areas of her life that provided fulfillment, despite her physical limitations. Her vitality was an elixir that affected everyone she knew. Dr. Mendez's dynamism arose from the strength of her unique personality, which was built on her positive attitude and her conviction that life still had much to offer despite her physical ailments.

Other people need support to arrive at the conclusion that adversity can be met and conquered, not through its disappearance, but rather through *mastery* of those things that can still be controlled in the situation. The emotional insight to face the consequences of catastrophic life events is not always readily accessible to people. Many individuals need supportive counseling to facilitate the emergence of their best coping mechanisms. Many older adults fear supportive counseling or mental health services because of lingering stereotypes that such services are needed only by people who are "crazy." Despite this, there is also a remarkable openness to the concept of *conflict resolution* as a means of finishing the business of relationships in the later stages of life. What is initially deemed a conflict resolution quickly moves into a more therapeutic approach that facilitates emotional insight and improves coping mechanisms. Furthermore, as older adults are exposed to the benefits of a therapeutic relationship, they experience greater acceptance of the impact these benefits can have on achieving mastery over their lives and the resolution of intergenerational relationships, end-of-life, and quality care issues.

Mrs. Tractenberg

The story of Mrs. Tractenberg provides one example of an individual achieving mastery over his or her life. She was a 97-year-old woman with multiple medical problems—including chronic obstructive pulmonary disease (COPD) that necessitated the regular use of oxygen—as well as hypertension; diabetes; and severe, disabling arthritis. She was homebound and often bed bound. Mrs. Tractenberg had two grown sons with whom she had a good relationship despite the fact that they lived at a great distance. She had several grandchildren, and although she communicated with them, it was becoming a "burden" for her to maintain contact with them. She began to feel guilty about having this sense of "burden" toward her family relationships.

Mrs. Tractenberg also experienced ambivalence when anticipating her own death and the loss that it would cause her sons. She felt that she could not "leave" them and therefore she could not die. In her perception of her cultural and faith tradition, a mother leaving a child was "abandonment." Because Mrs. Tractenberg saw many abandoned children due to historical events within the Jewish community during World War II, through which she lived, she felt a continuing responsibility to protect her children from such traumas. She held this belief despite the fact that her sons were nearing their own retirement ages!

Through a combination of *life review, supportive counseling,* and *reframing her present circumstance,* the care manager was able to help Mrs. Tractenberg understand that death as a result of longevity was a "goal," not a failure. She was able to revisit the good times she had had with her sons, including the manner in which she helped to prepare them for successful lives of their own. She found the courage to ask each son if he felt that his life provided a sense of fulfillment and contentment. She even spoke openly, for the first time, about the desire to be reunited with her husband and other family members who had died. In essence, she was ready to die peacefully if only she had the sanction of her sons whom she was leaving behind. Mrs. Tractenberg was able to work through her ambivalence, grieve for her own losses, achieve closure with her children, and have their permission to die in peace.

Often, counseling is part of the larger care management role because it becomes critical to the success of the process. In other words, each member of the system needs to move toward resolution of his or her own unique issues in order to cope effectively with concrete needs. Care management in its broadest terms is a holistic approach that empowers families to cope with the full range of biopsychosocial and environmental issues.

THE PROCESS OF CARE MANAGEMENT

In most popular and academic literature about care management, the process of care management is usually defined as outreach and intake, assessment, care planning, care implementation, monitoring and follow-up, reassessment, and termination. In their book, *Strengths-Based Care Management for Older Adults,* Fast and Chapin (2000) reframed this process into a strengths-based approach utilizing the following steps:

1. Engagement
2. Strengths inventory
3. Personal goal planning
4. Resource acquisition
5. Continuing collaboration
6. Graduated disengagement

The purpose of reframing the care management process in this way is to begin to move the practitioner away from the philosophical perspective of an illness model toward a strengths-based model. The reframing/redefining process is the first step in creating this paradigm shift.

ENGAGEMENT

Care management is based on a trusting relationship between consumers and providers. Engagement is the first step in the process, requiring the establishment of trust and mutual respect. These feelings can be fostered through the care manager's ability to relate to the consumer in a conversational manner that demonstrates genuine caring, warmth, acceptance, and open communication. During this phase of the process, the care manager must provide a clear definition of each person's responsibility in the relationship, including each family member and each provider of services, as well as a delineation of the roles among the various players in the process. The care manager also must identify and accept the consumer's definition of concerns and issues to be addressed.

To get a better understanding of this strengths-based shift, consider the difference between a casual conversation between new acquaintances and the typical assessment interview. Would you ever ask a new acquaintance about their toileting habits, their financial concerns, or their intimate family relationships? No? Yet professionals are surprised when consumers refuse to give such information. This is how consumers are often preemptively labeled as "resistant."

> WOULD YOU EVER ASK a new acquaintance about their toileting habits, their financial concerns, or their intimate family relationships? No? Yet professionals are surprised when consumers refuse to give such information. This is how consumers are often preemptively labeled as "resistant."

By first understanding a little about the consumer as a person, it becomes easier to explore the issues that have led the individual to seek assistance. This may take more time than a traditional assessment process, but it should have more effective results when it ultimately leads the consumer to need the provider less because of having learned to self-direct or manage his or her care.

STRENGTHS INVENTORY

Helen Kivnick (1993) pointed out that although most care managers are committed to maximizing client strengths, most assessment tools do not provide enough emphasis on this area to facilitate such a focus. By promoting the client's strengths through closer attention to these areas, the care manager is able to validate the individual's sense of dignity and self-worth.

Furthermore, by building on strengths, the client is able to benefit from successes that can lead to greater participation and ownership of the solution to problems. It also allows the consumer to re-evaluate and look to informal sources of support, as well as to rely on the formal services that are available.

Fast and Chapin (2000) reaffirmed that a strengths-based assessment offers the opportunity to understand each person holistically while promoting interaction and building rapport. The focus of the care manager is on the individual as a whole and not just on the "demographics" of the assessment tool. This individualized focus requires a more relaxed environment, with the time to get to know about the individual's interests, accomplishments, and hopes. It may also include a certain amount of self-disclosure as part of more conversational communication. The care manager needs to be sufficiently trained to understand the difference between becoming friends with the client and cultivating a therapeutically useful relationship.

A strengths-based assessment includes many of the components of a traditional assessment, but it places greater emphasis on strengths that relate to quality of life and relationships. It enables the care manager to elicit the wishes, preferences, and desires of the consumer based on the person's lifestyle, spiritual beliefs, values, interests, and activities. Therefore, a strengths inventory might be used to supplement a more traditional assessment tool that is likely to be required in many settings.

PERSONAL GOAL PLANNING

Personal goal planning facilitates the process of including the consumer in setting priorities, defining preferences, and drawing on strengths. It is only by including the client in defining the plan that his or her incentives for success can be aligned with those of the agency or care manager. Allowing clients to make their own decisions, no matter how small, builds their sense of self-esteem, competence, and dignity. This results in a greater sense of empowerment and the opportunity for growth.

It should be noted, however, that some individuals have been dependent for so much of their lives that they cannot make decisions for themselves. When this is the case, it is often necessary for the care manager or another surrogate decision maker to act in this capacity. To honor the dignity of the individual, it is still important to prepare the person for what will happen by including him or her in the discussion and providing information about what to expect. In this sense, the care manager partners with the consumer at the level that is tolerable for that person, remaining consistent with his or her life experience.

Mrs. Delecroix

Mrs. Delecroix had gone from her father's home to her husband's home and had never had to make her own decisions. She was well cared for and had the kind of privileged life in which she had other people to do most things for her. She rarely had to make even the simplest of decisions, such as what to wear or what to eat for a meal. When her husband passed away, she was totally lost. She was unable to navigate through a single day alone. The care manager and the in-home caregiver became responsible for making all decisions consistent with her former lifestyle. By establishing this type of care system, Mrs. Delecroix regained a sense of safety and security and was able to renew her activities.

The important part of this case example is that Mrs. Delecroix needed to be cared for in a manner consistent with her prior lifestyle of dependency.

In the vast majority of cases, however, the objective of setting goals together allows the care manager and the individual to collaborate in defining the best use of time and resources to meet concerns. Joint planning also helps to clarify the roles and expectations of those involved in the care plan so that all relationships can be helpful and mutually supportive.

Behaviorally specific steps are essential to building a successful care plan with the client. Fast and Chapin (2000) suggested setting goals that meet the following standards:

- *Goals should be stated in positive terms.* For example, what the client will do, as opposed to what the client will stop or refrain from doing.
- *Goals must have a high probability of success.* They must be realistic and achievable. It may be necessary to begin with very small goals.
- *Goals must be measurable and observable to reflect only one behavioral step.* In a provider's haste to "solve" problems, he or she often asks too much of a consumer. It is crucial to be specific, limited, and to review behavioral steps so that the plan can continue to be customized to the needs of each specific situation.
- *Goals must be specific, small, and time limited to assure a greater likelihood of achievement.*
- *Goals must be understandable and meaningful to the client.* Therefore, the provider must be able to confirm with the consumer that a particular goal is consistent with that person's wishes. (p. 65)

Another benefit of involving clients in defining long- and short-term goals is that it reveals how they are coping with issues of loss and grief. When consumers cannot understand realistic goal setting, it may be an indication that they have unresolved emotional issues that need attention before they can make appropriate progress. Evaluating emotional coping skills and potential therapeutic interventions may be a necessary step to advance the care plan. As significant a part of the process as this is, it is easy to overlook the emotional and therapeutic needs of the client if the care manager does not have sufficient training in that area. When this is the case, it is important for the care manager to have ready access to mental health services that can assist with the assessment and care planning process.

RESOURCE ACQUISITION

In a strengths-based model of services, it is usual to look to the "naturally occurring resources first before seeking support from the more traditional social service delivery system" (Fast & Chapin, 2000, p. 71). In this regard, the care manager's role often is to identify and provide clear guidance for the most effective use of those indigenous support services. Educating caregivers about care concerns and the best ways to maximize caregivers' input is an important role of the care manager in this model. This often means helping to structure the relationships within the consumer's natural support system to better serve the whole system. An example might include helping family members and friends to arrange their time and availability to be most helpful. If successful, no one individual has to carry an excessive burden and run the risk of "burnout," nor is the older adult faced with being left alone for many hours because everyone has visited at the same time. Still, some visitors may have reasons for arriving at specific times. For example, many people with cognitive impairments are most alert during the middle of the day. This would be a good time for socialization, errands, and doctor appointments, whereas late afternoon may need to be quiet time because of the possibility that the individual may experience disorientation, "sundowning," or the need for a rest. Conversely, times when a person receives medical treatment would *not* be appropriate times for social activities such as counseling, meal delivery, or a friendly visitor.

In this manner, care managers use clinical and advocacy skills to influence the allocation of community resources—formal and informal—to be responsive to each consumer's concerns rather than their own. In so doing, a more efficient service delivery system emerges because the client can be prepared to make the best use of the services at the mutually beneficial time.

Mrs. O'Malley

Mrs. O'Malley was her husband's caregiver. Her husband had multiple physical problems and required almost total care. Though the couple seemed to have enough resources to manage their current lifestyle, there was no room for extravagance, and that caused the couple to have financial concerns. Their marriage was a romance that had endured for more than 30 years. As such, Mrs. O'Malley felt that she was the "best" person to take care of her husband.

Mrs. O'Malley was heavily involved in her local church group, which had regular meetings that included lunch and educational activities. Participants in this group were very supportive of Mrs. O'Malley because they were aware of her intense caregiving responsibilities and the fact that she had no extended family. The doctor had advised Mrs. O'Malley to engage home care services or to place her husband in a nursing facility. She had not acted on his advice, and the doctor saw her as noncompliant. What neither he nor the church group knew was that Mrs. O'Malley felt that she could not afford the recommended help and that she believed she had the sole "responsibility" to care for her husband. Her private nature and sense of pride prohibited her from discussing her concerns with "outsiders."

Eventually, the unrelieved caregiving burden led to a crisis that required both Mr. and Mrs. O'Malley to be hospitalized. After that—and only when Mrs. O'Malley felt there were no more options—was she able to accept small offers of help that allowed her to care for herself while still caring for her husband. She allowed her church friends to stay with her husband for short periods of time to provide her some much-needed respite care, and another church friend who was a retired nurse began to help out a few mornings a week for a small fee.

The crisis could have been averted if someone had had the clinical skills to recognize her strong will, commitment, and determination as strengths rather than labeling her behavior as stubbornness, false pride, and noncompliance. After counseling, Mrs. O'Malley was able to recognize her strengths and use them to make efficient use of appropriate levels of help without feeling she was giving up her husband's care or being disloyal.

CONTINUING COLLABORATION

Care management is often seen as a time-limited service, especially in government-funded programs. The success of a care system, however, depends on the ongoing collaborative relationships among the client, family, agencies/community organizations, and informal supports. At the macro level, the care manager's job is to understand each program—its level of care, quality of the services, eligibility requirements, costs, and the culture of the environment. This level of knowledge must be cultivated over time and maintained so that the care manager can be efficient in getting access to services or in dealing directly with service delivery problems that might arise.

At the micro level, it is beneficial for the care manager to remain involved as a consultant to the family and the individual as they cope with significant changes over time. So much of the care for older adults is needed over extended periods of time because of chronic or degenerative disease processes. Ideally, relationships ebb and flow as the need for and intensity of care varies.

Concerns do not always increase over time; sometimes they decrease. This can be seen in the example of a healthy 80-year-old man who has had recent hip replacement surgery. After an appropriate course of rehabilitation with decreasing amounts of care, services may no longer be needed unless there is another change in circumstance. Although it would not be necessary in this case for all of the service providers to continue involvement, there is likely to be a need for some continuing relationship with medical providers, family, and informal support systems. The care manager's role might be to periodically monitor the older adult to determine if there are changes or emergent needs that could trigger intervention prior to a major crisis. This would be especially important if the family lives at a distance or if the support system is composed primarily of informal caregivers who need periodic direction and feedback for the services to be provided properly.

The continuity of the relationship is often the key to being able to move the client from one level of care to the next. The empathy, trust, and sense of security in a relationship that develops over time is critical to appropriately adjusting the levels of care and sometimes even the location where care is provided. Continuity in the care partnership enables the strengths-based model to be most effective.

GRADUATED DISENGAGEMENT

Graduated disengagement may seem like a contradiction to the concept of continuing collaboration. It is important to remember, however, that consumer-centered care requires individualization and personal ownership of the care plan. It is therefore possible to identify situations in which it is appropriate to disengage. It preferably does not occur abruptly, and a care manager often leaves open the possibility for future intervention with the individual. The need for additional assistance could arise, for example, if paid caregivers who have been involved for a long time and are quite proficient in their job performance have to leave the client for reasons of their own.

Disengagement or transition might also be necessary because of time limits on funded programs or the diminution of available private funds. In either of these two cases, it is important for the care manager to ensure that other appropriate services are in place to assure the well-being and safety of the client.

FAMILY SYSTEMS INTERVENTIONS

Most individuals live within a complex system of relationships. Often this is a family relationship issue, but many situations may also involve *fictive kin,* or the informal support system. To facilitate a strengths-based perspective with this complex system of related individuals, it is necessary to find strengths within each person involved and to build on them in order to facilitate the process of meeting some of the concerns of each participant. No single intervention will work with each family. Instead, by engendering growth within the system itself through various interventions, movement toward more mature, functional relationships can occur. These enhanced relationships begin to have multiplying effects, as individuals within the system engage in generalizing their newfound knowledge and ability to other relationships.

Roberta Greene (2000) described a revision of the functional age model that includes a strengths-based, culturally competent manner for social workers to use to serve the growing challenges of the aging population within the family constellation. This revised model

> Offers an approach for assessing the client system that is a composite of one particular member's biopsychosocial functioning within a family and societal context. As an intergenerational model, it addresses the *interdependence* among family members . . . allowing the family to *understand* behavioral patterns and to *choose* appropriate family-centered interventions. [italics added] (p. 52)

The care manager's role is also to provide the caregiver and care receiver with insights about realistic expectations of themselves and others, given their relationships and the need for appropriate boundaries. A manipulative, critical mother, for example, is not going to suddenly become sweet and endearing because she has a disability and is in need of care. The family member caring for her will not suddenly become compliant and understanding just because his or her mother is in need of care. The historical relationship of conflict, resentment, and guilt is likely to intensify for both parent and child as they embark on the caregiving journey.

Learning to express support and empathy for both mother (or father) and child (or other relative) is an essential role for the care manager to play and thereby teach through example. Helping each person with his or her own sense of disappointment, loss, grief, and anxiety is critical in maximizing the effect of any caregiving activities between them.

Sometimes, within a dysfunctional family system, a parent or child is not able to have or develop the insight needed to grow emotionally. When this is the case, it is important to maximize growth for the person who is capable of emotional growth while providing support for the grieving of the other party around the need to accept that the relationship will never be what they have yearned for or expected. Challenging relationships must be accepted without a value judgment on the part of the care manager in order to be clinically effective. This, again, is reinforcement of a strengths-based approach in which each participant is honored and supported for his or her contributions and abilities as well as for real limitations.

SOMETIMES, WITHIN A dysfunctional family system, a parent or child is not able to have or develop the insight needed to grow emotionally. When this is the case, it is important to maximize growth for the person who is capable of emotional growth while providing support for the grieving of the other party around the need to accept that the relationship will never be what they have yearned for or expected.

Mrs. Brown

Mrs. Brown had never had much of a relationship with her mother. The family had vast financial resources, and as a child Mrs. Brown had been left in the care of a series of nannies while her parents were absorbed in their business, social, and travel pursuits. In response, when Mrs. Brown began to raise her own family, she focused on creating a stable "home base" and being involved in the lives of her children.

When her mother developed ongoing care concerns and had difficulty gaining access to and successfully utilizing services, Mrs. Brown became quite involved with her care. It was apparent to the care manager that Mrs. Brown was driven to participate in the care of her mother even though it was emotionally difficult for her to do so. As her mother's care situation became more stable, Mrs. Brown continued her regular visits to her mother, which she attempted to make more social and less focused on care issues. This was difficult because of her mother's narcissistic personality traits, her constant demands for more attention and more material possessions, and her continual criticisms of her daughter.

The care manager became concerned about the potential for burnout and resentment and began exploring with Mrs. Brown her level of involvement with her mother. Mrs. Brown acknowledged that she had spent years in therapy dealing with resentment toward her mother. She further acknowledged that in order to make something positive out of a painful situation in her own life, she wanted to provide a different role model for her own family. Mrs. Brown was using her own strengths-based approach to teach future generations the importance of supportive familial relationships. The care manager cautioned, her, however, that if she were to burn out while caring for her mother, it would only add to the resentment she already felt at times. Mrs. Brown was eventually able to see that she could tap other sources of help, such as her father and her mother's friends, and still provide a good role model of forgiveness and reciprocity to her own family.

The case of Mrs. Brown is a powerful demonstration of the impact of a shift in perspective that facilitated the growth and future development of an extended family system. Family members often overextend themselves when caring for another family member. The reasons for doing so vary greatly. The care manager should alert family members to the signs that they may be overextended and at risk of burnout. The care manager must then help to set realistic expectations with the caregiver and the care recipient. When family members have a realistic expectation of each other's role in a caregiving situation—based on a diagnostic and developmental understanding of the consumer's personality, lifestyle, and historical patterns of relating—it has the impact of empowering the family, as well as the client, to be more successful in negotiating this stage of their relationship. Greene (2000) spoke about the need for families to be educated to the "various aspects of the aging process and . . . functional changes in their older member." Their education must include the fact that they can expect to see reverberating effects throughout the family from aging's functional changes because of each member's interdependence and interrelatedness, an effect referred to as *cogwheeling.*

In 1991, de Shazer wrote about a collaborative model used in working with families to identify strengths and goals. Using this approach, the care manager helps family members discover what they have been doing well and build on that behavior. In so doing, the care manager helps the family create a new vision for the future. With older adults, this may mean envisioning a future of successful coping as opposed to envisioning a future without a problem, because many of the problems and losses of aging are chronic or irreversible and require adaptation rather than cure. The perspective that is important in this approach is the assurance that helpful behaviors, communications, and relationships can be strengthened within the usual cultural norms and values of the family. In addition, it is possible for the care manager to collaboratively work with the family to build on what is already going well to enhance the positive outcomes.

Mr. and Mrs. Quade

Mr. and Mrs. Quade had been married for more than 60 years. They had two daughters. One daughter lived in another state and was married with a family and career. The other lived locally and had a complex combination of physical and mental health disorders. Despite many of their own losses and limitations, Mr. and Mrs. Quade were the family care managers for their local daughter, who was unable to manage her own care needs. In addition, they had been coping with the emotional trauma of Mr. Quade's recent heart surgery, which had forced them to examine the issues of their own mortality.

Mr. Quade, who had spent his life as a scientist and engineer, was having trouble dealing with the loss of control over his aging process and was frustrated that he could not "fix" his health situation or his daughter. After all, he had always been able to fix things in the past and to find logical answers to the puzzles of the universe. Because of his frustration, he pulled back from his relationship with his wife as a protective measure from the ultimate sense of loss and loss of control. Despite their intellectual recognition that they needed each other's mutual support more than ever, Mr. Quade's withdrawal left them with a sense of isolation from one another and an inability to be openly supportive.

This existential crisis drove the couple to confront the disappointments of a lifetime, primarily the dependence of their grown daughter and the lack of control over the course of their aging. They had envisioned a later life of peace and contentment, enjoying the fruits of a life well lived. Instead, they had to cope with the tragedy of an adult child with serious cognitive impairments who would never be what they had envisioned. They were also fearful of what would happen to her when they were no longer physically around or capable of being her "safety net."

Although numerous difficult issues existed within this family, its members possessed a great deal of strength on which to build coping strategies and to provide a framework for emotional resolution of many of the issues. Both Mr. and Mrs. Quade were willing to engage in an introspective exploration of their lives to find meaning in this crisis and in the totality of their lives. The ability of both husband and wife to articulate concerns and express fears, disappointments, needs, wishes, hopes, and dreams enabled the marriage to be revitalized through a re-emergence of the intimacy of their inner lives. This renewed open communication, which enabled them to share themselves on the feeling level, created opportunities for feelings of closeness and mutual support. They became more capable of expressing concerns and joys, which led them to a feeling of renewed connection to each other.

The process was not easy. It was a constant struggle to move from the concrete levels of daily concerns to the introspective discoveries needed to facilitate this process. The Quades were willing, however, to continue to explore deeper emotional levels to get their marriage back and not live separate lives. Another strength was their mutual commitment to the marriage and the family. A very strong sense of involvement, participation, and love extended not only to blood relations but to their community. This sense of connection to their family and community served as a bond with something larger than the two of them, which gave meaning and helped them to see the successes in their lives and not just the disappointments. The therapeutic tools that were helpful to this couple were the integration of *active life review* and *reminiscence* as a means of keeping perspective on the full continuum of their lives and not just the current issues. These tools restored their power to continue in their struggles.

The collaborative approach described in this vignette reaffirms and extends the regeneration discussed by Tice and Perkins (1999) in their work with aging and alcohol use. They described a process of "dialogue and collaboration" between the client system and the professional in which both individual and the communal wants and goals are achieved. The "synergy" created by the connections between the parts creates new energy within the system to facilitate positive change. This also enables families to cope along a continuum of care addressing biopsychosocial concerns in turn as they arise.

RESIDENTIAL CARE SETTINGS

Iecovich (2000) discussed the need for a different attitudinal and communication paradigm in working with clients and their families within residential care settings. In this model, staff need to be

Taught how their patients and their families feel in a foreign setting, why they behave and react as they do and what role diverse cultures play in these circumstances. Changing perceptions require exploration of previous experiences with elderly people and gaining insight into the roots of these attitudes and stereotypes. It also requires introspection by discussing one's own feelings, fears and perception of what is aging and old age. (p. 84)

When staff use their strengths to recognize their own experiences and feelings, as well as those of the residents, this will engender a more empathic relationship. Iecovich cited the work of others who have suggested a "multidisciplinary team that involves the geriatric patient and family members in assessing patients' problems, thus encouraging patients and their families to be active participants in developing and implementing a care plan, thus also reducing the sense of alienation and strangeness between staff and their patients" (2000, p. 85).

As each component of the team uses the communication technique to empower, each gets at the heart of the strengths-based approach. In many respects, this is parallel to the family systems approach in which the participation and attention to the needs of each member is vital.

STRENGTHS-BASED CARE MANAGEMENT WITH PEOPLE WITH DEMENTIA

Along with the increasing population of very old individuals has come a dramatic rise in the incidence of Alzheimer's and other dementing illnesses (including stroke, circulatory dementias, and Parkinson's disease). Because care managers work with a significant number of consumers with dementias, it seems appropriate to note the unique applications of the strengths-based approach with people with dementia.

In the introduction to Naomi Feil's book, *The Validation Breakthrough* (1993), Feil describes a life-altering relationship she had with a mentor who developed dementia while living in a nursing facility. Feil's experiences provided her with the determination to find a more supportive way to relate to individuals who may no longer live within our reality. She advocated a different type of relating to individuals—a concept she called Validation—that would enable

> Sons, daughters, nurses, doctors, neighbors, and friends to learn . . . to walk beside the very old person in this final life stage. They will learn empathy. They will learn to listen and talk with the disoriented instead of restraining them or patronizing them or telling them what to do. They will learn to respect them. (p. xxvi)

What the book describes is that even with the loss of memories, individuals have a way of "knowing and relating." This is not a cognitive knowing; rather, it is a more basic way of understanding how we are being treated based on a lifetime of experience with relationships. Rather than attempting to remold individuals into the way they were, the challenge of the caregiver is to honor the knowing and relating of individuals in a manner that provides reinforcement and validation for the way they live. Caregivers must find a means to build on whatever remaining strengths, memories, or feelings may exist. It is the caregiver's responsibility to build a bridge to the older adult in his or her world of dementia, based on who the individual had been before the dementing illness.

Feil suggested looking at "the whole human being, not just the condition of the brain, to understand the reason behind the behavior" as a means to connecting with the older adult (1993, p. 15). By looking at and attempting to relate to the entirety of the person, the caregiver can often find common ground to walk with the individual. Discovering this common ground may occur in the telling of a meaningful story, in recognizing prior achievements, or even in giving voice and consolation to old negative feelings. As with younger people involved with the therapeutic process, this often means a return to the past to find resolution in the future. Even when an individual cannot verbalize all of his or her old experiences and feelings, he or she continues to relate *with* them and *to* them. By providing Validation, care managers can help the individual regain a sense of dignity and, therefore, lessen some of the suffering of living with unresolved issues.

The principles of Validation often mirror the characteristics of the strengths-based approach used with cognitively intact individuals. Feil (1993) defined the basic principles of Validation with the 10 statements below. Each of Feil's principles is followed by a comparative statement expressed from within the strengths-based model.

1. *"All people are unique and must be treated as individuals."* In a strengths model, the corollary is connecting to the whole person not just the demographics or the diagnosis.

2. *"All people are valuable, no matter how disoriented they are."* In a strengths model, caregivers must recognize that all people still have wants, needs, hopes, and abilities.

3. *"There is a reason behind the behavior of disoriented old-old people."* In a strengths model, caregivers must understand that there is power and capacity in all people.

4. *"Behavior in old-old age is not merely a function of anatomic changes in the brain, but reflects a combination of physical, social, and psychological changes that take place over the lifespan."* In a strengths model, people still have volition and the ability to relate, however seemingly limited. In old age people continue as a composite of all that they have been and experienced throughout a lifetime.

5. *"Old-old people cannot be forced to change their behaviors. Behaviors can be changed only if the person wants to change them."* In a strengths model, older people can learn, grow, change, and even make decisions. Change must be generated internally by the older adult with facilitation from the caregiver. This must be based on an understanding of why the person acts as they do.

6. *"Old-old people must be accepted nonjudgmentally."* In a strengths model, judging imposes our standards and norms, rather than accepting those of the individual.

7. *"Particular life tasks are associated with each stage of life. Failure to complete a task at the appropriate stage of life may lead to psychological problems."* In a strengths model, again, it is necessary to recognize the ability of the older adult to continue to grow, and develop insight about prior unresolved conflicts/relationships.

8. *"When more-recent memory fails, older adults try to restore balance to their lives by retrieving earlier memories. When eyesight fails, they use the mind's eye to see. When hearing goes, they listen to sounds from the past."* In a strengths model, a person is not just the sum of their diagnoses, but rather the composite of all life experiences regardless of which senses or capabilities were engaged. These experiences must be validated.

9. *"Painful feelings that are expressed, acknowledged, and validated by a trusted listener will diminish. Painful feelings that are ignored or suppressed will gain strength."* In a strengths model, caregivers discover what is working and reinforce it, thereby helping the person to survive and perhaps thrive, even within the context of the chronic impairment.

10. *"Empathy builds trust, reduces anxiety, and restores dignity."* In the strengths model, cultivating capability through trusting relationships builds strength, capacity for coping, and a sense of security.

Rose (2000) learned that in empowering relationships

Meaning was restored to each person; earned trust was built into explicit acknowledgment of the purpose of the practice; interactions were explored for their links to social structures and their interests; and clients' lives were envisioned simultaneously as unique in terms of meaning, but collective or population-based in terms of patterns of domination and system barriers to validity. (p. 412)

Rose suggested that within certain universal patterns of growth and development, there is still uniqueness among our experiences based on our social/cultural norms and values.

Often, our institutions or social structures create barriers to strength building because caregivers tend to dominate the individual rather than allow the individual to dominate the system. In other words, the needs of the system take precedence over the needs of the consumer. In this manner, caregivers have excluded the possibility of a consumer-centered, strengths-based model of care because the consumer has no authority to make his or her unique concerns, wishes, or preferences known; therefore, these are left unattended. This tendency to override the consumer is particularly problematic for people with dementia who are no longer adequately able to express themselves. It is also apparent with older adults living in institutional care settings in which the need for safety has been given more importance than the need for self-expression.

> OFTEN, OUR institutions or social structures create barriers to strength building because caregivers tend to dominate the individual rather than allow the individual to dominate the system.

The necessity of *institutional routines* leads to defining the person who cannot comply with those routines as a problem. For example, someone who worked the night shift all of his or her life will not easily adjust to the sleep—wake cycle in a residential care facility without the use of medication. Institutions require uniformity and are not set up to handle the uniqueness of each person's situation. The residential care facility is but one example among many—including most community services for the aging—that have evolved out of a problem orientation that seeks standardized solutions, rather than a person-centered orientation that seeks the means to define solutions on a more individualized basis.

Mrs. Randall

Mrs. Randall was living in a senior residence that provided one meal at noontime, recreational activities, and light housekeeping and linen service. Personal laundry as well as personal and household management tasks were the responsibility of the individual. Although she had been social on first moving into the residence, it was apparent that she had some mild memory loss. As time progressed she became more confused and disoriented; she began to wander the halls, knocking on doors and looking for her mother. She also began to refuse to allow the staff to clean her apartment or linens. Furthermore, her attention to personal hygiene began to deteriorate and she was becoming offensive to the other residents.

Mrs. Randall's family received a call from the facility manager, who told them that they had 30 days in which to move their mother because she was "no longer appropriate" for this setting. The family had been unaware of the rapidity and the intensity of their mother's decline. They were shocked by her behavior, her lack of attention to personal care, and what they perceived as callousness from the facility staff. They decided to have a care manager intervene because they were afraid of the consequences of a move for their mother.

The care manager did an intensive intake interview with the family prior to making the first visit with Mrs. Randall. The family revealed that Mrs. Randall had left Europe with her parents before the beginning of World War II. In Europe, the family had been quite comfortable and traveled at a level in society that placed great emphasis on style and appearance. Prior to leaving Europe, they experienced some persecution and had many of their belongings taken from them. Whatever possessions they had left had to be abandoned when they left for America. As a result, Mrs. Randall was always meticulous about her appearance, even when financial times were tough. She also had a difficult time trusting strangers. She was very family oriented and she retained close ties with an extended system of relatives.

The care manager realized from the information provided that it would be important to gain Mrs. Randall's trust before any definite action could be taken to change the situation. The care manager made an agreement with the family that she would first approach the facility manager and let him know of her involvement and try to buy some additional time to see if a move could be avoided. It was also determined that the care manager would be introduced to Mrs. Randall as a friend of her daughter and that the daughter would call at the time of the visit so that her mother would not hesitate to allow the care manager to visit her.

Several of the initial sessions with Mrs. Randall involved the use of an informal assessment process that focused on getting to know her, her history, her wishes, concerns, and desires. It was discovered that despite all the people around her, Mrs. Randall felt very lonely because she could not remember the other residents and she wasn't sure if she could trust them. This was clearly an unresolved issue from her earlier experiences in Europe, in which her repressed anxiety toward strangers was displaced onto the other residents of the facility, leading to social isolation. She enjoyed the visits with the care manager and gradually agreed to go out to lunch with her. Mrs. Randall eventually allowed the care manager to take her to her doctor, who was asked to advocate for a neurological workup and to provide medication for her anxiety. The latter could be administered by the facility because there was a nurse whom Mrs. Randall trusted. The neurological workup found that Mrs. Randall did have the beginnings of dementia, but her symptoms were less severe once her anxiety was reduced and she had a trusting relationship with the care manager.

The care manager was able to help Mrs. Randall express her fears and to provide a sense of dignity, respect, and security. The facility management softened its position on Mrs. Randall's eviction because it became apparent that Mrs. Randall was not such a behavior problem. The biggest remaining concern was the issue of household and personal hygiene.

Again, with the family's involvement it was determined that an aide would be necessary to ensure that Mrs. Randall's personal care needs were being met. The care manager selected an aide with whom she had previously worked and who she knew had experience with people with dementia. The plan was for the care manager to introduce the aide as a friend. The aide was then instructed to visit with Mrs. Randall for 2 hours every morning. During these visits the aide did nothing but visit with the older woman. It was apparent that it would take time to create a sense of empathy, caring, and trust before the aide could attempt the intimate tasks of personal care.

When it was time to begin addressing these issues, it was done very gradually and with a sense of a shared adventure. For example, the first attempt to get Mrs. Randall to put on clean clothes involved the re-enactment of a memory of going to high tea with her mother. This meant selecting a very special outfit; paying careful attention to hair, nails, and makeup; and enjoying the pleasures of sharing secrets with a friend. The event was a success.

Gradually, the aide was able to help Mrs. Randall with the more intimate tasks of bathing, and together they went through her closets and drawers to remove the clothes that were no longer appropriate. This process occurred over several weeks but enabled Mrs. Randall to remain in her own environment for a very long time. Eventually, of course, the care was increased as Mrs. Randall became more impaired. She did not lose her ability to be sociable, however, and the problematic behaviors never returned. She maintained her home, her dignity, and her self-respect; she had a good quality of life in spite of a devastating illness. Her family was also able to maintain a sense of connection and pride in their mother.

We must be careful, when working with older people with cognitive impairments, not to assume that they do not *know*, simply because they cannot remember or articulate all that they feel and experience. Another client, who slipped into silence in the late stages of her illness, once turned to me after several months and stated very plainly: "It is terrible to be stuck in this big body and need care like a baby." She slipped back into silence until her death shortly thereafter. It was a moment of truth given to us both and in that instant I was aware that she knew about all of the attention that had been heaped on her in her confused world.

SUMMARY

Strengths-based care management is a means of addressing a situation that enables the individual to find one's own best self. By facilitating the growth toward what the individual knows has worked in his or her life, those working with older adults help them transform from the inside out. This transformation enables the individual to participate in his or her care to whatever extent is possible. This, in turn, facilitates a sense of personhood and wholeness that is sometimes over-looked in models that do not share that necessity. Building on strengths, whether the process is called validation, empowerment, or client-directed care, is critical if we are to provide services to a booming population within the framework of shrinking resources.

Although it may seem that the strengths-based approach is an expensive model, it is often more efficient in the long run because the mutual collaboration at all levels of the system facilitates the most effective use of resources and can produce more lasting solutions. In this way, the initial investment of time spent getting to know individual clients and the world within which they live means less time is spent in course correction and crises. Of course, there are those crises that are inevitable. By having partners in a collaborative system, however, all participants are better equipped to mobilize themselves effectively.

It must be emphasized that this approach is not confined to individual or family interventions alone. It is a pervasive approach at every level of the systems involved. Therefore, the care manager needs to have an array of skills to be able to negotiate within both large and small systems. The care manager also needs the clinical background to be able to comprehend the dynamics of the various interactions and to think critically so as to make the maximum use of each component in its appropriate turn.

We are each unique. In our uniqueness, we have sometimes found separate-ness, instead of richness and validation. What the strengths-based model has to teach us is that even within the constraints of a disastrous situation, it is possible to call on the individual uniqueness of character to discover the means toward success. The success may not be in healing of the flesh, but in the coping that leads to healing of the mind, the spirit, and the critical relationships of our lives.

REFERENCES

de Shazer, S. (1991). *Putting difference to work.* New York: Norton.

Fast, B., & Chapin, R. (2000). *Strengths-based care management for older adults.* Baltimore: Health Professions Press.

Feil, N. (1993). *The validation breakthrough.* Baltimore: Health Professions Press.

Greene, R.R. (2000). Serving the aged and their families in the 21st century using a revised practice model. *Journal of Gerontological Social Work, 34*(1), 43–62.

Iecovich, E. (2000). Sources of stress and conflicts between elderly patients: Their family members and personnel in care settings. *Journal of Gerontological Social Work, 34*(2), 73–88.

Kivnick, H.Q. (1993, Winter/Spring). Everyday mental health: A guide to as-sessing life strengths. *Generations,* 13–20.

National Institute on Consumer-Directed Long-Term Services, National Council on the Aging, in partnership with the World Institute on Disability. (1996). *Principles of consumer-directed home and community-based services.* Washington, DC: Author.

Rose, S.M. (2000). Reflections on empowerment-based practice. *Social Work, (5),* 403–412.

Rowe, J.W., & Kahn, R.L. (1998). *Successful aging.* New York: Random House.

Saleeby, D. (Ed.) (1997). *The strengths perspective in social work practice* (2nd edition). New York: Longman.

Tice, C., & Perkins, K., (1999). Family treatment of older adults who misuse alcohol: A strengths perspective. *Journal of Gerontological Social Work, 31*(3/4), 169–185.

SUGGESTED READING

Cress, C. (2001). *Handbook of geriatric care management.* Rockville, MD: Aspen Publishers.

5

THE SOCIAL PORTFOLIO

The Role of Activity in Mental Wellness as People Age

Gene Cohen

WHEN MOST PEOPLE THINK of aging well, they think in terms of, "What can I do to increase the likelihood of a healthy and satisfying later life?" Advice is typically offered in two domains: adopting good health habits that can reduce the risk of physical disease and disability, and developing a diversified and balanced financial portfolio to ensure economic comfort and security. In contrast, given a short shrift is advice of a mental health nature; the succinct old standby, "stay active," is commonly delivered, though not elaborated. The idea of an individual developing a *social portfolio* has not been deemed nearly as important as building a financial portfolio (Cohen, 1995, 2000). A social portfolio contains diversified activities and interpersonal relationships that become sound social assets to carry through later life.

HISTORICAL CONTROVERSY AND CONFUSION REGARDING ACTIVITY AND AGING

Activity theory, the view of aging that advocated social engagement and activity through interpersonal involvement and mental challenge (Havighurst, Neugarten, & Tobin, 1963), has generated considerable controversy over the years. Previously, many health care professionals rationalized that the goal or norm of aging was to *disengage.* The older *disengagement theory* maintained that high satisfaction in older

113

adulthood was associated with accepting the inevitability of reduced social and personal interactions (Cumming & Henry, 1961). Such a perception may explain why mental health promotion efforts related to staying active socially have been on a slow track, if not derailed. Over-reliance on the disengagement theory undermined both personal and societal motivation to foster social opportunity and activity for older adults.

Proponents of the *activity theory* challenged the disengagement theory by asserting that for individuals in later life, maintaining activity levels is important for obtaining and sustaining satisfaction, self-esteem, and overall health (Havighurst et al., 1963). Although findings from longitudinal studies on aging added support to the activity theory, the controversy highlighted both the confusion around mental health promotion practices in later life and the sparse research on successful aging strategies. Robert Atchely's *continuity theory* research also supports the role of activity, with findings that continuity in activity and lifestyle have positive influences on the course of aging (see Chapter 6).

BRAIN AND BEHAVIOR RESEARCH ON AGING

In the 1990s, findings from brain and behavior studies introduced a growing impetus for promoting not only social activity, but also mental challenge for older adults. This animal-based research showed that in response to cognitively and environmentally stimulating environments, the brain and its neurons responded both neuroanatomically and neurophysiologically (Diamond, 1993; Diamond, Krech, & Rosenweig, 1964). Figure 5.1 helps to illustrate these changes by showing a magnification of two neurons in the cerebral cortex, or gray matter, of a human's brain. These brain cells are responsible for higher intellectual functioning. On the left of the diagram is a depiction of one entire neuron with its different component parts: the cell body with its nucleus and the axon. The cell body, along with its nucleus, houses the genetic information and command information for the neuron. The long, thick offshoot to the right that projects from the cell body is the axon, which contains inner filaments that act like telephone wires, sending messages along the length of the neuron. The smaller extensions off the cell body and axon are dendrites (branch-like projections) that are involved in making communication connections between different neurons.

The cerebral cortex of human beings has more than 15 billion of these neurons. Neurons communicate with each other in two ways: through the release of neurotransmitters that function like chemical messengers and through their dendrites. Neurotransmitters are released and exchanged between the dendrites of neighboring neurons; the more dendrites that exist, the easier the communication. Researchers have discovered that when laboratory animals are exposed to a more challenging or an enriched environment, their brain cells sprout additional dendrites. For example, laboratory rats challenged in a more complicated and socially stimulating maze developed more dendrites than did rats in a less complicated and less stimulating maze. A given neuron can sprout hundreds or even thousands of these branch-like extensions. Moreover, additional *dendritic spines*—

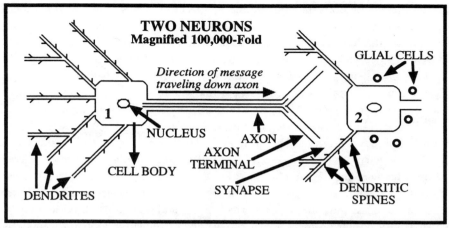

TWO NEURONS
Magnified 100,000-Fold

GLIAL CELLS

Direction of message traveling down axon

1

NUCLEUS AXON

AXON
TERMINAL

CELL BODY

2

SYNAPSE

DENDRITES

DENDRITIC
SPINES

Figure 5.1. Magnification of two neurons in the cerebral cortex, or gray matter, of a human's brain.

smaller branches extending from the dendrites and helping further with communication between brain cells—also sprouted.

Both anatomical and chemical changes resulted as well from increased brain challenge. While the number of neurons did not increase, the cell bodies and the nuclei increased in size; *glia*—supportive cells in the brain that help nourish the neurons—grew in number. The enzyme involved in the synthesis of *acetylcholine*, which is the neurotransmitter influencing memory and thinking, became more active. (Acetylcholine is deficient in the brain of a person with Alzheimer's disease.) Finally, research found that the cerebral cortex as a whole thickened, and the brain's weight actually increased in the more mentally and socially stimulated laboratory rats.

In contrast to the long-held belief that brain anatomy and functioning are on an irreversible course of reduction with age, environmental stimulation studies have shown that brain growth in response to environmental and behavioral challenges continues independent of age; a person's brain maintains plasticity and the ability for positive modifiability. In effect, findings indicated that the aging brain responded to mental exercise in much the same way that muscles respond to physical exercise regardless of age. This dramatic influence of behavior on biology, supported by a solid body of brain research, reflects the neurobiological mechanisms underlying the role of stimulating social activities in promoting mental health with aging. Neuroscience in the 20th century supported longstanding folk wisdom to "use it or lose it," but took it a step further, showing that there was no age limit for preventing loss.

> IN EFFECT, FINDINGS indicated that the aging brain responded to mental exercise in much the same way that muscles respond to physical exercise regardless of age.

Further findings on dendritic responses from biological brain plasticity studies revealed that between an individual's early 50s and late 70s there is actually an increase in both the number and length of branches from individual neurons in different parts of the brain involved with higher intellectual functioning (Flood, Buell, Defiore, Horowitz, & Coleman, 1985; Flood & Coleman, 1990). Martin (1999) referred to these neuronal changes that take place with aging as *reflecting saging* (in other words, the ability to accumulate wisdom with aging). These branching changes compensate for brain cell loss that can occur over time and further reflect the plasticity or modifiability of the brain as it ages.

Research by Glass, de Leon, Marattoli, and Berkman (1999) investigated the influence of social activity on the aging body. This collaborative study of social and productive activities as predictors of survival among elderly Americans selected adults who were age 65 and older and involved in limited physical exercise. For these individuals, the positive impact of social activity on their overall health was remarkable. Glass and colleagues reported, "Social and productive activities that involve little or no enhancement of fitness (e.g., visits to cinemas, sporting events, day trips, playing cards, attending church, gardening, community work, participation in social groups) lower the risk of all causes of mortality as much as fitness activities do." This suggests that, in addition to increased cardiopulmonary fitness, psychosocial activity may confer survival benefits through psychosocial pathways. Social and productive activities that require less physical exertion may complement exercise programs and may constitute alternative intervention for older adults. Research on social and mental activity demonstrates a significant effect on mental health with aging as well as on physical health and survival in later life.

> SOCIAL AND PRODUCTIVE activities that require less physical exertion may complement exercise programs and may constitute alternative intervention for older adults.

THE SOCIAL PORTFOLIO

How can these mental and social stimulation research findings be translated into effective practice? Trying to answer this question reveals the need for additional research addressing the application of mental health and aging advances into new health promotion practices for older adults.

In 1779, at age 70, Samuel Johnson wrote a letter to his friend James Boswell that stated, "If you are idle, be not solitary; if you are solitary, be not idle." The *social portfolio* approach developed into a practical protocol from an attempt to adapt Samuel Johnson's sage advice along with findings from activity theory research and brain stimulation studies (Cohen, 1995, 2000). Although people in the job force are advised to plan for economic security for their future by striving for a balanced financial portfolio, too little attention is paid to their developing a balanced social portfolio. Such a portfolio is based on an individual's investment in engaging activities, mental challenge, and interpersonal relationships that they can carry into old age.

The financial portfolio has three major concepts that influence its growth and development:

1. Assets from which to draw, with emphasis on diversification
2. Insurance backup should disability or related loss occur
3. The idea that you start early and build over time—though it is never too late

The social portfolio is designed with three major concepts that are analogous:

1. A person's assets are the diversified interests and relationships from which he or she can develop and draw.

2. The insurance backup is addressed by focusing on two areas: high energy/high mobility versus low energy/low mobility activities and group activities versus individual activities. The concept here is that should a loss occur in the form of a decline in physical health, not all of the interests a person has developed would require high energy or high mobility. Similarly, if the loss of a spouse or a friend occurs, in the transition of dealing with such loss, a person has interests that he or she can draw upon that do not require the involvement of another.

3. The idea that a person starts early and builds relationships and activities, though it is never too late to build. Thus, if a person has an interest in writing, he or she can start by taking a course on creative writing and in retirement write the great American novel.

The diagram shown in Figure 5.2 of a hypothetical social portfolio in preparation for later life reflects efforts to plan for the future—balancing individual with group activities, and balancing *high mobility/energy endeavors* (activities that require significant physical exertion) with low mobility/energy ones (those activities that require little physical exertion). Four categories of equal importance are created:

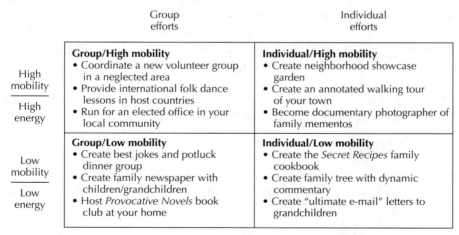

	Group efforts	Individual efforts
High mobility High energy	**Group/High mobility** • Coordinate a new volunteer group in a neglected area • Provide international folk dance lessons in host countries • Run for an elected office in your local community	**Individual/High mobility** • Create neighborhood showcase garden • Create an annotated walking tour of your town • Become documentary photographer of family mementos
Low mobility Low energy	**Group/Low mobility** • Create best jokes and potluck dinner group • Create family newspaper with children/grandchildren • Host *Provocative Novels* book club at your home	**Individual/Low mobility** • Create the *Secret Recipes* family cookbook • Create family tree with dynamic commentary • Create "ultimate e-mail" letters to grandchildren

Figure 5.2. An example of a social portfolio illustrating efforts that can be made toward tapping one's creative potential in later life. (From Cohen, G.D. [2000]. *The creative age: Awakening human potential in the second half of life.* New York: Avon Books; adapted by permission.)

Group/High mobility (e.g., dance group), Group/Low mobility (e.g., book club), Individual/High mobility (e.g., gardening), and Individual/Low mobility (e.g., writing one's memoirs). The social portfolio is a way of helping people develop new strengths and satisfactions while aging—even in the face of loss.

SOCIAL PORTFOLIO PLANNING STRATEGIES

ROUND-ROBIN STRATEGY   The *round-robin strategy* for social portfolio planning encourages individuals to arrange an advice-giving dinner with close friends. In this strategy, the individual hosting the dinner and the guests will be able to get perspectives about themselves from those who know about their attributes best. The dinner guests may each offer perspectives as to what might be areas of interests or areas of strengths for each to develop further. As the dinner progresses, everyone takes turns focusing their thoughts on one individual in the group. Each guest then shares his or her personal views about the strengths, talents, and areas that the individual focused on might consider for further involvement in their middle years and in retirement. For example, an individual who takes interesting snapshots might be encouraged to take a course on photography in his or her middle years. In retirement, he or she may be inspired to become the family's documentary photographer by arranging photo sessions with the extended family (Group/High mobility category). A person who likes exotic foods might be encouraged to take up cooking more formally and in retirement to develop an evolving loose-leaf notebook of the latest, popular recipes (Individual/Low mobility). If the individual likes reading and writing book reviews, he or she might be encouraged to set up a home book club (Group/Low mobility). A person who enjoys both physical activity and architecture might develop a walking tour of interesting buildings in his or her community for the local chamber of commerce (Individual/High mobility).

CONDUCTING AN AUDIT   For each social portfolio category, individuals should list the activities, friendships, or other relationships that are already part of their lives. What portion of a person's time is spent in a solo activity? Group activity? With close friends? Family? Co-workers or new acquaintances? How much of a person's activity is low energy or low mobility, and how much of it requires more energy or mobility? If a category on a person's list under any particular category is lacking or empty, that category may suggest the type of activity or relationship he or she needs to build. Some other ideas follow:

- *Create an activity reserve:* Individuals may want to consider creating a reserve of activities by listing several talents or interests; individuals should expand their options and be bold. A person does not have to skydive as President George H.W. Bush did in his 70s, but individuals should beware of limiting their options based on their past or on the wishes of family and friends. They should be open to the idea of trying something new.
- *Diversify and balance:* A person could aim for diversity and balance in the way he or she invests his or her time and energy among people and ac-

tivities. Depending on the nature of the under-represented social interaction in a person's current portfolio, he or she could develop opportunities for group and solo activities, low- and high-mobility options, and
low- and high-energy options.

- *Advance interests:* A person could advance his or her learning or experience in an interest by calling local colleges, universities, community
  colleges, community centers, and other resources for programs in areas
  of interest. Individuals could recruit friends or family members to join
  them from among those whom they believe will make their venture more
  enjoyable, or simply less daunting.

- *Pursue opportunities:* A person visiting a local bookstore's hobbies and
  jobs sections could find good ways to jog new activity ideas in areas that
  he or she never had the time or opportunity to pursue in the past.

- *Commit to self:* An individual can make a commitment to his or her self
  by choosing to develop a solitary interest, attend a class, or travel to socialize with others in a way that is different from what they are accus-
  tomed to doing. The individual should follow through with his or her
  plan of action. He or she could look for ways to get the most out of the
  experience by investing his or her time and attention in the activity and
  in any new relationships it offers.

- *Be adaptable:* A person should have a plan for any unforeseen changes in
  his or her social network of significant others and/or health status.

SOCIAL PORTFOLIO MARRIAGE/
RELATIONSHIP ENRICHMENT TRACKS

Collaborative approaches can be used to strengthen a person's relationships and
deepen emotional intimacy or sense of connectedness. The following exercises
were designed to expand—through various activities and efforts—the opportunity for personal growth for both partners in a significant relationship (marriages and other intimate relationships) (Cohen, 2000). These kinds of positive
experiences enhance self-esteem and satisfaction with each other and the relationship. To set the stage for a person's relationship work, individuals should
begin with a better understanding of their relationship's beginnings. They
should think about the basic internal and external forces at work in their relationship. For example, people marry for different reasons: finding love, intimacy,
sex, and companionship that is close and enduring, having a soul mate, gaining
personal identity and a sense of completion in the marriage partnership, having
children, and cultivating a family life. What brought the two individuals together? What has kept them together? What more do they desire from the relationship? What would they like to change?

Individuals should identify aspects of their relationship that they feel need
improvement. Too often, personal dissatisfaction with a person's situation is

APPEALING NEW activities not only help maintain and repair a relationship; they influence even more the growth of a marriage or relationship. Fundamentally, they are pathways for discovering new aspects of a person's self and new aspects of those close to that person.

taken out on the marriage. A couple should sort out the issues that undermine emotional intimacy and sense of connectedness. Individuals need to identify opportunities for growth in their relationships and in their individual lives; appealing, new activities nourish the chemistry of a close relationship. New activities enrich a relationship by helping both people feel good about themselves, each other, and the marriage. Appealing new activities not only help maintain and repair a relationship; they influence even more the growth of a marriage or relationship. Fundamentally, they are pathways for discovering new aspects of a person's self and new aspects of those close to that person. Interesting new activities with friends and family promote interaction, sharing, and communication.

MARRIAGE/RELATIONSHIP ACTIVITY TRACKS

Various strategies can be employed to help older individuals reconnect in their relationships.

ACTIVITY PLANS FOR PERSONAL INNER GROWTH

Activity plans focus on inner growth for an individual and his or her partner on a personal level and in relation to others, but not involving the two partners together.

- A person could explore new activities separate from his or her significant other. For example, a person could create a new home-based self-learning program regarding an engaging topic, such as 18th century American history or learning Spanish. He or she could build on this topic or program over time just for him- or herself. A person could read and collect books and other materials that support his or her interest.

- A person could explore new activities separate from a significant other that involves other people. For example, a person could take a class in which there is active interaction with others, especially one that is exciting and can be followed by other classes with the same group. Alternatively, a person could create a family tree or write a family history, ideally a project that has personal meaning for the individual and enables him or her to better understand him-or herself and familial roots.

- A person could encourage and support his or her partner's inner growth through activities that are separate from his or her own and solitary for his or her partner. For example, one partner who speaks Spanish as a foreign language, might encourage the other to learn French. Then, when they travel together to Europe, they will have two languages between them. Similarly, a person could encourage and support those activities that involve a person's partner with others but not with him- or herself. For example, one partner in a book club might encourage the other to join a movie club. They could share different experiences with one another.

Activity Plans for Shared Growth as a Couple

These activities focus on efforts in a person's relationship with his or her partner, first as a couple alone, and then as a couple in relation to others.

- A couple could explore together new activities that are exciting. The activity could offer a person something on which to build over time: for example, taking part in a sport or recreational pasttime, playing music, dancing, traveling, attending theater, or sampling ethnic cuisines.
- A person and his or her significant other could explore new activities that enable them, as a couple, to share meaningful time with old friends or to develop new friends to expand their shared circle of social relationships.
- A person should save a special activity or two just for him- or herself and partner. Some activities that can be enjoyed just as a couple may also be fun to share with others, but a couple should find ways to develop facets of these activities in ways that are uniquely intimate for each partner.

CONCLUSION

The social portfolio represents a balanced plan of action, with built-in contingencies, to keep a person socially and intellectually stimulated in later life. Its activities and relationships draw upon a person's inner strengths and also add to them. Though based on common sense and folk wisdom, it offers research-based, practical advice for maintaining mental health with aging and reminds people of the broader need and opportunity to advance research on mental health promotion in later life.

REFERENCES

Cohen, G.D. (1995). Mental health promotion in later life: The case for the social portfolio. *The American Journal of Geriatric Psychiatry, 3*, 277–279.

Cohen, G.D. (2000). *The creative age: Awakening human potential in the second half of life.* New York: Avon Books.

Cumming, E., & Henry, E.W. (1961). *Growing old: The process of disengagement.* New York: Basic Books.

Diamond, M.C. (1993). An optimistic view of the aging brain. In M.A. Smyer (Ed.), *Mental health and aging.* New York: Springer Publishing Co.

Diamond, M.C., Krech, S., & Rosenweig, M.R. (1964). The effects of an enriched environment on the histology of the rat cortex. *Journal of Comparative Neurology, 123,* 111–120.

Flood, D.G., Buell, S.J., Defiore, C.H., Horwitz, G.J., & Coleman, P.D. (1985). Age-related dendritic growth in dentate gyrus of human brain is followed by regression in the "oldest old." *Brain Research, 345*(2), 366–368.

Flood, D.G., & Coleman, P.D. (1990). Hippocampal plasticity in normal aging and decreased plasticity in Alzheimer's disease. *Progress in Brain Research, 83,* 435–443.

Glass, T.A., de Leon, C.M., Marottoli, R.A., & Berkman, L.F. (1999). Population-based study of social and productive activities as predictors of survival among elderly Americans. *The British Medical Journal, 319,* 478–483.

Havighurst, R.J., Neugarten, B.L., & Tobin, S.S. (1963). Disengagement, personality, and life satisfaction in the later years. In P. From Hansen (Ed.), *Age with a future.* Copenhagen, Denmark: Munksgoard.

Johnson, S. (1779). In a letter to Boswell as quoted in the Oxford Dictionary of Quotations. New York: Oxford University Press.

Martin, G.M. (1999). A comment made during the workshop "The Aging Fact in Health." New York: International Longevity Center–USA.

6

WHY MOST PEOPLE COPE WELL WITH RETIREMENT

Robert C. Atchley

AMERICAN CULTURE CONTAINS many negative beliefs about retirement. It is widely thought that retirement is an assault on the self-concept and detrimental to physical and mental health. Yet, research conducted over the past 40 years has repeatedly shown that a majority of people adjust well to retirement with no ill effects on health. In a culture that views aging and retirement so negatively, how do so many people manage it well? The key is in the adaptive strength that most people develop over the course of their lives. Most adults are not simply at the mercy of their circumstances. From their life experiences, they learn their strengths and focus their energies on developing them. They anticipate transitions such as retirement and prepare for them. By the time adults reach their sixties, most have clear ideas about what they enjoy, what their competencies are, and what brings them life satisfaction. This chapter explores these ideas in more detail.

In the 1960s, most scholars took for granted that retirement was a stressful transition for most people, particularly for men (Cumming & Henry, 1961; Rosow, 1967). Retirement was widely assumed to have negative effects on both physical and mental health. By 1975, however, several studies had documented that retirement was well within the coping resources of most people. The studies revealed that many of the mental health problems attributed to retirement were actually effects of ongoing medical conditions and disability (Atchley,

The case materials for this chapter are taken from the Ohio Longitudinal Study of Aging and Adaptation, which was funded by the National Institute of Mental Health and the Ohio Long-Term Care Research Project.

1971, 1974, 1975; Clark & Anderson, 1968; Palmore, 1964; Simpson & Mc-Kinney, 1966; Streib & Schneider, 1971). Poor health was a factor in retirement, not the other way around.

Although the evidence was mounting that retirement was not a crisis for most people, most studies were cross-sectional and therefore did not have data for the same people before and after the retirement transition. Results of longitudinal studies began to appear in the 1970s, with the Cornell Study of Occupational Retirement (Streib & Schneider, 1971). Further longitudinal studies of retirement, such as the National Longitudinal Studies of the Labor Market Experience of Mature Men (Parnes, 1981), the Normative Aging Study (Bossé & Spiro, 1995), and the Ohio Longitudinal Study of Aging and Adaptation (Atchley, 1999), collected data on retirees for a period of time before and after the retirement transition. When researchers followed the study participants through the retirement transition, they found no significant effects of retirement on the participant's physical or mental health.

How do most people manage to cope so well with retirement? Most people have used their life experience to construct a very robust system of ideas, activities, and relationships that they can use as resources for dealing with change. Because there is a great deal of continuity over time in these various elements, I called my theory of adaptation in later life *Continuity Theory* (Atchley, 1971, 1989, 1999).

Continuity theory presumes that most people *continuously* learn from their life experiences and intentionally continue to grow and evolve in directions of their own choosing. It is a general theory that attempts to explain why the continuity of ideas and lifestyles are central to the process of adult development. This theory also attempts to explain why continuity is such a common strategy for coping with the changes that occur in a person's middle and later life. Various investigators (e.g., Atchley, 1997; Bengston, Reedy, & Gordon, 1985; Cohler, 1993; Fiske & Chiriboga, 1990; Troll, 1982) observed a high prevalence of continuity in attitudes, beliefs, and values; self-conceptions; social relationships; and lifestyles and environments.

> CONTINUITY THEORY presumes that most people *continuously* learn from their life experiences and intentionally continue to grow and evolve in directions of their own choosing. It is a general theory that attempts to explain why the continuity of ideas and lifestyles are central to the process of adult development.

Aging brings about change, and that is undeniable; so how can I say that continuity is the most prevalent form of adaptation to aging? The key is to conceptualize continuity as the persistence of general patterns, rather than as a static sameness in the details contained within those patterns. Thus, an artist who has spent years drawing and who takes up printmaking is making a change in the details of life as an artist but is showing continuity of commitment to art as an element of self and lifestyle. Likewise, a person who has been religious during an entire lifetime can experience a spiritual deepening that places old values and beliefs in a new context. Religious values and beliefs may remain the same, but the meaning and interpretation that stand behind them evolve.

Over time, adults develop a considerable investment in their conceptions of themselves and the world around them. Individuals are presumed to be dynamic, self-aware entities who use patterns of thought created out of a lifetime of experience to describe, analyze, evaluate, decide, act, pursue goals, and interpret input and feedback. Through their own personal conceptions of how the world is and how it works, their personal strengths and weaknesses, what they are capable of, and what they prefer or dislike, individuals can make effective decisions and thus acquire a sense of personal agency.

Continuity theory assumes that the primary goal of adult development is adaptive change, not homeostatic equilibrium. It assumes that an adult's patterns of thought are about how best to adapt, to change, and to continue to develop through learning across the life span. As adults experience life-course changes, aging, and social changes, the goal of continuity is not to remain the same but to adapt long-standing individual values and preferences to new situations (Kaufman, 1986).

Because continuity theory is about adaptation, it presumes that individuals make choices, not only to achieve goals but also to adapt themselves to constantly changing circumstances. Accordingly, this theory deals with the development and maintenance of *adaptive capacity*. Adaptive capacity can be assessed by looking at the extent to which the person is able to maintain morale in the face of discontinuity.

Continuity is a constructionist theory. It assumes that in response to their life experiences, people actively develop individualized personal constructs (Kelly, 1955), ideas of what is going on in the world and why. Some of a person's most important personal constructs are ideas about the self, his or her relationships with others, and his or her personal lifestyle. Continuity theory assumes that personal constructs are influenced by the social constructions of reality learned from the social environment and from the mass media, but are not determined by them. No matter how strong a society's efforts are to influence personal constructs, individuals ultimately are free to decide for themselves how to construct their personal reality. An important implication of this aspect of the theory is that subjective perceptions of continuity are as theoretically relevant as researchers' perceptions of objective continuity.

> BECAUSE CONTINUITY theory is about adaptation, it presumes that individuals make choices, not only to achieve goals, but also to adapt themselves to constantly changing circumstances. Accordingly, this theory deals with the development and maintenance of *adaptive capacity*.

Continuity theory assumes that thought and patterns of behavior that endure over time are a result of a person's selective investment in time and energy. This theory is about personal evolution over the course of a long period of time and not about short-term fluctuations, such as changes in mood or transitory forays into new activities. It is about an individual's construction and use of enduring patterns designed to enhance his or her life satisfaction and adaptation to change. The theory posits that people make decisions, based on feedback from experience, about where best to focus their efforts to develop skills and knowledge. People select and develop ideas, relationships, environments, and patterns of activity based on their personal constructs of their desire to develop in a particular direction and of the available opportunity in that direction. Individuals invest themselves in the internal and external frameworks of their lives, and these relatively robust frameworks allow individuals to accommodate a considerable amount of evolutionary change without experiencing a crisis. If researchers assume that a primary motive for creating mental frameworks and lifestyle patterns is to allow people to adapt to their life circumstances and to pursue life satisfaction, then they would expect those individuals to use these highly personalized adaptive structures to make decisions about their future.

Continuity theory provides a conceptual way of organizing the search for coherence in life stories and of understanding the dynamics that produce basic story lines, but continuity theory has no ideology concerning which life stories are right or successful. Through its diagnostic concepts, however, continuity theory can help people understand why particular individuals have developed in the way they have and whether they have adapted well or not.

Nevertheless, continuity strategies seem to be adaptive for a majority of older adults in that they result in the maintenance of life satisfaction in most cases, even among those who experience disability (Atchley, 1998). However, a person's unyielding desire for continuity can also be maladaptive for those individuals who face life changes that cannot be assimilated within what they perceive as continuity of self and lifestyle. For example, an uncompromising desire for continuity is a major cause of depression connected with entry into nursing facilities (Lieberman & Tobin, 1983).

Using continuity theory requires information on four dimensions of an individual over time:

1. Idea patterns
2. Lifestyle
3. Personal goals
4. Adaptive capacity

Internal continuity can be seen in the maintenance of consistent frameworks of ideas, especially about the self and the phenomenal world. The consistency over time in the social roles, activities, living arrangements, and relationships that make up an individual's lifestyle express external continuity. Personal goals reveal the values an individual wants to actualize as he or she develops. They define an ideal self and an ideal lifestyle that constitute the benchmarks for assessing the results of adaptation.

INTERNAL CONTINUITY can be seen in the maintenance of consistent frameworks of ideas, especially about the self and the phenomenal world.

Six selected case examples from the Ohio Longitudinal Study of Aging and Adaptation (Atchley, 1999) show how continuity theory can help health care professionals understand how people adapt to retirement. For 20 years, this study followed more than 1,200 individuals who were age 50 or older in 1975. By 1995, there were more than 300 people ranging in age from 70 to 93 still participating in this study.

THE EFFECTS OF CONTINUITY

The four cases following illustrate unadulterated continuity. The two couples and two individuals used the structure of attitudes, values, beliefs, and lifestyles that they had created before retirement as a base for dealing with the changes retirement brought.

The Case of Ted and Gwen

When the study began in 1975, Gwen was 51 years old and Ted was 57. Both were college graduates. The youngest of their three children was a teenager still living at home. Ted worked as a guidance counselor, which was a good career choice because he put a high value on helping others. Gwen worked as an administrative trouble-shooter in a planning department, which supported her view of herself as someone who could "make things happen." Both individuals were very positive in their attitude toward their work. Gwen thought she would miss her job when the time came for her to retire, but Ted did not. Gwen also thought that retirement had a negative effect on health, whereas Ted did not. Perhaps as a result, Ted had a completely positive view of their future life in retirement whereas Gwen was generally positive but had some reservations.

Gwen and Ted were both highly self-confident, satisfied with their lives, and especially satisfied with the high quality of their marriage. They enjoyed frequent stimulating discussions with each other, often laughed together about life's foibles, and often had good times together. Both described their marriage as practically devoid of negative elements such as sarcasm, anger, criticism, or disagreement.

Although both led active lives, Gwen's activity level scored in the top 10%, whereas Ted's score was exactly average. Part of this difference in activity levels resulted from the fact that Gwen was much more inclined toward community volunteer work than was Ted. Also, at the beginning of the study, Ted was already experiencing some limitations in activity stemming from his chronic bronchitis. For example, in 1975 he reported being physically unable to do heavy work around the house. Despite the difference in their activity levels, their activity profiles were remarkably similar. To a great extent, they enjoyed doing the same types of activities at the same frequency.

Ted and Gwen were also quite congruent in terms of their personal goals, especially in their emphasis on close relationships with family and friends, and on the premier importance of their relationship with each other. Ted thought that being competent in and satisfied with his work was very important, whereas Gwen thought these goals were just important. Both were content to be workers in the community, not leaders. Neither participant placed any importance on mingling with the community elite or on being thought of as prominent in the community.

On the surface, it seems that a lot changed for Gwen and Ted between the years of 1979 and 1981. During this period, they launched their youngest child into adulthood and they retired. The endurance problems connected with bronchitis led Ted, at age 62, to retire earlier than he had planned. Health problems also played a role in Gwen's decision to retire early at the age of 56; subsequently, she fully recovered. Interestingly, neither launching their youngest child into adulthood nor their retirement seemed to have had a discernible impact on their values, life satisfaction, concepts about themselves, or lifestyle. For both Gwen and Ted, activity levels and patterns remained very consistent before and after these two transitions.

Ted had a very positive attitude toward life in retirement before he retired. He saw it as a life potentially filled with positive experiences—continued involvement, satisfying activity, independence, and freedom. He especially looked forward to the prospect of being able to spend more time with his family, especially his wife. As mentioned previously, Ted saw no negative aspects at all in the prospect of life in retirement. Gwen's attitude was not as positive as Ted's, but she was still very much in the positive range. Her major concerns were with the relationship between retirement and health, which she saw as a great unknown, and her feeling that she might miss her job.

After retirement, Ted's rating of life in retirement became even more positive, and Gwen's rating of it declined slightly, mainly because she saw her life as being slightly less involved and less mobile, primarily because of financial constraints on travel. She also saw herself as not being in good health. However, the overall patterns of their attitudes about life in retirement were very consistent across the retirement transition and both individuals scored well above average in their rating of life in retirement. After retirement, both Gwen and Ted downgraded the importance of having a satisfying job. Gwen compensated for this change by raising her priorities on friendships, being independent and self-reliant, and seeking new experiences. Ted was particularly pleased with his increased opportunity to observe the growth and development of his children and grandchildren.

After retirement, Ted's life revolved around home. He spent much of his time doing yard work and household paperwork, reading, and spending time with his wife and family. Ted enjoyed helping his wife with household work and doing things to help his children. Gwen's life also revolved around the household and family, but her commitments to volunteer work took her out into the community and created constructive "spaces in our togetherness." Gwen reported that being together more was a good experience but that it still "took some getting used to." Ted saw the change in totally positive terms, especially doing things together and sharing ideas and experiences. Both reported that retirement had improved an already high-quality marital relationship.

For this couple, launching their youngest child and retiring from their careers had trivial effects on morale, self-concept, values, and lifestyles because they remained in the same house and in the same community. Ted and Gwen maintained continuity in their social networks of friends and family, in their community involvement, and in their leisure pursuits.

They retained consistent value systems that provided a steady and highly compatible sense of life direction. Retirement enabled them to improve one very important element of their lives—their marriage.

The Case of Dale

At the beginning of the study, Dale was age 57. His work involved calling on schools within a 60-mile radius to sell kitchen equipment and to arrange to have kitchen equipment refurbished. He enjoyed his work. His wife worked as a secretary at the local university. Dale and his wife had three adult children, all of whom lived within a 30-minute drive of their small but comfortable home.

Dale's life revolved around his employment, his work around the house, and activities he did with his wife. He and his wife made trips in their recreational vehicle almost every weekend during good weather, and they visited many different parts of the surrounding country. They also enjoyed bowling, golfing, and fishing. The remainder of Dale's free time was spent visiting with family and watching television.

He was extremely satisfied with the quality of his marriage. He reported that he and his wife quite frequently worked together, particularly gardening and accomplishing the logistics of their trips. They also quite frequently discussed, laughed, and had a good time together. They had occasional disagreements, but they almost never were sarcastic, critical, or standoffish with one another.

Dale retired in 1980, but he continued to work for the same company part time through 1991, mainly during the company's busiest periods. He felt that retirement had improved his already strong marriage. He felt that the increased time together resulted in greater intimacy. His activities remained remarkably consistent over the entire 20-year study period. Slight reductions in gardening, television watching, participatory sports, and time spent with family and friends were offset by increases in travel, attending sporting events, and reading. His basic array of activities remained unchanged, including his total lack of involvement in other hobbies or in community organizations.

Dale's health continued to be good, although he developed a heart condition in 1992. Dale was in good health throughout the study, and it was only in 1995, when he was 77, that he had a bypass operation and, though fully recovered, reported that his lack of endurance prevented him from remaining employed. He scored very high on all preventive health measures. He had very high self-confidence, high morale, and a very positive attitude toward the prospect of retirement.

Dale's attitude toward life in retirement, which scored above average in 1975, was among the most positive in the study by 1995. Retirement had very definitely lived up to his expectations. He reported only minor fluctuations in morale and self-confidence throughout the study, and both scores remained above average.

His main goals in life were modest: to remain in good health, to have a close relationship with his wife, to remain in their home, and to enjoy their activities together. When asked how he coped with life's "ups and downs," he said, "a positive attitude and a wonderful wife." His strategy of focusing his life around his marriage very definitely worked for Dale. His attention to preventive health practices also was effective. He scored very high on the scale of predisposition toward continuity; his responses indicated that he perceived his life as having a high degree of continuity, which matched the longitudinal research data. He saw his continuity of attitudes, values, relationships, and activities as being the result of his own planning and conscious decisions. Dale is an example of someone who wanted continuity very much and whose good health, intact marriage, and modest but adequate retirement income provided every opportunity to realize this goal. Thus far, Dale has experienced aging as a very gentle slope, with no serious challenges to his preferred ways of thinking, relating, and living.

The Case of Gordon

In many ways, Gordon fits the stereotype of the "successful" retiree. He made the transition from middle age to later maturity with very little change in his life and thus had no need to make major life adjustments. Physically, mentally, and socially, aging had not imposed any limitations on his customary lifestyle. He remained in very good health, had very high morale and self-confidence, continued his customary patterns of activity, was happily married, continued to live in the same house, and enjoyed a very comfortable level of income throughout the study.

Gordon was in his early fifties in 1975 and his early seventies in 1995. He and his wife launched the last of their four children into adulthood when he was in his early sixties. At age 65, he retired from his position as a middle-level executive for a large company. Although he liked his work very much and felt a great deal of accomplishment from it, he did not miss it. He felt that he had achieved his occupational goals and was ready to move on with his life.

In Gordon's eyes, child launching and retirement improved the quality of his already strong marriage by giving the couple more time alone to enjoy one another and to travel. In addition, he continued to very often visit with his children, who lived in nearby cities. Thus, he was able to go through these transitions with either no change or an improvement in the relationships that formed an important part of his lifestyle.

After retirement, Gordon occupied himself by working around the house and engaging in a variety of physical activities, particularly golf in the summer and racquetball and swimming in the winter. He reported no difficulty whatsoever in "keeping myself productively busy." However, he did cut back substantially his involvement in professional organizations after he retired.

Gordon's smooth transition into later life did not occur by accident. His good health was in part related to the fact that he intentionally led a health-promoting lifestyle. He scored well above average on the study's preventive health practices scale. In addition, he had a strong sense of life direction that centered on keeping active and healthy and being attentive to his family and their concerns. He also scored high in gerotranscendence—he felt that his inner life had become more important, he felt less fear of death, and he felt a greater connection to the universe.

The Case of Lynn and Dennis

This couple illustrates the pattern of experiencing aging as a gentle slope. Both individuals were in their mid-fifties at the beginning of the study and in their mid-seventies in 1995. Through the launching of their children and Dennis's retirement, they maintained very positive morale, self-confidence, and expectations or ratings of life in retirement. They also remained active, enjoyed a comfortable level of income, and continued to live in the same home.

Although both Lynn and Dennis remained in good health, by 1995 they each reported that they could no longer do heavy work around the house. They compensated for this by hiring help, and their very adequate income allowed them to do so without feeling a financial pinch.

After Dennis retired from his position as a university administrator, his activity level remained high. He offset a decline in participation in professional organizations with increased time spent gardening, volunteering, and working on his hobby of genealogy, for which he had to learn some new computer skills. Dennis remained much in demand as a member of community boards, and in 1995, he continued to serve on several.

Early in the study, Dennis and Lynn were moderately involved in antique collecting, but by 1995, they had ceased this activity completely. They reported that they simply lost interest and increased their time in other activities.

Lynn's overall activity level dropped slightly from 1991 to 1995. She exercised less often, spent substantially less time on antique collecting, and cut back on her involvement in community organizations. Part of this change was offset by her increased involvement in church activities and in the senior center, but her feeling that she needed more time for ordinary housework offset most of the change. She remained an avid bridge player and shopper.

Lynn and Dennis enjoyed a very happy marriage throughout the study. They enjoyed traveling together, and they enjoyed the additional time together that retirement allowed. They also continued a pattern of having separate activities that gave them some time apart. Both Dennis and Lynn scored very high on the study's scale of preventive health practices. Both of them listed their religious faith, their marriage, their friends, and their family, in that order, as their major means of coping. They shared a common sense of direction, scoring more than 85% overlap in their ratings of the importance of various personal goals.

THE NEGATIVE EFFECTS OF DISCONTINUITY

What happens when continuity is not possible? We next look at two cases in which discontinuity had negative effects.

The Case of Mike and Elaine

When the study began, Mike was age 55 and employed as a professor at the local university. Elaine was 53 and director of a local social services agency. They had three children, all of whom had been launched into adulthood. Both enjoyed their jobs very much, and they focused their lifestyle around employment.

During the years from 1975 to 1981, both members of this couple showed a high degree of consistency in activities, psychological well-being, and goals. When he was not working, Mike's activities were woodworking, watching television, and reading. Elaine's most important activities were playing music, gardening, and participating in a variety of political, service, and professional organizations in the community. Both reported that they frequently spent time with friends and family, and they traveled frequently.

Both Mike and Elaine enjoyed positive psychological well-being. Elaine's scores were about average for the panel on self-confidence, morale, and attitude toward life in retirement, which is to say that she was generally positive. Mike's scores, on the other hand, suggested that he had very high self-confidence, average morale, and had a higher than average positive view of the prospects of life in retirement.

Mike's goals centered on self-acceptance and being with family, while Elaine's goals concerned maintaining good health, self-improvement, and helping others, especially her family. At the beginning of the study, neither Mike nor Elaine was sure if they would ever retire, although both of them expected that their quality of life in retirement would be quite positive. Elaine felt that being with Mike more would enhance the quality of their relationship.

From 1975 to 1981, both Mike and Elaine continued their customary lifestyles, and they each experienced aging as a gentle downward slope that required little conscious adaptation. Mike experienced some minor limitations in his activities because of asthma, but it did not affect his overall activity level or his psychological well-being.

In 1987, Mike and Elaine retired and moved from their community of long residence in Ohio to a new community in a distant Sunbelt state. Their choice of destination was in part determined by the fact that one of their sons and his family lived in that area. Mike and Elaine had expected their retirement to be active, involved, and healthy and to involve greater companionship.

These expectations were not entirely met, however. Elaine bought a partnership interest in a local retail franchise and, in 1991, her activities centered on the concerns of this business. She was very busy working in the store, attending work-related events, and doing business-related paperwork. She reported a significant reduction in seven activities she had done often in her previous community, especially involvement in community organizations.

Meanwhile, Mike's asthma continued to mildly restrict his activities, and the move from their community of long residence resulted in a significant drop in Mike's activity level, from an average score in 1981 to significantly below average in 1991. His major activities were cooking and fixing things around the house. He missed woodworking, gardening, traveling, and frequent visits with family and friends. Elaine said, "Since I continue to work and meet new people, I feel a certain guilt and frustration because he is home alone in a strange community and doesn't seem to have the initiative to get out and make a new life for himself." At this stage, Mike still rated his marriage as extremely satisfying. Elaine rated her marriage as satisfying, but not extremely so.

By 1995, Elaine had given up her involvement in the business, in part because she needed to provide care for her husband and another relative who lived in the area. She said, "We have too much togetherness sometimes. His physical limitations reduce our ability to do much outside the home. We can't travel because of his physical limitations, and I feel that I should stay and take care of him, so I can't travel by myself." Mike did not have significant functional impairments, however. He could not do heavy work around the house, or work in a full-time job, or walk half a mile, but he could walk up and down stairs, go out into the community, and do ordinary housework. Mike's asthma was troublesome but not severe, and he had no other disabling health conditions, so it was unclear what care he required other than companionship.

Elaine felt that things were much worse than she had expected. She wished they still lived in Ohio near their friends; she felt lonely a lot of the time; she was not satisfied with how she spent her free time; and she was not satisfied with her life in general. Mike's unwillingness to leave the house had restricted her to the household, which in turn, caused her to further reduce nine activities that she had done often in 1981. When Elaine's scores from 1995 were compared with her scores from 1981, both her self-confidence and her morale dropped to below average. By this time, her view of life in retirement had changed from very positive to much less positive, especially in terms of her feelings that her life in retirement was uninvolved, helpless, and meaningless.

Mike's activity level declined even further by 1995; his major activities consisted of watching television, feeding the birds, and helping his wife. He continued to do very few of the activities that made up his lifestyle in 1981. His morale and self-confidence scores dropped to significantly below average. His previously very positive view of retirement was challenged by new perceptions of retirement involving sickness, uninvolvement, and idleness.

Both Mike and Elaine seem to have significantly underestimated how much they would miss the social support from the friends they left behind in Ohio. Despite the fact that they had family nearby, Mike's increasingly homebound lifestyle caused a significant drop in the frequency of interaction with family members.

Elaine coped with her situation by relying on her feelings of connection with God and spiritual sources of inspiration, such as books and tapes. She also used social support from family to help her cope. Despite her frustrations with her caregiving role and what she saw as her husband's lack of initiative, Elaine continued to see their relationship as an important coping resource. Mike, on the other hand, cited "sense of humor" as his only coping resource. Perhaps because Elaine was there to provide the support he needed, he was more satisfied than she was with their marriage and with their life in general.

Mike and Elaine are a clear case of discontinuity far outweighing continuity. Their life before retirement was active and satisfying, and both of them were self-confident and satisfied with their life together.

But a combination of moving to a new community, Elaine's involvement in a new business, and Mike's increasing dependency combined to completely alter the structure and rhythm of their lives. Before these situations occurred, they were independent and active, and Elaine was very involved in the community. After these situations occurred, Mike was increasingly dependent and Elaine was increasingly constrained to life within their home, which was especially unsatisfying to her. Neither of them preferred this new life, as indicated by their significant declines in morale and self-confidence, but they felt helpless to do anything about it. Interestingly, Mike and Elaine both scored low on the disposition toward continuity scale, and the low priority they placed on continuity does not seem to have served them well.

The Case of Wayne

Wayne was in his early fifties when the study began. He was married with a child still living at home, and he worked as a university professor. His life revolved around his work and his family obligations. On one hand, he was in good health and had average self-confidence and morale. On the other hand, when compared with other research participants, his rating of his prospective life in retirement was much less positive—not negative but not positive. Wayne's activity level was slightly below average; the only activities he reported doing often were engaging in politics, reading, and listening to classical music on the radio.

In 1978, Wayne's wife died, leaving him to care for his teenage daughter who was still living at home. In addition, he developed a heart problem that limited his capacity to do heavy work but otherwise did not affect his lifestyle. He took these changes in stride. He increased the amount of time he spent with his child and took on more household obligations. He cut back on going to sporting events. Otherwise, his life remained a simple one focused on work and family obligations.

In 1983, his daughter left for college and was home only occasionally before moving into her own independent household in a distant city. In 1991, Wayne was still working, and his health and activity level remained about the same as in 1981. However, his self-confidence and morale suffered from his no longer having family obligations to organize his home life. Nevertheless, he remained satisfied with the amount and use of his free time.

In 1995, Wayne was in his early seventies. He had retired in 1992, and unlike most of the respondents, he had not been very positive about this change beforehand. Before retirement, he had expected his life in retirement to focus around sickness, immobility, incapacity, and dependency. In other words, he thought that poor health would force his retirement. But working conditions had more to do with his decision to retire. He began to feel that the issues that were important within the university community were no longer ones that held much interest for him. He had less and less empathy for his students and his younger colleagues. He had less patience with the bureaucracy and less respect for the university administration. He was befuddled by the compulsory student evaluations of his teaching, which were sometimes unfavorable. These socio-cultural factors, more than his health, led him to retire.

After retirement, Wayne felt inactive and uninvolved, that his life was empty, idle, and meaningless. He had expected sickness at this stage in life, but what he experienced was a crisis of life meaning. Not surprisingly, his scores in self-confidence and morale slipped even further below average. His activity level remained about the same, and he was satisfied with his amount of free time and how he used it. He still focused on reading, listening to classical music, engaging in politics, and playing cards. Wayne's customary lifestyle had focused around obligations, not self-affirming activities. He had reported that his major means of coping with life was to immerse himself in his obligations to work and family. But by 1995, he no longer had these obligations as coping resources because he did not work anymore and had only occasional contact with his daughter. These changes had very negative results for his psychological well-being.

INTERNAL CONTINUITY IN EXTERNAL DISCONTINUITY

Both of the previous examples of discontinuity illustrate the negative results that can happen when expectations for continuity are destroyed by circumstances. Sometimes continuity can be maintained at a deeper level, although substantial discontinuity may seem to be present. Jane's case illustrates this very well.

The Case of Jane

In 1975, Jane was 52 years old and at the top of her field as a full professor and chair of her department at a local university. She had never married, and she had no children. Jane maintained close ties with her family, and she had many close friends in the community.

Jane's life revolved around service to others. She put a high priority on her teaching and administrative work at the university, and she took an active part in regional and national professional organizations in her field. She was active in several community organizations, especially her church; she was an avid gardener, and she enjoyed many opportunities to travel. Jane had an active social life, attending many social gatherings and very frequently visiting with friends. During this period, when she was 52 to 58 years old, her overall activity level scores remained among the highest in the panel.

Jane was a highly self-confident woman with a very high morale and an extremely positive attitude toward her prospective life in retirement. There was literally no area of life in retirement that she did not see in completely positive terms, but she felt exactly the same way about her current life. Her worldview was rooted in a spiritual life of disciplined inner inquiry and enthusiastic participation in her church.

In the study's list of 16 personal goals, she found value in all of them. Her own list stressed being a useful member of society, being both respected and loved, having a comfortable life, being an active member of the community, and being dependable. She followed all of the preventive steps to ensure good health, and she rated her health as very good throughout this period. She reported that she had taken no medications in more than 20 years.

In 1988, Jane retired at age 65. In keeping with her past record, however, she continued to serve the university, using her many contacts with former students to encourage increased alumni contributions. She served the community by being elected to City Council, on which she served with her usual enthusiasm. Before the year 1990, Jane seemed destined to experience aging as a process with very gentle change, characterized by continued good health, satisfying activity, and distinguished service to the community.

In 1992, Jane began to experience severe pain in her hip. After a lengthy series of tests, doctors diagnosed her as suffering from bone cancer that had spread throughout her body. Her oncologist did not expect her to live another 6 months. She underwent radiation and chemotherapy and endured excruciating pain. She moved from her comfortable home to a skilled nursing facility in a nearby town in which, as a person medically defined as dying, she was given eligibility for Medicare hospice services.

Jane maintained her positive outlook, and she prevailed against seemingly insurmountable odds. Although the aggressive cancer therapy left her unable to walk, by 1994 she was cancer free. In late 1994, she lapsed into a coma and again she was not expected to live, but she recovered. In 1995, she continued to participate in the study.

Although Jane had experienced drastic negative changes in her physical health and appearance, functional capability, living arrangements, social relationships, and pattern of activities, her morale and self-confidence remained very high in 1995. However, her rating of her life in retirement realistically acknowledged her sickness and her dependency. She fully understood that she had lost many valued activities, and she wished she could still do them. But inside that body with disabilities, her inner faith and positive outlook remained strong. She said, "I get up in the morning ready to make the most of everything the day offers. I take part in all the activities to keep my mind stimulated. Given my previous life, I never thought I'd be playing Bingo, but I always try to find something good in my experiences here [in the retirement community where she still lives in the extended care facility]." The staff and the other residents saw her determination, optimistic outlook, and lack of self-centeredness as an inspirational example to others. Jane saw herself as just doing what she has always done—being positive and making the most of what she has been given.

Although the facility in which she lived was 16 miles from her former town, she took a keen interest in her visitors, and many more individuals visited her than any other resident of the facility. She was forced to leave behind her former lifestyle, and she proceeded to become as fully active a participant in her new community as she was physically able. She continued to serve others by simply being herself. She had a strong faith that she was in God's care. Compared with when she was 50 years old, she was less afraid of death, felt a greater connection to the universe, and took greater pleasure in her inner life.

Jane went from scoring above average to below average in her activity level; from being independent to needing help with bathing, dressing, and using the toilet; from vital and healthy to very sick; and from living in her own household to living in an institution. Yet, her lifelong approach to life provided her with enormous resilience. Her continuity of viewpoint and outlook triumphed over seemingly overwhelming changes in her circumstances. She is certainly a strong testimonial for the capacity of a clear and untroubled mind to prevail over illness and dependency. In an interview with her in 1997, she was still a confident but humble 74-year-old who fully appreciated that without the help and supportive environment, she would not be able to manage. She still took the fullest advantage of all opportunities. She continued to inspire visits from staff and residents of the retirement community, but perhaps more revealing was that after 4 years, a steady flow of visitors from her former town were still coming to see her.

SUMMARY

All of these cases illustrate that continuity theory can be a powerful tool for organizing information about a person's adaptation to retirement. In the overall study, continuity was much more prevalent for values (80%), self-confidence (70%), and frequency of contact with family and friends (70%) than for lifestyle (55%). Lifestyle changes were most commonly the result of changes in living arrangement caused by widowhood.

Continuity theory provides a conceptual framework for understanding how people see their world, make decisions about it, and adapt to changes in it. These cases illustrate that continuity is often—but not always—effective as an adaptive strategy. Those who share the idea of continuity as an evolutionary concept fare better in retirement than those who have a more static view of continuity and can be much more flexible in finding continuity in their life experience.

Retirement was seldom a negative experience for the more than 1,200 participants in the Ohio Longitudinal Study of Aging and Adaptation. The robust patterns of thinking and behaving that the participants had created in early and middle adulthood served as an effective platform for adapting to changes associated with retirement.

REFERENCES

Atchley, R.C. (1971). Retirement and leisure participation: Continuity or crisis? *The Gerontologist, 11,* 13–17.

Atchley, R.C. (1974). The meaning of retirement. *Journal of Communications, 24*(4), 97–101.

Atchley, R.C. (1975). Adjustment to loss of job at retirement. *International Journal of Aging and Human Development, 6,* 17–27.

Atchley, R.C. (1989). A continuity theory of normal aging. *The Gerontologist, 29,*183–190.

Atchley, R.C. (1997). *Social forces and aging: An introduction to social gerontology* (8th ed.). Belmont, CA: Wadsworth.

Atchley, R.C. (1998). Activity adaptations to the development of functional limitations and results for subjective well-being: A qualitative analysis of longitudinal panel data over a 16-year period. *Journal of Aging Studies, 12,* 19–38.

Atchley, R.C. (1999). *Continuity and adaption in aging: Creating positive experiences.* Baltimore: Johns Hopkins University Press.

Bengtson, V.L., Reedy, M.N., & Gordon, C. (1985). Aging and self-conceptions: Personality processes and social contexts. In J.E. Birren & K.W. Schaie (Eds.), *Handbook of the psychology of aging* (2nd ed.). New York: Academic Press.

Bossé, R., & Spiro, A. (1995). Normative aging study. In G.L. Maddox et al. (Eds.), *Encyclopedia of aging: A comprehensive resource in gerontology and geriatrics.* (2nd ed.). New York: Springer.

Clark, M., & Anderson, B. (1967). *Culture and aging.* Springfield, IL: Charles C Thomas.

Cohler, B. (1993). Aging, morale, and meaning: The nexus of narrative. In T.R. Cole, W.A. Achenbaum, P.L. Jakobi, & R. Kastenbaum (Eds.), *Voices and visions of aging: Toward a critical gerontology.* New York: Springer.

Cumming, E., & Henry, W.E. (1961). *Growing old: The process of disengagement.* New York: Basic Books.

Fiske, M., & Chiriboga, D.A. (1990). *Change and continuity in adult life.* San Francisco: Jossey-Bass.

Kaufman, S.R. (1986). *The ageless self: Sources of meaning in later life.* Madison: University of Wisconsin Press.

Kelly, G.A. (1955). *The psychology of personal constructs.* New York: Norton.

Lieberman, M.A., & Tobin, S. (1983). *The experience of old age: Stress, coping, and survival.* New York: Basic Books.

Palmore, E. (1964). Retirement patterns among aged men: Findings of the 1963 survey of the aged. *Social Security Bulletin, 27*(6), 3–10.

Parnes, H.S. (1981). *Work and retirement: A longitudinal study of men.* Cambridge, MA: MIT Press.

Rosow, I. (1967). *Social integration of the aged.* New York: Free Press.

Simpson, I.H., & McKinney, J.C. (Eds.). (1966). *Social aspects of aging.* Durham, NC: Duke University Press.

Streib, G.F., & Schneider, C.J. (1971). *Retirement in American society.* Ithaca, NY: Cornell University Press.

Troll, L.E. (1982). *Continuations: Adult development and aging.* Monterey, CA: Brooks/Cole.

THE REAL VOYAGE OF
discovery consists not in
seeking new landscapes but
in having new eyes.

—*Marcel Proust*

7

CONSCIOUS AGING

A Strategy for
Positive Change in
Later Life

Harry R. Moody

In his essay, *The Stages of Life,* Carl Jung wrote, "A human being would certainly not grow to be seventy or eighty years old if this longevity had no meaning for the species. The afternoon of human life must also have a significance of its own and cannot be merely a pitiful appendage to life's morning." But what is this "significance of its own" that belongs to later life? Conscious aging represents one answer to that question.

Conscious aging is a spiritual process that draws its inspiration from religion, art, lifelong learning, and other forms of self-transcendence that are reflected in the field of transpersonal psychology and wisdom traditions in the great world religions. Wisdom traditions such as yoga, Sufism, and Zen Buddhism are an important source for conscious aging because they espouse the second half of life as having a different, and more profound, purpose than that of the first half (Jewell, 1998). Conscious aging conceptualizes an individual's belief that the second half of life can be a time for becoming conscious in a deeper way than was possible earlier in life. It establishes the last stage of life as a time of transcendence—a time for going beyond the roles and values of mid-life. Old age can be a time when our deeper, inner faculties can begin to bloom, when we can achieve what psychologist Abraham Maslow (1971) called "self-actualization."

Edinger symbolically conveys the message of self-actualization when he describes this dream:

139

I have been set a task nearly too difficult for me. A log of hard and heavy wood lies covered in the forest. I must uncover it, saw or hew from it a circular piece, and then carve through the piece a design. The result is to be preserved at all cost, as representing something no longer recurring and in danger of being lost. At the same time, a tape recording is to be made describing in detail what it is, what it represents, its whole meaning. At the end, the thing itself and the tape are to be given to the public library. Someone says that only the library will know how to prevent the tape from deteriorating within five years. (1973, p. 218)

In Jewish folklore, Rabbi Zusya, an early Hasidic scholar and sage, told his followers, "When I reach the next world, God will not ask me, 'Why were you not Moses?' Instead God will ask me, 'Why were you not Zusya?'"

Both Edinger's symbolic language of the dream and Rabbi Zusya's statement point to a "nearly too difficult" task: namely, becoming the unique person each individual was meant to be ("something no longer recurring and in danger of being lost") and conveying the meaning of that singular life to others ("what it represents, its whole meaning"). This task is not merely "more of the same" but amounts to a developmental transition of inestimable value: a person's last chance for becoming the individual he or she was meant to be.

An important source for conscious aging appears in the world wisdom traditions, as described, for instance, by Rabbi Zalman Schachter-Shalomi (Schachter & Miller, 1995) in *From Age-ing to Sage-ing*. Schachter-Shalomi writes out of the Jewish mystical tradition, but Christian writers also depict later life as a period for "spiritual journey" (Bianchi, 1982). Robert Atchley (1993) has drawn on the Vedantic or Hindu mystical perspective to offer his description of the wisdom attainable in the last stage of life.

Not all varieties of conscious aging take their point of departure from religion, however. Late-life learning, involvement in the creative arts, and altruistic community contributions are also opportunities to attain greater consciousness in later life. Rosenmayr (1981) depicted a wide range of arenas for personal growth and late-life creativity that he called "the late freedom." Hazan (1996) described the practice of such freedom through older adult education in the University of the Third Age in Britain, which has its parallel in the American Elderhostel experience. Hazan accentuated the importance of community and social networks in the late freedom, as paralleled with the importance of social networks for mental health in general. Drawing on this theme, Drew Leder (1996) emphasized the importance of spiritual community for conscious aging.

JUST AS PREVIOUS SOCIAL movements have emerged favoring *conscious childbirth* or *conscious dying*, today there are signs of a broader movement on behalf of conscious aging.

Conscious aging is likely to appeal to individuals who are dissatisfied with conventional patterns for growing old. Just as previous social movements have emerged favoring *conscious childbirth* (e.g., natural childbirth) or *conscious dying* (e.g., practiced as part of the hospice movement), today there are signs of a broader movement on behalf of conscious aging. This tendency may increase as baby boomers approach old age. Theodore Roszak (1998) argues that the maturing of America's baby boomer population offers an opportunity to reshape society according to ideals of wisdom and compassion. Instead of a corporate or technocratic "wasteland," Roszak foresees an aging American population celebrating values once linked to the 1960s counterculture: autonomy, expressiveness, communal solidarity, and self-transcendence. Whether Roszak's vision comes to fruition, only time will reveal, but the values of the 1960s counterculture remain alive among a substantial segment of the aging cohort of boomers now in their fifties.

This brief account suggests why conscious aging can be considered a distinct direction for positive change in later life. But it leaves open questions for deeper consideration, including the following:

- Does conscious aging involve a genuinely new developmental stage or level of psychological functioning?

- How does the current call for conscious aging correspond to recent appeals in gerontology for a positive, vital, and optimal view of aging?

- Because conscious aging involves greater inwardness and focus on the *self,* how will this approach avoid the pitfalls of narcissism that challenge mental wellness in later life?

- What new approaches in research, psychotherapy, education, or health care can lay the groundwork for transpersonal gerontology responsive to the strategy of conscious aging?

CONSCIOUS AGING: A NEW LEVEL OF GROWTH IN LATER LIFE

What does it mean to say that conscious aging represents a new form of growth in later adulthood? It means that conscious aging amounts to a higher level of functioning correlated to a distinct chronological stage of later adulthood. Both level and stage, both hierarchy and chronology, are included in this definition of conscious aging. The importance of the correlation between one's level of consciousness and one's stage of life reflects the convergence of historical trends during the first decade of the 21st century: the evolution of humanistic psychology, transpersonal psychology, and life span development theory (Moss, 1999), and the widening impact of population aging in postindustrial societies. Our historical condition today makes possible a deeper view of the human being at exactly the moment when population aging demands the transformation of institutions to create new opportunities for positive development in later life.

One image of positive development in later life is the idea of successful aging made popular by the work of Rowe and Kahn (1998). But within the framework of life-span development psychology we can take a much wider perspective by drawing on the resources of humanistic psychology and transpersonal psychology. Gisela Labouvie-Vief (2000) draws a contrast between two very different trajectories for positive development in old age. The first, which I will label the *holistic line,* is a pathway characterized by increasing integration of divergent elements of an individual's self, both rational and emotional, to yield a more complex structure. This process is what Jung called *individuation,* a pathway that includes an increasing spiritual awareness in later life. The second trajectory for positive development, which I label *adaptation,* characterizes an individual's ability to maintain optimal well-being in the face of age-related losses. This trajectory is what Rowe and Kahn (1998) called *successful aging* and is correlated with multiple dimensions of life satisfaction extensively documented in the gerontology literature. The distinction between the holistic and adaptive trajectories is important in answering the question about why and in what sense conscious aging constitutes a higher stage of functioning.

Piaget's *cognitive-developmental theory,* in its classic form, pinpoints the highest level of function in formal operations as being achieved by early adulthood. Yet there has long been dissatisfaction with Piaget's formulation of cognitive development (Miller & Cook-Greuter, 1994). Critics of mainstream developmental psychology have called for a more comprehensive account of higher levels of consciences. Throughout the 1980s and 1990s, the discipline of transpersonal psychology documented higher stages of human development, described as transegoic or trans-rational stages, which go beyond formal operations that were identified with ego development in early adulthood (Walsh & Vaughan, 1993). These stages correspond to what Sinnott (1996) labeled "post-formal operations." Building on this body of work, Wilber (2000) defined and validated higher stages of psychological functioning.

Alternative views of life-span development appeared in the 1970s, and they have increased in number ever since. Following the pioneering work of Klaus Riegel's theories on dialectical operations, investigators began to hypothesize a higher level of so-called post-formal operations, linked to the development of wisdom throughout the course of adult life (Commons & Armon, 1984). This evolution of *dialectical thinking* or *post-formal cognitive operations* entails a movement beyond conventional interpretations in many domains of functioning (Pascual-Leone, 1990). For instance, in moral reasoning, Kohlberg characterized this higher level of moral development as *post-conventional.* Fowler (1995) gave a similar account of higher stages of cognitive development in religious orientation, and McFadden (1985) described a distinctive stage of "religious maturity" in later life.

UNTIL RECENTLY, few empirical investigators in the cognitive psychology tradition have looked at the link between hierarchical stage and life-span period in old age; this link is essential to the definition of conscious aging.

Many characteristics of higher levels of function coincide with phenomena investigated by transpersonal psychology. Until recently, few empirical investigators in the cognitive psychology tradition have looked at the link between hierarchical stage and life-span period in old age; this link is essential to the definition of conscious aging. Unlike the objective of traditional life-span development psychology, the agenda for a conscious aging approach to older adulthood posits a distinct possibility for growth in the last stage of life. This is the holistic path to growth that may be perceived, in the language of the dream, as the task that is "nearly too difficult" but remains still a possibility.

We do not want to suggest that conscious aging represents an inevitable or universal unfolding of human potential in later life. The potential is there but the holistic development needed to achieve this goal is not an easy path for a person to take and may not appeal to a majority of people entering old age. Other alternative approaches to aging, such as successful aging and productive aging, are far more appealing to people because both approaches represent efforts to sustain and support values already enshrined by mainstream culture: namely, *success* and *productivity.*

In a culture where old age is feared or denied, positive aging strategies that avoid anything that looks too much like aging will tend to be popular. In fact, both successful and productive aging strategies make old age a second middle age by denying the losses associated with aging altogether; denial can be an effective tool for positive aging. Depending on circumstances, individuals may be able to achieve positive life satisfaction and mental wellness without any greater inner growth of consciousness or wisdom. These individuals may simply remain the selves they are familiar with, adapting to changed conditions but sustaining mid-life habits. By contrast, the strategy of conscious aging typically entails a long struggle, described in greater detail in *The Five Stages of the Soul* (Moody, 1997).

Conscious aging is a process of going beyond the patterns of ego strengths that individuals acquire during their youth and mid-life. World wisdom traditions regard this course of transcendence as a human being's struggle to overcome the self. Rationality, assertiveness, moral certitude, mastery of the environment, and comparable active qualities are very different from the stance recommended by travelers of spiritual paths such as Zen Buddhism or Sufism, or by mystics in the Jewish and Christian traditions. By contrast, mystical traditions celebrate *the way of unknowing* (i.e., overcoming rationality), *emptiness* (i.e., giving up self-assertiveness), even entering what Buddhists call "the Great Doubt" in the face of cosmic mystery. Spiritual traditions typically entail a *dark night of the soul,* which might be described as *regression in the service of the ego.* In the most profound mystical traditions, the way to experience the pinnacle of transcendence involves the "loss of the self," that is, the dissolution of conventional ego structures altogether (Roberts, 1992). At this point, there is a stark contrast between the trajectories of the holistic path versus the adaptive paths of positive development in later life.

Religion plays an important but complex role in conscious aging. A growing body of empirical literature shows that "religion" as a global domain of human activity focuses generally on an adaptive path for promoting health and well-being in old age. For an individual, religious beliefs and practices can serve as buffers against losses that occur in later life and can help to sustain an individual's resilience—a kind of mental reserve capacity in coping with losses. For individuals, organized religion may also play a positive role because of the social networks it provides, including internalized social ties that protect individuals against a sense of isolation in the face of suffering.

Other resources serve to promote mental wellness in later life: for example, patriotism, family ties, networks of cultural solidarity, and ethnic identity (Putnam, 2000). Individuals can anchor themselves in these forms of *cultural capital* that transcend individuality and overcome isolation. Much like religion's way of providing mental wellness, these various forms of cultural capital serve to act as psychological buffers that strengthen people's reserve capacity for coping with losses of aging.

There is another side to the role of religion in conscious aging however. Religious institutions do not always favor higher stages of personal development. Rabbi Zusya's challenge from God to become the unique person he was meant to be poses a tension between the claims of individuation and the demands of conventional society. Conscious aging typically finds inspiration in underground mystical traditions, but it may not get an enthusiastic reception from the dominant authorities in churches, synagogues, or mosques (Moody, 1995). Conventional religion transmits the values of the wider society to the individual and thereby reinforces ego structures, while spirituality or mysticism tends to subvert these same structures. The dissolution of ego structures, as mystics themselves have recognized, is a risky approach for individuals and a controversial approach for social institutions. Indeed, conscious aging ultimately goes in a very different direction than the social assurances from literalistic faith identity or shared group identity. What Rosenmayr (1981) called "late freedom" may be inspiring for the late style of aging artists, but it can prove threatening for social groups when older people no longer behave according to social conventions.

In the early 21st century, across advanced postindustrial societies, conventional value structures are facing opposing cultural and economic currents on behalf of individuality and autonomy. Cultural and economic imperatives are pulling in opposite directions. The emancipatory imperative of culture—"do your own thing"—stands in stark contrast to the rationalizing tendency of the economic order, which demands more efficient and productive use of time. At the same time, the powerful demographic transition toward population aging means that various institutions—the family, the workplace, education, health care, and so on—will be forced to rethink the meaning of aging and the stages of life. In the United States, as unprecedented numbers of baby boomers enter old age, they may look for a way of life that promises to support values of autonomy, individuality, expressiveness, and self-transcendence outside the marketplace and the economic machine. In this sense, as growing numbers of people look for new meaning in old age, old arguments about the counterculture of the 1960s take on new importance. In this search for a new meaning, conscious aging can offer a strategy for positive change.

Conscious aging, I have argued, represents a genuinely new stage and level of psychological functioning. But its novelty is, in part, an historical artifact arising from the convergence between postindustrial culture and population aging. As a way of life and a level of consciousness, conscious aging is emerging at a distinct moment in history. Yet the holistic path of late-life development is not a new idea, but rather a prospect long familiar among the spiritual traditions of the world. Those traditions caution us to expect some inevitable degree of tension between dominant institutions on the one side, which have their own ruling ideas about successful aging, and, on the other side, the imperative of autonomy in becoming the person we were meant to be. This tension between dominant institutional values and the imperative of self-actualization is likely to endure and will set the stage for how we understand conscious aging as a strengths-based approach to mental wellness.

CONSCIOUS AGING: A POSITIVE IMAGE OF LATER LIFE

Many positive images of later life exist, and there are very different ways to grow older in a positive, optimal, and vital way. The wider culture tends to celebrate values of success and productivity, and those people who favor a more positive image of aging will urge their contemporaries to recast images of old age in terms of these conventional values. Even within the framework of those values, however, there will be different ways of coping with the losses associated with old age. Successful aging can include both extended good health and compensatory adaptation to declining health. Productive aging can include both wage-based employment, such as a second career, and volunteer or other non-monetized activities.

Conscious aging is also a multidimensional way to grow older: On the one hand, it embodies the concept of *ego-integrity* and, on the other hand, it postulates *ego-transcendence*. Ego-integrity, as the developmental task pychoanalyst Erik Erikson posited as characteristic of the final stage of life, is familiar to gerontologists. *Integrity* connotes a tendency toward closure, completeness, and life-satisfaction that incorporates previously rejected parts of the self: a return of the repressed aspects of the self that might have previously inspired disgust or despair but can now be assimilated and accepted. One method for achieving personal growth along this holistic line is through *life review,* a psychological process which was first defined by Butler (1980–1981) and later elaborated on by gerontologists (e.g., Woodward, 1986). Whether achieved through formal life review or through other processes of growth, ego-integrity corresponds to the holistic side of conscious aging.

As mentioned previously, another level of growth is represented by ego-transcendence. Chinen (1986, 1989) described transcendence in later life in his studies of fairy tales that involve older heroic figures, so-called *eldertales.* These stories, Chinen showed, present ego-transcendence as a major developmental task in later life. The typical pattern in the story is for an older person to move from an egocentric perspective after encountering magical or numinous elements outside of ordinary consciousness. These supernatural encounters lead to self-confrontation and struggle, whereby conventional egocentric thinking is eventually transcended. After a breakthrough into higher consciousness, the older heroic figure achieves a state of new innocence or emancipated maturity and may in turn become a guide for others.

Both ego-integrity and ego-transcendence involve coping with the limits of old age. Later life is typically a period of losses—role loss, bereavement, disability—that can threaten a person's self-esteem and well-being. The strategy of successful aging works according to a formula of optimization and compensation under the style of ego adaptation. According to this strategy, no lofty standard of holistic self-integration is required, simply skillful coping or, in the definition of successful aging, decrement with compensation. Ego-adaptation does not require deeper psychological work (e.g., therapy, meditation, life-review). On the contrary, the objective of ego-adaptation is for a person to maintain his or her habituated behavior, modifying it as required by changing circumstances.

> THE STRATEGY OF successful aging works according to a formula of optimization and compensation under the style of ego adaptation.

EGO-ADAPTATION AS A DEFENSE MECHANISM

Successful aging as a strategy is quite different from conscious aging. Ego-adaptation takes the path of optimal deployment of defense mechanisms, including denial, which can maintain tolerable life satisfaction even at the expense of self-knowledge or self-integration. Denial—which means sustaining long-term defense mechanisms—may not lead to consciousness or deeper wisdom; indeed, it can lead to blindness (the "old fool" syndrome). When a person walks a path of denial, it involves less pain than does acknowledging old wounds, as the hero in an eldertale must do. When individuals preserve their established defenses in later life, they could be described as unconsciously aging because they would succeed in keeping elements of the self in darkness. The ego maintains equilibrium and sustains positive self-esteem by warding off threats to so-called healthy narcissism.

The path of ego-adaptation takes some effort, yet it is an easier path. The pleasure principle, after all, favors doing what is familiar, comfortable, satisfying: The individual clings to customary opinions, congenial companions, established rituals, and tried-and-true habits. As a strategy for *optimization* and *selective compensation,* ego-adaptation will maintain stable personality characteristics and predictable habits without any deeper commitment to self-consciousness or integration. It amounts to what Robert Kastenbaum (1984) called *habituation* and what social gerontologists have formulated as the *continuity theory of aging.* Even individuals with the greatest philosophical minds, in their old age, may favor a path of habituation and ego-adaptation. For example, the citizens of 18th-century Konigsberg, in Prussia, knew they could set their clocks by observing the aged philosopher Immanuel Kant walk by at the same time each day.

Ego-adaptation's success depends, in part, on the cultural resources available to individuals in particular periods of time or a particular historical setting. Positive aging, then, becomes partly a matter of lucky historical fit. The path of ego-adaptation depends on congruence between habitual style and collective cultural possibilities that favor continuity between a person's past and present self.

What are the prospects for such congruence in the 21st century? It would seem that they are not so favorable. A postmodern culture threatens to disrupt all forms of cultural continuity, whether in marriage, the workplace, or in mass media (Kegan, 1995). The wider culture remains inhospitable to positive aging in many respects. Images of positive aging in the United States are increasingly linked to consumer culture: tourism, cosmetics, fashion, the entertainment industry, and advertising (Featherstone & Wernick, 1995). This consumer culture discredits old age and its imagery tends to reinforce a dual image of later life— the *well-derly* versus the *ill-derly*.

This bipolar pattern is increasingly tied to the emergence of successful aging as a cultural ideal. Success, after all, has its counterpart in failure, and the negative aspects of aging—including decline—can be treated as signs of failure. In a postmodern culture, aging is no longer a matter of fate but a voluntary act. Postmodernism means that nothing is a *given,* but rather, that everything can be deconstructed and refashioned. The spread of plastic surgery, for example, as well as prosthetic replacement parts for aging bodies, would open up the prospect of a world in which decline can be increasingly avoided or disguised under a "mask of age" (Hepworth, 1991).

In postmodern terms, everyday life and the aging body all become ingredients of virtual reality. We are what we are seen to be by others. The psychology of positive aging then becomes linked to social class and economic fortune. Consider, for instance, photographs of Dick Clark or Sophia Loren when these icons were in their seventies. Those who are wealthy and in good health can sustain a positive self-image far into advanced old age.

Individual psychology of positive aging is increasingly mediated by pervasive images of mass culture dominated by an uncritical ideal of successful aging. Some critics argue that these cultural representations of positive aging constitute a heroic struggle to achieve autonomy in opposition to "declinism" (Gullette, 1997), while another group of critics view the growing hegemony of positive aging as evidence of what German philosopher and sociologist Jurgen Habermas called the "colonization of the life-world." It is becoming clearer that aging itself, under postmodern conditions, is no longer a condition given by fate but is increasingly open and subject to individual or collective choice.

The strategy of conscious aging operates in this cultural and historical context in which the social definition of old age is contested and unclear. Many people who are considered healthy, wealthy, and wise—such as participants in Elderhostel—no longer think of themselves as *old* but rather as *ageless.* Indeed, some New Age philosophies promise that an individual can attain an ageless body and urge individuals to use the power of positive thinking to overcome all limits. This denial of aging is not far from the "culture of narcissism" decried by critics such as Christopher Lasch (1977). People who are not persuaded that culture and technology will enable us to overcome all limits need to reflect more deeply on the psychological significance of narcissism and its link with a postmodern condition of old age.

LATE-LIFE NARCISSISM

One predictable psychological risk in later life is a tendency toward narcissism, and this prospect poses dangers at both the individual and the societal levels (Kastenbaum, 1993). In the Freudian analytic perspective, aging was interpreted according to ideas of narcissism, aggression, and mourning. The psychoanalytic tradition views the aging body as a spectacle of unremitting impotence and decline (Woodward, 1991). Freudians have been deeply pessimistic about the prospects for successful psychotherapy among older people—meaning even individuals over the age of 50. Many analysts have been reluctant to treat older individuals, fearing that their rigidity makes them hopeless.

The Freudian account of aging and narcissism has not been the only view of the matter. The perspective of self-psychology represents an important alternative perspective. The work of Heinz Kohut went beyond traditional psychoanalytic thought in important ways, chiefly in arguing that the drive toward self-esteem is a central dynamic force in personality growth throughout the life span, including during old age (Goldmeier & Fandetti, 1992). In the perspective of self-psychology, narcissism even takes on an aspect of appropriate development. Individuals necessarily become attached to self-objects—that is, people whose images become internalized and are then psychologically used to maintain self-esteem (Kohut, 1976; Siegel & Kohut, 1996).

In this developmental account, empathic people play a critical role in the trajectory of life. The scope of an individual's self is widened enormously to include a range of significant psychological relationships. Instead of simple defense mechanisms, the human being is understood to have a complex structure involving mirroring, idealizing, and a subtle process of mutual transference. Inasmuch as predictable and normative declines of aging are a threat to the self, it is to be expected that a degree of typical and healthy narcissism in old age will serve as a buffer against losses of later life.

This more positive validation of healthy narcissism finds support in the experience of many clinicians and geriatric professionals. Practitioners familiar with older individuals who are tough, resilient, or even those who are considered mean, will immediately recognize the importance of healthy narcissism and its contribution to positive aging. For that reason, geriatric mental health professionals may understandably be skeptical of any doctrine of conscious aging that favors "loss of the self" as a good thing to strive for or to encourage among older people. Bouklas (1997), for example, urges geriatric psychotherapists to rely on a variety of approaches—transpersonal, psychodynamic, and behavioral—to enhance what he calls healthy narcissism in frail or ill older adults. This recommendation is entirely appropriate if the strategic goal is ego-adaptation. Clinical literature from long-term care suggests that older adults who are viewed as difficult or egotistical residents—those who are strongly assertive—are likely to survive and thrive in nursing facilities better than residents who are considered compliant.

Varieties of healthy narcissism have been documented earlier in the life course: for example, in the transition from youth through midlife. One longitudinal study of college women examined forms of narcissism, defined broadly to include individuals whose personality style is dominated by issues of self-definition, self-worth, identity, and autonomy. The "autonomy" group demonstrated a positive surge of personality growth in mid-life (Wink, 1992).

Late-life narcissism also has its negative side. One of the most powerful portraits of late-life narcissism ever drawn is King Lear. Lear's destructive behavior springs from a simple and primordial anxiety of old age: the fear of becoming helpless and abandoned. In Shakespeare's account, King Lear voluntarily retires, deliberately putting himself in a condition of dependency. He is thus compelled to rely on his daughters for "informal support," as geriatric social workers might say.

King Lear's case illustrates a classic problem with the continuity theory of successful aging. In Lear's case, the problem is that kingship is poor preparation for late-life dependency. Obviously this problem is not limited to royal rulers. Hess (1987) gives clinical analysis of common cases of late-life psychopathology that follow a pattern similar to that followed by Lear. One example is a stroke victim who behaves tyrannically because he is all too aware of his own helplessness. Another is the case of an aged writer near death who projects all difficulties onto sources outside of himself. The third case involves two older sisters locked in a pattern of tyrannical control. In this last instance, excessive demands for care result from motivations familiar to practitioners: fear of being left alone, a pattern of manipulation, and resentment (Lustbader, 1994).

If we read Lear's psychodynamic situation in terms of the strategy of conscious aging, the definitive diagnosis is given by one of Lear's own daughters, the monstrous Goneril. Goneril remarks that the aged king "hath ever but slenderly known himself." She puts her finger squarely on the problem. Lear's lifelong failure of self-knowledge comes back to haunt him in old age when unchecked narcissism creates the very destruction he long feared and resisted—a pattern of self-fulfilling prophecy well known to the ancient Greeks.

The fate of King Lear is a cautionary parable for those who would avoid the difficult path of conscious aging in favor of adaptation alone. In an allegorical sense, Lear as King represents the ego—king of the psyche. The king is successful as long as he is functionally in charge, but he flounders when exiled and vulnerable. Lear's fate, understood in allegorical terms, makes us wonder: what happens when the very strengths of earlier life become weaknesses in later life? Carl Jung, in *The Stages of Life* (Campbell, 1983), makes the point succinctly:

> What was great in earlier life becomes small in later years, and what was small may become great. Self-knowledge and consciousness represent a way out of the fateful pattern of narcissism and decline. Consciousness is precisely that "small thing" that can become greater and thus become a fulcrum for positive aging.

In the literature of geriatric psychiatry, narcissism is commonly described as either healthy or pathological. According to Bressler (1981), typical narcissistic gratification does promote self-regard and, through love and gratitude, strengthens investment of psychic energy in other people. But for the pathological narcissist, the pattern is quite different. Pathological narcissism tends to be manipulative and exploitative. The destructive habits associated with pathological narcissism may produce successful patterns of adaptation that flourish for decades, especially in a society that rewards selfishness and even cultivates sociopathic behavior (e.g., among celebrities). King Lear, too, was successful for many years before his retirement.

Nevertheless, as is common knowledge, success early in life is no guarantee of successful old age, as the pathos of aging movie star Norma Desmond in the film *Sunset Boulevard* makes vivid. Losses in later life are multiple. Role loss is one assault; the aging body is another, and they may work in tandem. Cumulative losses in later life involve narcissistic wounds, and it is appropriate to mourn for what is lost. Those who favor ego-adaptation as the supreme stage of human development will see mourning along with sublimation as the best that can be hoped for under adverse conditions. Healthy older people may hope to sublimate ego concerns, as Freud himself urged in praising of "Lieben und Arbeiten" (Love and Work) as the purpose of life.

This humanistic ideal has its heroic grandeur and courage, as Freud's old age and final illness demonstrate. At its best, the humanistic duality of love and work produces a personality devoted to compassion and wisdom—as in Erikson's accounts of generativity and ego-integrity as goals for the second half of life. Healthy narcissism, in the tradition of ego psychology, involves a strong sense of self-worth and an understanding of one's identity, both strengths and limits.

But these assets are vulnerable to time and loss. In Erikson's psychology, the humanistic ideal is ultimately based on preservation of the ego at all costs. A person who has achieved successful aging has stumbled on the good fortune of happy correlation between selfish concerns, physical and environmental resources, and social tasks that promote ego strength. This fortunate combination is what Aristotle called "moral luck" (Williams, 1981). Like other Greeks, Aristotle understood too well that time and chance are key factors determining whether an individual life will turn out to be happy or tragic. Contemporary scientific students of life satisfaction seem to have a less profound understanding of just how precarious the good life can turn out to be.

The ancient Greek imperative "Know thyself" was based on a sound conviction that chance and circumstance are all-important—yet inscrutable and unpredictable—forces. Self-knowledge would be the way out of this uncertainty. If an individual cannot know the world, then perhaps one can know one's self and so protect oneself from disaster—including disasters of one's own making.

Tragedy is not the final message of conscious aging, although the tragic sense of life is part of a deeper consciousness in old age. Out of the Greek understanding of tragedy arose the philosophy known as Stoicism. In other historical settings (e.g., ancient India), similar understanding gave rise to mysticism.

Reflection on archetypal tragic heroes like Sophocles's Oedipus and Shakespeare's King Lear will provide insights for us. A psychological realist might see both Stoicism and mysticism as clear-eyed views of the totality of life—a perspective that King Oedipus, for example, achieved only in old age. It was only in the last stage of life, Sophocles seemed to tell us in *Oedipus at Colonus,* that Oedipus, aged and physically blind, found a vision of an unseen world more profound than what was possible earlier in life. The transcendence of Oedipus at Colonus is much more than ego-adaptation. It constitutes the achievement of a genuinely new level of wisdom and detachment.

Consideration of the fates of characters such as Oedipus and Lear is bound to raise a question. Is their tragedy inevitable, or are some of the sufferings of old age preventable? In the dramatic cases of King Lear and Oedipus, failure of self-knowledge led to *hubris* (i.e., pride), another name for narcissism. Strengths-based approaches to mental health based on adaptation run a serious risk unless conscious aging is also part of the strategy for mental wellness. Primary prevention may be too much to hope for. At its best, psychology, through the skillful practice of psychotherapy, can offer older adults a version of self-knowledge that protects against disaster or at least reduces its catastrophic impact on them and their loved ones—a kind of secondary prevention.

But psychotherapy needs to widen its understanding of theory and method to include transpersonal psychology (Cortright, 1997; Deikman, 1982). Spiritual practices promoting self-discipline and increased consciousness (e.g., meditation) are well-established methods for countering the tendency toward narcissism (Epstein, 1995). The wisdom traditions of the world constitute a vast repository available to help people navigate the struggle between loss and gain in the last stage of life.

The revival of interest in ancient wisdom traditions—for example, in so-called New Age teaching—has fueled much of the recent appeal of conscious aging. It is important here to avoid stereotypes and oversimplification: New Age thinking is heterogeneous and displays many different facets (Lewis & Melton, 1992). Some New Age teachings, such as the writings of Deepak Chopra (e.g., *Ageless Body, Timeless Mind,* Harmony Books, 1993), foster the belief that reaching new levels of higher consciousness is a way of escaping altogether from the losses of age. Expressed in this way, conscious aging would simply amount to denial of aging—a message perilously close to the appeal promised by anti-aging technologies and quack medicine.

There is a danger that conscious aging, under postmodern circumstances, might become a vehicle for denial of aging. Critics have seen in New Age thinking a tendency toward irrationalism and a weakening of the reality principle (Faber, 1996), a dangerous form of regression and narcissism. Such criticism is not new. The psychoanalytic attack on New Age mysticism in terms of infantile regression and narcissism has a long history going back to Freud's (1968) critique of religion in *The Future of an Illusion.* During the 20th century, transpersonal psychology itself has been subject to the same kind of vigorous attack (Ellis, 1989).

Criticism of narcissism is not limited to those who are hostile to transpersonal psychology. Ken Wilber, one of the leading proponents of transpersonal psychology, has been eloquent in denouncing the threat of narcissism under the guise of New Age thinking (Wilber, 1988). Narcissism need not be a concomitant of transpersonal psychology, however, nor does the pursuit of higher levels of consciousness result in self-absorption at the expense of other values, as Wilber's own work demonstrates (Wilber, 2000).

People who are interested in conscious aging should not assume any intrinsic antagonism between psychoanalytic thought and transpersonal psychology. Writing from within the psychoanalytic tradition, Epstein (1995) argued for a version of Zen Buddhist meditation that is very close to what Freudians would call the Reality Principle. Epstein himself, trained in both orthodox analysis as well as Zen meditation, describes an approach that is utterly opposed to any tendency toward denial. In a different way, Washburn has defended a formulation of transpersonal psychology compatible with psychoanalytic thought (Washburn, 1994).

It is important to continue the dialogue between psychoanalytic thought and spirituality because both have important contributions to make to a comprehensive account of human development (Young-Eisendrath & Miller, 2000). To date, the most optimistic, popular psychology of life-span development is found in Erikson and his idea of ego-integrity as the optimal outcome for late-life development. Erikson's formulation is holistic because it reflects an awareness of loss and limitation. Despite its hopefulness, Erikson continues to stress the 'Reality Principle' in a tradition dating back to Freud himself. But Erikson's ideal of ego-integrity is not the only version of the holistic path. As noted previously, the other strand of the holistic trajectory is ego-transcendence, a path described by Chinen. The danger with all varieties of transcendence is that they may become mechanisms for denial and evasion of the Reality Principle, which would make an individual employing the strategy of conscious aging ill-equipped for coping with the genuine losses of later life.

A careful reading of the world wisdom traditions—in particular, the disciplined practice of meditation in Zen, yoga, Sufism, and Christian mysticism—shows that the temptation of evasion can be overcome. Indeed, skillful and experienced practitioners of meditation and other forms of spiritual practice show the way to achieve this (Goleman, 1988). The holistic path of self-transcendence may never become as popular as the promises of a second middle age or an ageless body. Nonetheless, the wisdom traditions remind us that meditative practices can help us recognize a divine reality coexisting with the world of material objects and human lives. Wisdom traditions remind us that paths of struggle and spiritual breakthrough have a nobility and power that have attracted some of the greatest minds in both East and West. Through the strategy of conscious aging, this holistic path may exert new power as an ideal for growth in the last stage of life.

TOWARD A TRANSPERSONAL GERONTOLOGY

In recent decades, the contemporary discipline of transpersonal psychology has documented higher stages of human growth going beyond what was conventionally identified with ego development in adulthood (Tart, 1990). The agenda for the future will be to incorporate the theory and practice of transpersonal psychology into the mainstream of research and practice in gerontology, thus creating the foundations for a transpersonal gerontology in the future.

At the outset of this discussion I emphasize that conscious aging involves transcendence of goals and patterns of mid-life in favor of higher consciousness. Some of the most groundbreaking work on conscious aging, combining theory and empirical investigation, has been that of Lars Tornstam (1997) and his concept of *gero-transcendence*. Tornstam argued that later life could be a time for a new feeling of cosmic connection with the universe. This cosmic communion involves a redefinition of time, death, and the self—a view close to what traditional mysticism has urged in all cultures.

What is important in Tornstam's work is that he sees a higher level of consciousness as a natural, though not inevitable, accompaniment of older adulthood. The "naturalness" of late-life spirituality, then, is akin to Atchley's (1997) idea of "everyday mysticism" in later adulthood. In Tornstam's account, gero-transcendence is the natural result of maturity and contemplative wisdom. Tornstam also recognizes that gero-transcendence could easily be confused by social disengagement, depression, and dementia. He argued that his evidence suggested that older people with a higher degree of gero-transcendence have complex patterns of coping with later life. He claimed that those with a higher degree of gero-transcendence also have higher levels of self-initiated social engagement and a higher score on scales of life satisfaction (Tornstam, 2000).

Ken Wilber, reflecting on the achievements of transpersonal psychology, has called for a "deep science" charting higher stages of human development, and his agenda is congruent with Tornstam's (2000) concept of gero-transcendence. Wilber identified some research questions such as the following:

- What happens to brain physiology when individuals move through higher developmental stages?
- What types of worldviews are generated from higher stages of development?
- What is the relationship between age-related changes in physiological functioning and the unfolding of higher developmental stages?
- What cognitive changes, such as wisdom, are correlated with higher stages?
- What interventions—therapies, spiritual practices, older adult education opportunities, delivery of services, and so on—can best facilitate the unfolding of higher stages in later life?

RESEARCH ON WISDOM

In recent years, an important body of empirical work on wisdom has been generated by Baltes, Staudinger, Maercker, and Smith (1995), who defined wisdom as "expert knowledge about ambiguous problems of life." Baltes and his colleagues were able to document empirically one version of *wisdom cognition*. But, contrary to expectations, they failed to find strong correlation between wisdom and aging. It seems that people may become wise (in their terms) at any period of adult life. But those who reach old age have no special claim on wisdom and people cannot presume any connection between wisdom and positive development in later life (including happiness or life satisfaction).

These findings lead to an important conclusion: If the holistic strategy of conscious aging is a path toward greater wisdom, then conscious aging may not be the typical path for positive aging for most people. Conscious aging represents an option, but only one pathway, perhaps not even a typical pattern, for coping with the challenges of later life.

People do not automatically grow in consciousness or become wiser as they age. Many individuals can achieve mental wellness without becoming more conscious as they adapt to age-related losses and changes. The holistic and the adaptive pathways are both viable but different alternatives to mental wellness in later life. Individuals may combine elements of both coping styles, but they represent distinct trajectories for positive development.

Staudinger (1999) provided a valuable summary of the wisdom paradigm emerging from the work of Baltes and his colleagues. This paradigm, based on cognitive psychology of adult development, understands wisdom to be a kind of expert-level judgment in the pragmatics of living, operationalized in *wisdom-related performance*: namely, factual knowledge, procedural knowledge, life-span contextualism, value relativism, and awareness and management of uncertainty. Chronological age seems to show no particular correlation with wisdom-related knowledge.

The result of the empirical work by Baltes and colleagues (1995) is highly ambivalent. On the one hand, age brings richer experience; on the other hand, it may also bring decreases in intellectual functioning and changes in personality that undermine wisdom-related performance. There is no guarantee that extended life will ever bring hoped-for gains in wisdom unless supportive conditions serve to promote that goal. Defining what those supportive conditions might be must become part of the agenda for conscious aging.

A transpersonal gerontology approach to wisdom might take a very different approach from the one developed by Baltes and colleagues, an approach that is more comprehensive and looks at deeper aspects of the person. Some empirical investigators are already working along lines congenial to a transpersonal perspective. For example, Ardelt (2000), like Labouvie-Vief (1994), sees late-life wisdom as an inclusion of cognitive, reflective, and affective components: a much wider view than the exclusively cognitivist line developed by the Berlin group.

McKee and Barber (1999) view wisdom as "metacognition" enabling the wise person to "see through" deep and widely shared illusions. This approach to wisdom is compatible with empirical work on the operational measurement of late-life wisdom summarized in Sternberg (1990), among others. The idea of "seeing through" is also close to the idea of "unknowing" urged by many strands of mysticism in the Zen, Sufi, and Christian traditions.

NEW INSTITUTIONAL PRACTICES AND PROGRAMS

Theory alone will not drive the future of conscious aging. A variety of institutional practices that reflect the strategy of conscious aging have emerged and are likely to shape the way people think about old age in the future. New organizational settings can become arenas for research and social experimentation contributing to transpersonal gerontology.

One of the most important institutional settings is the Spiritual Eldering movement, launched in 1989 by Rabbi Zalman Schachter-Shalomi. The experience of Spiritual Eldering groups sheds light on some of the concerns about the future of conscious aging. For example, Spiritual Eldering groups around the country avoid some of the dangers of narcissism and self-absorption by emphasizing intergenerational mentoring and community service. Interest in a residential community is shared by the Elderspirit Center sponsored by the Federation of Communities in Service, as well as the Senior Spirit Program linked to the United Church of Christ (Leder, 2000).

Late-life learning is another important arena for the practice of conscious aging. One organization that promotes late-life learning and can help test and refine ideas of conscious aging is Elderhostel, a national network of collegiate programs founded in 1975. Elderhostel has now grown to become the largest educational travel organization in the world, enrolling more than a quarter of a million participants each year. Courses offered are drawn from the liberal arts tradition with a focus on personal growth and exploration rather than practical skills. Some courses are inspired by ideals of conscious aging and include topics such as Eastern mysticism, artistic creativity, holistic health care, and recovering the roots of Jewish and Christian mysticism. Closely akin to these course offerings is the practice of "guided autobiography" as developed by gero-psychologist James Birren (Birren & Feldman, 1997).

THE POWER OF THE NEGATIVE

Throughout this discussion, conscious aging is emphasized as a strategy for positive change. But individuals must never overlook what Hegel called "the tremendous power of the negative." Thus, this discussion of narcissism fuels an important conclusion: namely, emphasis on greater consciousness requires that negative elements of aging not be excluded or denied, but rather, they should be embraced. Conscious aging can be conceived as a dialectical strategy: It achieves positive growth by embracing negative life events, not repressing them. As the Sufis say, "When the heart grieves for what it has lost, the Spirit rejoices for what it has found."

Negative events of later life have corresponding positive attributes when viewed according to the wisdom traditions in skillful spiritual practice. Thus, role-loss and disengagement can become a basis for contemplative detachment; depend-

ROLE-LOSS AND disengagement can become a basis for contemplative detachment; dependency can become a basis for gratitude and receptivity.

ency can become a basis for gratitude and receptivity (Ram Dass, 2000); even the loss of self in dementia and death can become symbolic of ego-transcendence (Ewing, 1999).

These suggestions about positive attributes should not be misunderstood as literal direct equivalents: That is, loss of the self in dementia is not the same as loss of the self in higher states of consciousness. The concept of positive attribution is a way of reframing the meaning of negative life events; a reframing that could have powerful consequences for caregiving, morale, and adaptation to late-life losses. Far from being a New Age version of happy talk about old age, the strategy of conscious aging has substantial implications for how we experience negative late-life events such as disengagement, dependency, dementia, and death.

SUMMARY

Conscious aging can be defined as a strategy for approaching late life as an opportunity for increased consciousness. Instead of repressing or rejecting age, conscious aging means becoming more aware of both gains and losses in the last stage of life. This greater awareness is a matter of individual consciousness but also has implications for the critique of societal practices that limit human potential at all ages. Thus, support for conscious aging is likely to come from parallel movements such as holistic health care, progressive education, environmental advocacy, and transpersonal psychology. All emphasize a broader, more humanistic orientation in contrast to the mechanistic or instrumental approaches that have dominated mainstream gerontology.

Gerontology, until recently, took little account of developments in humanistic and transpersonal psychology or even acknowledged what Maslow called "the farther reaches of human nature." As the 21st century advances, we may hope that students of aging and of life courses will take seriously a wider sense of human possibilities.

Developing a theory and practice of conscious aging will require systematic reconstruction of gerontology to take account of elements previously excluded, and this new approach is what I have here described as transpersonal gerontology. The task of creating this new approach to aging may seem formidable, even impossible, when we consider the forces that conspire to keep individuals from looking on the world with new eyes. But recall the wonderful example of Edinger's dream about finding a log of heavy wood lying deep in the forest and wondering whether the task of carving it can be completed. The task, the dreamer suggests, is not impossible, only "nearly too difficult." So, too, with the task of reconstructing a new vision of positive aging: it is not impossible, only "nearly too difficult." In any event, it is a task not only for the next generation but also for anyone who believes that older adulthood represents our future selves.

REFERENCES

Ardelt, M. (2000, July). Antecedents and effects of wisdom in old age. *Research on Aging, 4*(22), 360–394.

Atchley, R.C. (1993). Spiritual development and wisdom: A vedantic perspective. In R. Kastenbaum (Ed.), *Encyclopedia of adult development.* Phoenix, AZ: Oryx Press.

Atchley, R.C. (1997). Everyday mysticism: Spiritual development in later adulthood. *Journal of Adult Development, 2*(4), 123–134.

Baltes, P.B., Staudinger, U.M., Maercker, A., & Smith, J. (1995, June). People nominated as wise: A comparative study of wisdom-related knowledge. *Psychology and Aging, 2*(10), 155–166.

Bianchi, E.C. (1982). *Aging as a spiritual journey.* New York: Crossroads.

Birren, J.E., & Feldman, L. (1997). *Where to go from here: Discovering your own life's wisdom in the second half of your life.* New York: Simon & Schuster.

Bouklas, G. (1997). *Psychotherapy with the elderly: Becoming Methuselah's echo.* Northvale, NJ: Jason Aronson.

Bressler, & Feiner M. (1982). Narcissism and role loss in older adults. *Journal of Geriatric Psychiatry, 1*(14), 91–109.

Butler, R.N. (1980–1981). Life review: An unrecognized bonanza. *International Journal of Aging and Human Development, 1*(12), 35–38.

Campbell, J. (Ed.) (1983). *The Portable Jury.* New York: Viking Press.

Chinen, A.B. (1986). Elder tales revisited: Forms of transcendence in later life. *Journal of Transpersonal Psychology, 2*(18), 171–192.

Chinen, A.B. (1989). *In the ever after: Fairy tales and the second half of life.* Wilmette, IL: Chiron.

Commons, M., Richards, F., & Armon, C. (Eds.). (1984). *Beyond formal operations: Late adolescent and adult cognitive development.* New York: Praeger.

Cortright, B. (1997). *Psychotherapy and spirit: Theory and practice in transpersonal psychotherapy.* Albany: State University of New York Press.

Deikman, A. (1982). *The observing self: Mysticism and psychotherapy* Boston: Beacon Press.

Edinger, E.F. (1973). *Ego and archetype.* Baltimore: Penguin.

Ellis, A. (1989). *Why some therapies don't work.* Buffalo, NY: Prometheus Books.

Epstein, M. (1995). *Thoughts without a thinker.* New York: Basic Books.

Ewing, W. (1999). *Tears in God's bottle: Reflections on Alzheimer's caregiving.* Tucson: AZ. Whitestone Circle Press.

Faber, M.D. (1996). *New Age thinking: A psychoanalytic critique.* Canada: University of Ottawa Press.

Featherstone, M., & Wernick, A. (Eds.). (1995). *Images of aging: Cultural representations of later life.* New York: Routledge.

Fowler, J. (1995). *The stages of faith: The psychology of human development and the quest for meaning.* San Francisco: HarperSanFrancisco.

Freud, S. (1968). The future of an illusion. In J. Strachey (Ed. and Trans.), *The standard edition of the complete psychological works of Sigmund Freud* (Vol. 21). London: Hogarth Press. (Original work published 1927)

Goldmeier, J., & Fandetti, D.V. (1992, April). Self psychology in clinical intervention with the elderly. *Families in Society: The Journal of Contemporary Human Services, 73*(4), 214–221.

Goleman, D. (1988). *The meditative mind: The varieties of meditative experience.* Los Angeles: Jeremy Tarcher.

Gullette, M.M. (1997). *Declining to decline.* Charlottesville: University Press of Virginia.

Hazan, H. (1996). *From first principles: An experiment in ageing,* Westport, CT: Bergin & Garvey.

Hepworth, M. (1991, October). Positive ageing and the mask of age. *Journal of Educational Gerontology, 6*(2), 93–101.

Hess, N. (1987). King Lear and some anxieties of old age. *British Journal of Medical Psychology, 60,* 209–215.

Jewell, A. (1998). *Spirituality and ageing.* London: Jessica Kingsley Publishers.

Kastenbaum, R. (1984, March). When aging begins: A lifespan developmental approach. *Research on Aging, 6*(1), 105–117.

Kastenbaum, R. (1993). Encrusted elders: Arizona and the political spirit of postmodern aging. In T. Cole, W.A. Achenbaum, P.L. Jakobi, & R. Kastenbaum (Eds.). *Voices and visions of aging: Toward a critical gerontology* (pp. 160–183). New York: Springer-Verlag.

Kegan, R. (1995). *In over our heads: The mental demands of modern life.* Cambridge, UK: Belknap Press.

Kohut, H. (1976). *The restoration of the self.* Madison, CT: International Universities Press.

Labouvie-Vief, G. (1994). *Psyche and eros: Mind and gender in the life course.* New York: Cambridge University Press.

Labouvie-Vief, G. (2000). Positive development in later life. In T.R. Cole, R. Kastenbaum, & R. Ray (Eds.), *Handbook of humanities and aging* (2nd ed., pp. 365–380). New York: Springer-Verlag.

Lasch, C. (1977). *The culture of narcissism.* New York: W.W. Norton.

Leder, D. (1996, Summer). Spiritual community in later life: A modest proposal. *Journal of Aging Studies, 10*(2), 103–116.

Leder, D. (1999–2000, Winter). Aging into the spirit: From traditional wisdom to innovative programs and communities. *Generations, 23*(4), 36–41.

Lewis, J., & Melton, G. (1992). *Perspectives on the New Age.* Albany: State University of New York Press.

Lustbader, W. (1994). *Counting on kindness.* New York: Free Press.

Maslow, A. (1971). *The farther reaches of human nature.* New York: Viking Press.

McFadden, S.H. (1985, Spring). Attributes of religious maturity in aging people. *Journal of Religion and Aging, 1*(3), 39–48.

McKee, P., & Barber, C. (1999). On defining wisdom. *International Journal of Aging and Human Development, 49*(2), 149–164.

Miller, M.E., & Cook-Greuter, S.R. (Eds.). (1994). *Transcendence and mature thought in adulthood: The further reaches of adult development.* Lanham, MD: Rowman & Littlefield.

Moody, H.R. (1995). Mysticism and aging. In M.A. Kimble, S.H. McFadden, J.W. Ellor, & J.J. Seeber (Eds.), *Aging, spirituality, and religion: A handbook.* Minneapolis, MN: Fortress Press.

Moody, H.R. (1997). *The five stages of the soul: Charting the spiritual passages that shape our lives.* New York: Doubleday Anchor Books.

Moody, H.R. (2001). Productive aging and the ideology of old age. In N. Morrow-Howell (Ed.). *Productive aging.* Baltimore: Johns Hopkins University Press.

Moss, D. (Ed.). (1999). *Humanistic and transpersonal psychology: A historical and biographical sourcebook.* Westport, CT: Greenwood Press.

Pascual-Leone, J. (1990). Reflections on life-span intelligence, consciousness, and ego development. In C.N. Alexander & E. Langer (Eds.), *Higher stages of human development.* New York: Oxford University Press.

Putnam, R. (2000). *Bowling alone: The collapse and revival of American community.* New York: Simon & Schuster.

Ram Dass (2000). *Still here: Embracing aging, changing, and dying.* New York: Riverhead Books.

Roberts, B. (1992). *The path to no-self: Life at the center.* Albany: State University of New York Press.

Rosenmayr, L. (1981). *Die Spaete Freiheit* (Late Freedom). Vienna: Severin & Siedler.

Roszak, T. (1998). *America the wise: The longevity revolution and the true wealth of nations.* Boston: Houghton Mifflin.

Rowe, J., & Kahn, R. (1998). *Successful aging.* New York: Pantheon.

Schachter, Z., & Miller, R.S. (1995). *From age-ing to sage-ing: A profound new vision of growing older.* New York: Warner Books.

Siegel, A.M., & Kohut, H. (1996). *The psychology of the self.* New York: Routledge.

Sinnott, J. (1996). Postformal thought and mysticism: How might the mind know the unknowable? *Aging and Spirituality, 8,* 7–8.

Staudinger, U.M. (1999, September). Older and wiser? Integrating results on the relationship between age and wisdom-related performance. *International Journal of Behavioral Development, 23*(3), 641–664.

Sternberg, R.J. (Ed.). (1990). *Wisdom: Its nature, origins, and development.* New York: Cambridge University Press.

Tart, C. (Ed.). (1990). *Altered states of consciousness* (3rd ed.). New York: HarperCollins.

Tornstam, L. (1997, Summer). Gero-transcendence: The contemplative dimension of aging. *Journal of Aging Studies, 11*(2), 143–154.

Tornstam, L. (1999–2000, Winter). Transcendence in later life. *Generations, 23*(4), 10–14.

Walsh, R., & Vaughan, F. (Eds.). (1993). *Paths beyond ego: The transpersonal vision.* Los Angeles: Jeremy Tarcher.

Washburn, M. (1994). *Transpersonal psychology in psychoanalytic perspective.* Albany: State University of New York Press.

Wilber, K. (1988, July/August). Baby boomers, narcissism, and the New Age. *Yoga Journal, 46–50.*

Wilber, K. (2000). *Integral psychology: Consciousness, spirit, psychology, therapy.* Boston: Shambhala Publications.

Williams, B. (1981). *Moral luck.* Cambridge, UK: Cambridge University Press.

Wink, P. (1992, March). Three types of narcissism in women from college to mid-life. *Journal of Personality, 60*(1), 7–30.

Woodward, K. (1986). Reminiscence and the life review: Prospects and retrospects. In T.R. Cole & S. Gadow (Eds.), *What does it mean to grow old? Reflections from the humanities* (pp. 135–161). Durham, NC: Duke University Press.

Woodward, K. (1991). *Aging and its discontents: Freud and other fictions.* Bloomington: Indiana University Press.

Young-Eisendrath, P., & Miller, M. (Eds.) (2000). *The psychology of mature spirituality.* London: Brunner-Routledge.

8

CHANGING INSTITUTIONAL CULTURE
Can We Re-value the Nursing Home?

Judah L. Ronch

CONTEMPORARY ADVOCATES for nursing home reform (Fagan, Williams, & Burger, 1997) contend that quality of life for nursing home residents will improve only when their lives are more like life in the world outside the facility. These voices have built on the message of earlier advocates moved by the long history of de-humanization that traditionally characterized the life of people living in old age homes and similar institutions (Bowker, 1982; Goffman, 1961; Gubrium, 1975; Henry, 1963). Since the 1960s, however, little has been achieved in the continuing fight to change the culture of care in nursing homes.

Bowker's (1982) work *Humanizing Institutions for the Aged* still offers one of the most useful overviews of the problem and contains some of the most comprehensive recommendations for reform. His analysis and common-sense suggestions for institutional change, some of which eventually became widely accepted standards of quality care, appear in retrospect to have been both self-evident and non-controversial. Yet most of his ideas for humanization, especially those that treat the residents and care providers as equals in an "I-thou" relationship (i.e., in which each person is valued because of his or her humanity) (Buber, 1970), are absent in most institutions and in the regulations that govern them.

Goffman first detailed the essence of dehumanization in his classic *Asylums* (1963). What he termed the *total institution* is an environment in which life goes on in one place, during scheduled intervals of time developed by administrators.

161

People who live in total institutions, he observed, eat, sleep, and socialize at the same time, on a permanent 24-hour basis, with groups of other residents according to a schedule developed and imposed by institutional authority. Rationally organized activities in these environments meet the goals of the institution, rather than the needs of the residents. Unless the behavior of the caregiver is questioned or the residents violate the rules, the underlying social rationale and cultural rules operate covertly. If and when residents attempt to display signs of individuality, their attempts are treated as deviant and are usually met with a range of negative sanctions. At the least, the offending resident is labeled a *problem,* and all subsequent behavior likely will be seen in a context of *problem behavior.* Staff–resident relationships in total institutions are caste-like, which implies "considerable social distance between the two groups as well as reciprocal negative stereotypes" (Bowker, 1982, p. 4).

> THE PCM FURTHER identified ways that institutional totality and the medical model together can accelerate the process of rapid deterioration commonly found among nursing home residents, a status previously considered to be a function of aging and chronic illness per se.

Bennett (1963) described institutional totality as existing on a continuum of environmental severity rather than as a dichotomous variable. Her findings provided a valuable dimension by which to assess the degree and location of institutional control of residents' lives, with "totality" at one pole and "humanization" at the other. Nicholson's (1979) *Personalized Care Model* (PCM) was a comprehensive and pragmatic effort to move institutions toward greater humanization. It was one of the first systematic programs for institutional change to specify the necessary role transitions that staff would have to undergo if nursing facilities for the older adult were to care for the whole person. Her proposed changes in the relationships between care providers and recipients required a departure from the medical model of acute care. The PCM further identified ways that institutional totality and the medical model together can accelerate the process of rapid deterioration commonly found among nursing home residents, a status previously considered to be a function of aging and chronic illness per se.

ACHIEVING GREATER HUMANIZATION

Bowker's (1982) quintessential advice about how to achieve greater levels of humanization, though deceptively simple, remains a stubbornly elusive goal for most nursing homes. Institutions, he suggested, must focus on the needs of individuals rather than on cost-effective service delivery to a class of people. This requires that the *how* of care (e.g., quality, personalization) must have priority over the *what* of care (e.g., speed at which tasks are completed, adherence to schedules). The *how* of care directs attention to-

> THE *HOW* OF CARE directs attention toward the relationship of those who participate in the act of care (i.e., provider and recipient) and how cultural norms that define their participation affect them.

ward the relationship of those who participate in the act of care (i.e., provider and recipient) and how cultural norms that define their participation affect them.

Dr. Alvin Goldfarb, one of the founding fathers of geriatric psychiatry, advised, "Take care of the staff and you'll solve more than 50% of the residents' problems." Usually, administrators see staff concerns as a secondary issue. Staff concerns are typically (and incorrectly) viewed as being at odds with the concerns of residents when institutions consider changes in the *how* of care. An institution that seeks to humanize its environment must consider the needs of the care provider as equally important with the needs of residents.

CULTURE: FAMILY VERSUS CAREGIVER

Thomas Kitwood, the late British social psychologist who pioneered the systematic development of person-centered dementia care, defined culture as "a settled, patterned way of giving meaning to human existence in the world, and of giving structure to action within it." He detailed three components of culture that are relevant here:

1. Institutions through which social power is clearly allocated: families, houses of worship, institutions of education, systems of justice, government, and health care facilities

2. Norms: Standards for behavior within institutions (They show individuals what behavior is acceptable, draw praise or other reward, and elicit criticism or punishment.)

3. Beliefs that define the nature of what *is* and what *ought to be* (undated, pp. 1–2)

A culture's power resides in the immersion of people in the norms, institutions, and beliefs that create it and the meanings that it gives to their behavior. Culture's influence on people's behavior seems like it should be self-evident to everyone, yet it remains invisible until an outsider observes it in reference to his or her own culture. Moreover, Kitwood claimed that institutions develop organically and through people's social interactions they establish ways of demonstrating power and control first. Only then are beliefs formally articulated or codified into rules to create "facts" that fit the environment (i.e., that show "this is the way things are done"). Putting it another way, the purpose of institutions is to perpetuate their existence, and the cultures they establish are *operating systems* at the heart of their attempts at perpetuity.

An example of the powerful effect of culture on those immersed in it can be seen in the struggles between families and nursing home personnel over whose view of the resident shall prevail during the admission process when initial assessments are completed, or in the battle over whose cultural values will guide care practices when a person en-

> A CULTURE'S POWER resides in the immersion of people in the norms, institutions, and beliefs that create it and the meanings that it gives to their behavior. Culture's influence on people's behavior seems like it should be self-evident to everyone, yet it remains invisible until an outsider observes it in reference to his or her own culture.

ters the acute medical setting (Levine & Zuckerman, 1999). The tendency to demonize the family, and label as *dysfunctional* the family members who strive to bring a family culture into the health care setting, is almost universal but not addressed.

The movement to humanize institutions and enhance the quality of life for residents with dementia in nursing homes has perhaps been the most potent catalyst for accelerating the pace of nursing home reform. Because of a resident with dementia's inability to negotiate the covert rules of institutions, he or she becomes *a problem.* In health care professionals' attempts to alleviate residents' distress, the residents have functioned as the proverbial canaries in the coal mine who alert observers to the toxic, dehumanizing, and "malignant" (Kitwood, 1997) aspects of the nursing home environment.

CONTEMPORARY INSTITUTIONAL CULTURE

The fact that long-term care institutions in the 21st century have remained largely unchanged since the 1960s, when calls for reform began is a sad commentary on the way people in the United States view aging, the chronically ill, and the very old (Bowker, 1982; Goffman, 1961; Henry, 1963; Stannard, 1973; U.S. Senate, 1975; Vladek, 1980). Though many of the dehumanizing conditions and systematic failures have been partially addressed in some nursing facilities and by some regulators, contemporary replays of nursing home horror stories remind health care professionals that no matter how they try to shine up the current model of long-term care, it is fatally flawed and ultimately unacceptable to a society that is increasingly sensitive regarding gerontological issues.

A major barrier to cultural change in nursing homes is that the acute care medical model constitutes the defining core of the philosophical and operational blueprint of nursing home care. A historical perspective of the lineage of the nursing home—from poorhouses to old age homes (descendants of the almshouses of colonial times) to homes for "incurables," reveals a foundation that was not designed to support humanization. As poorhouses evolved into contemporary nursing facilities and regulations became the responsibility of the government, they focused on medical care of residents, even though many of these individuals had chronic, not acute, illnesses that brought about functional impairment and the need for nonmedical help. Homes for the aged maintained fewer humanistic, homelike characteristics as they adopted a greater number of practices characteristic of the acute care environment (Cohen & Eisendorfer, 2001). Rosenberg (1995) noted that the hierarchic, paternalistic culture of care in hospitals for the acutely ill originally aimed to contain infection and illness and protect the upper classes from both, hence the need for all of the rigid rules, regulations, and procedures that serve the professionals' needs. The culture created by an acute care hospital, even now, is acceptable to patients of all classes, in part based on their understanding that the hospital stay is for a short period of time, after which they will return to their home and community and resume usual habits, status, and other cultural markers of familiar modes of daily living.

Although hospitalized, individuals temporarily surrender their autonomy and status indicators (e.g., clothing, personal effects, privacy, control over one's daily social contacts) while they receive care, with the understanding that these will be returned after the duration of their hospital stay; they do not have to surrender their personhood forever. Ironically, most long-term care facilities operating according to the culture of the medical model still require the surrender of most of these aspects of life outside the institution, but the resident rarely gets them back. These items are viewed as unnecessary for good long-term care. To the individual, what had once been temporary and necessary for a brief period of time becomes permanent.

According to Bowker (1982), the acute care medical model is the very antithesis of humanization in its patriarchal/hierarchical organization, its orientation toward treating clinical problems rather than treating people as individuals, and its impositional model of care. The acute medical model approach considers staff to be experts in the treatment of illness and views people as *patients,* not participants in their own care. Nursing homes to this day are characterized by an 18th-century industrial model of management and service delivery in which a hierarchically organized group of employees are accountable to a small group of middle managers (department heads) for the efficient delivery of a requisite number of care procedures per unit of time (usually referred to colloquially as "cares"; e.g., bathing, dressing, toileting).

This model views aging, chronic illness, and functional dependency as being passively experienced conditions. It subordinates the experience of the individual who is aging and the younger person with a chronic medical condition to care practices organized around institutional needs, and treats individual preferences about care that arise from these experiences as "noise," or as barriers to efficiency. Such a system is predicated on ageist stereotypes of group homogeneity and loss of individuality with advancing years, but more critically, the system and its processes are essentially mismatched to the myriad day-to-day, nonmedical, quality-of-life concerns and the years-long length of stay common to most nursing home residents.

This antiquated system has survived in part because the state and federal regulators that monitor and reimburse long-term care providers have not stimulated adequate reform in any systematic way or adequately championed and supported efforts at true paradigm change. Regulators, and the political system to which they are accountable, are more comfortable with quantifiable indicators about the impact of care, and data that fit and reflect the processes of care essentially in the more medical and biological domains (see BASICS on page 167 for an example). Until an acceptable data set is developed that captures and quantifies the impact of qualitative changes in institutional culture and how they affect quality of life, the tenacious hold of the acute medical care model will remain. Meanwhile, the public is largely unaware of this sequestered population, possibly because it represents what they fear will become of them if they live long enough. Issues of nursing home care can be overlooked until a personal encounter with a nursing home breaks through the denial and arouses strong emotions—but, typically, inadequate responses for true reform.

Factors that prevent or subordinate humanization for nursing home residents affect staff who care for them as well. Just as treatment for residents is chosen from

HUMANIZATION CAN occur only when caregiver–recipient relationships define the quality of care. Simply stated, an *I–thou* relationship is a significant source of clinical benefit for the resident and a significant source of job satisfaction for the employee because it considers the needs, concerns, and characteristics of the care recipient as well as the caregiver to be the foundation of a mutually enriching relationship.

a fixed repertoire of procedures that the facility has to offer, staff are likewise treated as interchangeable parts in an impersonal process of turning out a quota of care procedures on each shift. Individual caregiver characteristics are seen as extraneous to the resident's experience of the quality of care. In Bowker's (1982) sense, the state of equality is the balance point for humanization and thus the point of leverage for culture change. Humanization can occur only when caregiver–recipient relationships define the quality of care. Simply stated, an *I–thou* relationship is a significant source of clinical benefit for the resident and a significant source of job satisfaction for the employee because it considers the needs, concerns, and characteristics of the care recipient as well as the caregiver to be the foundation of a mutually enriching relationship.

The changing demographic and psychographic (i.e., how people think of themselves, e.g., "informed," "with it," "preferring only the best") nature of the current and future aging cohorts, not regulators, is driving the development of innovative residential models for the aging (e.g., assisted living, board-and-care homes, other congregate settings) that are less like the acute care medical model. In this consumerist age, the value of the *brand* of care a nursing home provides will be seen in the relationships it creates and perpetuates with consumers. Baby boomers are especially instrumental in driving this change by virtue of what they say and as a result of how the long-term care industry perceives them. Older adult long-term care residents and their children who are their advocates will not be content with industrial-age notions for their long-term care (i.e., the worker is responsible to management and the management is responsible to the regulators for the quality of their work). Long-term care workers will demand to work in an environment in which they may achieve greater personal satisfaction in addition to more equitable reimbursement.

INTERDISCIPLINARY CARE

Since the mid-1970s, the term *interdisciplinary care team* has become the description preferred by nursing facility providers to describe their model of care. It is unfortunate that a truly interdisciplinary model—a collaborative, holistic approach among colleagues in which all participants' knowledge is respected and valued equally—has not yet been fully developed in many facilities. Rather, a multidisciplinary one—without the integration of knowledge forming a whole picture of the resident—prevails.

Nursing facilities remain largely organized, staffed, regulated, and reimbursed according to the acute medical model of care, a system that values and rewards curing illness, and, therefore, those who possess the most advanced medical knowledge and can deliver the cure. This model is a poor fit with the nature of the nursing home population, which typically includes residents with multiple, chronic health problems, functional dependency, and complex psychosocial needs rather than acute illnesses. Because the medical model relies on a hierarchic, *top down* management structure, it concentrates the power to make the most critical decisions about residents' lives at its apex. The departments responsible for treating physical illnesses and caring for biological and activities of daily living needs have the highest priority with regard to institutional resource allocation and represent the greatest power block with whom the facility administration must align. Despite the advent of supposed *interdisciplinary* models of care that are designed to integrate the needs of each resident holistically, the traditional, hierarchic distribution of power and influence on the lives of residents characteristic of the acute medical care model, and its artificial segmentation of people's needs according to the institution's organizational model, is maintained.

THE BASICS APPROACH

One way to determine whether a facility is using a holistic, interdisciplinary model is to contrast the needs of the whole person with how the organization of the nursing home meets the needs of residents at various levels through the BASICS model (Ronch, 1987; Vickers, 1975). Built on Maslow's (1962) original hierarchy of needs model and the PCM (Nicholson, 1979), the BASICS hierarchy demonstrates one way of conceptualizing the range of human needs and how those needs relate to each other. BASICS is a biopsychosocial model of needs arranged hierarchically in ascending order of how needs are satisfied in succession, that is, from the most essentially life sustaining to the higher order domains that give life its meaning (Maslow, 1962). The levels of the BASICS are

- *Biological:* The need for food, water, oxygen, safety, shelter, rest, and human stimulation
- *Activities of daily living (ADLs):* Access to the resources to meet personal concerns (e.g., eating, mobility, dressing, toileting, personal hygiene) that support lifestyle and optimal self-dependence
- *Societal:* Preserving one's unique personal identity in society (e.g., as in a congregate setting) through opportunities for privacy, choice of groups, cultural expression, family, choice of association, and celebration of uniqueness, among others
- *Interpersonal:* Belonging and connectedness to others while building self-esteem through social role expressions, support of interpersonal and social skills, and living in an atmosphere in which one is cared about and cares about others
- *Creative:* Being able to act independently to achieve personal expression, humor, creativity, and decision-making and problem-solving skills in ways that bring a "spark of life" to the person's eyes
- *Symbolic:* Living with hope and self-fulfillment according to the spiritual and religious beliefs one holds and achieving through them a sense of peace and oneness with the universe

The greatest shares of resources in nursing homes are devoted to both the biological and the ADL levels of need. There are far fewer staff available to satisfy resident needs at higher levels: social workers, activity specialists, clergy, and the like. This is especially problematic because a quality nursing home will satisfy the more essential biological and ADL needs and, in the process, prepare residents to satisfy their intrinsic demand for need satisfaction at higher levels.

Evolving out of the philosophy of the acute medical hospital model, traditional long-term care nursing homes assign staff various tasks based on systems of organization that are in line with regulatory standards. This model creates a layering of discrete departments (silos) that are primarily and singularly responsible for satisfying one level of need. Treatment of the resident is by a management system based on a silo model, as if the resident were a collection of separate and disconnected concerns. Through its organization and staffing, the traditional long-term care facility creates a traditional culture of nursing home care that communicates what it values and how it ascribes meaning to the various aspects of residents' lives. What is lost in the process is how these needs are interrelated in each human being and how they have traditionally been satisfied in each resident throughout his or her life. To the degree that this integration is incomplete, "interdisciplinary care" is an illusion.

Culture change is difficult for an organization and its employees, and indeed counterintuitive, when old role relationships are reinforced and standards of care are tied to an acute care medical model that is neither holistic nor person-centered. Multidisciplinary care may be possible, but true interdisciplinary relationships are difficult to achieve under the current conditions of hierarchical organization and the biomedical approach favored by regulations. The supposed "interdisciplinary" care models presently being tried have not been able to rectify problems of fragmented care approaches precisely because the systems that are in place to provide care perpetuate the original hierarchic system that is not functionally interdisciplinary.

The dilemma faced by long-term care facilities can be appreciated by using the BASICS model. How can they adequately promote the societal, interpersonal, creative, and symbolic needs of residents and satisfy these needs despite the low ratio of social workers, recreational specialists, and other trained caregivers who possess the skills to help meet these needs?

Interdisciplinary care is merely a goal for the future of long-term care unless an individual's higher levels of need are given adequate resources and the whole person's needs are met. Care plans that are truly interdisciplinary in nature are the best hope of meeting all of a resident's needs (such as are illustrated in BASICS), but they are written *pro forma* if there are inadequate resources and decision-making power available to meet these needs specifically and individually across the aggregate resident population.

The Dangers of Failing to Meet Needs

By focusing staff attention on how quickly they complete their tasks rather than on the preferred I–thou relationships they form with residents, the traditional nursing home culture devalues the personal attributes of the people providing the care as well as the residents and deprives residents of essential emotional nurturing. A telling parallel exists between the "failure to thrive" among residents seen in many nursing homes, and the anaclitic depression (Spitz, 1946) (i.e., a behavioral syndrome characterized by weepiness, apprehension, sleep disturbances, and refusal to eat) seen in infants and toddlers in orphanages in which the children received only physical care without adequate interaction with caregivers. The acute medical model as transposed into the nursing home fails to provide adequate personnel and fiscal resources to meet higher order needs of all residents and deprives staff of opportunities to have their needs and concerns met as well. In this model, when care is sub-optimal, everybody loses.

THE RE-VALUED CULTURE

Cultural re-valuation suggests that if nursing homes changed their cultures of care from a medical model to a humanizing, holistic one, they could initiate a process of increasing their value or perceived worth in the eyes of society and, in turn, increase the status of those who live and work there. The humanistic culture of care would operate around a different cluster of interpersonal, regulatory, and organizational values and produce greater levels of resident, family, and staff satisfaction.

SOCIETAL VIEWS OF NURSING HOMES: THE CULTURE OF CHRONICITY

Perhaps the greatest source of de-valuing the nursing home, and those in it, is what Kleinman (1988) called "the *culture of chronicity*." Society sees older adults, especially those in institutions, as somehow different, apart from, and less than the rest of the human race. "Ageism" (Butler, 1975) and "gerontophobia" (Comfort, 1977) are two of the terms used to describe bigoted and hostile views of aging people held by many in our productivity-oriented society, views that produce and justify physical and psychological distancing between younger people ("us") and older adults ("them"). By casting aging solely as a chronic condition, a society supports a belief system that implies that nothing can be done to improve the lives of people as they age; aging is viewed as the unfolding of nature's destructive processes at the end of life.

> SOCIETY SEES OLDER adults, especially those in institutions, as somehow different, apart from, and less than the rest of the human race.

This view of aging people permits an undetected rationalization for being sparse with the resources allocated to quality aging and allows people to feel ethically satisfied in caring for the biological and ADL aspects of life while ignoring the other levels of concern (e.g., the BASICS). It appears that societies who do not value the humanization of the older adult believe that resources needed to optimize quality of life and support individual identity for older adults—especially nursing home residents—do not matter that much, if at all.

Myths about aging collude well with the values of the culture of chronicity to create a system of negative expectations and self-fulfilling prophecies, which blame the older adult victims and disempower their caregivers. "Patients," wrote Kleinman, "learn to act as chronic cases; families and caregivers learn to treat patients in keeping with this view. . . .We place complex individuals in simple one-dimensional roles (the old, the disabled, the terminally ill) as if this were all they are and can be" (1988, p. 180). Nursing home culture is both victim and creator of this view of its residents. By treating aging as a chronic condition and reinforcing this account of the residents' conditions, society justifies models of dependency-oriented and safety-need–based caring (Maslow, 1998). People remain insensitive to residents' normal attempts at psychosocial mastery and to their natural developmental imperatives to retain a strong sense of identity and growth as human beings.

The paid care provider, especially the certified nursing assistant, suffers in a similar manner in the culture of chronicity because he or she is taught to be—and comes to see herself or himself as—an observer of the inevitable deterioration that the chronicity model defines as normal. The care provider is trained primarily to provide care procedures; any natural skills in forming relationships are secondary to task efficiency. The worker learns to leave at the institution's door any legitimate need for personal agency and creativity that could contribute to quality of care. In all probability, these are the same skills he or she may need with family and friends. Thus, care providers are at risk of becoming demoralized and devalued as they come to see themselves as unable to intervene or to do anything to reverse the assumed cause—age—of everything the older adult resident does.

Revisiting the *total institution* idea, health care providers may now understand how the daily routines and allocations of resources in nursing homes align with and support the chronicity model. Our society seems to accept the suboptimal environment and the culture of chronicity, viewing people within nursing homes—residents and staff—as being less valuable than people in the extra-institutional world. One possible basis for this mind-set is that at some level people believe that the larger mandate of "honor thy mother and thy father" is in conflict with the concept of institutionalization, and that institutionalization of family members is seen by people in general as a social failure whose perpetrators deserve second-class treatment. The "social failing" model used to rationalize a view of people in institutions for the elderly as less entitled to being treated as "whole" human beings recalls those instances in our history when medical or mental health diagnoses were used to rationalize the tolerance of poor treatment (Wolfensberger, 1985), and as a "scientific" basis for punishing political dissidents and justifying punishment of resistors (Comas-Diaz, 2000).

A new paradigm of care is required, one in which the institutional culture humanizes residents and staff by eliminating their competition over satisfying safety and other lower needs and thereby preventing the conditions for self-actualization. By departing from norms of institutional totality and the nihilism of the chronicity model, health care professionals should be able to create a culture of care within which the mutual and complementary needs of resident and staff are synergized and the quality of life for the aging *and* their care providers is optimized.

CREATING THE RE-VALUED CULTURE

As in any setting, cultural change is a long, ongoing process in nursing homes and requires a great deal of planning and constant self-evaluation by institutional leadership. Contributions in management and business literature (Kotter, 1996) pointed out how difficult a struggle culture change could be even when a determined leader is committed to change. The issues in health care are somewhat more complicated because the interplay of regulation, the rapidly changing health care delivery environment, and correlated reimbursement practices add uncertainty to culture change initiatives. Culture change in health care and the values conflict between stakeholders (e.g., individuals, families, providers, unions, insurers, government, and professional interests) are other confounders that necessitate innovative models of person-centered, collaborative care in nursing homes.

CULTURAL CHANGE

Changes toward humanizing the culture of the nursing home environment have already begun at the better and more enlightened homes, such as those participating in the Pioneer movement (Fagan et al., 1997). Their leaders have realized the ethical, economic, and demographic impetus for culture change. The essence of leadership in the current culture-change movement (Weiner & Ronch, in press) is to adopt and advocate convincingly for a humanistic view of how people, residents, staff, and family should be treated in a nursing home. The essential process of humanizing institutions for the aged involves going beyond traditional approaches of task-based care in order to help co-workers and residents satisfy their higher order, altruistic motivations. Humanization of long-term care cannot happen if residents and care providers are competing for resources to satisfy more essential, defensive needs in an environment in which both groups experience a scarcity of resources. For the residents, this lack of resources involves losing their usual access to the people, places, and things they desire and the freedom to pursue their personal goals that supported self-identity before institutionalization. The prevailing degree of institutional totality (Bennett, 1963) will determine residents' specific experiences in this regard. For staff, scarce resources are manifested in relatively low wages, difficult working conditions, and risk of injury from residents with cognitive impairments, or from heavy lifting and other physically taxing work.

Ryden and Feldt (1992), when writing about caring for nursing home residents with dementia who are aggressive, proposed six goals for caregivers to achieve in order to reduce or eliminate difficult behaviors. These goals have since been adapted to reflect the parallel goals of care recipients and care providers across the board in the same situation (Bradley, Ronch, & Pohlmann, 1999) and reflect one approach to identifying "win-win" aspects of humanized culture. Building on this research, I posit that in every aspect of their lives in the nursing home, residents and staff each want to

1. Feel safe
2. Feel physically comfortable
3. Experience a sense of control
4. Feel valued as a person
5. Experience optimal stimulation
6. Experience pleasure

When residents and staff are engaged in relationships that provide a context for needed care and when autonomy is supported through appropriate guidance, then these six goals are attainable. As these mutual needs and goals of resident and caregiver are explained to staff, their relationship with residents can be redefined. Performing tasks or doing care procedures is replaced by establishing and building relationships among people in the I–thou framework discussed by Buber (1970). Furthermore, each participant can be at his or her best and feel positive about his or her role without having to struggle for who will be in the subordinate position. Conversations with co-workers about what they have in common with residents as human beings allow them to reconnect with the altruistic aspects of why they continue to work in the health care field and can increase humanization of the culture of care by simultaneously reinforcing these needs of both the caregiver and residents. Howard (1978) proposed that caregivers and residents each have a need for

- Inherent worth (as a person regardless of role)
- Irreplaceability (uniqueness and nonstereotyped view of each)
- Holistic self (each is more than the sum of their problems or job tasks)
- Freedom of action (forcing either participant to engage with the other against their will is dehumanizing)
- Status equality (the I–thou basis of the relationship despite role differences)
- Shared decision making and responsibility (each has the duty to participate in the decisions about how care can best be accomplished)
- Empathy (the ability to sympathize and identify with each other)
- Positive affects (conveying emotion with reciprocity and empathy)

The culture change leaders in a nursing home may also identify and support staff who interact with residents and demonstrate humanizing qualities. This involves recognizing care providers who abandon the medical model tradition with its status distinctions, lack of reciprocity, and inadequate communication of caring feelings (Bowker, 1982) and celebrating the *positive deviants* (insightful problem solvers), a minority among staff who solve problems with existing resources in ways that the majority of staff do not while affirming both the value of residents as people and of themselves (Sternin & Choo, 2000). The act of celebrating staff who—by their everyday behavior and attitudes embody the values of the humanized culture of care—has been found to be a powerful way of setting the process of change in motion. This practice has been found to be even more effective than importing best practices. People immersed in a culture respond better to peers as exemplars of better ways to do things once the success of the positive deviants has been pointed out and their approach to successful problem solving has been shared with others. In addition, it is difficult to import "best practices" with any success unless the workers who created those best practices are hired to become the enterprise's work force.

Culture change is built by developing a *community of practice* in which *know how* (learning how to behave according to humanistic values and knowing what these values are) replaces *know that* (knowing what they are) (Bruner, as cited in Brown & Duguid, 2000; Ryle, 1949). By highlighting the work of those staff who are the insightful problem solvers (positive deviants who see exceptions to the generally accepted ways a group does things), the nursing home can set the stage for communities of practice to develop along the lines of cultural change they prefer. Lessons from other industries illustrate how communities of practice arise and how the process of analyzing individual differences among service recipients — whether humans or, in the case described below, machines — generates spontaneous and innovative problem solving processes among staff (Orr, 1996).

> PEOPLE IMMERSED IN A culture respond better to peers as exemplars of better ways to do things once the success of the positive deviants has been pointed out and their approach to successful problem solving has been shared with others.

CULTURAL ADAPTATIONS

Orr described three adaptations developed by service personnel at Xerox who, without administrative mandates, overcame serious quality problems in a process that was highly procedure driven. Because of the similarity to nursing home protocol and the typical policy- and procedure-driven approaches to care found in nursing homes, these adaptations merit serious consideration as elementary mechanisms that would support nascent efforts at culture change, especially because positive deviants are undoubtedly at work in most, if not all, nursing homes.

COLLABORATION The first of these factors was collaboration. Staff pooled their knowledge on their own time and created an *inventory of solutions* from which they all could draw when unsure about how to proceed with a problem. Though there may be formal occasions in nursing homes in which staff collaboratively problem solve (in-services, care planning meetings, and case reviews), the informal chats at lunch, on breaks, and in the hallways among staff and between staff and relatives are when staff do most of their creative problem solving. Because it is not the practice in many nursing homes to have nursing assistants at care planning meetings, collaboration is the best way to highlight what works to provide care in line with the new culture and to institutionalize the innovations supportive of the new culture generated through the collaboration channel. Collaboration is easy to promote, probably already in place on an informal basis as staff converse during their workday, and recognizes instances of *positive deviancy* that demonstrate the actual know how of co-workers when they provide humanistic care.

STORYTELLING The second activity is narration—telling stories informally about problems and solutions, successes, and failures, as staff members interact with each other throughout the day. Because stories have a linear structure (beginning, middle, and end), they help people understand what happened and give coherence to separate items of information (Brown & Duguid, 2000). They create and convey principles of practice that bind the community of practitioners together. Stories are essential and universal cultural devices used by people throughout the world to communicate cultural values and meaning without formal teaching. They operate in the same fashion in nursing homes to embody and spread the culture of care to new arrivals.

> STORIES ARE ESSENTIAL and universal cultural devices used by people throughout the world to communicate cultural values and meaning without formal teaching. They operate in the same fashion in nursing homes to embody and spread the culture of care to new arrivals.

A story that is told and retold, such as one that demonstrates a situation in which successful care or care that met a particular resident's needs through staff creativity, is a powerful yet informal way to spread the desired aspects of the new culture to co-workers and newly hired staff. The stories are at their most powerful when residents and staff tell how care was given in line with the new culture, or when accounts of the residents' past or current behavior illustrate autonomy and coping skills. When management celebrates such stories, they acknowledge the staff's self-actualizing behavior consistent with the new culture. Stories in which the resident is able, heroic, wise, triumphant, or creative dispel ageist myths about older residents and help staff focus on resident attributes other than frailty, dependency, medical diagnoses, and care needs.

IMPROVISATION The third activity is *improvisation,* or what people do to fill the gaps between the real world of work in which they are immersed and the codified, formalized routines of the workplace (Remember the fictional worlds represented in *Catch-22* by Joseph Heller and *M*A*S*H* by Ron Hornberger?) This activity constantly takes place without the supervisor's formal approval or actual awareness as the practitioner goes about his or her work and improvises, creating solutions to everyday practicalities that the rules do not take into account. Such "practical subversion" (Suchman, 1996) is how workers find ways to get around the rigid and dysfunctional barriers that many rules impose and that nobody really follows anyway—often because supervisors realize that improvisation is a necessary way to get work done despite formal policies. These creative responses are needed if individualized, humanistic care is to be given in nursing home cultures in which the tightly regulated and rigidly paternalistic medical model holds sway. Improvisation may lead to innovations in nursing home care when hands-on staff and the families, who know the most about a person's historical preferences, develop creative modes of problem solving together. Policy and practice can be adapted to reflect the innovative culture-change care approaches that are developed. As the rules that supported the old culture become obsolete, they can be modified to support the new culture and its values.

These three activities help promote a community of practice in which *know that* is replaced by *know how.* This is an essential step for achieving a culture that is both effective and efficient in meeting the needs of whole people, be they residents or workers, and of creating conditions within the new culture that support achieving the humanizing needs and shared personal goals discussed above.

LIFE-SPAN DEVELOPMENT

A final paradigm shift is needed if the values outlined above are to be realized through the activities just cited. The shift involves abandoning the chronicity model of geriatric care and replacing it with the *life-span developmental framework* of older adult individuals (Baltes & Baltes, 1993).

Although most nursing home care workers are unlikely to think much about which (if any) model they use as they try to do the best job they can, embedded in how they think about older people is a mental model of how they understand and explain the aging experience. Models are the frames of reference or predominant views through which people structure and interpret their experiences and interactions with the older adult. Models form the basis for what people think is normal, desirable, and even possible, as they try to be helpful to older adults. Most important, models determine what people feel called on to do for and with older adults and how they view their jobs, and create the standards of successful behavior for themselves. Models create expectations in our minds of our work with residents and with our co-workers and further determine which resources will be devoted to residents in attempts to be cost effective, clinically adept, and successful. Models guide the way people go about their business. Unexamined or tacit models tend to remain unchanged, and as the world changes, tacit models become increasingly unproductive (Senge, 1994).

Models of aging run the gamut from the medically influenced "aging as catastrophe" view of the older adult as incapable of new growth (Gutmann, 1994) to the more optimistic, positive views of aging as a period of growth and continued development (Baltes & Reese, 1984). In previous work, Ronch and Crispi (1997) advocated for the value of the life-span developmental approach as a model from which to help nursing home residents integrate the reality of nursing home placement into their developmental narrative (Marshall, 1986), or life story, to achieve improved mental health. By understanding that the individual's characteristics (e.g., personality traits, preferences, culture, demographics, history, how he or she experiences his or her health/illness status), the cultural characteristics of the nursing home (policies, procedures, rules, economic stability, staffing patterns, location, auspices), and the characteristics of the staff as individuals and as an aggregate (personalities, attitudes about aging and the residents, goals, personal values, culture and history) all interact to influence and be influenced by each other (Lerner, 1989), individuals can begin to appreciate the dynamic properties of the nursing home environment. All of these variables affect the wellbeing of the residents and staff, and in turn, determine their quality of life.

If the staff and the institutional culture in which they are embedded view aging according to the chronicity model (Kleinman, 1988), then both residents and staff suffer the demoralization that comes from characterizing and attending to deterioration, respectively. Opportunities for growth and continued development are denied in such environments because they are deemed unimportant and without the potential to add value or increase the success of the institution or its inhabitants. The chronicity model's most damaging influence arises from the stereotyped way it explains the behaviors of older people and attributes their behaviors to agedness and its supposed inevitable physical, mental, and other infirmities. The result of such views is that because everything is seen as resulting from aging per se, and is entirely rooted in pathology, there is nothing to be done but to be the custodian of deterioration in all its (often peculiar and/or endearing) manifestations. It is important to reiterate that in the chronicity model, staff are as de-valued as the residents. Contrary to the life-span developmental model, neither is viewed as having the need or opportunity for personal growth, a view that prevents self-respect and self-actualization from being achieved in hierarchic organizations.

The nursing home industry, like other parts of the health care sector, has evolved within a culture of care that has remained remarkably homogeneous, and therein may lie one of its major problems. Because close-knit industries such as nursing homes are especially vulnerable to relying on internal, consensual mental models or "best practices" (Senge, 1994) presented at professional conferences where providers essentially talk only to each other, nursing institutions are especially vulnerable to maintaining approaches that lead to counterproductive actions and a widening of the gap between the mental models of the insiders and market realities.

CONCLUSION

Changes in views on aging and the older adult and of the cultural context of illness (Morris, 2000) predict a move toward understanding aging as a time of active mastery (see Chapter 7). Older adults will increasingly be viewed as separate from their infirmities as the biomedical model and its emphasis on cure is increasingly influenced by postmodern concepts of wellness and nonscientific models of healing (Morris, 2000). The ultimate goals of humanizing institutions for older adults will benefit from an overall shift in attitude in the workplace from an "instrumental" to a "sacred" view of work (Yankelovich, 1981). When people are valued for themselves apart from the instrumental use they serve, humanistic care will be realized.

The humanistic culture of care envisioned for nursing homes must adopt a sacred view of its older adult residents, the staff, and its defining work if it is to grow beyond the culture of chronicity embodied in its medical model origins. The people responsible for the culture of care in nursing homes and the population they serve will need to establish a new set of core values about aging for these nursing homes to become truly humanized. Culture change will have successfully re-valued the nursing home and those who inhabit it when its mental model is to create a "covenential relationship" between residents and staff that is built on "a shared commitment to ideas, to issues, to values, to goals and to management processes." (dePree, 1989).

REFERENCES

Baltes, P., & Baltes, M. (Eds). (1993). *Successful aging.* New York: Cambridge University Press.

Baltes, P.B., & Reese, H.W. (1984). The life-span perspective in developmental psychology. In M.H. Bornstein & M.E. Lamb (Eds.), *Developmental psychology: An advanced textbook* (pp. 493–531). Mahwah, NJ: Lawrence Erlbaum Associates.

Bennett, R. (1963). The meaning of institutional life. *Gerontologist, 3,* 117–125.

Bowker, L. (1982). *Humanizing institutions for the aging.* Lexington, MA: Lexington Books.

Bradley, A., Ronch, J., & Pohlmann, E. (1999). *The EDGE Project.* Available at www.dementiasolutions.com.

Brown, J., & Duguid, P. (2000). *The social life of information.* Boston: Harvard Business School Press.

Buber, M. (1970). *I and thou.* New York: Charles Scribner's Sons.

Butler, R. (1975). *Why survive: Growing old in America.* New York: Harper and Row.

Cohen, D., & Eisdorfer, C. (2001). Wanted: A new look at nursing homes in America. *Journal of Mental Health and Aging, 7*(3), 299–300.

Comas-Diaz, L. (2000). An ethnopolitical approach to working with people of color. *American Psychologist,* 1319–1325.

Comfort, A. (1977, April 17). Review of *Growing old in America. New York Times Book Review.*

dePree, M. (1989). *Leadership: An art.* New York: Doubleday.

Fagan, R., Williams, C., & Burger, S. (1997, October 1). *Final report: Meeting of pioneers in nursing home culture change.*

Goffman, E. (1961). *Asylums: Essays on the social situation of mental patients and other inmates.* Garden City, NY: Anchor Books.

Gubrium, J. (1975). *Living and dying in Murray Manor.* New York: St. Martin's Press.

Gutman, D. (1994). *Reclaimed powers.* Evanston, IL: Northwestern University Press.

Henry, J. (1963). *Culture against man.* New York: Random House.

Howard, J. (1975). Humanization and de-humanization in health care. In J. Howard & A. Sharon (Eds.), *Humanizing health care* (pp. 57–107).

Kitwood, T. (1997). *Dementia reconsidered.* Buckingham, England: Open University Press.

Kitwood, T. (undated). *A contrast of cultures: consider what we bring.* Bradford, England: Bradford Dementia Group.

Kleinman, A. (1988). *The illness narratives: Suffering, healing and the human condition.* New York: Basic Books.

Kotter, J.R. (1996). *Leading change.* Boston: Harvard Business School Press.

Lerner, R.M. (1989). Developmental contextualism and the life-span view of person-context interaction. In M. Bornstein & J.S. Bruner (Eds.), *Interaction in human development* (pp. 217–239). Mahwah, NJ: Lawrence Erlbaum Associates.

Levine, C., & Zuckerman, C. (1999). The trouble with families. *Annals of Internal Medicine, 130,* 148–152.

Marshall, V. (1986). A sociological perspective on aging and dying. In V. Marshall (Ed.), *Later life: The social psychology of aging* (pp. 125–146). Beverly Hills: Sage Publications.

Maslow, A. (1962). *Toward a psychology of being.* Princeton, NJ: D. Van Nostrand.

Maslow, A. (1998). *Maslow on management.* New York: John Wiley & Sons.

Morris, D. (2000). *Illness and culture in the postmodern age.* Berkeley, CA: University of California Press.

Nicholson, C. (1979). *Personalized patient care in the nursing home: Problems and practice.* Paper presented at the annual meeting of the Gerontological Society.

Orr, J. (1996). *Thinking about machines: An ethnography of a modern job.* Ithaca, NY: IRL Press.

Ronch, J. (1987). Specialized Alzheimers units in nursing homes: Pros and cons. *American Journal of Alzheimers Care and Related Disorders and Research, 2,*10–19.

Ronch, J., & Crispi, E.L. (1997). Opportunities for development via group psychotherapy in the nursing home. *Group, 21*(2), 135–158.

Rosenberg, C.E. (1995). *The care of strangers: The rise of America's hospital sytem.* Baltimore: Johns Hopkins University Press.

Ryden, M., & Feldt, K. (1992). Goal directed care: Caring for aggressive nursing home residents with dementia. *Journal of Gerontological Nursing, 18*(11), 35–41.

Ryle, G. (1949). *The concept of mind.* London: Hutchinson.

Senge, P. (1994). *The fifth discipline: The art and practice of learning organization.* New York: Currency Doubleday.

Spitz, R.A. (1946). Anaclitic depression. *Psychoanalytic Study of the Child, 2,* 313–342.

Stannard, C.I. (1973). Old folks and dirty work: The social conditions for patient abuse in the nursing home. *Social Problems, 20,* 329–341.

Sternin, J., & Choo, R. (2000, January–February). The power of positive deviancy. *Harvard Business Review,* 14–15.

Suchman, L. (1996). Supporting articulation work. In R. Kling (Ed.), *Computerization and controversy: Value conflicts and social choices* (2nd ed., pp. 407–423). San Diego: Academic Press.

U.S. Senate, Special Committee on Aging. (1975). *Nursing home care in the United States: Failure in public policy.* Washington, DC: U.S. Government Printing Office.

Vickers, R. (1975). Psychogeriatrics. In A. Kraft (Ed.), *Psychiatry and medical practice.* New York: Arco Medical Publishers.

Vladek, B.C. (1980). *Unloving care: The nursing home tragedy.* New York: Basic Books.

Weiner, A., & Ronch, J. (Eds.). (in press). Culture change in long-term care. *Journal of Social Work in Long-Term Care.*

Wolfensberger, W. (1985). An overview of social role valorization and some reflections on elderly mentally retarded persons. In M.P. Janicki & H.M. Wisneiewski (Eds.), *Aging and developmental disabilities: Issues and approaches* (pp. 41–58). Baltimore: Paul H. Brookes Publishing Co.

Yankelovich, D. (1981). *New rules: Searching for self-fulfillment in a world turned upside down.* New York: Random House.

From Symptoms to Strengths
in Therapy and Counseling

9

FUNDAMENTAL CONCEPTS OF MILTON H. ERICKSON AND THEIR RELEVANCE TO OLDER CLIENTS

Joseph A. Goldfield

MILTON H. ERICKSON (1901–1980) was an innovative psychiatrist and hypnotherapist who is considered by many clinicians to be the founder of strengths-based therapy. He was a proponent of utilizing client strengths and tendencies to achieve therapeutic goals. Dr. Erickson preferred to develop approaches based on his clients' unique personalities and circumstances rather than developing or applying a universal model of therapy.

THE DEVELOPMENT OF ERICKSON'S IDEAS

Erickson attributed many of his clinical ideas to experiences he had in his youth and in his early psychiatric career. Although he made occasional reference to contemporary colleagues, he considered himself to be self-taught. Erickson grew up on a farm in rural Wisconsin. He credited the development of his intense curiosity and acute observational capacities on being tone-deaf, color-blind, and dyslexic (Haley, 1985; Rossi, Ryan, & Sharp, 1983). One example of his acute observational skills was that early in his childhood, he observed how people's nonverbal patterns, such as breathing rates, could be altered in others:

> This served to convince me that people communicate with each other at "breathing levels" of awareness unknown to them. I did not then have an ade-

quate vocabulary nor clarity of concepts to come to a good understanding. But I did know that communication with another could be achieved at a nonverbal and actually unrecognized fashion. (Erickson, in Rossi, 1980a, p. 364)

As a child, Erickson also learned that patterns tended to guide peoples' behavior. For example, he delighted in making a crooked path in the snow and observing how people automatically followed that inefficient, curved path instead of creating a direct path of their own (Mead, 1977).

There were two books on Erickson's family farm: a book about American history and a dictionary. Erickson loved reading the dictionary but because of his dyslexia, he had difficulty in looking words up efficiently. Serendipitously, Erickson amassed a huge vocabulary as well as a thorough knowledge of the multiple meanings of words (Rossi, Ryan, & Sharp, 1983). This knowledge would form the foundation of his ability to understand how his clients used language, thereby fostering his ability to enter their *experiential* world. These linguistic skills would also lead to Erickson's pioneering use of therapeutic language in an *injunctive* (i.e., action-oriented) form as opposed to an *indicative* (i.e., descriptive, explanatory) form (Watzlawick, 1985). Anecdotal storytelling, the use of metaphor, multiple-level communication, and reframing are all tools that issued from Erickson's love and command of language and his understanding of how language influences human behavior (Brown, 1991; Geary, 1988).

At age 17, Erickson was stricken with polio and was totally paralyzed with the exception of being able to move his eyes. Although his doctors expected him to die, he survived and in his ensuing self-rehabilitative experiences, made further pivotal discoveries. Once, while secured in a rocking chair, he observed that the intense desire to be closer to the window lead to a slight rocking of the chair. He thus experienced directly the known *ideomotor principle* that thought can stimulate subtle neuromuscular mechanisms.

He continued to observe other aspects of ideomotor activity and discovered that the vivid recalling of previous learned physical activities, such as squeezing an apple, handling a pitchfork, or climbing a tree, resulted in slight body movements. He would later write, "At age eighteen, I recalled all my childhood movements to help myself relearn muscle coordination" (Erickson, in Erickson & Rossi, 1977, p. 40). Thus, Erickson had learned of the existence of experientially acquired and unconsciously stored knowledge that he would later refer to as *experiential learnings*; that this knowledge needed to be accessed indirectly; and that these learnings could be utilized to overcome difficulties. He had also learned that strong motivational forces can play an important role in creating change.

During this time, his baby sister was going through the developmental stages of crawling, standing, and walking. Erickson carefully studied the sequences of movements she was employing as she progressed through these stages. He committed these sequences to memory, relying on them as he gradually taught himself to stand and walk. Within 1 year he had recovered sufficiently to be able to walk with crutches; within 10 years he was able to walk with only a subtle limp (Haley, 1985). Erickson had learned the importance of scanning for resources and information in one's environment that could catalyze, or reinforce, change. Erickson had also discovered that being able to envision a future that went beyond current limitations could be a powerful tool in organizing an individual's response to present circumstances. His goal of re-learning to walk served to organize his response to having polio, as well as his understanding of the small incremental nature of the steps needed to achieve that goal.

Realizing that he would be too weak to be a farmer, Erickson decided to go to college and to medical school. As a pre-medical student at the University of Wisconsin, Erickson attended a seminar on hypnosis given by the psychologist Clark Hull. While this was his first, formal introduction to hypnosis, Erickson later realized that many of his previous experiences were actually *auto-hypnotic* in nature (Erickson & Rossi, 1977). The seminar covered topics such as the psychological nature of hypnotic trance, possible transcendence of normal capacities, and whether the hypnotist or the subject was the primary contributor to the development of a trance state.

Erickson eventually broke from the prevailing theoretical tradition that the hypnotist was primary. Because of his own experiences with polio and the results of studies he later conducted by hypnotizing hundreds of college students, he believed the subject was most important in the development of the hypnotic state. He further believed that the unique personality characteristics and responses of each subject determined the elicitation, manifestation, and use of hypnotic phenomena. Erickson also objected to the standardized, uniform methodology employed in the administration of hypnotic suggestions. Instead, Erickson preferred to approach each subject in an individualized, tailored way (Erickson, 1954).

Throughout his college and medical school experiences, Erickson conducted extensive research on hypnotically induced trance states and the inherent capacities that these states evoked. He also studied the manifestations in everyday life of hypnotic phenomena, such as having the pain of a toothache diminish on the way to the dentist (analgesia); or having a sudden childhood memory when smelling fresh-cut grass (age regression). Rossi noted,

> No longer were rote suggestions automatically imprinted into the "blank" mind of a person in trance; instead, Erickson recognized the hypnotic trance state as one of dynamic complexity and individuality wherein the person's own capacities could be used to facilitate the healing process. (Rossi, Ryan, & Sharp, 1983, p. 22)

Early in his psychiatric career, Erickson worked at various state and county hospitals, where he continued to research hypnotic phenomena and its use in the treatment of a wide variety of psychological and medical problems. In these settings, while working with patients with psychotic and delusional symptoms, he began formulating nonhypnotic therapeutic approaches. Respecting his client's reality orientation, he learned to work from within his clients' worldview to achieve therapeutic change (Haley, 1985). This is illustrated by a case he had in the early 1930s:

There was one patient who said he was Jesus Christ. He was very paranoid and yet he was harmless and had ground privileges. And Worcester tried to use patients with ground privileges at useful tasks. And the Psychology Laboratory wanted a handyman. And here was this patient, wrapped in a sheet, walking, communing with God . . . very polite and courteous. So I was told to do something with him. I told him how desirable it was for the doctors to play tennis in the recreation hour. They were using muscles and skills and abilities that God had endowed them with. And it was very imperative that the tennis grounds be kept in good shape . . . dirt court. And we wandered down to the tennis court. We made a lot of comments about the trees that God had made, the beautiful grass, the creation of the earth itself, and then I noticed that there were some rough spots on that dirt court and I told him I was sure that God didn't want those rough spots there and could he in some way succeed in having the tennis ground leveled carefully and smoothed out? He said he certainly would TRY, he was there to serve Mankind. So I left him. He was an excellent tennis court groundskeeper. As for the Psychology Laboratory, they wanted some bookcases built. I happened to mention Jesus was a carpenter. So he built the bookcases. He became a handyman around the Psychology Laboratory. (Erickson, in Gordon & Meyers-Anderson, 1981, p. 43; reprinted by permission)

RELEVANCE OF BASIC ERICKSONIAN PRINCIPLES TO OLDER CLIENTS

Milton Erickson's psychiatric career spanned more than 50 years. During that time, he worked with clients of all ages who had a wide range of psychological and physical problems. While Erickson is credited with many clinical innovations (Geary, 1988; Haley 1973), a few basic principles permeate his work; a discussion of these principles follows.

PRINCIPLE 1: THE UNIQUENESS OF EACH INDIVIDUAL

Erickson believed that a therapist's reliance on theories of behavior and models of therapy influences him or her to assess and intervene with clients in preconceived and limited ways: "Each person is a unique individual. Hence, psychotherapy should be formulated to meet the uniqueness of the individual, rather than tailoring the person to fit the Procrustean bed of a hypothetical theory of human behavior" (Erickson, in Zeig, 1985, p. viii).

The principle of individual uniqueness, when applied to the therapeutic treatment of older adults, guides the therapist away from normative assumptions about aging or mental health as the basis for understanding and intervening. Instead, the client's unique worldview, his behavioral and cognitive tendencies, his view of his problems, and his therapeutic goals, inform and organize a clinician's understanding and therapeutic behavior (verbal and nonverbal). This process, which is inherently respectful, helps to deconstruct stereotypical generalizations that a therapist might have—consciously and/or unconsciously. This could protect older adult clients from any age-based, negative stereotyping that they themselves might have internalized.

Adopting this principle initiates a *collaborative context* for therapy. Erickson stated, "There are no two people alike. No two people understand the same sentence in the same way. And so, in dealing with people you should try not to fit them into your concept of what they should be . . . you try to discover what their concept of themselves happens to be" (Erickson, in Gordon & Meyers-Anderson, 1981, p. 18).

> THE PRINCIPLE OF individual uniqueness, when applied to the therapeutic treatment of older adults, guides the therapist away from normative assumptions about aging or mental health as the basis for understanding and intervening.

The establishment of a collaborative context is an empowering experience and one that may be contrary to many day-to-day, social interactions older people may have. Collaboration, by definition, means *doing with* or *doing together,* as opposed to *doing to* or *doing for.* Thus, a collaborative context in therapy prevents an older client from being put in a *one-down (inferior) position,* or rendered dependent. In initiating a collaborative context, the therapist adapts him- or herself to the client's perspective. "This matter of psychotherapy requires your appreciation and appraisal of the working of the human personality . . . then you must adapt your own behavior to the patient's needs on the basis of your appraisal" (Erickson, in Rossi, Ryan, & Sharp, 1983, p. 215). Therapy outcomes have shown that a client's perception of therapist–client congruence is highly correlated with a client's satisfaction and a client's ratings of therapeutic change (Duncan, Hubble, Miller, & Coleman, 1998).

One way Erickson adapted himself to his client's worldview was by synchronizing his verbal and nonverbal language with that of his clients:

> Too often, psychotherapists try to deal with their patients by using their doctoral degree language, trying to explain the ego, superego and the id, conscious and unconscious, and the patient doesn't know whether you're talking about corn, potatoes or hash. Therefore, you try to use the language of the patient. (Erickson, in Gordon & Meyers-Anderson, 1981, p. 49)

Duncan et al. (1998) studied the therapeutic benefits of clinicians being guided by their clients' use of language. After reviewing the literature on therapy outcome studies, they concluded that high ratings of client satisfaction are significantly related to similarity in client–therapist linguistic styles. They also proposed that therapeutic progress is enhanced.

It is essential that clinicians tune in to the uniqueness of every aging client because of the heterogeneity of the older population. The diversity of ages—ranging from 65 to older than 100—cultural backgrounds, current and past economic and living situations, family constellations, variations in health status, and diversity of interests gives a sense of the differences within this population. Marilyn Albert, professor of psychiatry at Harvard, noted, "in no other group except infants do we find individuals so different from one another as in the elderly" (Albert, in Restak, 1988, p. 66). Finally, the individual goals in seeking therapy are as unique to that individual as are the skills, strengths, and resources that each client brings to achieve those goals.

Notably, nursing facilities and other institutions that serve elderly clients are beginning to incorporate processes of *individualizing* and *tailoring* into the structure of service delivery. Institutional values, such as *efficiency* and *uniformity of services* are being challenged by resident-centered values, such as expansion of *resident's choice* and *control over their (one's) environments, activities,* and *lifestyles* (see Chapter 8). Research has shown that residents in nursing facilities who have more control over their lives through increased responsibility and decision making are more alert, active, happy, healthy, and long-lived than residents who do not have such control (Langer, 1997; Langer & Rodin, 1976).

PRINCIPLE 2: UTILIZATION OF CLIENT RESOURCES

Erickson believed that a client enters therapy with a multitude of capabilities and that these capabilities can be utilized for the resolution of his or her problems. However, a client is often unaware of his or her abilities or how to gain access to and channel them in order to achieve his or her goals. Erickson illustrated this principle with a story from his youth:

> I was returning from high school one day and a runaway horse with a bridle sped past a group of us into a farmer's yard looking for a drink of water. He was perspiring heavily. And the farmer didn't recognize it. I hopped on the horse's back. Since it had a bridle on, I took hold of the tick rein and said, "Giddy up." Headed for the highway, I knew the horse would turn in the right direction. I didn't know what the right direction was. And the horse trotted and galloped along. Now and then he would forget he was on the highway and start into a field. So I would pull on him a bit to call his attention to the fact that the highway was where he was supposed to be. Finally, about four miles from where I had boarded him, he turned into a farmyard, and the farmer said, "So that's how that critter came back. Where did you find him?" "About four miles from here." "How did you know you should come here?" I said, "I didn't know, the horse knew. All I did was keep his attention on the road." I think that's the way you do psychotherapy. (Erickson, in Gordon & Meyers-Anderson, 1981, p. 6; reprinted by permission)

Erickson was able to discern potentials and skills in his client's present repertoire of behaviors, motivations, likes and dislikes, worldview, and value systems. "In rendering the patient aid, there should be full respect for and utilization of whatever the client presents" (Erickson, in Rossi, 1980a, pp. 170–171). For Erickson, helping a client often included the utilization of behavioral, cognitive, or affect-related aspects of the presenting problem:

> By using the patient's own patterns of response and behavior, including those of their actual illness, one may effect therapy more promptly and satisfactorily. Indeed, it often seems absurd to re-educate patients when all that may be needed may be a re-direction of their endeavors, rather than a change or a correction of their behavior. (Erickson, 1973, p. 217)

According to Gilligan (1992), Erickson often stated that the mechanism of a problem frequently contains the mechanism of the solution. He was able to find the seeds of strengths in apparent liabilities.

Erickson believed that people have latent, experientially acquired learnings that are stored in a vast reservoir he called the unconscious mind. Making these unconscious resources available to his clients was Erickson's reason for employing hypnosis, which he defined as follows:

> Hypnosis is essentially a communication of ideas and understandings to a patient in such a fashion as to maximize his receptivity to what is presented and thereby, motivate him to explore his own bodily potentials toward control of his psychological and physiological responses. The average person is unaware of the extent to which his capacities and accomplishments have been learned through the experiential conditionings of his body behavior via his life experiences. (Erickson, in Rossi, 1980c, p. 237)

Erickson felt that hypnosis had special value in the treatment of psychophysiological problems, such as pain, which is a problem many older adults deal with. Estimates of community-dwelling older adults suffering from chronic pain range from 25% to 50%; for nursing home residents, the range is from 55% to 80% (Roberto, 1994; Schuster & Goetz, 1994). Often accompanied by fatigue, chronic pain reduces an individual's capacity to perform activities of daily living (Gold, 1994). Also, chronic pain is highly correlated in older adults with depression, anxiety, and substance abuse (Schuster & Goetz, 1994). In addition to pain associated with chronic medical conditions, the incidence of cancer-related pain is higher in the older population than in younger generations (All, 1994).

> ERICKSON BELIEVED that people have latent, experientially acquired learnings that are stored in a vast reservoir he called the unconscious mind. Making these unconscious resources available to his clients was Erickson's reason for employing hypnosis.

Sole reliance on pharmacological treatments of pain in older clients is problematic. Many older people have a lower level of tolerance to drugs, metabolize drugs at a slower rate, and are more likely to be on multiple medications, rendering them more susceptible to adverse drug interactions (Morris & Gali, 1994). Much of Erickson's experience with older clients involved assisting people who were suffering either chronic pain or pain associated with terminal cancers (Erickson, 1959). He adhered to the principles of utilization of each person's unique experiential background and understandings when working with these clients (Erickson 1966; Rossi, Ryan, & Sharp, 1983).

In addition to the utilization of a client's manifest and latent capacities, Erickson also looked to the client's natural environment for resources that could serve as catalysts or reinforcers of positive, therapeutic momentum:

> No matter what problem the patient brings you, there are always psychological and personality significances in relation to the patient's total life situation. You never consider a case without wondering about family implications, living situation, work situations, because the patient's problem is entirely concerned

with the disturbance of daily living. Therefore, you ought to have an open mind . . . a curious, scientific mind, wondering just what the real situation is. It is very important that you have a comprehensive view of the total situation. (Erickson, in Rossi & Ryan, 1992, pp. 117–118)

Sullivan (1992) noted that when the environment is viewed as a source of opportunities as opposed to an obstacle, a dramatic increase in the number of resources reveals itself and thus becomes available. The utilization principle is useful to clinicians working with older clients for a variety of reasons:

- Looking for resources within an older client's current repertoire of behaviors and beliefs facilitates rapport. Because the therapist cannot know, a priori, which elements of the client's repertoire will prove useful, an attitude of curiosity, respect, and acceptance is naturally engendered.

- The client receives the credit for, as well as satisfaction of, actual goal achievement because the skills used to resolve the client's problems come from the client's personality and ability. This could further empower older clients to undertake other endeavors of interest.

- The utilization paradigm deconstructs ageist assumptions. Erickson believed that, "We ought to expect to find solutions rather than passively accepting a decree of 'incurable.' Such an attitude is far more conducive to our task of exploration, discovery and healing" (Erickson, in Rossi, 1980b, p. 202). Therapists who work with older adults and look for strengths and capacities are more likely to discover them; not only will this benefit their clients, but also it will positively influence their own ideas about the aging process (including their own aging).

- Clients are not placed in a position of having to learn a totally new vocabulary and set of tools to resolve their problems. The message that they have the requisite skills needed to resolve their problem is one of respect and optimism that change will occur.

- Many problems that older people face are related to experiencing changes in their lives (e.g., changes in health, social networks, financial resources, and family and work-related roles). When facing these problems, the potential exists for people to experience a disruption in the stability of their sense of self. The utilization of an older client's existing experiential learnings and tendencies in dealing with these problems is likely to promote stability and continuity in the sense of self (longitudinal continuity). In addition, the maintenance of the continuity of self can be important if an older person is experiencing the trauma of loss and bereavement (see Chapter 13).

PRINCIPLE 3: PRESENT AND FUTURE ORIENTATION

Erickson broke with the prevailing psychiatric practice of focusing primarily on a client's past. Instead, he believed that the present and future well-being of the client was paramount.

The *sine qua non* of psychotherapy should be the present and future adjustment of the patient, with only that amount of attention to the past necessary to prevent a continuance or a recurrence of past maladjustments . . . the purpose and procedures of psychotherapy should involve acceptance and utilization of what the patient presents and represents. These should be utilized in such a fashion that the patient is given an impetus and a momentum, making the present and future become absorbing, satisfying, and constructive. In this way, the patient can be recognized as a living, sentient human being with a present and future, as well as a past. (Erickson, in Rossi, 1980a, p. 171)

Erickson's emphasis on the present, as discussed in the section on utilization, was related to his ability to see potentials in his clients' current behaviors and frame of reference. Erickson's emphasis on a client's future is especially valuable to older clients.

Although a youth-oriented culture might suggest that life is over when an individual is defined as old and that all a person can do is reminisce, it is a truism that all people have a future until they actually die. The support of an older person's ability to envision a future and to organize his actions in alignment with this vision humanizes the aging process by validating his right to function psychologically within the three time frames in which he has always functioned: past, present, and future. This inherently promotes longitudinal continuity, the importance of which has been discussed. When an individual is assisted in shaping his own future, empowerment, satisfaction, and self-confidence are facilitated through the establishment of proactive self-reinforcing patterns.

> THE SUPPORT OF AN older person's ability to envision a future and to organize his or her actions in alignment with this vision humanizes the aging process by validating the person's right to function psychologically within the three time frames in which he or she has always functioned: past, present, and future.

PSYCHOLOGICAL PROCESSES AND TIME DIMENSIONS ARE INTERRELATED How people function in the present tends to influence how they envision their future. A person's future vision not only involves anticipated life events but also includes how he or she envisions his or her self while interacting with these events. For example, it is a common experience that if a person is depressed in the present, the future appears bleak. Moreover, the person's attitude toward him- or herself is likely to be one of hopelessness regarding his or her ability to change his or her situation in the future. In contrast, a person who is enjoying and actively involved in life in the present is more likely to be able to envision a future of satisfying possibilities. This person's future vision is likely to be characterized by confidence in his or her ability to enjoy positive events and successfully adapt to difficult events that might occur in the future.

Similarly, a person's vision of the future influences his or her moods, thoughts, actions, and attitudes in the present. A fulfilling vision of the future is generally associated with a positive mood in the present, attitudes of positive expectancy and curiosity, and patterns of activity that are in accord with individual needs and preferences. In contrast, if a person has visions of a morbid future, including a vision of his or her self as lacking the capacity to influence that future, it is likely to be associated with depressed and/or anxious moods in the present.

It is in this realm of moods and future visions that the perniciousness of ageist myths can occur. Generally, ageist myths portray aging as a period of time dominated by loss, decline of mental and/or physical capacities, and correspondingly, an increased dependency on others. Not only is the future vision that these myths portray a morbid one but it also contains the message that because of a loss of powers, a person cannot prevent this inevitable scenario.

Evidence suggests that many older people have internalized these ageist myths (Langer, 1989; 1997). To the degree that they have, their ability to envision a satisfying, fulfilling future is potentially compromised, interfered with, or replaced by nihilistic scenarios. The artificial limitations these myths suggest impede an older person's rights to discover their actual capacities, present and future, and to proactively negotiate their goals and interests accordingly.

Much of Erickson's work was aimed at helping clients to overcome those unnecessary limitations that impeded them from achieving their goals. These limitations involved patterns of thought, behavior, attitude, and emotion (Gordon & Meyers-Anderson, 1981). Erickson found that introducing small changes could alter the influence that these patterns had on a client's future. He noted,

> What you need to do is try to do something that induces a change in the patient . . . any little change and they follow that change and that change will develop in accordance with his/her own needs. It's much like rolling a snowball down a mountainside. It starts out as a snowball, but as it rolls down it gets larger and larger and it starts an avalanche that fits to the shape of the mountain. (Erickson, in Gordon & Meyers-Anderson, 1981, p. 123)

CASE ILLUSTRATIONS

Throughout most of Milton Erickson's career, he was involved in teaching professionals hypnosis and the art of psychotherapy. Toward the end of his career he was confined to a wheelchair and thus he taught and practiced primarily by offering instructional seminars out of his home office. He used *teaching tales*, which included case material as well as anecdotal storytelling, as educational tools. According to Sidney Rosen, M.D. (2001), a longtime student of Erickson's, "Erickson used teaching tales as a medium for transmitting ideas. He wanted to teach therapists how to think." The following two cases of Erickson's are culled from his teaching tales:

CASE NUMBER 1: AFRICAN VIOLET QUEEN

Once while I was in Milwaukee, lecturing, William asked me, 'My mother's sister lives in Milwaukee. She is independently wealthy, very religious, she doesn't like my mother and my mother doesn't like her. She has a housekeeper come in, a maid comes in every day to do the housework, the cooking, and she stays alone in that big house, goes to church, has no friends there. She just attends church and silently slips away. And she's been horribly depressed for nine months. I'm worried about her and I'd like you to stop in and do something for her. I'm the only relative she has that she likes and she can't stand me. So call on her and see what you can do.' So, a depressed woman . . . I introduced myself and identified myself thoroughly . . . asked to be taken on a tour of that house. In looking around I could see she was a very wealthy woman living alone, idle, attending church but keeping to herself, and I went through the house, room after room . . . and I saw three African violets and a potting pot with a leaf in it being sprouted as a new plant. So I knew what to do for her in the way of therapy. I told her, 'I want you to buy every African violet plant in view for yourself . . . those are yours. I want you to buy a couple hundred potting pots for you to sprout new African violets, and you buy a couple hundred gift pots. As soon as the sprouts are well rooted, for every birth announcement you send an African violet, for every Christening, for every engagement, for every wedding, for every sickness, for every death, every Church bazaar.' And one time she had two hundred African violets . . . and if you take care of two hundred African violets you've got a day's work cut out. And she became the African Violet Queen of Milwaukee with an endless number of friends. Just that one little interview, I just pointed her nose in the right direction and said 'giddyup.' And she did all the rest of the therapy. And that's the important thing about therapy . . . you find out the potentials that are possible for your patients and then you encourage your patient to undertake them and sooner or later he'll get all wrapped up in it. (Erickson, in Gordon & Meyers-Anderson, 1981, pp. 124–125; reprinted by permission)

CASE DISCUSSION   Erickson appraised the different sub-components that comprised the pattern of the woman's depression and social isolation. What does she actually do? She spends most of her time alone, isolated. Where does she do it? She spends most of her time at home, and some of her time in a church. She also spent a little time tending African violet plants. (Erickson noted elsewhere that these delicate plants require some considerable care [Zeig, 1980].) The behavioral suggestion used in this case reveals acceptance and utilization of components of this client's behavioral repertoire and value system.

Erickson was aware that she was a religious woman. He utilized this value system to redirect her behavioral repertoire, speaking her language in doing so: 'for every Christening, church bazaar. . . . ' Thus, her tendency to spend time alone at home was respected, but it subtly shifted to include purposeful activity such as tending many plants and potting new ones. Similarly respected was her tendency to spend some time at church alone, but also with a subtle addition: to get information about upcoming events. This task was small enough to be within the range of her current capacities and also had built into it the potential for the development of curiosity about events in the near future.

Growing newly sprouted plants for upcoming events reframed the total situation by recontextualizing her activities in the two environments in which she spent most of her time. Going to church becomes related to contributing something of value: this is congruent with her religious beliefs. Sprouting new plants and tending to their growth in her home creates an expectancy of a positive social interaction when each plant is grown enough to be a gift.

At this point, the client is in a win-win situation. She can interact from a distance (i.e., as an anonymous donor of gifts), which will raise her self-esteem due to her religious values. Or, as actually happened, her gift giving can snowball into making personal relationships and friends. Ultimately, the level and nature of social interaction is under her control and develops according to her personality and needs. Over time, as the woman implements the purposeful activity, being at home alone becomes associated with the social interactions and relationships being built. The circular and limiting nature of the original pattern (i.e., depression leads to social isolation which leads to depression . . .) is transformed. It is replaced by an open pattern that is full of ongoing potential (i.e., purposeful activity leads to positive interaction, which leads to positive self-esteem, which empowers this client to undertake further purposeful activity that could lead to a variety of additional social interactions). Erickson's suggestion strongly enhanced the likelihood of improved morale and the lifting of depression, as well as a more enjoyable lifestyle.

Erickson's handling of this case is consistent with findings from gerontological research on social interaction and how it improves health, morale, and longevity (Potts, 1997). Furthermore, by growing plants that mark occasions through the life-span (e.g., births, weddings, deaths) the client was able to participate in intergenerational events. Research has shown that an older person's self-esteem level increases significantly when he or she receives respect and appreciation from younger people (Brabazon, personal communication, 2000).

CASE NUMBER 2: THE RETIRED POLICEMAN

A man about eighty pounds overweight entered and said, "I'm a retired policeman—medically retired. I drink too much, I smoke too much, eat too much . . . I have emphysema, high blood pressure, I like to go jogging, I can't . . . the best I can do is walk. Can you help me?" I said, "All right. Where do you buy your cigarettes?" He said, "There is a handy little grocery around the corner from where I live." I said, "Who does your cooking?" He said, "I'm a bachelor . . . I usually do all my own." "And where do you shop?" "At a handy little grocery around the corner." I said, "How do you buy your cigarettes?" "Usually three cartons at a time." "And you usually do your own cooking . . . where do you dine out?" He said, "At a very nice restaurant, around the corner." I said, "Now the liquor?" "There's a handy little liquor store around the corner." I said, "Well, you are an ex-policeman and you want to correct your blood pressure and your obesity, emphysema and you buy your cigarettes three cartons at a time. Now your therapy isn't going to require very much. You can do all the smoking you want . . . buy your cigarettes one package at a time by walking to the other side of town to get the package. As for doing your own cooking, well you haven't much to do so shop three times a day. Buy only enough for one meal but no leftovers. As for dining out, there are a lot of good restaurants a mile or two away . . . that'll give you a chance to walk. As for your drinking . . . I see no objection to your drinking. There are some excellent bars a mile away. Get your first drink in one bar, your second drink in a bar a mile away. And you'll be in excellent shape before very long." He left the office swearing at me in the most eloquent fashion. Now why would I treat him that way? He was a retired policeman . . . he knew what discipline was and it was entirely a matter of discipline. And there would be no way for him to refuse from any other way. He left swearing at me . . . he was very eloquent. About a month later a new patient came in and said, "A friend of mine referred me to you. My friend was a retired policeman. He said you were the only psychiatrist who knows what he is talking about." (Erickson, in Gordon & Meyers-Anderson, 1981, pp. 111–112; reprinted by permission)

CASE DISCUSSION   In this case, Erickson again made suggestions that led to changes in the client's patterns of behavior. His client had two goals: the reduction of unhealthy behaviors and the increase of healthy activity, namely walking. Walking was also related to something he enjoyed. Erickson helped him achieve his goals simultaneously. He inserted walking into the man's current drinking, smoking, and eating patterns in such a way as to automatically reduce these behaviors to a level of moderation, as opposed to the existing level of excess. At the same time, more walking (healthy exercise) assisted the man in achieving his goal of improved health. Not only is exercise important in the treatment of obesity, high blood pressure, and emphysema but also walking is a commonly prescribed delay technique for people dealing with the cravings that accompany the reduction or elimination of addictive and compulsive behaviors. As people outlast their cravings (three to fifteen minutes), their confidence in their capacity to abstain and not feel out of control also increases (Lesser, personal communication, 2001). In addition, by varying the contexts in which the man ate, drank, and smoked, Erickson reduced the probability that environmental cues would trigger these behaviors in an automatic way.

Erickson commented on the utilization of his client's background as a police officer. He stated, "It was purely a matter of discipline." Since the attribute of discipline necessary for the accomplishment of the man's goals was not manifest in his current behavioral repertoire, Erickson evoked this skill from the client's latent, unconsciously stored repertoire of experience. It appears that Erickson revivified and activated the client's discipline of receiving and carrying out orders by providing specific instructions regarding the behaviors the client wished to modify. The referral a month later indicated that the client had maintained the discipline he needed to accomplish his goals.

CASE OVERVIEW

These cases demonstrate how Erickson used the three principles discussed in the previous section (uniqueness of the individual, utilization of resources, and present and future orientation) in an integrated way. Erickson aided these clients in overcoming their difficulties by accepting and redirecting what they already were doing. He did this in such a way that they became absorbed in the process, which built on its own momentum in accordance with their personalities. These cases also revealed how his interventions were informed and structured by the behaviors, goals, and values that these clients brought with them to therapy.

SUCCESSFUL AGING

As more people live longer, scholars and researchers are investigating the varieties of ways people can experience the later stages of life. Partly in opposition to negative stereotypes of old age, many gerontologists have proposed the concept of "successful aging." Morgan and Kunkel asserted that "successful aging does not mean 'optimal' or 'problem free' or 'better than average' . . . for psychologists successful aging implies that individuals are satisfied or contented with their lives—that they have found ways of maximizing the positive in their lives while minimizing the impact of inevitable age-related losses" (1998, p. 146).

Some research has focused on and identified certain factors that are generally associated with successful aging. Important factors are *social support* (Morgan & Kunkel, 1998; Pierlin & Skaff, 1995; Rowe & Kahn, 1998); *active involvement in physical and cognitive activities* (Restak, 1999; Rowe & Kahn, 1998); *cultivation of attitudes of self-efficacy, mastery, and curiosity* (Albert, 1999; Rowe & Kahn, 1998); *avoidance of unhealthy behaviors* (Albert, 1999; Rowe & Kahn, 1998); and *successful adaption to stressful events* (Pierlin & Skaff, 1995). The benefits of such factors can be obtained, to varying degrees, at any point in an individual's life—it is never too late to profit from any or all of them (Restak,1999; Rowe & Kahn, 1998).

UTILIZATION OF CLIENT RESOURCES

Erickson's utilization of his client's capacities and skills allowed them to resolve their problems (as in the case of the "African Violets" woman dealing with depression), or to diminish the impact of their problems on their lives. In both types of situations, clients were able to discover and use their capabilities proactively so that they had a positive impact on their lives. This promotes an attitude of self-efficacy that is associated with an increase in active involvement (physically and cognitively) in a person's life, increased self-esteem, and greater resiliency in dealing with present and future stressors (Pierlin & Skaff, 1995; Rowe & Kahn, 1998).

The utilization approach can also be helpful to older clients who would like to make health-related lifestyle changes. Clients' ability to make these changes in a sustained fashion is facilitated when latent skills and/or aspects of their current patterns are respected, utilized, and built upon in the development of new patterns (as in the case of the retired policeman). Clients are able to discover for themselves that it is never too late to change.

PRESENT AND FUTURE ORIENTATION

Erickson believed that clients should be "actively involved in present activities that are influenced by future goals" (Rosen, personal communication, 2001). For older clients, being active in such a way is likely to stimulate involvement in cognitive, physical, and social activity that is self-perpetuating due to the satisfaction obtained by setting goals and achieving them. This process is also likely to generate a sense of self-efficacy, which can raise the probability that an older client's interest will lead him or her to newer environments and spheres of activity. In turn, this variety and novelty stimulates ongoing curiosity, learning, decision making, and other cognitive processes. The ongoing use of such cognitive processes is known to maintain and promote healthy brain functioning (Goldberg, 2001).

Involvement in self-determined interests can also serve to provide structure and distraction to people who might be dealing with the trauma associated with a major loss and bereavement. Not only can this facilitate their ability to integrate experiences in their own rhythm, but also it might reduce their vulnerability for developing secondary stressors (e.g., the insomnia that often accompanies the bereavement process).

Finally, being actively involved in present activities that are influenced by future goals can diminish the anxiety and stress of anticipating future stressful events, such as major medical procedures and losses. Rose (1991) noted that this anticipation is often more detrimental, physiologically, then the stress associated with the stressful event itself.

UNIQUENESS OF EACH INDIVIDUAL

Being interested in, and guided by, a client's unique situation, resources, and goals helps ensure the appropriate amount and type of support a clinician offers a client. Rowe and Kahn (1998) noted, "Unneeded or unwanted support—or the wrong kinds of support—can cause more harm then good, reducing older people's independence and self-esteem." In addition, having clients use their lifetime of experiential learnings when addressing their problems expands the number of ways they can adapt to stressful events.

Encouraging older clients to experience themselves as unique individuals supports them in making lifestyle decisions that are in accordance with their standards; this is consistent with what some gerontologists propose about successful aging (Baltes & Cartensen, 1996)—that it should be defined not in generalities but according to each individual's goals and preferences.

Erickson's view on successful aging is best illustrated by a teaching tale he told concerning his father:

> My father died at ninety-seven and a half. My father was planting fruit trees, wondering if he would live long enough to eat any of the fruit. . . . My father had a massive coronary attack at eighty. He was unconscious when he was taken

to the hospital. My sister went with him, the doctor told my sister, "Now don't have too much hope. Your father is an old man. He worked hard all of his life and he's had a very severe coronary."

My sister said, "I snorted at the doctor and said, 'You don't know my dad!'"

When my father recovered consciousness, the doctor was there. My father said, "What happened?"

The doctor told him, "Don't worry, Mr. Erickson. You've had a very bad coronary attack, but in two or three months, you'll be home as good as new."

My father, outraged, said, "Two or three months my foot! What you mean is I've got to wait a whole week!" He was home in a week's time.

He was eighty-five when he had his second and similar heart attack. The same doctor was there. My father recovered consciousness and said, "What happened?"

The doctor said, "Same thing."

My father groaned and said, "Another week wasted."

He had a drastic abdominal operation and had nine feet of intestine removed. When he came out of anesthesia in recovery, he asked the nurse, "Now what happened?"

She told him and he groaned and said, "Instead of a whole week it'll be ten days."

His third heart attack occurred when he was eighty-nine. He recovered consciousness and said, "Same thing, doctor?"

The doctor said, "Yes."

My father said, "Now this is getting to be a bad habit of wasting a week at a time."

He had his fourth coronary at ninety-three. When he recovered consciousness he said, "Honest, Doc, I thought the fourth would carry me off. Now I'm beginning to lose faith in the fifth."

At ninety-seven and a half, he and two of my sisters were planning a weekend trip to the old farming community. All of his peers were dead and some of their children.

They planned whom to visit, what motel to stay in, what restaurants to eat in. Then they walked out to the car. When they reached the car my father said, "Oh, I forgot my hat."

He ran back for his hat. My sisters waited a reasonable length of time and then looked at each other coolly and said, "This is it."

They went in. Dad was dead on the floor, of a massive cerebral hemorrhage.[1]

This teaching tale illustrated that Erickson didn't believe that a person necessarily had to change how they approached their lives, even as their longevity became uncertain. While his father made adjustments that he needed to make, he continued to be organized by his present and future interests. He continued to discover his actual abilities rather than be constrained by any artificial limitations

---

[1]From *My Voice Will Go With You: The Teaching Tales of Milton H. Erickson* by Milton H. Erickson and Sidney Rosen, M.D. Copyright © 1982 by Sidney Rosen, M.D. Used by permission of W.W. Norton & Company, Inc.

suggested by his diagnosis or by other people's assumptions and expectations of him, based on his age.

Like his father, Erickson was actively absorbed in the present and oriented to the future when he died. He had been teaching a seminar on a Friday and was looking forward to teaching another the following Monday. That Sunday, he became ill and died a few days later at age 78.

REFERENCES

Albert, M. (1988). In R.M. Restak (Ed.), *The mind* (p. 66). New York: Bantam Books.

All, A. (1994). Current concepts and management of pain in older women. In K. Roberts (Ed.), *Older women with chronic pain.* Binghamton, NY: Harrington Park Press.

Baltes, M.M., & Cartensen, I.I. (1996). The process of successful aging. *Aging and Society, 16,* 397–422.

Brown, P. (1991). *The hypnotic brain: Hypnotherapy and social communication.* New Haven, CT: Yale University Press.

Duncan, B., Hubble, M., Miller, S., & Coleman, S. (1998). Escaping the lost world of impossibility: Honoring clients' language, motivation and theories of change. In M. Hoyt (Ed.), *The handbook of constructive therapies.* San Francisco: Jossey-Bass.

Erickson, M.H. (1954, October). Initial experiments investigating the nature of hypnosis. *The American Journal of Clinical Hypnosis, 1,* 152–162.

Erickson, M.H. (1959, January). Hypnosis in painful terminal illness. *The American Journal of Clinical Hypnosis, 1.*

Erickson, M.H. (1966). The interspersal hypnotic technique for symptom correction and pain control. *The American Journal of Clinical Hypnosis, 8,* 189–209.

Erickson, M.H. (1973). Psychotherapy achieved by a reversal of the neurotic processes in a case of ejaculato praecox. *The American Journal of Clinical Hypnosis, 15,* 217–222.

Erickson, M.H., & Rossi, E.L. (1977, July). The autohypnotic experiences of Milton H. Erickson. *The American Journal of Clinical Hypnosis, 20,* 76–84.

Geary, B. (1988). The psychotherapeutic legacy of Milton H. Erickson. *Arizona Counseling Journal, 1* (13), 40–44.

Goldberg, E. (2001). *The executive brain: Frontal lobes and the civilized mind.* New York: Oxford University Press.

Gordon, D., & Meyers-Anderson, M. (1981). *Phoenix: Therapeutic patterns of Milton H. Erickson.* Capitola, CA: Meta Publications.

Haley, J. (1973). *Uncommon therapy: The psychiatric techniques of Milton Erickson, M.D.* New York: Norton.

Haley, J. (1985). *Conversations with Milton H. Erickson, M.D. Volume II: Treating couples and families.* New York: Triangle Press.

Langer, E. (1989). *Mindfulness.* Boston: Perseus Books.

Langer, E. (1997). *The power of mindful learning.* Boston: Perseus Books.

Langer, E., & Rodin, J. (1976). The effects of enhanced personal responsibility for the aged: A field experiment in an institutional setting. *Journal of Personality and Social Psychology, 34,* 191–198.

Mead, M. (1977). The originality of Milton H. Erickson. *The American Journal of Clinical Hypnosis, 20,* 4–5.

Morgan, L., & Kunkel, S. (1998). *Aging: The social context.* Thousand Oaks, CA: Pine Forge Press.

Morris, C., & Gali, V. (1994). The physiology and biomedical aspects of chronic pain in later life. In K. Roberts (Ed.), *Older women with chronic pain.* New York: Harrington Park Press.

Pierlin, L., & Skaff, M. (1995). Stressors and adaptation in late life. In M. Gatz (Ed.), *Emerging issues in mental health and aging.* Washington, DC: American Psychological Association.

Potts, M. (1997). Social support and depression among older adults living alone: The importance of friends within and outside of a retirement community. *Social Work, 42*(3), 348–362.

Restak, R. (1988). *The mind.* New York: Bantam Books.

Restak, R. (1999). *Older and wiser: How to maintain peak mental ability for as long as you live.* New York: Berkley Books/Simon & Schuster.

Rose, R. (1991). Normality and stress: Response and adaptation from an endocrine perspective. In D. Offer & M. Sabshin (Eds.), *The diversity of normal behavior.* New York: Basic Books.

Rosen, S. (1982). *My voice will go with you: The teaching tales of Milton H. Erickson.* New York: Norton.

Rossi, E. (Ed.). (1980a). *The collected papers of Milton H. Erickson, M.D. Volume I: The nature of hypnosis and suggestion.* New York: Irvington Publishers.

Rossi, E. (Ed.). (1980b). *The collected papers of Milton H. Erickson, M.D. Volume II: Hypnotic alteration of sensory, perceptual and psychological processes.* New York: Irvington Publishers.

Rossi, E. (Ed.) (1980c). *The collected papers of Milton H. Erickson, M.D. Volume IV: Innovative hypnotherapy.* New York: Irvington Publishers.

Rossi, E., & Ryan, M. (1992). *Creative choice in hypnosis.* New York: Irvington Publishers.

Rossi, E., Ryan, M., & Sharp, F. (1983). *Healing in hypnosis.* New York: Irvington Publishers.

Rowe J., & Kahn, R. (1998). *Successful aging.* New York: Random House.

Schuster, J., & Goetz, K. (1994). Pain. In E. Coffrey & J. Cummings (Eds.), *Textbook of geriatric neuropsychiatry.* Washington, DC: The American Psychiatric Press.

Sullivan, W. (1992). Reconsidering the environment as a helping resource. In D. Saleedey (Ed.), *The strengths perspective in social work.* White Plains, NY: Longman Publishing Group.

Watzlawick, P. (1985). Hypnotherapy without trance. In J. Zeig (Ed.), *Ericksonian psychotherapy. Volume I: Structures.* New York: Brunner/Mazel.

Zeig, J. (1980). *A teaching seminar with Milton H. Erickson.* New York: Brunner/Mazel.

Zeig, J. (1985). *Ericksonian therapy: Clinical applications.* New York: Brunner/Mazel.

SUGGESTED READINGS

BOOKS

Brown, P. (1991). *The hypnotic brain: Hypnotherapy and social communication.* New Haven, CT: Yale University Press.

Duncan, B., Hubble, M., Miller, S., & Coleman, S. (1998). Escaping the lost world of impossibility: Honoring clients' language, motivation and theories of change. In M. Hoyt (Ed.), *The handbook of constructive therapies.* San Francisco: Jossey-Bass.

Erickson, M.H., & Rossi, E.L. (1979). *Hypnotherapy: An exploratory casebook.* New York: Irvington Publishers.

Erickson, M.H., & Rossi, E.L. (1981). *Experiencing hypnosis: Therapeutic approaches to altered states.* New York: Irvington Publishers.

Goldberg, E. (2001). *The executive brain: Frontal lobes and the civilized mind.* New York: Oxford University Press.

Gordon, D., & Meyers-Anderson, M. (1981). *Phoenix: Therapeutic patterns of Milton H. Erickson.* Capitola, CA: Meta Publications.

Haley, J. (1973). *Uncommon therapy: The psychiatric techniques of Milton Erickson, M.D.* New York: Norton.

Haley, J. (1985). *Conversations with Milton H. Erickson, M.D. Volume II: Treating couples and families.* New York: Triangle Press.

Keeney, B. (1983). *The aesthetics of change.* New York: Guilford Press.

Langer, E. (1997). *The power of mindful learning.* Boston, MA: Perseus Books.

Langer, E. (1989). *Mindfulness.* Boston, MA: Perseus Books.

Miller S., Duncan, B., & Hubble, M. (1997). *Escape from Babel.* New York: W.W. Norton.

Morgan, L., & Kunkel, S. (1998). *Aging: The social context.* Thousand Oaks, CA: Pine Forge Press.

Restak, R. (1999). *Older and wiser: How to maintain peak mental ability for as long as you live.* New York: Berkley Books/Simon & Schuster.

Rosen, S. (1982). *My voice will go with you: The teaching tales of Milton H. Erickson.* New York: Norton.

Rossi, E. (Ed.). (1980a). *The collected papers of Milton H. Erickson, M.D. Volume I: The nature of hypnosis and suggestion.* New York: Irvington Publishers.

Rossi, E. (Ed.). (1980b). *The collected papers of Milton H. Erickson, M.D. Volume II: Hypnotic alteration of sensory, perceptual and psychological processes.* New York: Irvington Publishers.

Rossi, E. (Ed.). (1980c). *The collected papers of Milton H. Erickson, M.D. Volume IV: Innovative hypnotherapy.* New York: Irvington Publishers.

Rossi, E., & Ryan, M. (1985). *Life reframing in hypnosis.* New York: Irvington Publishers.

Rossi, E., & Ryan, M. (1992). *Creative choice in hypnosis.* New York: Irvington Publishers.

Rossi, E., Ryan, M., & Sharp, F. (1983). *Healing in hypnosis.* New York: Irvington Publishers.

Rowe J., & Kahn, R. (1998). *Successful aging.* New York: Random House.

JOURNALS

Erickson, M.H. (1954, October). Initial experiments investigating the nature of hypnosis. *The American Journal of Clinical Hypnosis, 1,* 152–162.

Erickson, M.H. (1959, January). Hypnosis in painful terminal illness. *The American Journal of Clinical Hypnosis, 1.*

Erickson, M.H. (1966). The interspersal hypnotic technique for symptom correction and pain control. *The American Journal of Clinical Hypnosis, 8,* 189–209.

Erickson, M.H., & Rossi, E.L. (1977, July). The autohypnotic experiences of Milton H. Erickson. *The American Journal of Clinical Hypnosis, 20,* 76–84.

Geary, B. (1988). The psychotherapeutic legacy of Milton H. Erickson. *Arizona Counseling Journal, 1*(13), 40–44.

Mead, M. (1977). The originality of Milton H. Erickson. *The American Journal of Clinical Hypnosis, 20,* 4–5.

10

SOLUTION-FOCUSED THERAPY

Elders Enhancing Exceptions

Marilyn J. Bonjean

SOLUTION-FOCUSED THERAPY helps clients tap their latent resources by focusing their attention on feelings, thoughts, and behaviors that are exceptions to the problems discussed in therapy. *Exceptions* are those times when the problem does not occur or the problem is a little less intense or somehow different than usual. I have found solution-focused therapy useful when working with older adults and their families because it emphasizes a respectful appreciation of individuals' abilities and very quickly mobilizes their energy to make changes.

A solution-focused therapist develops a collaborative relationship with clients and helps them define their goals. The therapist must assume that each client has a unique manner of self-expression, personal values, and way of thinking about life. The therapist must then adapt to these to assist the client in achieving satisfactory outcomes from therapy.

The solution-focused approach is characterized by 1) assumptions that help guide the therapist's behavior during the therapy sessions, 2) questions that assist clients' thinking about a positive future and achieving goals they define, and 3) messages the therapist delivers to clients at the end of the session that summarize the session and suggest methods to continue progress toward goals.

HISTORY AND DEVELOPMENT
OF SOLUTION-FOCUSED THERAPY

The practice of working on constructing solutions with clients instead of exploring the cause of problems was a shift in the field of mental health that a group of psychotherapists at the Brief Family Therapy Center (BFTC) in Milwaukee, Wisconsin, originated during the late 1970s and 1980s. The core group of founders consisted of Steve de Shazer, Insoo Berg, Jim Derks, Elam Nunnally, Marilyn LaCourt, and Eve Lipchik.*

   The founders credit several other mental health professionals with influencing their thinking. One primary resource was renowned psychotherapist and hypnotherapist Milton H. Erickson (de Shazer, 1982). (See Chapter 9.) In his article, "Special Techniques of Brief Hypnotherapy," Erickson (1954) described interacting with individuals' neurotic symptoms to meet their unique needs. He successfully utilized whatever capacities his clients made manifest in therapy to solve their problems without trying to find and solve causative underlying maladjustments. Erickson perceived people as having social systems that allocated resources for changes to occur. In an Ericksonian model, the therapist and client work together to use these resources to solve the client's problems. Erickson emphasized a therapist's responsibility to respect the abilities of his or her clients and to help focus these abilities toward behaviors that enable the client to achieve goals.

   Another influence on the development of solution-focused therapy was the approach espoused by the Mental Research Institute (MRI) in Palo Alto, California. Members of this group, Weakland, Fisch, Watzlawick, and Bodin (1974), wrote a paper titled "Brief Therapy: Focused Problem Resolution," which described their ideas about how human problems form, how individuals maintain these problems, and how change can take place so that the problem is no longer a problem. The MRI therapy model is based on the belief that problems develop

---

*I was fortunate enough to be a part of the Brief Family Therapy Center from 1983 through 1988 and to learn from my interactions with the founders. Since establishing a private practice in 1988 (ICF Consultants, with my business partner Eve Lipchik), I have continued to pursue interests in applying a strengths-based, solution-focused approach to client situations. My work as a gerontologist in private practice has been with older families or in settings with adults with chronic medical illnesses and their families. The clients with whom I work often have little time for change to occur before they may be facing very serious consequences such as loss of family support, placement in a nursing home, or increased health problems (Bonjean & Bonjean, 1996). Disempowerment of the older person may have occurred as a result of multiple losses, failing control over physical functions, or involvement in hierarchical relationships with community service providers.

   I have chosen the solution-focused model as my way of working with clients because its philosophical tenets fit well with my worldview, values, and beliefs about human beings. It allows me to work with people who have potential for change and healing, are viewed as cooperative, and are willing to share their difficulties and eventually their achievements with me. I find that it promotes my own sense of gratefulness and growth and helps me to construct a positive model for my own aging.

from, and are maintained by, the way that normal life difficulties are perceived and the attempts that individuals make to solve them.

Attempted solutions that are motivated by a particular belief framework result in circular patterns of unsuccessful behavior. These patterns are self-reinforcing as individuals try to solve problems by doing more of the same behaviors that have not worked—and then eventually the "solution" becomes incorporated into the problem. The goal of this model is to interrupt the well-intentioned solution behaviors that maintain the problem so as to help clients start to do something different.

> THE GOAL OF THIS model is to interrupt the well-intentioned solution behaviors that maintain the problem so as to help clients start to do something different.

In 1978, the staff of the BFTC was also problem focused and interested in the question of how doing more of the same unsuccessful solution behaviors maintained problems. They interacted with the staff of MRI to discuss their evolving ideas about therapy. Over several years, a solution-focused therapy model developed. It retained certain theoretical beliefs in common with MRI such as the lack of emphasis on the history of a problem and on discovering underlying pathology in an individual's personality. The solution-focused model emphasized exceptions to the problem rather than the problem behavior itself or what maintained it. This model centered around gathering information about what was happening when the problem was not occurring or was a little less intense or different somehow, instead of on gathering information about what was wrong and not working for the client. For example, a person who is generally overwhelmed with stress copes with that stress a little at times, and a person who is mourning experiences some ebb and flow to that mourning process while it is occurring. It is the thoughts, feelings, and behaviors that support these variations in the problematic experiences that are of interest to the solution-focused therapist and that form the basis for continuing change. De Shazer described this development toward better-understanding solutions rather than exploring information about problems:

> Over the last three or four years we have shifted significantly from a concern with problems, complaints, and how to solve them; to a concern with solutions and how they work. Over this time, we have become convinced that solutions, from case to case, have more in common with each other than with the problems they solve. We used to think that solutions had to bear a fairly high degree of correspondence to the problems and complaints brought in by families or clients. We have now come to the conclusion that very little correspondence may be necessary. (as cited in Cade, 1985, p. 96)

As the solution-focused model shifted toward an interest in solution construction, its philosophical stance also changed toward a valuing of the subjective experience of clients. The goal of therapy changed from interrupting interactional patterns that the therapist identified as faulty attempts at solutions to a more collaborative goal established by the client. Instead of the therapist knowing what was in the best interest of clients, the clients' own values were a guide to establishing goals. The therapist and client were considered a therapeutic suprasystem and together developed new, nonproblematic ways of interacting with others.

This philosophical change was part of a larger trend in the humanities and behavioral sciences toward constructivism and social constructionism. *Constructivism* is a relativistic point of view emphasizing the subjective construction of reality. An emphasis is placed on the individual's unique, personal, subjective experience of the world and of relationships. *Social constructionism* addresses holding this subjective reality in common with others within a particular linguistic/cultural context such as a family or social group (Held, 1995).

In 1984, the BFTC began a project in artificial intelligence—BRIEFER—to develop a computer software program to assist in formulating messages to deliver to clients after the first therapy session (Goodman, Gingerich, & de Shazer, 1989). To work on this project, the core group conducted an analysis of how a therapist makes decisions in relation to clients, both as an interviewer and as a team member. The analysis stimulated a theory of solution that was a decision tree of the therapeutic process (De Shazer, 1988). It also emphasized the importance of nonverbal language and emotions as a context in which the therapeutic interview took place (Lipchik, 1993, 1997, 1999). Core group members went on to explore different areas of interest. De Shazer expanded the theoretical aspects of language use to convey and shape subjective experience (Miller & de Shazer, 2000). Other members, such as Eve Lipchik, continued to expand on the importance of the collaborative relationship between therapist and client and the role of emotion in solution-focused therapy (Kiser, Piercy, & Lipchik, 1993; Lipchik, 1999; Piercy, Lipchik, & Kiser, 2000). As the core group tried to be clear about the steps they took in making decisions related to client interaction, the underlying assumptions of the solution-focused model became very clear.

THEORETICAL ASSUMPTIONS
OF THE SOLUTION-FOCUSED MODEL

Therapy models are based on certain assumptions about the nature of a person, problem formation and problem maintenance, creation of change, role of the client, and role of the therapist. Making these assumptions explicit is important because it allows the therapist to understand his or her motivation for the techniques that are used in interviewing clients. The assumptions are a philosophy that remains consistent even though the situations that clients bring to therapy may have great variety and the environment in which the therapist practices may vary from that of a nursing facility to a hospital to the client's own home. Having a consistent guiding philosophy or set of beliefs keeps the therapist from applying a collection of techniques or becoming mechanistic in approaching client issues.

GUIDING PRINCIPLES

The guiding principles of solution-focused therapy have been well described (Lipchik, 2002; Walter & Peller, 1982). A summary of the guiding principles follows.

PRINCIPLE 1: EVERY CLIENT IS UNIQUE When solution-focused therapists believe in their own uniqueness and that of their clients, it keeps them from thinking they know what solution should work for a particular client because it worked in a particular case or in their own personal life. One older adult may find that getting more involved with other people will be helpful in engendering a feeling of being more connected to the social world whereas another may find that reading and walking in the forest promote a feeling of connection.

PRINCIPLE 2: EACH CLIENT WILL HAVE HIS OR HER OWN SPECIAL WAY OF REACHING GOALS Clients have the inherent strengths and resources to help themselves. Often, when a client comes for therapy, the description of complex problems and the intensity of feelings around the problems presented can make the therapist feel overwhelmed and question where to begin or what to offer this client. The assumption that each client has a unique way of reaching goals is often one of the hardest to deeply believe but it is the foundation for practicing the solution-focused model.

The therapist begins by noticing what the client is doing, such as coming to the office or tolerating the intensity of the discussion about the problem. The therapist may then continue with questions asking the client about how problems have been managed or coped with to this point. Acting on this assumption emphasizes clients' resources and promotes a positive relationship between therapist and client.

PRINCIPLE 3: EXCEPTIONS TO EVERY PROBLEM CAN BE CREATED BY THE THERAPIST AND CLIENT AND CAN BE USED TO BUILD SOLUTIONS This may seem to be an impossible task in therapy if the definition of exception and solution are not broad enough. An exception can be any fluctuation in the problem situation itself, variations in coping ability, or increased acceptance . . . anything that implies change for this client. Solutions may include utilizing a community resource so that a caregiver for a frail family member can have short periods of respite, or helping an individual learn to communicate more clearly with a physician so that medication can be evaluated and used more effectively. Finding a solution often does not mean dramatic differences in the client's life, but rather, enough change to move toward the client's goals.

PRINCIPLE 4: CLIENTS ARE ALWAYS COOPERATIVE The client has a way of going about change, and it is the therapist's responsibility to be flexible enough to find ways to assist each client in change. Labeling a client resistant or noncompliant usually happens when the client does not accept the therapist's point of view or do what the therapist thinks the client should do. When this happens, the therapist may perceive the client as resistant or noncompliant and fail to seek more information about what will work for the client. As human beings, therapists will naturally feel frustrated at times. These feelings will often happen when the therapist is taking too much responsibility for change.

PRINCIPLE 5: CLIENTS CAN ONLY CHANGE THEMSELVES This assumption emphasizes a person's nature as free to choose responses to situations and to be the ultimate decision maker about behavior. The therapist can make suggestions, offer information, review alternatives, and discuss feelings with a client, but in the end, the client will choose a path for him- or herself. This assumption can be very hard to follow when the therapist believes the client will regret a decision. This can be seen in the case of a spouse caregiver whose frail husband's or wife's condition has deteriorated. The caregiver may be unable to face the necessity of nursing home placement for his or her spouse and may decide to continue home care, despite the fact that all the professionals involved may have advised not taking the spouse home from the hospital. Often, the guilt is more powerful than the advice and logic offered by professionals. Supporting the caregiver's feelings and the need to try home care again will make it easier to eventually face the need for using the nursing facility.

PRINCIPLE 6: CHANGE IS OCCURRING ALL THE TIME As human beings, we may create patterns and habits, yet our environment also contains much variation of experience. Often when a client feels stuck in painful feelings or circumstances, the variety of experience is obscured by the awareness of pain. The therapist can be useful by helping the client do one thing differently, such as thinking about something that had seemed unthinkable, noticing something to report more clearly about in the next session, or performing a minor behavior such as making a telephone call. Returning to talk more with the therapist might be the next helpful step. Taking some action, no matter how small, can create a feeling of movement toward solution and generate hope. Hopeful feelings can provide the energy to continue changing. Small changes lead to larger changes. Hope is important for the therapist as well as the client, to keep from being overwhelmed by the sadness, complexity, or multiplicity of client problems.

PRINCIPLE 7: THE PAST CANNOT BE CHANGED It is important to concentrate on the present and the future. Clients may have experienced many hurtful and difficult events in the past and need to tell the therapist their story. The therapist's listening to the narrative attentively may provide the first experience the client has had of sharing this personal history. It is the impact of that past on the client in the present and an emphasis on a more positive future that will be useful to consider in therapy, however. After listening to the client's story, the solution-focused therapist is interested in the lessons the client learned from the past that can be useful in the future or the strengths and coping mechanisms that the individual learned through adversity that can be used to solve problems now.

PRINCIPLE 8: BOTH THE THERAPIST AND THE CLIENT ARE EXPERTS The therapist will bring knowledge of human development, models of change, information about community resources, and an ability to assist clients in focusing energy on solution construction. The client will bring an experience of personal circumstances, definitions of the problems and their solutions, strengths, solution-finding abilities, and a preferred manner of going about change. Respecting the client as an expert will help the therapist to emphasize client goals and have confidence in the possibilities for change.

Assumptions are important because they shape the therapist's attitude and relationship with clients. They provide a guiding framework for decision making and lead the therapist to ask questions about certain thoughts, feelings, or behaviors. The structure of the first therapy session and subsequent meetings is built around these assumptions.

SOLUTION-FOCUSED THERAPY IN PRACTICE

The following text describes ways in which solution-focused therapy can be woven into each therapy session.

THE FIRST SESSION

A short, social interchange usually happens at the beginning of the first session in which the therapist and client get to know a little about each other. Then a getting-down-to-business transition happens as the therapist asks what brings the client to therapy or what the client is hoping to achieve. The client often provides a description of the problem as an attempt to try to help the therapist understand the situation. As the client describes difficulties, the therapist listens for variation in the client's experience of the problem, the client's use of language such as metaphors or other descriptive words that can help the client feel understood if the therapist uses them, and the client's value system and worldview.

EXCEPTION QUESTIONS   After respectfully listening to a client's unique descriptions of difficulties, the therapist tries to understand a client's ideas about a more positive future. The therapist guides the client's focus on a positive future orientation by asking questions that elicit a description of the desired state of being. This allows goals to become clear so that client and therapist have a direction for therapy. The following are some examples of exception questions:

- How will you know that you no longer need to come to therapy?
- If a miracle happened and your problem disappeared, what would be different?
- Who would notice if the problem disappeared? How would it affect those who noticed?
- How would it affect you if the problem disappeared?
- How would you know if things were better? When that happened, who would be affected and how? (Berg, 1991, pp. 97–100)

The therapist can continue to focus on solutions by asking the client whether any of these more-positive experiences are currently occurring. Often there is some fluctuation in the client's painful experiences that has been dismissed because it did not last or was taken for granted. Fluctuations may be discussed by making a distinction between the generally painful experience and those times when that general state is either worse or better. When the generally painful state is worse and then ebbs, it may be useful for the client to explore how such ebbs happen and how the state could be controlled to prevent exacerbations. This exploration would describe movement, even if it were among degrees of pain, and might help the client feel less stuck. Positive exceptions to the difficulty can also be explored.

COPING QUESTIONS   Some clients are unable to identify any exceptions to their problems; it is not in the best interest of the therapeutic relationship for the therapist to struggle with the client to get acknowledgment of exceptions. The structure of the therapeutic relationship needs to be flexible and built around the client's wants. If the therapist becomes attached to the form of the interview such as a certain order of questions or a rigid structure, the interview can become formulaic instead of individualized and personalized. The practice of interviewing in a mechanistic way has been referred to as "solution-forced" (Nyland & Corsiglia, 1994).

> THE STRUCTURE OF the therapeutic relationship needs to be flexible and built around the client's wants.

Questions about exceptions or positive futures may be very difficult for clients to answer because they require clients to focus on positive emotions when they may feel bad; it may be more congruent for them to talk about problems (Kiser, Piercy, & Lipchik, 1993). Clients may try to protect themselves from the disappointment or the consequences of change. Solution-focused therapists tend to encourage their clients to translate feelings into observable behavior; for example, they may ask the client, "How will you act when you are feeling better?" For some clients, sharing the story of the problem may be the beginning of change and talking about behavior is too large a step for them. Clients who are unable to identify exceptions may relate better to questions about their coping ability. "With circumstances as difficult as you describe, how have you managed to cope?" " . . . to not give up?" " . . . to have the energy to come for therapy?" Such questions may communicate more understanding and form a useful basis for progress. The power of the therapist's human presence should not be underestimated in gradually helping clients express feelings in ways that are likely to lead to their greater satisfaction in daily life.

CONSEQUENCES OF CHANGE QUESTIONS   If clients are ambivalent about change, it will be useful to explore the good reasons they have for going slowly or not considering change. Client autonomy extends to all aspects of the change process. A therapist's respectful help in examining decisions about change may be different for the client and may itself lead to changes.

As people age, their uniqueness becomes increasingly apparent; no two sets of clients' circumstances will be the same. The therapist's ability to craft approaches that fit each client is an important component of respect. Even if clients make a decision not to change, they may be in a more satisfying position because they have weighed their consequences and have chosen not to do anything.

It is especially important for the therapist to be willing to examine the negative consequences of change when working with the problems of adults who are physically frail. For these individuals, remaining independent may be based on a carefully balanced set of interactions with other people or community agencies. If a change is made, this balance may be disrupted and the client's independence could be at risk. When a therapist examines the positive and negative possibilities of change with the client, this communicates a real concern for the client's welfare and removes the therapist from a position of being a change advocate to being a client advocate.

SCALING QUESTIONS Scaling questions may help clients examine change by creating a subjective measure of their present location on the change continuum and mark progress toward goals: "On a scale of 1–10, where 1 represents *the worst,* and 10 *the way things will be when problems are resolved,* where would you place yourself now?" (These numbers can be transposed, with 1 as the best-case and 10 as the worst-case scenario, as is illustrated in the case studies that follow.) Berg suggested many uses of scaling questions: "Scaling questions can be used to assess the client's self-esteem, self-confidence, investment in change, willingness to work hard to bring about desired changes, prioritizing of problems to be solved, perceptions of hopefulness, evaluation of progress, and so on" (1991, p. 8). Collaboratively, the therapist and client create the scale, a process that encourages change as the therapist records the progress and shares it with the client from session to session. It can also help the client describe steps necessary for additional progress as clients define the behaviors needed to move from one number on the scale to another.

PHYSICAL HEALTH STATUS QUESTIONS To be most useful to older adults with whom the co-occurrence of physical and mental health issues is well documented, the therapist should ask a client about physical and pharmacological factors that may need to be examined in the change process. Some of the factors that the therapist should consider in identifying resources available to achieve the older individual's goals are the medications being taken (especially those just started or discontinued), including over-the-counter products and preparations by community healers; the involvement of family members or significant others; and the presence of community agencies. Considering this information as steps the older adult has been taking to try to solve problems makes them part of the solution. When the therapist asks about health issues with which the older adult is coping or medication taken to maintain physical stability or comfort, these factors should be included in the strengths profile of the client, rather than collected to complete a picture of disability.

Mental health professionals will often work collaboratively with physicians around the biomedical issues of older adult clients. Both psychotherapy and pharmacological therapy can be useful approaches to creating change for clients. Utilizing descriptions of change that support the combined use of therapy and medication is important so that clients do not experience the therapist as excluding or discouraging the use of medication. For example, when a client is clinically depressed and the number of physiological symptoms indicates medication would be useful, describing the use of medication as helpful to the psychotherapy process can support clients in considering an antidepressant. Griffith and his colleagues (1991) described metaphors that may promote considering action from more than one perspective. The *psychophysiological metaphor* suggests that stress may have exhausted the systems of the brain built to process worry and that medication may restore the chemicals to normal baselines so energy is there to work in psychotherapy. The *stress-diathesis metaphor* suggests that a strong family history of depression may dispose the client to become depressed under great stress. Medication may lower that vulnerability so that psychotherapy can help clients learn behaviors that mediate against stress. The *protective physiological reflex metaphor* labels depression as a natural protective response to great stress and medication as a buffer to the nervous system so that psychotherapy can help create behavioral buffers. If the physician and therapist use the same metaphor in discussing the antidepressant, the client may consider this option without sorting through inconsistencies in the information provided by professionals.

SUBSEQUENT SESSIONS: DEVELOPING GOALS

As the first session progresses, the therapist and client try to define together what the client wants to accomplish. As discussion continues from session to session, these goals will often become clearer, more specific, and better defined. Therapists, influenced by the current managed care emphasis on brief therapy, may believe that a well-defined goal should be stated by the end of the first session. For some clients this works well; however, others will need more time. It may be useful for the therapist to think about goal development as a process that will continue throughout the duration of therapy. As clients change, more information becomes available to them about the consequences of changing and they may modify their ideas about desirable outcomes or be better able to consider the behaviors needed to achieve goals. The following guidelines may help the therapist in formulating collaborative goals:

> IT MAY BE USEFUL FOR the therapist to think about goal development as a process that will continue throughout the duration of therapy.

1. *Goals are whatever the client wants to accomplish.* Although the therapist may think that the client could benefit from a number of changed behaviors, suspending these judgments is important so that the focus is on change that is meaningful to the client.

2. *Goals must be realistic and achievable.* A realistic goal will be something the client can achieve within a week or two. In the beginning, a goal of thinking about the conversation in the session, reading some material about community resources, or noticing some behavior that is already occurring are types of goals that can be achieved. Experiencing success is important to reinforce the client's efforts and confidence in the usefulness of therapy. It is especially difficult to focus on small, achievable goals when clients present many problems and are overwhelmed. It is

especially in this situation that achieving something different is so important, however, and moving one step at a time will promote incremental change that may be better tolerated by someone who is already overwhelmed. Goals describe desired behavior.

3. *Solution-focused therapy emphasizes the strengths of the client and the description of a positive future.* In keeping with this focus, state goals so that the behaviors to be achieved are described. Instead of the client stating, "I will be stopping . . . " or "I will no longer be doing . . . " encourage the client to phrase goals positively, such as "I will be thinking, feeling, or doing . . . " and insert the desired new behavior. Often, clients can describe problems or what they wish would stop, but it is not as easy to carefully state the new behaviors, and their definition stimulates the change process.

4. *Describe goals in interpersonal terms.* As a client changes, new behaviors will have an impact on people in the client's environment, and the reactions stimulated by this impact will affect the client's continued change. As goals are stated, part of the description of the desired state should include helping clients anticipate and adjust to behaviors of others. For example, a client whose goal is to say "No" more often when requested to help baby-sit grandchildren will need to anticipate the reaction of adult children to these new limits. Predicting reactions of others will help the client think through more specifically how he or she will implement the desired behaviors.

5. *Goals develop and change.* It is not unusual for the goals clients want to accomplish to change. As their circumstances change, clients often become clearer about the way they would like to construct their futures. For example, it is not unusual for someone to seek therapy for difficulty in adjusting to retirement. Some individuals adjusting to retirement try certain different behaviors only to find that activities that seemed promising are not. For some individuals, finding meaning in this stage of life consists of behaving in ways not thought useful until behaviors had been tried and discarded. Throughout the therapy process, clients can discover new information and redefine what they want. Both client and therapist will know therapy is over when the evolving goals have been met to the satisfaction of the client.

The following case example emphasizes the importance of constructing questions and goals as well as exceptions. The therapist in the example builds on behaviors the client is already exhibiting. Goals are negotiated so that they are achievable and do not raise the anxiety level of the client. By acknowledging the usefulness of many approaches to achieving goals, the therapist encourages an openness and creativity in accomplishing change.

One of the most difficult clinical situations therapists face is the attachment some clients develop to medication that may cause dangerous side effects. Another difficult situation is the belief of some clients that only medication can cause change and that they can contribute little to their own improvement. When these difficulties present themselves in the first session, it is an opportunity for the therapist to respectfully explore the goals of the client and to create a therapeutic relationship in which change can be considered.

Mrs. Browning

When Mrs. Browning came for consultation, she had been referred by her physician because the medication she was using to reduce her anxiety was affecting her memory and concentration. Her physician requested that she learn behavioral methods of relaxation so that her anxiety medication could be reduced or eliminated. Mrs. Browning described how anxious she had become after her best friend moved away and how the medication had helped her. On a scale of 1–10, she scaled the problem at 10 as *maximum intensity*. She did not want to experience the painful anxiety again without something to help her reduce it. This situation opens an opportunity for the therapist to explore the part that client behavior already plays in relaxation.

Therapist: Do you cooperate with your medication?

Client: What do you mean, cooperate?

Therapist: Well, some people expect medication to work but they fight it. They take a sleep medication but get up and run around. Others take something to relax but keep doing what was making them nervous.

Client: Well, I think I cooperate.

Therapist: What do you do?

Client: I usually take my medication and then sit down for a little while until I feel better.

Therapist: What do you do when you are sitting there?

Client: I read or pray; I do something to take my mind off of my nerves.

Therapist: So you do things to help your medication work. I think your doctor would like those helping behaviors to grow strong enough that the medication could be gradually reduced so that these behaviors would take over influencing the anxiety. What do you want?

Client: I don't want to have the painful anxiety like I did, but I don't want to have memory lapses either—I guess I could try more relaxing things if I know I don't have to go off the medication right away. I could gradually reduce it but I would have to know the other things were really working.

Therapist: Could we say that right now your goal is to become more relaxed and keep the medication the same? Then eventually, as you feel confident in your ability to relax, you could experiment with lowering the medication?

Client:	That sounds right. I need to know I can control being so nervous.
Therapist:	When you are feeling more relaxed, how is that different than when you are feeling nervous?
Client:	My chest feels loose, and I keep my hands open and not clenched. My mind can think of something other than worries. I am more patient with other people.
Therapist:	Does that happen now when you are helping your medication to work?
Client:	A little, but not enough.
Therapist:	When it is enough, how will you know?
Client:	I will feel like I can go out and do more things with other people. My body will feel looser, and my breathing will be regular even if I have to make a decision or something unexpected comes up.
Therapist:	What do you think other people will notice when you are relaxed enough?
Client:	I will laugh more and suggest doing activities rather than waiting for them to invite me. I used to be very outgoing. I'm not sure what happened to me.
Therapist:	You have already started making progress toward your goals. It sounds as though you are doing some of the relaxation when you sit down and help the anti-anxiety medication to work. Together we can decide how to expand what you have been doing.

As therapy progresses, emphasis continues to be placed on what is changing and how the client is bringing this about. The first session of therapy is used to understand the life situation of the client and to create a picture of what the client's life will be like when goals are achieved.

CREATING THE SUMMATION AND SUGGESTION MESSAGE At the end of the first and subsequent sessions, the therapist will construct a structured response to what the client has shared in the interview, the summation message, and a suggestion for change (Lipchik, 2002). The therapist may want to step out of the session for a few minutes to do this and can explain to the client that he or she needs a few minutes to think and will come back with some ideas to share. Sometimes the therapist may write out the message and give it to the client to think about between sessions. Other times the therapist may know what to say at the end of the session, will not need to leave the room, and will be able to convey a short summary and suggested action to the client. The summation message includes

- A summary of what brought the client to therapy
- Strengths and changes the client has already started to make

- A summary of the feelings that the client has shared
- Goals that the client has described

Clients may respond to the summation message with agreement or with a correction of some aspect they do not find accurate. The therapist will acknowledge the client's responses. After the summation message, the therapist will offer the client suggestions for something to notice, to think about, or to do. Because this is a collaborative relationship, the tone is tentative and not prescriptive. If positive changes have already begun, then the suggestion will support their continuation. When the client does not appear to experience any variation in painful circumstances, suggestions can center on having the client observe situations for some indications of variety.

In Mrs. Browning's case, a summation message after the first session would include her referral from her physician and a description of the difficulty she is having and what she wants—good concentration and freedom from high anxiety. Feeling anxious is a unique kind of pain, and the therapist would empathize with her about this problem. Mrs. Browning would be complimented for agreeing to come when her physician suggested it and for her helpful description of her thoughts and feelings. The relaxation she is doing would be described as a good basis for more work in lowering anxiety behaviorally. The therapist suggests continued behavioral changes that Mrs. Browning could make, such as noticing the effect of the relaxation, seeking a distraction while waiting for medication to work, and thinking about what she can do to expand her efforts. Perhaps rhythmic breathing could be added to the behaviors she is already using.

THE SECOND AND SUBSEQUENT SESSIONS

The second and subsequent sessions focus on what has been different since the last session. Progress is often taken for granted, and the therapist's goal is to identify any variation in the situation and give it attention through questions and comments. Seeking detail about change that has occurred between sessions and the behaviors used to achieve it underscores clients' strengths and competence. When therapists and clients gather details about the progress of change, it reinforces the behavior and helps the clients notice a difference in their present. Often, clients report change and then state that it was very short-lived or only slight. They will then go back to describing the problem. Unless the therapist continues to be interested in small changes, progress can be lost in the description of problems. The meaning clients assign to these changes is a very important factor in whether the change will be viewed as making a difference and also whether the change will be continued. The attention the therapist gives to small change can raise it to a meaningful level.

Defining solutions in very realistic terms so that problems are solvable is crucial to outcomes. The most important question the therapist will ask is not "What is the problem?" but "How will you know when the problem is solved?" The definition of solution may keep changing and become more and more realistic. Although Mrs. Browning may wish she would never feel nervous, for example, anxiety may be very appropriate at times. She may decide that "relaxed enough" means that her anxiety will not make her body uncomfortable or keep her from being outgoing and doing activities. She will be able to live with little or no medication. At times she will feel nervous because that is a normal human reaction, and the goal is not for her to become reckless.

> THE MOST IMPORTANT question the therapist will ask is not "What is the problem?" but "How will you know when the problem is solved?"

The structure of the sessions is built around ongoing events and experiences and, so, is less predictable than the first session. Each session is composed of "purposive questions" (Lipchik & de Shazer, 1987), which are questions aimed at eliciting distinctions between what is happening during periods that are more like what clients want and times that are more difficult for the clients.

Clients will have a variety of responses to the summation and suggestion. They may follow the suggestions and then the subsequent session may be dedicated to detailing the changes that ensued and next steps that could be taken with this new behavior as a foundation. The client may redesign the suggestion so that its intent is accomplished even though the method is not what was suggested in the session. Often, clients who are creative or like to feel more in control of their efforts will redesign suggestions. For example, when the therapist suggests gathering more information about a community resource by reading through a pamphlet, the client may do the information gathering by another means such as talking to friends or calling an agency. When clients do not follow the suggestion, their response is information for the therapist to consider before another suggestion is offered. Perhaps there is good reason the suggestion was not accomplished and the clients are basically willing to take suggestions. Certain clients do not like to take suggestions from others, however, and the therapist will need to find the best way to offer ideas for different behavior to these clients. Sometimes it may be more useful to give written information for discussion with the therapist, to use metaphors, or to tell stories that suggest changes more indirectly (de Shazer & Kral, 1986).

SUMMARIZING A SOLUTION-FOCUSED APPROACH

Following is an example of a therapist following the solution-focused assumptions outlined earlier, asking questions to describe a positive future, setting goals, and making suggestions to a client. It also addresses the issues related to providing care for a family member who is in frail health. Balancing the physical, emotional, and financial costs of caregiving with the rewards of the relationship and the personal development of the caregiver is never easy (Tennstedt, 1999). Therapists working with older adults and their families will find that caregiving issues are common problems motivating clients to seek consultation with a therapist.

Mrs. Roberts

Mrs. Roberts made an appointment with the therapist because she was becoming increasingly depressed and unwilling to leave her house. She was caring for her husband after his two heart attacks had affected his ability to concentrate and his confidence in his capacity to make decisions. Mrs. Roberts, like so many spouses, had become the first line of caregiving assistance when her partner became ill. Her daughter had referred her because she was concerned for her mother and the increasing isolation from friends and family. Her daughter lived about a half hour away, and a son lived in another state.

Mrs. Roberts explained that she seldom left her husband alone because she was afraid of returning home to find him dead; she worried that he would suffer and have no one to help him. Mrs. Roberts had terminated her club memberships and church work in which she had been very active; she left the house only for short intervals while her husband stayed alone. He did not accept the intervention of a volunteer or a professional, stating, "I'm not that bad."

When the therapist asked Mrs. Roberts to scale the intensity of her problem, she said it was at the maximum of 10. She would like to reduce the problem's intensity to a 2 because she felt it was realistic to expect to have some difficulties. Describing how she would feel and what she would be doing differently when she reached 2 on the scale, Mrs. Roberts stated that she would be able to have some of her old life back. She would be able to meet with her friends and attend church. The guilt she felt when she went out would go away and she could enjoy herself.

One of the first steps in building a therapeutic relationship with clients is acknowledging and/or normalizing their feelings. Mrs. Roberts visibly relaxed when the therapist framed her concerns as normal under the circumstances and very realistic. Mrs. Roberts described her feelings of guilt. She loved her husband but she was becoming more impatient with him, saying things she regretted and wanting to get away from him. She did not want to feel she had neglected or hurt him if he died in her care. Mrs. Robert's demeanor brightened when the therapist wondered how she was able to cope under the circumstances. Someone else might have broken down but she was still trying to find her own balance, she noted. Exploring the strengths a client already utilizes outlines a foundation on which additional change can take place. She answered by describing various ways that she had tried to help herself adjust and the changes she had made since her husband's heart attacks. Prior to his illness, she and her husband had made most of the financial decisions for the household together. Now she had to do more decision-making alone and she felt very overwhelmed.

For the remainder of the session, Mrs. Roberts discussed the feeling of being stuck between undesirable alternatives. She could continue as she had been, but she thought that would result in things getting worse for her and hurt her relationship with her husband, which would make her feel very guilty. She could go out more, but then she would worry about her husband and feel guilty for leaving him. The therapist agreed that there appeared to be no completely satisfactory choice. Envisioning a more positive future may not mean totally changing a difficult circumstance. She asked Mrs. Roberts what it would be like when a balance was found between her own needs and those of her husband. Mrs. Roberts stated it would be less of a worry to her children, she would feel less guilty all of the time, and she would be more positive in her attitude and comments to her husband. When the therapist asked her if any of those things happened even a little bit now, Mrs. Roberts said no. She just felt very stuck and didn't know if it could ever get any better. Rather than push Mrs. Roberts to consider changes that seemed impossible, the therapist empathized with how hard it was to find answers when each seemed to have drawbacks.

At this point, the therapist focused on those behaviors that Mrs. Roberts was already doing that even slightly resembled those she would be doing when her goals were met. The therapist asked how she was able to leave the house at all.

Client:	Well, I have to. We need food, and I go to the bank to pay bills. I wait until it is absolutely necessary and become very tense. I know I snap at him when I tell him I'm going out.
Therapist:	So when you feel you have to do it, you do go out but you are very anxious something will happen to your husband.
Client:	Yes, I'm getting more and more angry with him. He was so independent before and now I can't ask him to do anything. I feel guilty because he couldn't help having the heart attack. We were very close, you know. The doctor said he could stay alone but I know he doesn't like it and I'm so afraid something will happen, like when he had the last heart attack and had to call the ambulance himself.
Therapist:	This situation seems to be creating a lot of pressure on your marriage. It sounds as though reducing the anger toward your husband is an important goal. If he were able to discuss the decision of staying alone or having someone else with him, would you consider that a step in the direction you want to go?
Client:	Yes, but I am so tense that when I finally mention it, I snap at him and then he just says I should go. But I know he doesn't mean it when he says that.

By the end of the first session, the therapist had formed a relationship with Mrs. Roberts by listening to her story. The feelings of guilt and anger had been expressed as well as the experience of entrapment in her situation. Goals had been discussed and some exception to the problem had been identified. Mrs. Roberts felt very stuck and continued to express her frustration. She would have liked an immediate solution, but she also knew progress would come in steps. The therapist left the room at the end of the session, composed the summation and suggestion message, and on returning to the room, shared it with Mrs. Roberts:

Therapist:	As I understand what you were telling me, the situation is very difficult with your husband. You have been doing a good

job of making decisions and keeping your household running. However, you know that you need to have some breaks and do things outside the house. When you do, the worries, anger, and guilt are overwhelming. You go out to accomplish practical matters, but it is very difficult and you can never relax or enjoy yourself. One concern that I have in listening to your circumstances is how your marriage is being affected. The anger and guilt make you feel estranged from your husband and you would like to feel close again. I know it is hard to think about, but without some time to be away and relax, I'm afraid the resentment toward him will just keep growing. I don't know of any caregiver who can be responsible for everything and not have a break. Will you think about what you would need to feel comfortable going out, even if you think it is impossible to have it? We could talk about that next time.

Mrs. Roberts opened her session the following week with her thoughts about what the therapist had suggested:

Client:	All week I thought about the concerns you raised about my marriage. Since the heart attacks, I've been thinking of my husband more as a patient than a spouse. I don't like that—it makes me feel so far away from him.
Therapist:	How is it different if you think of him more as a spouse?
Client:	I expect him to make a contribution—I've been taking everything on myself and feeling very guilty if I ask him for anything.
Therapist:	What keeps you from expecting things from him now?
Client:	I feel like I should protect him. I know I can't but I still feel I should. The strange thing is that I also resent him and I think he can tell.
Therapist:	I think most people would resent feeling trapped and lonely, but I know you want the guilt and anger to go down.
Client:	Yes; if he dies, I don't want us to be having problems like this. We were very close, you know, and now I just want to get away.
Therapist:	If you began to treat him more like a husband, not a patient, and expected a contribution from him, what would you want him to be doing?
Client:	To accept someone being with him when I'm gone. He would just have to allow that.
Therapist:	How would it be different for you if he allowed someone to be with him?

Client:	I could relax and not rush back. Maybe I could meet with a friend or do something enjoyable. I haven't done that in a long time.
Therapist:	Do you think he realizes how much you need some time?
Client:	I don't know; I haven't told him but I would think he would realize I don't go out like I did before he got sick.

As the session continued, Mrs. Roberts explored how she might tell her husband about her feelings and needs. At the end of the session, the therapist shared a summary and suggestion message with the client:

Therapist:	I appreciate the thought you gave to your own needs. I know it is not easy to think about yourself when you are worried about someone you love. However, you are also realizing that in order to have a good relationship with your husband, you need to have some time away. To get that and be relaxed enough to enjoy it, you need to know someone is with your husband. I think you are beginning to believe it is not so unreasonable to expect some time away. You have good ideas about how to talk with your husband, making clear how much you need him to accept a companion even if he doesn't think he needs one. It seems as though the next step is to look for the right opportunity.

When Mrs. Roberts returned for her third session, she described the conversation she had with her husband.

Client:	I rehearsed ahead of time so I wouldn't snap at him because I was so tense. Then I explained how terrible I felt whenever I left the house.
Therapist:	I know that was a very difficult step for you to make. How did your husband react?
Client:	He said he hadn't realized it and didn't want me to rush back. He felt that if he told me he would be all right, I should just be able to go and not worry.
Therapist:	Could you accept his idea?
Client:	No. That is when we had our first argument since the heart attack. I couldn't help myself. I yelled at him about how he needs to help me and stop being so insensitive. I have needs, too. He yelled back at me, and I don't know why but that made me feel better.
Therapist:	How were you able to work out this issue?
Client:	Well, the argument cleared the air somehow and we both felt closer. We had sex for the first time since the heart attack. The

> doctor had said we could, but I still wasn't sure. So I just thought that if his heart could take an argument, it could take making love.

Therapist: I'm glad to hear you're both trying to get your marriage back to more the way it was before the heart attacks. I know that is what you wanted. What about leaving the house?

Client: We will hire someone. Even if he thinks it is a waste of money, we can afford it and I need this time. So he agreed because I insisted I have to feel comfortable leaving.

During the remainder of the session, Mrs. Roberts discussed her concerns about finding a person to stay with her husband. The therapist was able to give her information about community resources and common issues caregivers have when hiring a companion for a spouse. At the end of the session, the therapist shared a summary and suggestion message:

Therapist: You accomplished a lot by having the courage to talk to your husband about how you really felt. Now it seems you are both treating each other more as you did before the heart attacks. I have some brochures I can give you about hiring a companion. Maybe you and your husband can review them together before you both interview people.

By the fourth session, Mrs. Roberts was setting up the companion services and was preparing to go out for the first time for a more extended period.

Therapist: I know that even though you need to do things for yourself, the first time you go out and leave your husband for an extended period, it will be difficult. When you have accomplished challenging things in the past, how have you helped yourself be successful?

Client: I'd talk to myself and say that it would work out. I'd also visualize myself being able to do whatever was difficult and solve problems as they came up.

Therapist: How would you use those behaviors when you go out for the first time?

Client: I've started thinking about what I am going to do. I'll go to a movie with a friend. I thought a movie would be good because I couldn't worry too much about what was happening at home.

Therapist: What could prevent you from reaching your goal of going out?

Client: If, at the last minute, my husband asks me not to go and I feel guilty enough to stay home.

Therapist: What will you need to visualize yourself doing so this would not keep you from going?

Client: I'd let myself get mad, because he promised to try this. When I'm angry, I don't feel sorry for him and I can stay strong.

The session continued with the therapist and Mrs. Roberts discussing a positive outcome and the behaviors that would be needed for Mrs. Roberts to move closer to her goal of getting her life back by resuming her activities. The therapist ended with a summary and suggestion message.

Therapist: You have been doing some very useful planning with your husband. I think that interviewing companions together has helped both of you to believe it can work out for you to re-sume some of your activities. It has taken a lot of courage to keep going and continue to work toward the future you want. I think the visualization and the self-talk you use as encour-agement will be useful in making the time away from home enjoyable. Usually there are some problems whenever one tries something new, but I think you know that and will keep solving problems as they come up.

The fifth session was scheduled to allow an interval for Mrs. Roberts to experi-ence going out several times. When she returned, Mrs. Roberts reported how much she enjoyed resuming her activities. After reestablishing a sexual relation-ship with her husband, she had shifted toward thinking of him as a spouse and not as a patient. Now she was able to consider her own needs and to feel less guilt. The therapist reviewed the goals Mrs. Roberts wanted to accomplish when she came for therapy and the progress she had made. Mrs. Roberts now scaled her dis-tress level at a 2. She had some worries but felt that she could cope with prob-lems as they came along, just as she had all her life. Mrs. Roberts felt ready to fin-ish therapy with the understanding that she could call at any time and return if she wanted. The therapist concluded the session with a summary of the accom-plishments Mrs. Roberts had made and a suggestion:

Therapist: When we began our work together, you were still in shock from your husband's heart attacks and you were trying to pro-tect him. Your distress level was at a 10. You wanted to have some time for yourself but it seemed impossible. Sometimes illness interferes with the way a couple has always solved problems and faced issues together. I think that happened for you. Once you could feel close to your husband again, the strength of your relationship and your problem-solving abil-ities could come forward and help you get your life back. Now your distress level is a 2. In the future, if you feel ten-sion rising, it may help to just stop and think how you would have handled the problem before the heart attacks and decide if those behaviors would be useful to you. I think you are starting to find a balance between your husband's needs and your own and that you will be able to keep making the adjustments needed for both of you to be happy.

The example of Mrs. Roberts provides an overview of applying the solution-focused model to client issues of chronic illness and caregiving. The ultimate measurement of the effectiveness of a therapy model is the response of clients to its usefulness in helping them solve problems. As a model develops, is structured in its application, and becomes more widely practiced, however, more formal research about efficacy is conducted.

EVALUATION OF MODEL EFFECTIVENESS

The assumptions found in solution-focused therapy make it difficult to systematically evaluate because diagnosing a client is often viewed as unnecessary and even harmful, so it is difficult to get comparable samples. In order to conduct well-controlled research studies, specification and use of a defined procedure is necessary, such as the use of detailed treatment manuals and measures that ensure the same method is used with each client in a treatment group. Gingerich and Eisengart (2000) have completed a review of 15 studies investigating the effectiveness of solution-focused therapy and found that only five could be considered well controlled for validity and reliability. All five of the well-controlled studies reported significant benefit from solution-focused therapy. The studies represented investigations of different client groups in various settings. Four of those studies (Cockburn, Thomas, & Cockburn, 1997; Lindforss & Magnusson, 1997; Seagram, 1997; Zimmerman, Jacobsen, MacIntyre, & Watson, 1996) found it to be significantly better than standard institutional services or no treatment at all.

The other study (Sundstrom, 1993) compared solution-focused therapy with problem-focused, interpersonal therapy and found that it produced equivalent outcomes. The authors concluded that these five studies provided initial support for the efficacy of solution-focused therapy, but urged continued research, moving from the pilot or open trial phase to the efficacy phase of developed research. When more research about outcomes is completed it will give greater insight into the usefulness of solution-focused therapy with clients.

SOLUTION-FOCUSED THERAPY AND AGEISM

The cooperative relationship so necessary between the client and the therapist makes ageism an important issue when utilizing solution-focused therapy with older people. Ageism is a chronologically age-based process of systematic stereotyping and discrimination (Butler, 1969). The therapist and client may make assumptions based on ageist stereotypes that influence the process and outcomes of therapy. Common ageist assumptions include overlooking the importance of sexuality to older people (because they are assumed to have lost sexual interest), accounting for physical symptoms as part of normal aging rather than disease process, or failing to encourage learning new information because older people are assumed to be less intellectually capable than younger people.

The mental health field gives little notice to issues of ageism in mental health (Ivey, Wieling, & Harris, 2000; James & Haley, 1995; Reekie & Hanson, 1992) or in psychotherapy (Hughston, Christopherson, & Bonjean, 1988; Van Amburg, Barber, & Zimmerman, 1996). Older adults have often been viewed as poor candidates for psychotherapy, too rigid to make changes, and physically ill or cognitively impaired (Lewis & Johansen, 1982; Reekie & Hansen, 1992).

The solution-focused model's roots in a constructivist philosophy help protect the therapist from stereotyping and categorizing older adults by emphasizing the unique aspects of each older adult client. An individual's abilities and strengths are stressed rather than his or her pathology. When therapists have a strong belief in the abilities of clients to create change, this attitude is communicated to clients and their autonomy is encouraged. The therapist can build on the older adults' long, rich, life histories and glean examples of successful change. The therapeutic collaboration of client and therapist supports reviewing the lessons older clients have learned from life experiences and applies them to present problems: Life—not therapy—is the best teacher.

> WHEN THERAPISTS have a strong belief in the abilities of clients to create change, this attitude is communicated to clients and their autonomy is encouraged.

The objective is to help clients achieve their goals, not to change their personality to an ideal or normative type. Some models of psychotherapy place the source of a client's problems as his or her personality. This approach allows the therapist to take responsibility in identifying the problem and setting the course of treatment. In this scenario, clients are compared against a normative standard that suggests what changes should be made and what are useful goals for therapy. In solution-focused therapy, the goals of therapy are the client's goals, except in cases of illegal activity or endangerment of the safety of the client or others. In risky circumstances the therapist is bound by professional ethics and legal stipulations to meet certain standards of society and assist clients in meeting those standards.

Although the solution-focused philosophy helps protect therapists against ageist attitudes, the social context in which psychotherapy occurs does not. Learning about the later stages of life and increasing interaction with older people from a variety of backgrounds and situations is useful for the therapist to offset narrow views of the roles and capabilities of older people.

Many professionals find that their clientele are increasingly older, but their professional training has not prepared them for this type of work. In the early stages of a person's life, individuals strive to define themselves whereas in stages of late life, maintaining a sense of personhood and mastery over the environment becomes paramount. Older people often express problems that include their families and families seek assistance in difficulties with older relatives, yet the family therapy field has few resources for therapists who will increasingly assist older families. Van Amberg, Barber, and Zimmerman (1996) analyzed 873 articles published in four major journals during an 8-year period, evaluating the extent to which gerontological issues were addressed in the literature of the family therapy field. The fact that less than 4% (or 28) of these journal articles were related to aging points to the need for family therapists to have more information available to them about working with older people. Gatz and Finkel (1995) pointed to a lack of training at all levels of the mental health care field and a pattern of economic disincentives for service providers to specialize in geriatrics and for older adults to see trained professionals.

DEFINITION OF SUCCESSFUL AGING

The bias of ageism deeply affects the definitions of appropriate goals and outcomes for older people in therapy. Acknowledging that all people involved have assumptions that may need to be questioned can be useful to minimizing the influence of prevailing social norms and stereotypes. The emphasis in solution-focused therapy on the client's worldview, values, and goals makes the definition of successful aging in this model very subjective. One cannot predict what another person's successful aging will look like until one knows the functional abilities and goals that the individual considers both able to achieve and personally meaningful. The individual client, family members, helping professionals, and psychotherapists will all be influenced by prevailing assumptions about the social, biological, and cultural norms for older people. A normative standard does not allow for the heterogeneity among aging people and the diverse standards for success. One person may be physically strong but have economic problems, worry about family relationships but feel well balanced spiritually, live in poor housing conditions but be able to perform meaningful work. Considering how each individual measures aging successfully is important in solution-focused therapy rather than adhering to a general norm for successful aging.

CONSIDERING HOW each individual measures aging successfully is important in solution-focused therapy rather than adhering to a general norm for successful aging.

Early theories of aging emphasized either a disease-and-decline model of aging or a highly idealized description of optimal adaptation to aging. The implementation of the Older Americans Act of 1965 (PL 89-73) and similar government policies was both useful and problematic to older people. The view of aging as a time of decline was reinforced by advocates and politicians who sought funding for services but described older adults as ill and financially needy in order to obtain support. Scientific research focused on the problems of aging—isolation, dependence, physical illness, and decline (Estes & Binney, 1989). At the beginning of the 21st century, more emphasis is being placed on the unused or latent capacities of older people, however. In keeping with this trend, the MacArthur Foundation Study of Successful Aging (Rowe & Kahn, 1998) has made an important contribution to the field. This study provided more than $10 million to support interdisciplinary research on the methods older adults can use to maintain and enhance physical performance and mental functioning in later life. It moved away from supporting a disease-and-decline model toward an emphasis on potential and the process used to achieve it. In the early 21st century, the national research agenda on aging reflected the MacArthur Study perspective of learning more about what encourages and supports individuals' wellness and enjoyment of later life.

Historically, many theories of psychological aging proposed very idealized states for those who had truly accomplished successful aging. Jung (1931) proposed moving beyond gender constraints toward full humanity and wisdom. Erik Erikson and colleagues (1986) described ego integrity and generativity as the outcomes of successful aging. Cumming and Henry (1961) proposed the disengagement theory that promoted reconciliation with the losses of power as success. Havighurst and Albrecht (1953) developed the activity theory that viewed replacement of lost roles and involvement in social and personal relationships as the means to success. Ryff (1989) posited a broader perspective including six dimensions of positive functioning: self-acceptance, positive relationships, autonomy, environmental mastery, purpose in life, and personal growth. Baltes and Baltes (1990) suggested a model of compensation with optimization that views successful aging as a blend of gains and losses. This theory is more compatible with the assumptions of solution-focused therapy. It allows a clinical gerontologist to blend a solution-focused approach to psychotherapy with older adults and a model of successful aging that considers the social construction of aging and a highly individualized description of how people age successfully. Three processes are explored:

1. *Selection.* Increased restriction of life domains as a consequence or in anticipation of changes in personal and environmental resources
2. *Compensation.* Alternate means to reach the same goal
3. *Optimization.* The enrichment and augmentation of reserves or resources and, thus, the enhancement of functioning and adaptive fitness in selected life domains

The criteria of goal attainment can vary by type of assessment (i.e., objective or subjective), authority (i.e., individual, group, family, culture), judging success, and norms (i.e., statistical, ideal, functional). Theories such as the compensation with optimization theory allow for much more consideration of the individual in context, ethnic and cultural influences, and the meaning of loss and gain. This model encourages research into the creative potential that older people utilize when accomplishing their life goals and consideration of the complex nature of the aging experience in which strengths and weaknesses or problems and solutions can be present in the same experience. Solution-focused therapy emphasizes an acceptance of the tension between the parts of this complexity and the importance of attending to resources that elders utilize to compensate and optimize their experiences.

ADAPTING THE BASIC SOLUTION-FOCUSED MODEL

Working with older adults will often require adaptation of the basic model of solution-focused therapy. A primary contribution to the field of mental health has been the emphasis that solution-focused therapy places on exceptions to problems and on behaviors that would expand those exceptions. The basic theory is very behavioral and describes psychological processes. To be an effective therapist for older adults, the therapist must be interested in both the psychological and physical status of the client. The therapist must be aware of normal physical and psychological aging and able to help clients decide when more medical assessment or intervention is needed.

Knowledge of community resources will be important because many issues may include the need for help from outside the family. Often, coordination of the activities of other service providers will be useful and the therapist will be providing some case management as part of psychotherapy. Realization of the impact that ageist assumptions about personal capabilities may have on clients' views of a more positive future will stimulate the therapist to discuss the issues of ageism affecting the client. The types of problems expressed by clients will often be about adjustment to loss and grief over losses. Solution-focused therapy is a behavioral model and the emphasis in its development has been on identifying and changing what clients do. Adapting this emphasis to include the emotions of clients is important for older people because healing from grief and loss requires managing deep feeling.

Working with clients who are grieving offers a good example of the importance of respecting the feelings of clients and carefully pacing the rate of change the therapist suggests. The following case highlights some of the skills the therapist will need to adapt the basic solution-focused model to be helpful to a grieving client. Grief is often experienced late in life as relationships, physical abilities, or environmental supports change. When clients enter therapy with almost overwhelming feelings of grief, they need the therapist to adapt language and pace the rate of change to the clients' needs. Clients often struggle with fears of disloyalty or loss of clear memory of the loved one if the strong emotion decreases. Labeling this dilemma and discussing it is an example of the collaboration between the therapist and client in constructing a solution.

Mrs. Abbott

During Mrs. Abbott's first session, she tried to convey the amount of pain she was experiencing after the loss of her spouse 6 months ago: "Sometimes the waves of grief come over me and I feel that I'll be drowned by an ocean of pain. We were married more than 35 years, you know. My daughter suggested coming to see you, but I really don't think it will do any good. I'm not mentally ill, you know. I'm just lost without him." During this interview, Mrs. Abbott sat facing the therapist, twisting a handkerchief between her fingers and wiping away tears. She talked about herself and her family, cried often, and described how lonely she felt. She was concerned about whether the therapist understood her feelings.

In solution-focused therapy, the client often interviews the therapist in the beginning of their relationship to determine if the match will be useful and the relationship safe enough for healing to take place during their interchanges (Kantor & Kupferman, 1985). The therapist responds by listening carefully, asking questions to understand the client's situation thoroughly, reflecting his or her feelings, and making empathic statements. Clients who have been grieving for a while will be very sensitive to the therapist's response to their emotions of pain and grief because they will have experienced others who are tired of listening to their grief story and have indicated they should move on with life and not talk of pain any longer.

The solution-focused therapist does not ask future-oriented questions at this point in the process because the client is already overwhelmed and unsure about the future. Effective therapy goes slowly at first. As the therapist develops patience with him- or herself and a deep belief in the capacity and strength of the client to change, it is easier to maintain an environment that is conducive to a natural, not forced, change.

In the case of Mrs. Abbott, the therapist asked Mrs. Abbott how she had managed to have the energy to cooperate with her daughter's suggestion and come in for therapy. While making empathetic statements, the therapist also added questions such as "How did you manage to keep going?" and "How did you survive that or cope with a certain situation?" Mrs. Abbott incorporated into her narrative short statements that she had always been a person who faced reality or who pushed herself when she needed to do so. She also pointed out how important her children were to her and how supportive they had been. The therapist made sure to clarify that he did not view Mrs. Abbott's grief as a mental illness, but as a response that honored a long and rewarding relationship. The therapist also mentioned that when a person is experiencing mourning, it is helpful to talk to someone outside the family and friendship circle to avoid a common tendency to shy from topics that might stir up shared feelings of intense grief. In her therapy sessions, Mrs. Abbott could discuss whatever she wanted and did not have to protect anyone.

At the end of Mrs. Abbott's first session, the therapist constructed and shared a summary of her story with additions of a few examples of the coping mechanisms she used to help or comfort herself. The therapist suggested that these behaviors seemed to be very useful and expressed the hope that discussing her situation would be helpful to Mrs. Abbott.

SETTING GOALS During the second session, Mrs. Abbott continued to share her feelings of pain, but she cried a little less. She scaled the intensity of her feelings of grief and isolation at a maximum of 10. She wanted to reduce them to a 2 or a 3. At that level of intensity, she saw herself able to engage with life again and to feel connected to other people. It was hard for her to imagine being able to make any progress, however. The therapist began the goal-setting process, utilizing exception and coping questions. The most useful exception questions for grievers may be coping questions: "How have you managed these circumstances so far?" "How have you kept the situation from getting worse?" "Do you think things could get worse?" "What would that be like for you and for others?" "What is the smallest thing that could make a difference?" Language needs to be adapted when asking about exceptions because people who are grieving may not relate well to questions about times when the grief is better or different and these words may seem insensitive and diminishing to the intensity of their pain. Instead, the therapist can ask about when their experience is a little less painful or about anything that brings them a little comfort.

When Mrs. Abbott described the waves of pain, the therapist asked her what helped her hold on when the flow of pain was very intense. Again, she explained that praying during those times and telling herself that the intensity would ebb comforted her. In this instance, the therapist considered influences that might be part of a holistic solution for the client that may not be mentioned unless specific questions are asked. Such information can increase the therapist's ability to offer suggestions to the client if it appears that a medication would be useful or if a substance may be contributing to the intensity of the client experience. The therapist explored what happened when the pain ebbed and how Mrs. Abbott kept up her strength during her mourning. Was she eating, sleeping, and exercising as before and keeping social contacts? Did she have physical problems that might grow worse during mourning? Was she taking any prescribed medication, over-the-counter items, or herbal preparations from friends or community healers? Even though a client may complete a document containing such information during registration at the therapist's practice, questions will often prompt him or her to share more information.

The therapist continued to set goals more directly with Mrs. Abbott by acknowledging both her doubts and her hopes.

Therapist: I understand it is difficult to think that anything could have an impact on the pain you feel, but I wish our sessions could be useful to you somehow. You must have hoped for something when you came; what was it?

Client: Well partly I wanted to please my daughter and partly I wanted to feel a little better. I have my grandchildren, you know, and I would like to have energy for them again. I know my husband would want me to.

Mrs. Abbott described how she was comforted a little at times. She thought about good memories with her husband and felt grateful for their years together. As Mrs. Abbott answered the therapist's inquiries, she also reinforced to herself that there were variations in her experience without any one of them being pointed out to her. As the therapist attended to both parts of her experience, Mrs.

Abbott could develop a more balanced self-appraisal. As therapy continued, the therapist helped Mrs. Abbott label parts of her experiences as she recovered from her loss and reinvested in life again. The therapist, knowing the trajectory of grief and the problems of recovery often faced by grievers, brought an expertise that helped Mrs. Abbott identify her experiences and find behaviors useful in recovery. Mrs. Abbott may come to a juncture in her recovery when she has to choose between deliberately holding on to painful grief emotions or allowing peaceful feelings to develop.

Therapist: When you have more energy to invest in life again, what would be happening?

Client: I would be able to have the grandchildren over and take care of them like I used to when my husband was with me.

Therapist: What did you do with them?

Client: I would take them for the day or overnight. We would play games or go shopping.

Therapist: Can you do any of that now?

Client: No, I have so little energy for them.

Therapist: I understand that grief takes enormous energy. Yet, you miss the way it was with the grandchildren. As the energy comes back, what do you think you will notice first?

Client: I'll be able to touch them again and hug them. Now I'm afraid I'll just break down and frighten them.

Therapist: When you start to touch them again, who do you think will notice besides you?

Client: My granddaughter, probably. She keeps trying to sit next to me on the couch and touch my arm.

Therapist: Who else?

Client: My daughter. She has mentioned noticing that I'm not as energetic as usual. I feel so pressured to be all right again, and I'm not.

Therapist: You know best the pace of recovery that will work for you. Others love you and want more peacefulness for you but they can't know the right timing. It takes time.

Client: I know, but it would make me feel so much better to cuddle the children again. I would feel closer to my husband, too.

Therapist: What would be the smallest thing you would do that would make you feel you were being more expressive but it wouldn't be overwhelming?

Client: I would smooth my granddaughter's hair. I always did that and she would notice and smile up at me.

At the end of this session, the therapist again constructed a message that summarized Mrs. Abbott's feelings of being overwhelmed by grief and her dual wishes of feeling better and being more physically expressive to her grandchildren. The therapist suggested that Mrs. Abbott think about the pace that she felt she needed to have in her grief recovery.

At the beginning of the third session, the therapist asked Mrs. Abbott about her experiences since the last meeting. Together, they explored the variations in the intensity of Mrs. Abbott's grief and examples of her returning energy to engage in life. Mrs. Abbott shared that she had been able to touch her grandchildren and that it eased some of her loneliness. "I think I was afraid to feel close to them again because losing someone I love hurts so much; so I just stopped touching to form a barrier. I'm glad I reached out to them. It makes me less lonely for my husband."

As Mrs. Abbott reflected on the pace she needed for her recovery, she realized that she had not been telling her daughter how she felt. She didn't want to worry her and Mrs. Abbott realized that her daughter was also grieving. This, too, created a barrier that kept her from feeling close, however, and now she expanded her goal to include wanting to feel close to her daughter again.

Therapist:	Before your husband's death, how would you have told your daughter about difficult feelings?
Client:	I would just tell her straight out. But now I'm afraid to do that because if she knows how bad I feel at times, she will really worry about me. She keeps saying I'm all she has left now and nothing can happen to me.
Therapist:	So you feel very protective of her but you also want to be able to talk to her directly like you did before.
Client:	Yes. Touching the grandchildren helped me a lot. I don't want to feel separated from my daughter, but I'm the mother and I should be helping her—not adding to her problems.
Therapist:	When you imagine talking to your daughter, do you think mainly of telling the feelings of deep grief?
Client:	I guess so. I've been trying to act like I'm myself even though I don't feel that way. Now that I think about it, she probably knows I'm not. She did ask me to come here.
Therapist:	I wonder how your daughter would react if you shared both the times when your grief is a little less intense as well as the times when you feel very bad? If she knew about both times, she might get a more balanced impression of how you are.
Client:	Maybe I could. I've been trying to avoid saying much about how I feel—good or bad. When she asks me how I am, I just say I'm all right and change the subject.

The remainder of the session consisted of discussing how Mrs. Abbott could convey the variety of experiences she had. The therapist concluded the session with a summary and a suggestion that Mrs. Abbott consider telling her daughter some of the positive feelings she had and a little of her grief reaction. Then she could observe her daughter's response and judge how much of the grief to continue to share.

During the fourth session, Mrs. Abbott described how she had continued to do activities with her grandchildren and how she had tried to share more with her daughter. As she told her daughter more about her feelings, she was surprised to discover her daughter was relieved by her sharing.

Client:	I think we were trying to protect each other by not saying anything, but we were both feeling worse—isolated. She was very worried about how I was and didn't feel she could ask me because I seemed so sad at times. I'm so glad to feel connected to her again.
Therapist:	So in a strange way, you protected her more by telling her how you felt. What will you need to do to keep this positive change going?
Client:	I have to keep believing it is worth investing in life again and worth getting close to other people. For a while, I thought I would lose my connection to my husband if I let myself feel better. Now I know my connection to him just changes; it isn't lost. It isn't disloyal to engage with life again.

The rest of the session centered on the continued connections Mrs. Abbott believed she would make as her healing continued. The session ended with a summary and a suggestion that Mrs. Abbott continue to notice how the feelings of connection to others influenced her.

Mrs. Abbott began the fifth session with a description of changes in her grief experience.

Client:	Now I notice there is more time between the really deep grief feelings and when I feel better. Sometimes I go through part of a day and feel all right.
Therapist:	Is that different?
Client:	Yes. When I first came here, I was having surges of grief constantly. Now I will suddenly realize I haven't had one in a few hours.
Therapist:	How do you explain that change to yourself?
Client:	I think that when I could get closer to other people again, it helped. I was afraid I'd get lonelier for my husband, but surprisingly, it made me more peaceful.

As the session progressed, the therapist reviewed the progress Mrs. Abbott had made toward her goals. She now scaled her distress at a 3 and felt that level was appropriate for her circumstances. She felt more energy to engage with life but knew that she would continue to miss her husband and mourn the loss of the relationship. She had begun to reconnect with her grandchildren and her daughter and felt she could continue to do so. The therapist discussed with Mrs. Abbott whether she felt she had accomplished the goals she wanted to attain or if she had more work to do in therapy.

Mrs. Abbott replied that although she had doubted that therapy could help her, she had been able to make changes and felt much better. Her goals for therapy seemed accomplished, but she had been thinking of joining a grief group for women who had lost a spouse and wondered if the therapist could suggest some resources. She felt ready to share her experiences with others and believed she could benefit from learning about theirs.

The session ended with a summary and a suggestion. The therapist complimented Mrs. Abbott on her perseverance in therapy when she was unsure about its benefit. She reviewed the goals they had set for working together and the progress Mrs. Abbott had made in engaging with life again and overcoming her isolation. The therapist gave Mrs. Abbott information on community resources for grief groups and stated that her interest in a group seemed further progress toward engaging with other people and with life. The therapist also mentioned that Mrs. Abbott could expect normal reactions to being without her husband for the first time on anniversaries or holidays and that would not mean a setback in her recovery but would be part of the progress she was making as she shared these with her daughter and grandchildren. If, at any time, she felt she wanted to return, she could come and talk for a session or two as part of continuing her healing, but for now the therapist agreed that the goals were achieved and that Mrs. Abbott would continue to heal.

SUMMARY

The solution-focused model is based on therapists' deep faith in the resources and capacities of their clients. Faced with the difficulties that life brings, older people may have trouble recalling the lessons they have learned and the strengths they have shown over a lifetime and worry about being overwhelmed by their problems. Psychotherapy can provide a therapeutic relationship in which clients can remember their competency and have their self-esteem restored. In this model, the therapist responds with a respect for the clients' views and a curiosity about how they have found solutions in the past. The therapist's background in human development, methods of change, and community resources can help to enhance the solutions clients construct toward a more satisfying future. When therapist and client envision the future through questions that stimulate a description of more positive outcomes, it stimulates hope that gives energy for change.

REFERENCES

Baltes, P.B., & Baltes, M.M. (1990). Psychological perspectives on successful aging: The model of selective optimization with compensation. In P.B. Baltes

& M.M. Baltes (Eds.). *Successful aging: Perspectives from the behavioral sciences* (pp. 1–34). New York: Cambridge University Press.

Berg, I.K. (1991). *Family preservation: A brief therapy workbook.* London: B.T. Press.

Berg, I.K. (1994). *Family-based services: A solution focused approach.* New York: Norton.

Bonjean, M. (1988). Psychotherapy for families caring for a mentally impaired elderly member. In C. Chilman, E. Nunnally, & F. Cox (Eds.), *Chronic illness and disability* (pp. 141–155). Beverly Hills: Sage Publications.

Bonjean, M., & Bonjean, R. (1996). Working with the family. In C. Kovach (Ed.), *Late-stage dementia care guide.* Washington, DC: Taylor and Francis Publishing Company.

Butler, R.N. (1969). Age-ism: Another form of bigotry. *The Gerontologist, 9,* 243–246.

Cade, B.W. (1985). The Wizard of Oz approach to brief family therapy: An interview with Steve de Shazer. *The Australian and New Zealand Journal of Family Therapy, 6,* 95–97.

Cockburn, J.T., Thomas, F.N., & Cockburn, O.J. (1997). Solution-focused therapy and psychosocial adjustment to orthopedic rehabilitation in a work hardening program. *Journal of Occupational Rehabilitation, 7*(2), 97–106.

Cummings, E., & Henry, W.E. (1961) *Growing old: The process of disengagement.* New York: Basic Books.

de Shazer, S. (1982). *Patterns of brief family therapy: An ecosystemic approach.* New York: Guilford Press.

de Shazer, S. (1988). *Clues: Investigating solutions in brief therapy.* New York: Norton.

de Shazer, S., & Kral, R. (Eds.). (1986). *Indirect approaches in therapy.* Rockville, MD: Aspen Publishers.

Erickson, M. (1954). Special techniques of brief hypno-therapy. *Journal of Clinical and Experimental Hypnosis, 109*(2), 109–129.

Erikson, E.A., et al. (1986). *Vital involvement in old age.* New York: Norton.

Estes, C.L., & Binney, E.A. (1989). The biomedicalization of aging. *The Gerontologist, 29,* 587–596.

Gatz, M., & Finkel, S. (1995). Education and training of mental health service providers. In M. Gatz (Ed.), *Emerging issues in mental health and aging.* Washington, DC: American Psychological Association.

Gingerich, W., & Eisengart, S. (2000, Winter). Solution focused brief therapy: A review of the outcome research. *Family Process, 39*(4), 477–498.

Goodman, H., Gingerich, W.J., & de Shazer, S. (1989). BRIEFER: An expert system for clinical practice. *Computers in Human Services, 5,* 53–67.

Griffith, J.L., et al. (1991). A model for psychiatric consultation in systemic therapy. *Journal of Marital and Family Therapy, 17*(3), 291–294.

Havighurst, R.J., & Albrecht, R. (1953). *Older people.* New York: Longman.

Held, B.S. (1995). *Back to reality: A critique of postmodern theory in psychotherapy.* New York: Norton.

Hughston, G.A., Christopherson, V.A., & Bonjean, M.J. (Eds.). (1988). *Aging and family therapy: Practitioner perspectives on golden pond.* New York: Haworth Press.

Ivey, D. (1993). *The influence of gender on family leadership, family roles, and observer training in comparisons of selected measures of family functioning.* Unpublished doctoral dissertation, University of Nebraska, Lincoln.

Ivey, D., Wieling, E., & Harris, S. (2000, Summer). Save the young—the elderly have lived their lives: Ageism in marriage and family therapy. *Family Process, 39*(2), 163–175.

James, J.W., & Haley, W.E. (1995). Age and health bias in practicing clinical psychologists. *Psychology and Aging, 10,* 610–616.

Jung, C.G. (1931). Life's turning point. *Psychological problems of today.* Zurich: Rascher.

Kantor, D., & Kupferman, W. (1985). The client's view of the therapist. *Journal of Marital and Family Therapy, 11*(3), 225–244.

Kiser, D., Piercy, F., & Lipchik, L. (1993, July). The integration of emotion in solution-focused therapy. *Journal of Marital and Family Therapy, 19*(3), 233–242.

Lewis, J.M., & Johansen, K.H. (1982). Resistances to psychotherapy with the elderly. *American Journal of Psychotherapy, 36,* 497–504.

Lindforss, L., & Magnusson, D. (1997). Solution focused therapy in prison. *Contemporary Family Therapy, 19,* 89–103.

Lipchik, E. (1993). "Both/and" solutions. In S. Friedman (Ed.), *The new language of change: Constructive collaboration in psychotherapy* (pp. 25–49). New York: Guilford Press.

Lipchik, E. (1997). My story about solution-focused brief therapist/client relationships. *Journal of Systemic Therapies, 16*(2), 159–172.

Lipchik, E. (1999). Theoretical and practical thoughts about expanding the solution-focused approach to include emotions. In W. Ray & S. de Shazer (Eds.), *Evolving brief therapy: In honor of John Weakland.* Galena, IL, & Iowa City, IA: Greist & Russell Companies.

Lipchik, E. (2002). *Beyond technique in solution-focused therapy: Working with emotions and the therapeutic relationship.* New York: Guilford Press.

Lipchik, E., & de Shazer, S. (1987). The purposeful interview. *Journal of Strategic and Systematic Therapies, 5*(1), 88–99.

Lipchik, E., & Kubicki, A.D. (1996). Solution-focused domestic violence views: Bridges toward a new reality in couples therapy. In S.D. Miller, M.A. Hubble, & B.L. Duncan (Eds.), *Handbook of solution focused brief therapy* (pp. 65–99). San Francisco: Jossey-Bass.

Miller, G., & de Shazer, S. (2000). Emotions in solution-focused therapy: A reexamination. *Family Process, 30*(1), 5–23.

Molnar, A., & Lindquist, B. (1989). *Changing problem behavior in the schools.* San Francisco: Jossey-Bass.

Nyland, D., & Corsiglia, V. (1994). Becoming solution focused in brief therapy: Remembering something important we already knew. *Journal of Systemic Therapies, 13*(1), 5–11.

Older Americans Act of 1965, PL 89-73, 42 U.S.C. §§ 3001 *et seq.*

Piercy, F., Lipchik, E., & Kiser, D. (2000). Commentary on Miller and de Shazer's article on emotions in solution-focused therapy. *Family Process, 39,* 25–27.

Reekie, L., & Hansen, F.J. (1992). The influence of client age on clinical judgments of male and female social workers. *Journal of Gerontological Social Work, 19,* 67–82.

Rowe, J., & Kahn, R. (1998). *Successful aging.* New York: Pantheon Books.

Ryff, C.D. (1989). Possible selves in adulthood and old age: A tale of shifting horizons. *Psychology and Aging, 6,* 286–295.

Seagram, B.C. (1997). *The efficacy of solution-focused therapy with young offenders.* Unpublished doctoral dissertation, New York University, New York, Ontario, Canada.

Tennstedt, S. (1999, March). *Family caregiving in an aging society.* Paper presented at the U.S. Administration on Aging Symposium: Longevity in the New American Century, Baltimore, MD.

Van Amburg, S.M., Barber, C.E., & Zimmerman, T.S. (1996). Aging and family therapy: Prevalence of aging issues and later life concerns in marital and family therapy literature. *Journal of Marital and Family Therapy, 22,* 195–203.

Walter, J., & Peller, J. (1992). *Becoming solution-focused in brief therapy.* New York: Brunner/Mazel.

Weakland, J., Fisch, R., Watzlawick, P., & Bodin, A. (1974). Brief therapy: Focused problem resolution. *Family Process, 13,* 141–168.

Zimmerman,T.S., Jacobsen, R.B., MacIntyre, M., & Watson, C. (1996). Solution-focused parenting groups: An empirical study. *Journal of Systemic Therapies, 15*(4), 12–25.

THERE ARE FEW
presumptions in human
relations more dangerous
than the idea that one
knows what another human
being needs better than
they do themselves.

—*Ignatieff, 1984, p. 11*

11

NARRATIVE THERAPY
WITH OLDER ADULTS

Raymond Grimm

IN 2001, A REPORT TO THE SURGEON GENERAL of the United States from the Department of Health and Human Services, Administration on Aging (DHHSAA) stated, "The design and delivery of mental health services to older persons is a vital societal challenge, in light of the enormous increase in the elderly [older adult] population" (p. ix). The report concluded that older adults are under-identified and underserved by mental health professionals. It then presented multiple traditional models for the treatment of older adults. Binney and Swan (1991) examined the cultural assumptions of those traditional mental health delivery systems and concluded that they were embedded in discourses of capitalism's market economy and politics and discourses of individualism. They suggested that both discourses frequently act against and disenfranchise many older adults. Binney and Swan called for new institutions and mental health delivery systems and new models for thinking about the mental health treatment of older adults. These new models would address the social and political contexts, including race and social class, which influence the lives of each older adult. Citing the research work of Scheper-Hughes and Lovell, Binney and Swan concluded their findings by calling for the development of communities that would be "receptive, responsive, and responsible, and more than just passively tolerant" of the mental health concerns of older adults (p. 184). A community that practices narrative therapy with its older adult population meets these challenges.

NARRATIVE THERAPY

Narrative therapy focuses on an individual's unique life stories. It believes that these stories are more than reflections or mirrors of an individual's life. Stories are situated in larger social, cultural, political, and economic ecologies (Freeman & Lobovits, 1993). Individuals' beliefs, identities, present experiences of themselves, memories of their histories, and future experiences are all affected by their personal life stories.

Life stories provide the frame within which a person interacts with others. As identities are performed in relationships with other individuals, a person experiences multiple stories of their life; at times, these stories may conflict with one another. The performance and what the "audience" notices have constitutive effects in how the person and the audience see the individual. In effect, both the performer and the audience are in a parallel process of writing and performing unique life stories. Consider, for example, an older person who may have a personal story of competence, reflected in the belief that he or she was a competent worker, a good parent, and a satisfying partner. Those stories, however, may conflict with other stories that were caused by a change in the older person's circumstances or status in life. This individual may now sense that he or she is no longer useful, is a poor patient dependent on others for personal care, or is living a meaningless life in forced retirement. In this case, life stories of competence conflict with life stories of incompetence. This conflict can result in the development of a dominant discourse of incompetence that totalizes a person's experience of him- or herself. Either the individual forgets alternative stories of competence or no longer believes they are applicable to his or her life. The dominant life story is then enacted by the person, which frequently results in his or her diagnosis of depression. A trained therapist may feel invited to diagnose and then to prescribe corrective therapeutic interventions, including a possible medication regime (often the only intervention offered to older people). Alternatively, the therapist may also feel pressure to develop theories such as detachment to explain the person's withdrawal behavior. Terms such as life stories and others associated with narrative therapy are listed in Table 11.1.

NARRATIVE THERAPY rejects the essentialist position whereby the problem is viewed as resulting from some state of internal dysfunction that needs to be corrected, adjusted, or eradicated by an expert in order for the person to resume a normal life.

Narrative therapy rejects the essentialist position whereby the problem is viewed as resulting from some state of internal dysfunction that needs to be corrected, adjusted, or eradicated by an expert in order for the person to resume a normal life. As suggested by the quotation at the beginning of this chapter, narrative therapists do not take an "expert" position on people's lives; nor do they confuse problems with people. Narrative therapists believe that individuals have the knowledge, skills, beliefs, values, and competence to overcome the effects of their problems. Through a collaborative, deconstructive, and reflective questioning process, people notice and revive subjugated knowledge that allows them to enact and

Table 11.1. Common narrative therapy terms and phrases and their definitions

Narrative term/phrase	Definition
Alternative/preferred story	A story that contradicts the dominant, problem story as identified by the person who seeks therapy. It is a story on which the individual prefers to base his or her life. The alternative story is developed from externalizing and re-storying conversations that help the person to identify and enact unique outcomes
Constitutionalist perspective	A perspective that suggests that dominant cultural discourses (e.g., patriarchy, individualism, social interaction) influence and define how a person experiences his or her life
Deconstruction	A process that involves analyzing the historical and present conditions that influence how one makes meaning of the world and taken-for-granted truths
Deconstructing questions	Deconstructing questions help an individual to examine the ideas, beliefs, and conclusions that he or she has made about him- or herself that support the problem story
Discourse	Reflects the prevalent social structures of power and knowledge that are actively constitutive of people's lives. Discourses operate through language, cultural practices, and social institutions to achieve a common worldview
Essentialist position	In psychology, the position that states an essential truth exists about human behavior and can be discovered through the systematic study of human behavior. Professional knowledge is privileged over personal experience
Externalizing questions	Questions that help an individual separate from his or her identity as the problem by examining the social contexts that contributed to the development of the problem, the effects of the problem in his or her life, and how those factors maintain the existence of the problem
Externalizing the problem	A process that separates the person from the problem identity

(continued)

Table 11.1. *(continued)*

Narrative term/phrase	Definition
Individualizing discourse	Social discourses that focus on the individual, including self-reliance, self-determination, hard work, and opportunity to get ahead based on his or her own merits. Problems are viewed as deficits within the person
Landscape of action questions	These questions inquire about the events of a unique outcome. Questions about the unique outcome event may be asked across time, relating to the history of the event, its present effect in the person's life, and future projections of what the action might have for the person. Linked together with landscape of meaning questions, responses to landscape of action questions set the foundation for the alternative story
Landscape of meaning questions	These questions encourage a person to reflect on the meanings behind one's action and the intentions and beliefs that support one's preferred view of oneself. Like the landscape of action questions, these questions also may be asked across time: past, present, and future
Problem story	A dominant story in which the person is identified as a problem and that construes the person's life in a problematic manner
Reflexive questions	Facilitative questions that a therapist uses to help an individual or family reflect on the nature of the problem and its underlying belief system, as well as to identify new possibilities for their lives
Re-membering	A process of emotionally linking an individual to significant people in the individual's past. The goal of the re-membering process is to help the individual identify significant people from the past who supported a preferred account of the individual. Through this process, options become available to the individual that support new ways of thinking about and enacting the preferred story

Narrative term/phrase	Definition
Re-storying questions	A series of questions that include land-scape of action and landscape of meaning questions that support the re-authoring and enactment of the individual's preferred story
Social constructionism	A theory that suggests that a person's ideas, beliefs, actions, and so on arise from social discourses and social interactions; one whose experiences of social events are mediated by language
Statement of Position Map	A specific sequence of questions utilized in deconstruction of the problem and re-authoring of the preferred story. The sequence involves 1) defining the meaning of a thought, action, and so forth, 2) asking about its effects, 3) evaluating the effects, and 4) giving justification for the evaluation. Once a justification has been given, the therapist may start the process again, asking the individual about the meaning behind the justification
Unique outcomes	Actions and thoughts that contradict what one would expect from the problem-saturated story. For example, a person influenced by depression would not be expected to experience moments of happiness. When such a moment is identified, that moment of happiness would be a unique outcome. Unique outcomes provide the entry points into the alternative story

live their preferred lives. Viewed from this perspective, many clinicians interpret narrative therapy as a strengths-based therapy because of its focus on revived skills and knowledge that helps clients change as such skills are used to bring forth preferred lifestyles. Most narrative therapists would not state that they were strengths-based, however, as this concept introduces an evaluative component that most narrative therapists attempt to avoid. People experience narrative therapy as both respectful and nonblaming.

The following case study sets the scene for a discussion of narrative therapy.

Ricki

When 74-year-old Ricki, a former client, learned that I was writing a chapter on narrative therapy with older adults, she asked that I include her story. Ricki was initially referred to me by a hospital social worker. I was unable to see her because of my large number of clients, so I referred her to other therapists in the community. She called back in tears 3 months later. She stated that the other therapists were either unavailable or unable to understand her situation. I agreed to see her. At our first meeting, she stated that her husband had attacked her. This was very unusual for him, as they had been married for more than 40 years and had what she described as a very close relationship. Their relationship had not had a violent incident prior to this attack. Following the advice of others, she moved into a shelter for abused women, received counseling, and was advised to divorce him. She stated that she was committed both to him and to their relationship, so she had sought counseling. She became very distressed when one therapist told her that Ricki was unconsciously provoking her husband into attacking her because she had been emotionally abused by her father in the past. (A discussion of the power effects of dominant discourses appears later in this chapter.)

Another therapist was counseling Ricki's husband for anger management; however, he did not seem to understand why he was receiving therapy and even denied the attack had occurred, Ricki related. When I inquired about potential neurological indicators of a variety of dementias, she stated that her husband had been asked "a few questions about presidents and other such nonsense." She stated that she was told the magnetic resonance imaging (MRI) tests were inconclusive. As a result of these tests, Ricki felt that her husband's doctors believed she was overly hysterical and responsible for much of his aggressive behavior. Reinforcing the blame she was experiencing, Ricki's therapist told her that if she would change her behavior, her husband would not be aggressive.

Ricki told me that she felt blamed by her therapist and had stopped therapy, but continued to feel guilty because she thought she was the person who initiated the aggressive incident. As Ricki related her story, I was astounded by how the expert knowledge imposed on her by her therapists and doctors had influenced her experience of herself. I asked Ricki, "If you were able to put aside all the advice and counseling given to you, what would you be able to tell me about yourself?" She told me an incredible story: that she was one of the first women to break into and succeed in an industry totally dominated by men. In addition, she related a series of stories that reflected her competence and skill. When I asked what she felt was occurring in her current family situation, she related a story of her husband's slight behavioral changes for the past 2 years. She said he had lost some of his skills as a former mechanic and construction worker, but until he had attacked her she had attributed the changes to his "growing old." She felt that he did have "a problem with his brain." Ricki thought the tests her husband's doctor and therapist had given to him were either too easy or lacked test sensitivity needed to reliably measure any neurological changes that may have caused the behavioral changes she noticed. Her belief was confirmed when he was diagnosed a year later with an unspecified form of dementia in addition to his prior diagnosis of lung cancer.

During our therapy, Ricki and I discussed what her husband's diagnosis of dementia meant to her. We deconstructed both her personal and social ideas about dementia in a manner that would allow her to remain respectful of him and their relationship while ensuring her safety. Furthermore, over the course of our work together, we examined how she was negatively influenced by the discourses of patriarchy and professional knowledge in a manner that did more harm than good. We also had sessions with her husband and invited him to discuss his experiences. During therapy, Ricki was emotionally reconnected to experiences of her own competence and to occasions when her knowledge was correct, even though it countered dominant beliefs of the time. For example, she had been one of the first women to work in an industry dominated by men. She was told that she would not be able to compete with men, yet she knew she could; in fact, she did very well professionally in her field.

This emotional connection is more than memory; it is a reconnection with the original experience, a process that Meyerhoff (1992) termed *re-membering*. The effect of such an experience is to bring into the present the experience of competence and personal expertise. Shedding the restrictive professional discourse associated with psychopathology, Ricki was able to utilize and build on those exceptional moments to restory her life as a competent, compassionate, and loving person. As she enacted her new descriptions, she discovered that she felt better about herself and her husband.

Her relationship with her husband improved, as did her feelings toward herself. No more aggressive incidents occurred, and the couple was able to enjoy the last 2 years of their marriage until his death. Ricki continued to do well, and connected with her many friends as she traveled around the world. I asked Ricki if there was a statement she would like to include in this chapter. She wrote the following:

I have met every neighborhood professional in counseling. It has both hurt me and helped me. There are some who go by the book and forget that some of the books undermine humanity. It [the previous counseling] made me feel I was an undeserving human being; stupid and without feeling as if I had set out to destroy my life, my marriage, my children, and everything else around me. It made me doubt my basic beliefs in my essence and my being. It shook my faith and almost destroyed me through despair, hopelessness, and anger. I felt my life and life experiences were for nil and all I put into trying was in vain, in spite of 70-plus years of living.

Now, the positive. The good counseling [the narrative therapy] gave me hope in my judgment when I knew I was right in the decisions I was making. I needed the support and love, and most of all, the understanding of what I was feeling and trying to do, even if others were not in agreement with me. It spurred me on even though we [Ricki and her husband] knew what the end result [his death] would be. Because of all this, I now live in harmony and am at peace with myself and all those around me. (Ricki, personal communication, 2001)

THEORIES OF NARRATIVE THERAPY

Narrative therapy, a concept first introduced by Michael White and David Epston (1990), continues to evolve. Likewise, the work presented here also continues to evolve. The next sections of this chapter review theories of the social construction of people and of the aging process and theories of the narrative metaphor. It specifically addresses the utilization of the narrative metaphor and its relationship to therapy, as introduced by White and Epston (1990), through a discussion of the central tenets of narrative practice. Strategies for using narrative therapy with older adults are then presented through individuals' stories.

SOCIAL CONSTRUCTIONISM AND THE CONSTITUTIONALIST PERSPECTIVE

Social constructionism is concerned with understanding the processes by which people come to describe and understand the world in which they live. Social constructionism challenges the modernist perspective that suggests people can learn universal truths about the world through scientific inquiry. Gergen (1985, 1999) outlined four working assumptions of social constructionism that have implications for a narrative practice:

ASSUMPTION 1   The first assumption is that for any situation an unlimited number of possible explanations exists. When people describe their experiences of a problem, they often attribute the problem to a single cause. For example, a person might ascribe his or her depression to a chemical imbalance, whereas another person might state that the depression is caused by a personality disorder. The person's belief of the cause of his or her problem leads to the person's enacting that belief (e.g., seeking medication or long-term psychotherapy to change his or her personality structure). For example, a client, Linda, stated that she had "killed her oldest daughter." When asked to tell her story, Linda said that her daughter was driving her home from a care facility when Linda decided she needed to smoke a cigarette in her daughter's car. Her daughter was concerned about her mother's health and raised her voice in protest. At that moment, the daughter suffered an aortic aneurysm and died instantly. Linda felt that if she had not wanted to smoke, her daughter would not have gotten upset at her and would not have died. Linda felt she had caused her daughter's death. Her religious beliefs prompted her to believe she had a spiritual responsibility for the death and she was doomed to hell. Her experience of the incident was that there was no longer any hope for her either in this world or the next. She explained that her hopelessness was the cause of her depression. At the beginning of our work together, she was unable to identify any other explanation for the cause of her daughter's death or for her depression.

ASSUMPTION 2 Assumption 2 is that people make meaning of the world, including descriptions and modes of explanation, in relationships with others: "The individual mind (thought, experience) does not thus originate meaning, create language, or discover the nature of the world. Meanings are born of co-ordination among persons—agreements, negotiations, and affirmations" (Gergen, 1999, p. 48). The implications of this assumption are important to narrative therapists for multiple reasons. Implied in this assumption are the following:

- Problems are an effect of people's interactions with each other.
- Problems are an effect of people's interactions with dominant cultural discourses, such as discourses of gender, individualism, capitalism, and so forth.
- Therapy provides a context for change.
- Psychotherapists have a responsibility to inform their clients that they will be co-authoring a preferred story about their clients' lives and experiences and these stories have real effects in clients' lives.
- It is a myth to assume that psychotherapists can adopt a completely neutral or objective position in relation to their clients because all therapist–client interactions affect how clients experience and live their lives.
- Therapists must acknowledge their position of power in the relationship.
- Therapists have a responsibility to reflect on the dominant discourses that influence them so that they do not unknowingly participate in subjugating discourses toward their clients (e.g., what Ricki had experienced in her therapy).

ASSUMPTION 3 Assumption 3 is that a person's meaning systems are bound in relationships and these relationships are bound by broader social practices and discourses (Gergen, 1999). For example, Hazan (1994) stated that the social discourse on aging includes a vocabulary of words such as *handling, managing, organizing, looking after, caring for, placing,* and *planning.* The effect is the development of what Estes (1999) has called "the aging enterprise." In society's attempt to assist older adults, it may be constructing an image of aging that acts against the best interests of those whom society is attempting to serve. Hazan noted, "Social action is indivisible from the socially constructed ideas that define and provide images of the phenomena of old age and aging—whether or not these images are empirically demonstrated" (1994, p. 135). Social constructionism provides us with the opportunity to examine the effects of our institutions and the language used to support the subjugating aspects of those institutions. In the process, it offers us the invitation to transform our social lives and institutions, generating new meanings that will offer new possibilities for action. In therapy with older individuals, this translates to generating new meanings and possibilities for their lives.

ASSUMPTION 4   Assumption 4 holds that an individual's future well-being within this complex society is dependent on a critical reflection of societal forms of understanding and practice (Gergen, 1999). This final assumption invites people into a state of reflexivity, one in which they question their premises, suspend obvious beliefs, listen to alternative belief systems, and critically examine the effects of multiple outcomes. As Gergen noted, to accept one discourse means the rejection of alternatives. This practice does not necessarily lead to the rejection of all current beliefs, practices, or traditions. It recognizes such traditions as being historically and culturally situated and, as such, as legitimate. It invites the excitement of creativity and new possibilities for everyone's future. The following case example illustrates how assumptions three and four translate into clinical practice.

Mary

Mary was a 75-year-old woman referred to me because she was diagnosed with "complicated mourning." She and her husband had been married for more than 40 years and their life together had been good. After his death (which had occurred 3 years previously) she could not seem to do anything, she told me. She spent most of her time sitting in her chair thinking about him and their life together. Mary's friends had stopped coming by. Her daughter was frustrated with her and told Mary to get on with her life. Mary stated that she did not know how to do that. She had received grief counseling but it did not help, she said. She just could not let go of her husband. She believed that to let go of him meant that she would no longer love him. She said she could never stop loving him. So, Mary sat in a state of unhappiness and grief. After listening to her story about her wonderful life with her husband, we began to deconstruct her beliefs about her relationship with Grief.[1] We also discussed how she might live her life if Grief were not entirely present. Utilizing a "saying hello again" metaphor (White, 1988), we explored an alternative system of thinking about grief and loss that suggests a person can invite the wisdom and voice of the deceased back into his or her life. We reflected on the possible effects that this discourse might have on her life. She decided that the effects of "saying hello again" to her deceased husband would allow her to rediscover in herself the qualities her husband knew and loved about her and that she could enact those strengths in relationships with others. She believed that the enactment of those strengths would result in a significant improvement in her life.

After three sessions, Mary was too busy to see me for more sessions. She had re-established her relationship with her daughter and several of her friends and had established a number of new friendships. She felt happy with her life again and was overjoyed that her husband would always be a part of her future.

---

[1]Grief and other terms are capitalized to emphasize narrative therapy's focus of separating problems from people by naming the problem.

CONSTITUTIONALIST PERSPECTIVE

The *constitutionalist perspective* developed from the work of Michel Foucault (1990, 1995) identifies the processes by which dominant discourses and practices "constitute" peoples' lives and their understanding of themselves and others. White suggested that "persons' lives are shaped by the meaning that they ascribe to their experience, by their situation in social structures, and by the language practices, and cultural practices of self and of relationships that these lives are recruited into" (1991, p. 27). These processes and practices can be critically examined and deconstructed through the course of therapy. Therefore, narrative therapists are not interested in traditional perspectives that locate problems within the person. Rather, they focus on examining and deconstructing the operations of power and subjugating cultural practices and institutional meanings that negatively affect people's lives. Neal (1996) surmised that much of the excitement about narrative therapy is based on social constructionist's and constitutionalism's critical practices that invite therapists to challenge the destructive effects of cultural beliefs and practices in the lives of their clients, as opposed to the maintenance of those practices that were previously attributed to the psychology of the individual.

> NARRATIVE THERAPISTS are not interested in traditional perspectives that locate problems within the person. Rather, they focus on examining and deconstructing the operations of power and subjugating cultural practices and institutional meanings that negatively affect people's lives.

SOCIAL CONSTRUCTIONISM OF AGING Writing about a particular age group from a social constructionist position presents the writer with a dilemma. When a person defines a specific population by age, it is possible to reify the dominant discourses that may subjugate the group and promote segregationist practices. Indeed, in later life there exists more heterogeneity than similarity.

Hareven (1995) traced the social construction of old age as a developmental period. Although age and aging are related to biological phenomena, she noted that their meanings are socially and culturally determined. Like Burman (1994), Hareven stated that the identification of developmental stages was caused by the rise of industrialization and the resulting social worth of older adults in a capitalistic system. Characterizations of older adults as "useless," "worn and unattractive," "dependent," and "senile" have resulted in *ageism,* the systematic stereotyping and discrimination against older people based on their age alone (Harevan, 1995).

Among the multitude of discourses affecting older adults is what critical gerontologists (Estes & Binney, 1991; Robertson, 1991) called the "biomedicalization of aging." Although acknowledging the contributions of medical science, this view suggests that identifying the problem of aging as primarily a result of physiological decline in later life totalizes and dehumanizes the experience of older people. As old age is medicalized and brought into the realm of medical expertise, people are identified as having an individual pathology that needs to be treated and cured (Robertson, 1991). Alternative discourses that focus on non-medical issues such as poverty, racism, isolation, loss of roles, life partners, and friends are ignored. Maintaining a biomedical discourse of aging depoliticizes other problems of aging that result from the dominant culture's social and economic policies. The effect of equating old age with illness has been that medical professionals and the larger society think of aging as a pathological or abnormal process and ignore cultural and social factors that contribute to a person's illness and aging process. As a result, interventions address only the medical processes of aging and tend not to address or change social factors that contribute to the problems associated with aging, such as inadequate medical care, insufficient financial assets, or lack of low-income housing.

Estes and Binney (1991) suggested that there are two aspects of the biomedicalization of aging. The first is the social construction of aging as a medical problem and the second is the praxis or practice of aging as a medical problem. Biomedicalization practices are the behaviors and policies that arise when society sees aging as a medical problem. There are four dimensions of the praxis of aging:

1. The scientific consequences that shape the overall discipline and knowledge base
2. The professional consequences of the professions serving older people, including status, training, and the conceptualization and organization of work
3. The development of policy
4. Lay perceptions and the consequences of those perceptions

Accompanying the discourse of the biomedicalization of aging is what Robertson has called the "gerontologization" (1991, p. 136) of the experience of aging. She stated that as the disciplines of gerontology and geriatrics seek scientific laws and theories about aging, they emphasize the physical and psychological aspects through the lens of scientific methodology. Thus, the process of aging is viewed more as an observed phenomenon rather than as lived experience. Older adults become objects of study and are both individually and collectively subjected to professional scrutiny, social and political definition, and management by experts in the field of gerontology. Robertson related this process to Foucault's example of the clinical gaze, in which people's lives are objectified, defined, and colonized by others.

Estes (1991) stated that these social constructions dominate both attitudes toward older adults and public policies. Among the perceptions that result from the biomedicalization and gerontologization of older adults are the following (Binney & Swan, 1991):

• These processes link physical and psychological decline with aging such that the decline begins to be viewed as part of typical aging.

- Although some older adults are seen as deserving of assistance, most of them, essentially, are seen as having outlived their social usefulness and thus are perceived as less deserving of time, attention, and resources than are younger people.
- Older adults are viewed as receiving more than their share of scarce national resources, thereby putting the future of younger generations in jeopardy.

Critical gerontologists (Binney & Swan, 1991; Estes, 1991; Wallace & Villa, 1999) systematically refuted each perception through an analysis of the social policies affecting older adulthood. Of note, Wallace and Villa (1999) showed that beginning in the late 1970s through the 1980s there was an effort to counter the image of older adults as a deserving group and instead to promote an image of the older adult as generally healthy and financially stable. In reviewing the economic realities of older adults, they concluded that the image of the financially stable older adult is sexist, racist, and insensitive to people in lower socioeconomic classes. They noted that a disproportionate number of women and minority older adults have low incomes and are in poor health. Therefore, the policies that weaken public programs for the older adult affect minorities and immigrants in particular. The effect of what Robertson (1991) called "apocalyptic demography" is reflected in a study by Silverstein, Angelelli, and Parrott (2001). Their study revealed that the attitudes of Americans have become less supportive of entitlement programs for the older adult and more supportive of cutting the costs of those programs.

Binney and Swan (1991) reviewed the consequences of social discourses and policies on mental health in the United States. They stated that mental illness in a class society has a class character and is not reflective of an individual pathology. They reported that older adults are less likely to be seen as experiencing emotional difficulties; however, if emotional difficulties are identified, older adults are prescribed medication more often and are less likely to receive therapy. Also, fewer training opportunities are available for individuals interested in careers that specialize in working with older adults. Furthermore, fewer students are interested in learning how to work with older adults than they are in working with children and families. Binney and Swan suggested that one effect of the biomedicalization of mental health problems is that the majority of research attention and funds have been diverted to biomedical disease research. As a result, funds that once were targeted to serve older adults affected by mental health issues are no longer available.

Finally, therapeutic discourses may unwittingly discriminate against the older adult. Many individuals, including older adults, are unable to go to a therapist's office for a number of reasons, however, such as poor health or unreliable transportation systems for those unable to drive. The majority of private and public therapists practice out of their offices, however. The discourse of therapy mandates that this be done in order to protect the boundaries of the therapy process and the confidentiality of the individual. A prevailing mythology exists in the psychotherapy field that when therapy services are provided in someone's home, professional boundaries are being violated. The violation, according to the myth, is that a therapist must remain in a neutral environment (the office) in order to remain objective. From a critical perspective, however, the establishment of boundaries may be interpreted as an effect of a capitalist economy. The time spent driving to and from client homes is perceived by a capitalist economy as neither productive nor financially sound.

The capitalist underpinnings of the profession make access difficult for many older adults who are most in need of psychotherapeutic services. The low economic status of many older individuals does not allow them to set aside funds to pay for individual therapy. Whereas most government funds will support access to basic services for older adults who have very low incomes, very few provisions will pay for mental health services. Although adjustment problems can have a significant negative impact on an older person's later life, they rarely require or result in hospitalization. Thus, the majority of older adults in California, for example, do not receive mental health support services. As Wallace and Villa (1999) stated, these policies have their most negative impact on women and minorities.

Therapies that support an individualizing discourse engender a therapy of private endeavors. Individualizing may restrain and restrict the involvement of community participation in the clients' lives. When working with older adults who may be lacking the most basic resources due to limitations of health and income, therapy as a private endeavor is ineffective. Reflection without access to food or other basic concerns reinforces dominant subjugating discourses that blame the victim.

From a narrative perspective, working with older adults necessitates multiple collaborations with social workers, agencies, friends, churches, and others interested in contributing to the lives of clients. Social workers and senior service agencies can assist the therapy process by providing medical, social, housing, and legal assistance to clients. When friends, church members, and others are invited into the therapy process, they can provide invaluable social support for individuals. In discussing her need for physical contact from others, my client Ruth stated, "It's a known fact that even babies, if they're left alone in cribs, even children without physical contact, even animals if they're not physically touched, they don't do as well. So, why don't old people . . . receive hugs? I haven't had physical contact for more than a year [crying]" (personal communication, 1999). Collaborations challenge individualizing discourses by acknowledging social, economic, and political contexts within which clients live.

> FROM A NARRATIVE perspective, working with older adults necessitates multiple collaborations with social workers, agencies, friends, churches, and others interested in contributing to the lives of clients.

Narrative therapy invites such participation from others in support of clients' preferred lives. The following story illustrates the effects of both biomedicalization and social construction on a former client.

June

June was a 63-year-old woman who was initially referred to me after she made a statement about wanting to die. Her husband had recently passed away, and she herself had multiple health complications (for a fuller description of the case, see Grimm, Maki, & Morales-Long, 1995). After our initial work together, June called me, tearful and in crisis. During the session she stated that she had just seen her doctor to complain about an experience of intense pain in her side. She reported that her doctor had told her he was tired of all of her complaints. He could find nothing wrong with her; and if she complained one more time, he would have her admitted to the psychiatric ward of the hospital. During the session, I asked how well she knew her body and her symptoms. She felt that she was more aware than her doctor was of her health because she did not believe that the doctor took the time to know her and her health problems. I asked if she thought she was "crazy"—the self-construction she interpreted from her doctor's response. She said no—she was not crazy, but since the doctor told her that her pain was "all in her head," she could not understand why she was experiencing pain. Throughout the session, we addressed the knowledge she maintained about her body. June described being perceived by her doctor as a medical problem and a person with emotional problems. Toward the end of the session, she decided to seek a second medical opinion regarding her pain. She set an appointment with another doctor. On the day of the appointment, the new doctor immediately hospitalized her because she had a severe infection. The doctor told her that had it gone untreated she would likely have died within 2 weeks.

The Narrative Metaphor

In exploring how people make meaning of their lives, White and Epston (1990) suggested that narratives provide the frame for people's experiences. White stated, "It is through the narratives or the stories that persons have about their own lives and lives of others that they make sense of their experience" (1991, p. 28). The narrative metaphor proposes that people live their lives by their stories and that those stories shape, frame, and have real effects on their lives. Narratives are not simple descriptions of people's lives; rather, these stories constitute life, meaning, and memory (Zimmerman & Dickerson, 1995). Becker suggested that narratives "reflect people's experience, as they wish to see it and as they wish others to see it" (1997, p. 25). She stated that narratives are both performative and empowering.

Bruner (1986, 1990) contended that narratives are composed of a sequence of events and mental states involving people as characters within the narrative. He suggested that narratives are composed of two landscapes: one of action and one of consciousness or meaning. The landscape of action includes events that are linked sequentially and temporally, according to specific plots (White, 1991). People link experiences in their lives across time. The events they notice and the manner in which they interpret those experiences have implications for past, present, and future experiences.

Included in landscapes of meaning are beliefs, feelings, meanings, perceptions, and conclusions that result from reflections by the person as well as others. As these become elaborated on through a narrative text, they "coalesce into 'commitments' that determine particular careers in life" (White, 1991, p. 28). Thus, these meanings are enacted within landscapes of action. For example, if a person believes he or she is no longer useful because of his or her age and he or she believes self-worth is related to being useful, the person may become influenced by Hopelessness. This person may then enact those beliefs of self-worth into symptoms reflective of a depressed lifestyle (Madigan, 1998).

Narratives are not radically constructed within the person. Rather, narratives are constructed within the context of culture. As White (1991) noted, personal stories about who we are have been historically constructed and negotiated within the context of social structures and institutions. Framed by a dominant culture, these social discourses are defining of personhood (as described earlier in this chapter in the section on social constructionism). As a result, narratives have a determinant quality about them based on social and cultural discourses that define personhood: how one should think and act within the dominant culture.

Despite a determinant quality to stories, it is not possible for those stories to account for all contingencies that arise in life. The stories people live by are filled with gaps, inconsistencies, and contradictions (White, 1991). Therefore, White stated that within determinacy there exists indeterminacy. Bruner (1990) stated that one function of the story is to make comprehensible these indeterminate deviations from dominant cultural discourses. This understanding of indeterminacy provides people with the opportunity to actively engage in the performance of unique meaning. It also provides the opportunity to identify alternative experiences that may go unnoticed by people when they are under the influence of their dominant stories. When people are able to identify multiple scenarios to achieve a desired end, this phenomenon is referred to as the subjunctivizing element of narratives. Its effect is to engage people in the realm of "human possibilities rather than in certainties" (Becker, 1997, p. 28).

Exploration of these possibilities and alternative meanings are a central aspect of narrative therapy.

PRINCIPLES OF NARRATIVE THERAPY

Although there may be a great deal of diversity in how narrative therapists work with people and problems, some underlying principles guide the work of most narrative therapists.

THERAPEUTIC POSITIONS

The first principle is that narrative therapists do not see the person as the problem but the problem as the problem. This stems from the social constructionist and constitutionalist stances that meaning and lives are constituted by larger cultural discourses and interpersonal relationships. Thus, narrative therapists do not accept individualizing discourses that attribute problems to personality disorders or dysfunctions. As Dickerson and Zimmerman stated,

> The problem occurs when we have been so subjugated by the culture's normative specifications and by some of our personal experiences that we can no longer distinguish between what some of our personal experience and preferences are telling us to believe or value and what the specifications have subjected us to. (1996, p. 82)

Thus, narrative therapists will work with clients to identify the discourses and experiences that invite them into nonpreferred lifestyles. Deconstructing the nonpreferred effects of dominant discourses through questioning results in the naming of the problem and the identification of the problem's negative effects. White (1991) referred to this process as participating in *externalizing conversations.* Older adults are frequently influenced by ageist discourses, such as old age being equated with a lack of personal value, increase in memory problems, and so forth that may negatively affect their lives.

Max

Max suffers from depression as a result of his isolation. He states that he does not want to be a burden on anyone because he is old. Utilizing externalizing conversations with older adults such as Max is especially important because once the problem is named and negative effects are identified along with personal strengths and preferences, older adults are then empowered to make preferred changes in their lives.

ETHICAL RELATIVISM Several narrative writers (Dickerson & Zimmerman, 1996; Freedman & Combs, 1996; Freeman & Lobovits, 1993; Madigan, 1998; White & Epston, 1990) discussed the political and ethical stances of narrative therapy. Freeman and Lobovits (1993) addressed the issues of ethical relativism. They cautioned against the risk of clinicians accepting dominant cultural constructions such as individualism or ageism, which oppress and victimize people, in settling for what they believe will work strategically. For example, if a therapist were to externalize depression when the individual's problem was actually related to the denial of needed medical services, the externalization would support an individualizing discourse promoted by the market economy of the health care system. The therapist would not be advocating on behalf of the client's interest, but rather, the therapist would be participating in the client's continued subjugation.

It is important that externalizations take into account the effects of social and political discourses that influence clients' lives. Citing the work of Waldegrave and his colleagues (1991), Freeman and Lobovits (1993) suggested that therapists have a social responsibility and accountability to their clients when therapists participate in the construction of a person's experiential reality. Likewise, Dickerson and Zimmerman debunked the myth that narrative therapy takes a relativistic position. "The cultural narratives are the problem, and our stance is clearly against any subjugating narratives that specify how persons should be or that have harmful effects on others" (1996, p. 80).

TRANSPARENCY   Transparency is a position espoused by narrative therapists. The work of Epston, Freeman, and Lobovits (1993) suggested that transparency involves including clients in a discussion of the ideas, dilemmas, and choices that therapists struggle with when working with individuals. This means that a therapist situates or reveals to the client what the therapist's thoughts, ideas, and intentions were for asking a particular question. This process acknowledges the client's personal wisdom and knowledge about his or her life. Transparency requires therapists to be more accountable to their clients by acknowledging the therapists' own cultural biases that may have a negative, albeit unintentional, impact on their clients.

> TRANSPARENCY requires therapists to be more accountable to their clients by acknowledging their own cultural biases that may have a negative, albeit unintentional, impact on their clients.

Finally, taking a position of transparency and accountability challenges the hierarchical nature of therapist–client relationships. Acknowledging clients' expertise regarding their own lives invites a more equal partnership between therapist and client. The effect is a therapy of collaboration and creativity rather than a therapy based on professional expertise.

REFLEXIVE QUESTIONS   Another principle that guides the work of narrative therapists is the practice of asking *reflexive questions.* Tomm stated, "by definition then, reflexive questions are questions asked with the intent to facilitate self-healing in an individual or family by activating the reflexivity among meanings with pre-existing belief systems that enable family members to generate or generalize constructive patterns of cognition and behavior on their own" (1987, p. 172). Reflexive questions are developed and asked in direct response to clients' narratives of their experiences. These questions are asked from a position of curiosity about what is important to clients and how they experience themselves rather than what is of interest to therapists who are trying to justify the use of professional and individualizing discourses. Questions are not asked for the strategic purposes of guiding, teaching, or otherwise influencing clients. Finally, when therapists ask reflexive questions, they are asking questions of which they truly do not know the answers. The effect on clients is an experience of active participation in the re-authoring process of their lives.

THERAPEUTIC LOVE   Another stance that I have found clinically helpful when working with older adults is reflected by Karl Tomm in work by Tomm, Hoyt, and Madigan (1998), in which Tomm discussed the concept of *therapeutic love.* A similar concept is Weingarten's *intimate interaction,* which she defined as "occurring when people share meaning or co-create meaning and they are able to coordinate their actions to reflect mutual meaning making" (1991, p. 47). Therapeutic love means "opening space for the enlivened existence of the other" (Tomm et al., 1998, p. 208). This stance invites the participation and collaboration of clients during the course of their work together. Because many older adults have been influenced by fears of institutionalization, these moments of connection reassure them of the therapist's support for their rights of self-determination.

THE PROCESSES OF NARRATIVE THERAPY

People have innumerable experiences in their lives, many more than they could ever remember. They make meaning of these life events using narratives. Meaning systems arise as a result of people's attempts to understand their lives. People's meaning systems are enacted within a social context of others. The responses of others may also influence and modify how people experience and understand their lives. A person's actions, interpretations of his or her social interactions with others, and cultural discourses all influence his or her meaning systems. Thus, a person's meaning systems about his or her self co-evolve within the context of others.

For many people, the multiple stories they develop about themselves are generally preferred stories. Stories may include themes such as being a good parent, partner, or friend. People experience and lead their lives in a manner that reflects their stories. Some people's lives, however, have been taken over by problem stories. Once problems occur in people's lives, those problems can begin to constitute their lives. People assign meaning to their problems and enact those problems in interactions with others. In addition, they find that others assign individualizing and pathologizing meanings to their actions, reinforcing their troubled meaning systems. Thus, problems co-evolve in relationships with others.

Narrative therapy is a nonpathologizing approach to working with people. Reviewing the works of White and Epston (1990) and other narrative writers (Freedman & Combs, 1996; Morgan, 2000; Zimmerman & Dickerson, 1995), narrative therapy varies among people and interactions, in narrative therapy's attention to individual discourses, a general narrative therapy process can be identified. Essentially, the process involves externalizing problems, exploring the effects that problems have on the person's life, deconstructing the problem, noticing moments that contradict the dominant discourse, and utilizing those unnoticed experiences to bring forth a re-description of the person's life and to speculate on new possibilities for his or her future.

EXTERNALIZING THE PROBLEM AND DECONSTRUCTION

White (1991) stated that deconstruction allows therapists a procedure by which they can work with people to subvert the taken-for-granted truths and meanings that negatively influence their clients' lives. Externalizing the problem objectifies problems that affect people. It moves the course of therapy away from internalizing conversations to externalizing conversations that invite people to examine how problems influence their lives in nonpreferred ways. Zimmerman and Dickerson stated that externalizing problems is much more than a technique:

> When externalizing problems, therapists must continually be aware of the effects that externalizations have on their clients. Thus, when therapists externalize problems but continue to think of them as internal to individuals or families, they are acting from an inherently contradictory position. It is important—no, necessary—to understand the sociopolitical perspective that informs our therapeutic approach. Without that perspective, the practice makes no sense. (1995, p. 86)

Externalizing problems reflects a particular orientation to therapy. As conveyed by Zimmerman and Dickerson (1995), utilizing externalization of problems as a technique can actually have an effect opposite of that which was intended. Externalizing conversations require therapists to listen closely to an individual's descriptions of problems. Utilizing these descriptions, a narrative therapist will name a problem that attempts to encapsulate the individual's experience of the problem. During the course of an externalizing conversation, it is possible to externalize a variety of things such as behaviors, habits, thoughts, meaning systems, problems between people, and sociocultural specifications. Among the many problems that I have externalized with people are depression, conflict, anxiety, bereaved lifestyles, isolation, health-directed lifestyle, and voicelessness.

Narrative therapists may utilize a variety of externalizations as they proceed through multiple levels of a problem.

Helen

Helen was referred to me for depression. She reported that she had recently seen her doctor because she did not feel well. After a medical examination, he told her that there was nothing medically wrong with her and she should see a counselor. She initially stated that her doctor told her she was depressed and she agreed. I began to talk about how Depression was affecting her life.

Discussing a problem such as Depression as an entity unto itself affords the individual an opportunity to separate his or her identity from the identity associated with the problem. Once an individual's identity begins to separate from the problem's identity, the person is able to objectively examine the effects of the problem in his or her life and make preferred changes based on that examination, thereby altering one's relationship with the problem. This act of talking about the problem as a thing allows individuals the opportunity to separate their identities from problems, opening space for them to examine the effects of problems in their lives and alter their relationships with problems.

It quickly became evident that isolation contributed significantly to Helen's experience of depression. Our discussion about the effects of an "an enforced isolation" revealed that Helen felt unable to control her life. We discussed the social elements that contributed to her isolation, such as lack of transportation, a sense that nobody was interested in her, and minimal income from Social Security, all of which limited her socialization opportunities. As we discussed the negative social influences in her life, I asked how those social influences affected how she felt and thought about herself, as well as its effects on "an enforced isolation." She stated that she felt that there must be something wrong with her or she would not be alone. Furthermore, she felt that her circumstances increased not only the experience of being isolated but also the depression. At this point, Helen began to separate from being the problem (Depressed) to understanding the multiple factors in her life that contributed to the Isolation and Depression. Once she separated from her problem, she began to discuss her history of competence. Reviewing her life history, she stated she had been able to maintain a positive attitude all her life, she was a "people-person" and had several friends, although many had died over the years. Furthermore, she felt she had managed to resolve multiple problems that arose throughout her life and saw each of those abilities as personal strengths that she felt she still possessed. As these conversations continued, Helen experienced herself as a competent individual who could also overcome the current Isolation and resultant Depression. Utilizing a variety of community services, such as paratransit, senior center programs, and a friendly visitor program, Helen's personal sense of competence increased and she became more involved in the community. As she became more active, the depression subsided.

To promote the separation between people and problems, narrative therapists will collaborate with individuals to reflect on the nature of the problem. Once the problem has been personified, narrative therapists will ask about the problem's intentions, tactics, purpose, motives, allies, and goals (Morgan, 2000). As individuals personify a problem and identify its effects, they are empowered to take action against problems and the ideas that support the problem. For example, Helen stated that Depression and Isolation wanted to keep her from solving problems for herself and seeking aid from others, both of which would cause Depression and Isolation to lose their influence over her. As the problem's tactics and intentions are identified, an individual is able to identify times when the problem did not have influence over his or her life. Narrative therapists notice those times when the problem does not have an influence over the individual's life and ask about them. White and Epston (1990) and White (1991) called these events *unique outcomes*. Unique outcomes can be thoughts, actions, intentions, or any other occurrence that *could not* be predicted by the presence of a problem in a person's life. Unique outcomes are in past, present, and future events. For example, an older person who experiences depression attends a social luncheon and plans a short trip with the senior center. Neither attendance at the luncheon nor the plans for a trip are consistent with the intentions of depression; both activities can be explored as unique outcomes to the problem story.

As the unique outcomes are combined and expanded, the individual begins to experience an alternative description of him- or herself separate from the problem identity. As the alternative description is enacted in the individual's life, the individual experiences a preferred change.

Stella

Stella, a 78-year-old woman, was slightly injured in a car accident. Fear entered her life. When asked about Fear's intentions for her, Stella stated that Fear was planning on imprisoning her in her small apartment. The primary tactic that Fear used against her was to tell her she would die if she left her home. It also stole from her the desire to do the things that she enjoyed doing. Depression was a constant partner to Fear, imprisoning her further. As we identified Fear's tactics, Stella also began to identify times when she was able to overcome the effects of Fear. For example, she was able to go to bingo with friends and she continued to feel the desire to leave her house. I asked if there were other times in her life when she was able to overcome Fear, and she identified a history of events when she was able to overcome its effects. For example, she left an abusive relationship despite not having financial resources she could rely on and she attended college at a late stage in her life despite her fear that others would ridicule her. Through our conversations, she began to experience herself as being brave in the face of Fear. As she internalized the preferred description of herself as being brave, she began to leave her home more often.

A final note of concern regarding externalizations comes from a variety of writers (Dickerson & Zimmerman, 1996; Freeman & Lobovits, 1993; Morgan, 2000). They warned that therapists must account for the larger social context within which problems occur before externalizing a problem, or therapists might unwittingly externalize a problem that essentially blames the victim. For example, a therapist would not want to externalize Depression when an older adult is a victim of physical or emotional abuse. If the therapist focuses on Depression, questions will likely address how the Depression influences the individual's thoughts and behavior without addressing the abusive circumstances sustaining the Depression. Furthermore, as the focus on Depression persists, it is less likely that the older person will report the abuse to the therapist. A preferred approach would be to challenge the effects of an "abuse-dominated" story (Adams-Wescott & Dobbins, 1997). That externalization shifts the problem from the individual to the social conditions and discourses that perpetuate abuse toward older adults.

EXPLORING THE PROBLEM'S EFFECTS Narrative therapists are interested in the effects that problems have on a person's life. Each individual has a different story, and it is important that a therapist's questions reflect a client's unique experiences.

Narrative therapy does provide some guidelines on the types of questions to be asked during the course of therapy, however. Externalizing questions are developed that ask about the effects that problems have on a person's sense of self, and on his or her relationship with family members, partners, friends, siblings, or other people involved in his or her life. Externalizing questions about how problems affect an individual's social life, spiritual life, life with caregivers, and leisure life as well as questions of how problems affect moods, thoughts, feelings, and desires are also employed. An example of these questions might be:

- How do you think Hopelessness has influenced how you think about yourself?
- How does Conflict get you to interact with your children when they try to assist you? Do you feel it acts for or against you and your family?

- When Fatigue of Caregiving overwhelms you, what effect does that have on your relationships with others? Do you find it invites support from others or does it isolate you further?
- What effect has Uselessness had on your thoughts about your future?

As people engage in these externalizing conversations, they continue to separate from problems that negatively affect their lives. Morgan (2000) stated that there are at least five effects of externalizing-the-problem conversations:

1. As people separate from problems, they find that problems no longer reflect the truth about their identities, opening space to alter their relationships with those problems.

2. When problems are seen as being less fixed or true, people are able to notice their abilities, skills, and competencies. This self-knowledge empowers people to take responsibility for and action against problems.

3. Externalizing conversations challenge the power of professional discourses that rely on labeling, pathologizing, and diagnosing. Rarely do these reflect an individual's experience of oneself, although frequently labeling, pathologizing, and diagnosing will have a negative impact on the older person. As a result of our dominant culture's use of professional discourses that utilize labeling, many older adults have been diagnosed and labeled as depressed, anxious, paranoid, resistant, and so forth, much to their detriment. Many people fear institutionalization if they receive a mental health diagnosis; as a result, they avoid seeking therapy. Other older adults fear that once they are diagnosed, their identities will be taken over by the meaning of diagnosis. Thus, if a doctor states that an individual is depressed, he or she must *be* depressed and any experience other than depression goes unnoticed. To exacerbate the problem, when medical doctors and psychotherapists assign an older adult a Diagnostic Statistical Manual (DSM) diagnosis, they frequently prescribe medication as the only intervention, believing that their patient is too old to benefit from psychotherapy. Therefore, many older adults feel that they have never had an opportunity to live their lives free from the effects of labeling. When older clients participate in externalizing conversations, they have the opportunity to challenge the thin descriptors of diagnosis and labeling and explore alternative and preferred descriptions of themselves.

4. Once a person experiences him- or herself apart from the Problem, options and alternatives become available to the person because he or she is able to discuss the personal effects of the Problem. The person is no longer the Problem. The individual begins to notice times when he or she has not given in to the Problem or when he or she openly acted against the Problem.

5. Frequently, conflict arises between family members, particularly in caregiving situations. Externalizing conversations help family members see problems as separate entities and notice how problems infect the lives and relationships of all family members. Through the use of externalizing conversations, family members are invited to unite against the effects of problems and, as a result, they spend less time blaming one another.

DECONSTRUCTING PROBLEM STORIES

Whereas externalizing questions bring to light the influence of the problem stories, deconstructing questions examine how problem stories influence conclusions people make about their lives and their relationships. Furthermore, deconstructing questions ask about the strategies and techniques the Problem has used to recruit an individual into a problem lifestyle and how those techniques direct the individual's life and interactions in a nonpreferred manner (Zimmerman & Dickerson, 1995). The purpose of deconstructing questions is not to challenge the existing narrative or to replace one bad story with a good story, but rather, to examine the problem story from multiple perspectives (White, 2000).

Deconstructing questions can address meanings and experiences from multiple domains. They ask an individual to analyze the problem story by closely examining the specific events, thoughts, interactions, intentions, beliefs, social contexts, and cultural discourses that have contributed to the individual's meaning system regarding the problem. These deconstructing questions ask about the meanings of the events across time: past, present, and future. The purpose of these questions is twofold. First, it helps the individual understand the etiology of his or her problem story. Second, it opens up space for the individual to notice those times when he or she acted outside of the problem story or noticed alternative explanations of the events that set the foundation for a preferred re-description of the life experience. These explanations set the foundation for change. Zimmerman and Dickerson (1995) noted that deconstructing questions must capture a person's meaningful experiences in order for deconstruction to be effective.

When a narrative therapist is working with an individual to deconstruct a meaning of an event that contributes to the problem story, it is important for the therapist to map or track the effects of the event. Although there are a number of ways to ask deconstructing questions about the effects of a problem, White (1999) proposed a model for systematically asking a sequence of questions that assists individuals to examine, evaluate, and map each effect of the Problem. He called this sequence of questions a *Statement of Position Map.* It literally asks the clients to examine and take a position on each component of the Problem. During the process of asking deconstructing questions about a problem, a narrative therapist who is using the Statement of Position Map begins by asking questions about what meaning an individual would give to a particular event, thought, or other experience. It may include giving the event a name that fits with the individual's experience.

Lisa

During therapy, Lisa stated that she was depressed and overwhelmed from caring for her parents for the past 10 years. She noted that she rarely leaves her parents' home, even though she has her own home that she feels she has ignored. Lisa believed that she needed to put her life aside while she cared for her parents. When she was asked about why she does not have her four other siblings (who live in the same area as her parents) help her, she stated that helping her parents is "her role." The therapist then asked the first of the Statement of Position Map questions: what "her role" means to her. Her answer revealed multiple meanings, the foremost of which was that she would not be a good daughter if she did not take complete care of her parents all of the time.

The second question in the Statement of Position Map addresses the *effects* that the problem has on the individual. Lisa's answers indicated that she felt compelled to care for her parents. She believed that no one else in the family was willing to help. She could not assert herself to her siblings for fear that they might become angry with her, and she felt helpless, angry, and resentful.

The third question in the sequence asks that the individual evaluate those effects. When the therapist asked the evaluation question, Lisa stated that it was not fair that her family should treat her this way and fail to assist her.

The final question in the Statement of Position Map asks the individual to justify one's evaluation. When Lisa was asked to justify her evaluation, she gave a variety of reasons why she felt that she was unfairly treated, including the fact that, without offering any assistance, her siblings frequently criticized what she did for her parents. As the work continued with Lisa, she asserted herself and insisted that her siblings care for their parents every weekend. Her siblings complied, and Lisa's stress significantly decreased over the course of therapy.

The following example illustrates the use of deconstructing questions.

Dorothy

Dorothy was a 78-year-old woman who left her home in Alabama to visit her daughter in California. During her visit, Dorothy had a heart attack and required major heart surgery. Despite this episode, Dorothy still planned to return to her home in Alabama. After the surgery, however, the cardiac surgeon in California informed her that her health problems would likely prevent her from ever returning to Alabama. Dorothy was overwhelmed by hopelessness. Dorothy reported that she could not take more than two to three steps before becoming fatigued and that she felt useless and burdensome. I asked her to identify at what point the problem of Hopelessness had entered her life. We explored how Hopelessness made her feel that there was nothing she could do to affect her health and then we discussed the effects of turning her life over to the medical profession. Discussing the effect of Hopelessness on her relationship with her daughter and her daughter's partner, I asked

Dorothy how Hopelessness had recruited them into the truth about her medical condition and how that truth recruited them into particular behaviors that reinforced her story of Hopelessness. As each effect of the problem was discussed, she was asked to evaluate the multiple effects of Hopelessness on her life and on the lives of her daughter and partner. Dorothy stated she did not feel it was right that Hopelessness had taken away her life. When asked to justify her response, she stated that she still had plans for her life—one of which was to return to her home in Alabama. She committed herself to learning relaxation skills through meditation in order to decrease her cardiac symptoms and to increase her energy. As Dorothy felt empowered to do something about her health, she began to take more action. In addition to the ongoing therapy, she learned how to meditate. Within 1 month after the start of therapy, she began to walk across the living room without assistance, then she could help her daughter cook meals, and finally she was able to do light housework. Each time she visited her doctor, he was surprised by her progress. These changes in her life reinforced her idea that she was in charge of her life. Psychotherapy ended after 3 months, when her doctor in California agreed she was well enough to return to her home in Alabama.

INVITATIONS TO ALTERNATIVE STORIES

When a person participates in externalizing conversations, he or she begins to notice times when a problem's totalizing description does not have control over him or her. A problem's grip over a person's life is powerful and blinding, so many people do not give meanings to such experiences, which can be classified as unique outcomes described earlier in this chapter.

Unique outcomes provide entry points to alternative stories. Because clients generally discount unique outcomes, therapists must listen carefully for the occurrence of unique outcomes within the telling of dominant stories. For an experience to qualify as a unique outcome, it must be directly related to clients' experiences. In collaboration with clients, therapists must be interested in exploring the details of unique outcomes. Furthermore, therapists influenced by narrative models do not believe that unique outcomes exist in isolation. Problems do not completely take over people's lives. Unique outcomes can be connected to other unique outcomes, resulting in a movement away from the thin descriptions of labels and pathology and toward the rich descriptions of personal experiences and preferences. Initially, it is through this collaborative exploration of unique outcomes that a re-authoring process begins to occur.

UNIQUE OUTCOMES can be connected to other unique outcomes, resulting in a movement away from the thin descriptions of labels and pathology and toward the rich descriptions of personal experiences and preferences.

In order to facilitate the re-authoring process, White (1991) suggested that a variety of questions be asked of the individual's experience, especially within the realms of *landscape of action* questions and *landscape of meaning* questions, terms he has incorporated from Bruner's (1986) work. Landscape of action questions focus on specific events. These questions ask what, where, and when an event occurred, as well as how the unique outcome event happened, and what skills were needed to make it happen (Zimmerman & Dickerson, 1995).

Furthermore, landscape of action questions may also ask clients to situate unique outcomes in a sequence of events that support their re-authoring experiences, or they may ask about a sequence of events that led up to the performance of unique outcomes. For example, therapists might ask their clients what steps they took to prepare themselves to take action against their problems. Landscape of action questions also seek to link the preferred developments of the present with experiences in the past, and they encourage the client to develop a history of unique outcomes by situating them across time. As a history of unique outcomes is identified and linked with the present, the client recovers alternative narratives that challenge the totalizing demands of problems.

Landscape of meaning questions (White, 1995) invite clients to make meaning of the sequence of events or unique outcomes described in the landscape of action. Clients are asked about what the unique outcome might reveal about their preferences, wishes, or desires. They are also asked to identify what personal values and beliefs were reflected by their unique outcomes, what personal skills or abilities were needed to perform the unique outcomes, and what commitment was reflected in the performance of the unique outcomes. As with landscape of action questions, landscape of meaning questions can explore the history and development of a client's "personal commitment in life" (White, 1991).

Neither landscape of action nor landscape of meaning questions are asked in isolation of one another. Rather, therapists weave them together to bring forth a coherent alternative experience to the problem story. As clients reflect on the meanings of alternative experiences in the landscape of action, they clarify their preferences, values, and motives. Therapists can then ask questions about what other events may have occurred that are consistent with those values and preferences; landscape of meaning questions then ask about those events, and so forth.

> As persons respond to landscape of action and landscape of consciousness (meaning) questions, they engage in a reliving of experience, and their lives are "retold." Alternative knowledge of self and of relationships are generated and/or resurrected; alternative modes of life and thought become available for persons to enter into. (White, 1991, p. 32)

Just as the Statement of Position Map is useful in deconstructing the Problem story, it is also a useful model to use during the re-authoring process. An individual is asked what meaning he or she ascribes to a unique outcome in the context of one's preferences, goals, personal motives, and so forth.

Eleanor

Eleanor was a 66-year-old woman who had a severe medical condition that resulted in chronic pain and physical limitations. She was initially referred for depression. After we deconstructed factors that contributed to depression, such as dependence on others, fiscal concerns, the recent death of her husband, decreased memory capability related to the illness, and lack of confidence in herself, she began to identify what she considered personal strengths. Among those strengths was her ability to access needed medical help, a desire to socialize with others despite her pain, times when her ability to think clearly would return so she could make plans, and a willingness to learn new ways of coping. Using landscape of action questions and landscape of meaning questions, I asked what those self-described strengths *meant* to her. She replied that they meant she was still a competent human being with something to offer the world. They also meant that she was a good person who had to live and take action on her own behalf under very difficult conditions. I asked her to describe the *effect* (the second set of questions in the Statement of Position Map) that each of those strengths had on her current life. She replied that each effect allowed her to focus on what she needed to do to improve her life and make her plans accordingly. It also meant that she would have to monitor herself so she would not overexert herself and bring on the pain. She also stated that she would make plans to have others help her when the pain became unbearable and she could not think clearly. Consistent with the Statement of Position Map, I asked if those outcomes were preferred. She replied they were and she went on to *justify* (the fourth set of questions in the mapping process) why they were preferred. Essentially, she felt more empowered to take action on her own behalf. The effect of her empowerment was that she was able to minimize her pain to some degree and feel more in control of her life. It should be noted that the sequence described is simply a template rather than a prescription of how to do narrative therapy.

Naming the counter-plot or re-authored story or alternative story has multiple benefits (Morgan, 2000; Zimmerman & Dickerson, 1995). It extends the separation between people and problems and allows clients to consider what preferences they desire for their lives. It also helps clients to set a framework by which they can compare and contrast actions and thoughts that support a preferred lifestyle or a problem lifestyle. Zimmerman and Dickerson (1995) noted the benefits of using the client's name in conjunction with some metaphor as a title for the re-authored story. For example, I might talk about "Mary's Voice," or "Bob's Resolve." Naming the alternative story also allows clients to speculate on what future steps they might take to further support the alternative story (see Chapter 9 for more on the importance of future vision).

SUPPORTING THE ALTERNATIVE STORY   New and preferred stories develop over the course of narrative therapy. In order for new stories to become dominant stories, however, they must be performed and circulated in interpersonal contexts. Unless the new stories are performed in interpersonal contexts, clients may have difficulty maintaining their preferred ways of being. Therapists influenced by narrative ways of working with clients seek witnesses who can act as a supportive audience to the preferred changes.

Although it is beyond the scope of this chapter to detail the many different methods that narrative therapists use to support preferred changes, among these methods are definitional ceremonies in which people outside of the therapy are asked to observe the therapeutic conversation in a particular manner that promotes either questions about or acknowledgment of changes the individual in therapy has made. Other methods include outsider witness groups, who comment in specific ways about the individual's experience, leagues, certificates, videotapes, and therapeutic letters (Morgan, 2000). *Re-membering conversations* are particularly useful when working with older adults. Citing the work of Barbara Meyeroff, White (1997) stated that *membered* lives evoke an image of a *club of life* that is composed of individual members with whom one has interacted in his or her past. Some of these members were invited into a person's life, whereas other members were uninvited but were included in the club because of circumstances beyond the person's control. They all participate in how a person's life is constituted, however.

Re-membering practices invite a special type of recollection in which people may engage in a revision of the membership of their clubs of life. This metaphor suggests that people can change the status and importance of those in their lives. White stated "It is in this way, through re-membering practices, that persons can have more say about whose voices are to be recognized on matters of their identity, and about who might be authorized to speak on such matters" (1997, p. 23). Many older adults have lost opportunities to perform a preferred story to a supportive audience because of deaths of significant people in their lives, poor health, poverty, ageism, and other social factors. The lack of opportunities to enact preferred stories in an interpersonal context may lead these individuals to enact nonpreferred stories. Significant benefits when one engages in re-membering conversations with older adults include the following:

- Re-membering conversations can reactivate dormant relationships by reengaging clients with others from their past.

- Through re-membering conversations, clients can experience the presence of important relationships even when others cannot be present, such as when the other person in the relationship is deceased.

- Re-membering conversations bring forth an experience of being with important others that extends beyond the passive images and feelings of typical memories.

- Re-membering is "calling attention to the reaggregation of members, the figures who belong to one's life story, one's own prior selves, as well as significant others who are part of the story. Re-membering, then, is a purposive, significant unification" (Meyeroff, 1992, p. 240).

- Re-membering conversations can provide an entry point to recover preferred stories in older persons' lives.

As therapy proceeds, it is important to try to provide opportunities for a client to perform his or her alternative story in the context of supportive others.

Alice

Alice was a 68-year-old woman referred to our office because of depression and suicidal ideation. During our first session, she stated that she did not think she could continue living. She said her husband of 15 years had recently left her and she did not know why. She felt it must be because of some personal defect. We initially externalized Hopelessness and examined the effects it was having on her life. She stated that it told her that her marriage was a lie. In fact, she continued, she felt that her whole life was a lie. She felt abandoned by two prior husbands and her children from each of her marriages. Alice stated that Hopelessness told her that she had no true significant relationships throughout her life.

Furthermore, Hopelessness told her she would be alone and unloved for the rest of her life. She had few personal friends because she had devoted herself to her relationship with her husband. Hopelessness told her that without her husband she would lose her home and become homeless. Hopelessness felt she should end her life because her pain was unbearable. When the initial session ended, she stated that she would not kill herself despite her feelings. We explored what it was about her that was able to keep her from carrying out the demands of Hopelessness. She began to talk very tentatively about her hope for the future. I experienced this as a unique outcome because having hope and thoughts about one's future is not consistent with or could not be predicted to occur under the conditions of Hopelessness.

During the course of our meetings together, we began to deconstruct Hopelessness. I asked her what ideas supported Hopelessness in her life. Alice responded that Hopelessness relied on her experience of never being loved, despite giving "everything" to her former husband. It enlisted Worthlessness to make her feel as if no one could ever care about her. As sessions proceeded, we also discussed the influence of Voicelessness, a reflection of her fear to state what she wanted from others. Voicelessness was eventually linked to the dominant patriarchy discourse.

As we explored the histories of her externalizations, she felt the problems had been with her all of her life. She related a history of events that included verbal and physical abuse from her mother and domineering husbands. She stated that she accepted whatever happened to her because "that was what a woman was supposed to do." We did not explore her history in search of an individualizing discourse of pathology but rather as a way of mapping the development of a problem narrative.

Landscape of action questions were included in our discussions. I asked her what actions Hopelessness, Worthlessness, and Voicelessness invited her to take. Integrating landscape of action questions with landscape of meaning questions, we pursued what meaning she made of those actions. What did she feel when Hopelessness, Worthlessness, and Voicelessness consumed her life? As these questions were asked, Alice began to separate from her internalization of having a psychological defect and was able to critically examine the influence and histories of her externalizations.

The separation of her identity from problems influencing her life was made possible by utilizing Statement of Position Map questions. For example, during one of our sessions, Alice was discussing how Hopelessness had increased her isolation from others. When I asked what tactics Hopelessness was utilizing, she stated that it told her she was ugly, and people would notice her ugliness and avoid her, so why go out. She felt that the ugliness they would notice was not only external but also an internal ugliness. I asked what effects this tactic had on her image of herself and others. She stated that it increased her experience of Hopelessness, Depression, and Isolation from others. I asked her if she felt those effects had a positive or negative impact on her life. She responded that she felt the effects were negative. We then explored why she felt the effects were negative. She stated that deep down, she knew she was a good person and she was not ugly. She wanted to be with people because she cared about others. Over the course of the next few sessions, we discussed the tactics that Hopelessness used against her. Among the tactics were fear of losing her house, critical voices from her past and present, a belief that as a woman she should remain subservient to her husband, the feeling that she had somehow done something wrong in the marriage, and a belief that to be a complete woman she needed to be married. As we deconstructed each of these beliefs, she began to vocalize times when she felt she did not have to be subservient to a man, nor was she to be blamed for his leaving. Furthermore, she had begun to socialize with other people and she discovered that they liked her. At these times she experienced the unique outcome of liking herself, which she felt decreased the influence of Hopelessness in her life.

For Alice, there were two particular events that opened the space for a re-authoring of her story. One was historical, and the other was centered on an act of assertiveness. During a session, I asked re-membering questions; in this particular instance, the questions had to do with identifying someone in her past who she felt truly supported her. She became tearful as she discussed a former supervisor who she said had "loved me for who I truly was." She said they could be honest with one another and she had never had a friend such as he in her life. When he died, it broke her heart. I asked her what she thought he would say if I was to ask him what he had noticed about her that invited him to "see and love her as she truly was." As she re-experienced his presence and her emotional connection to him, she began to tell about an alternative experience in her life that included both connection and compassion. As the re-membering questions proceeded in accordance with her experience, she began to see herself in a different light. She began to remember with other people in her life who had supported her. Landscape of action questions and landscape of meaning questions were asked about those relationships. Alice stated that she appreciated re-experiencing her relationships, both with her former supervisor and others who had supported her in her life. She stated she wanted to keep all those re-membered friends as consultants and to use their mutual relationships as a model for all future relationships.

The second most notable unique outcome occurred when Alice disagreed with someone she had known for several years. She stated that she had never voiced her opinion because she felt she had always been "put down" by the other person. She stated, however, that she stood her ground and let her Voice be heard. She said, afterward, that she was surprised, delighted, and somewhat frightened that her Voice could be so strong. We labeled the Voice "Alice's Voice." Again, several landscape of action and meaning questions were asked in relationship to "Alice's voice," such as

- Was this a preferred development for you?
- How do you think you prepared yourself for this step?
- Have there been other times in your life when the voice was present?
- Do you feel the voice speaks for you or for Hopelessness?
- What do you think standing your ground says about you as a person?

Both of these unique outcomes served as points for Alice to enter into an alternative story about herself. As she continued to re-author her life, she started to see herself in a new light and she began to enact and perform her alternative story. She took a more active role in her life. In defining how she preferred her life and relationships, she began to develop new relationships that supported her preferred lifestyle. Hopelessness became less and less a part of her life as she assumed more control over her decisions. She developed a network of friends who offered her the type of support she wanted. She took active control of her divorce instead of letting Hopelessness make her a victim again. She refused to give in to the demands of patriarchy in relationships with men. Finally, Alice volunteered for a Friendly Visitor program for isolated seniors as her way to help others break the chains of isolation and hopelessness.

SUMMARY

Narrative therapy is an effective approach for working with older adults. Developed from theories of social constructionism, constitutionalism, and narrative metaphors, narrative therapy acknowledges the dominant cultural discourses and interactional contexts that constitute people's lives. It provides an alternative to the individualizing discourses that place problems within people. Therapists influenced by a narrative practice view problems as problems. Utilizing reflective questions, narrative therapists collaborate with their clients to deconstruct the meanings, intentions, and strategies of problems. A re-authoring process results from the critical analysis of problem stories and the identification of unique outcomes. Narrative therapy promotes client empowerment and choice.

Narrative therapy provides multiple opportunities for older adults to re-experience and remember past knowledge and relationships. Utilizing clients' expertise about their own lives, narrative therapists are able to act as co-authors to bring forth alternative narratives that provide options to problem stories. Furthermore, narrative therapists work with clients to invite supportive people into their preferred stories. Most important, clients report experiencing respect, support, and preferred life changes.

REFERENCES

Adams-Westcott, J., & Dobbins, C. (1997). Listening to your "heart ears" and other ways young people can escape the effects of sexual abuse. In C. Smith & D. Nyland (Eds.), *Narrative therapies with children and adolescents* (pp. 195–220). New York: Guilford Press.

Becker, G. (1997). *Disrupted lives: How people create meaning in a chaotic world.* Berkeley: University of California Press.

Binney, E.A., & Swan, J.H. (1991). The political economy of mental health care for the elderly. In M. Minkler & C.L. Estes (Eds.), *Critical perspectives on aging: The political and moral economy of growing older* (pp. 165–188). Amityville, NY: Baywood Publishing Company.

Bruner, J. (1986). *Actual minds, possible worlds.* Cambridge, MA: Harvard University Press.

Bruner, J. (1990). *Acts of meaning.* Cambridge, MA: Harvard University Press.

Burman, E. (1994). *Deconstructing developmental psychology.* New York: Routledge.

Department of Health and Human Services, Administration on Aging. (2001). *Older adults and mental health: Issues and opportunities* [On-line]. Available: http://www.aoa.dhhs.gov/mh/report2001/default.htm.

Dickerson, V.C., & Zimmerman, J.L. (1996). Myths, misconceptions, and a word or two about politics. *Journal of Systemic Therapies, 15,* 79–88.

Estes, C.L. (1991). The new political economy of aging: Introduction and critique. In M. Minkler & C.L. Estes (Eds.), *Critical perspectives on aging: The political and moral economy of growing older* (pp. 3–17). Amityville, NY: Baywood Publishing Company.

Estes, C.L. (1999). The aging enterprise revisited. In M. Minkler & C.L. Estes (Eds.), *Critical gerontology: Perspectives from political and moral economy* (pp. 135–146). Amityville, NY: Baywood Publishing Company.

Estes, C.L., & Binney, E.A. (1991). The biomedicalization of aging: Dangers and dilemmas. In M. Minkler & C.L. Estes (Eds.), *Critical perspectives on aging: The political and moral economy of growing older* (pp. 117–134). Amityville, NY: Baywood Publishing Company.

Foucault, M. (1990). *The history of sexuality: An introduction* (Vol. 1.) New York: Vintage Press.

Foucault, M. (1995). *Discipline and punish: The birth of the prison.* New York: Vintage Press.

Freedman, J., & Combs, G. (1996). *Narrative therapy: The social construction of preferred realities.* New York: Norton.

Freeman, J.C., & Lobovits, D. (1993). The turtle with wings. In S. Friedman (Ed.), *The new language of change: Constructive collaboration in psychotherapy* (pp. 188–225). New York: Guilford Press.

Gergen, K.J. (1985). The social constructionist movement in modern psychology. *American Psychologist, 40,* 266–275.

Gergen, K.J. (1999). *An invitation to social construction.* Beverly Hills: Sage Publications.

Grimm, R., Maki, B., & Morales-Long, L. (1995). Developing narrative approaches with the elderly. *Journal of Collaborative Therapies, 3,* 4–14.

Hareven, T.K. (1995). Changing images of aging and the social construction of the life course. In M. Featherson & A. Wernick (Eds.), *Images of aging: Cultural representations of later life* (pp. 119–134). New York: Routledge.

Hazan, H. (1994). *Old age: Constructions and deconstructions.* Cambridge, MA: Cambridge University Press.

Ignatieff, M. (1984). *The needs of strangers.* Harmondsworth, UK: Penguin Books.

Madigan, S. (1998). Destabilising chronic identities of depression and retirement: Inscription, description, and deciphering. In S. Madigan & I. Law (Eds.), *Praxis: Situating discourse, feminism and politics in narrative therapies* (pp. 207–230). Vancouver, British Columbia, Canada: The Cardigan Press.

Meyeroff, B. (1992). Life history among the elderly: Performance, visibility and re-membering. In M. Kaminsky (Ed.), *Remembered lives: The work of ritual, storytelling, and growing older* (pp. 231–247). Ann Arbor: The University of Michigan Press.

Morgan, A. (2000). What is narrative therapy? An easy-to-read introduction. *Gecko, 1,* 1–132.

Neal, J.H. (1996). Narrative therapy training and supervision. *Journal of Systemic Therapies, 15,* 63–77.

Robertson, A. (1991). The politics of Alzheimer's disease: A case study in apocalyptic demography. In M. Minkler & C.L. Estes (Eds.), *Critical perspectives on aging: The political and moral economy of growing older* (pp. 135–150). Amityville, NY: Baywood Publishing Company.

Silverstein, M., Angelelli, J.J., & Parrott, T.M. (2001). Changing attitudes toward aging policy in the United States during the 1980s and 1990s: A cohort analysis. *Journal of Gerontology: Social Sciences, 56B,* S36–S43.

Tomm, K. (1987). Interventive interviewing: Part II. Reflexive questioning as a means to enable self-healing. *Family Process, 26,* 167–183.

Tomm, K., Hoyt, M.F., & Madigan, S.P. (1998). Honoring our internalized others and the ethics of caring: A conversation with Karl Tomm. In M. Hoyt (Ed.), *The handbook of constructive therapies: Innovative approaches from leading practitioners* (pp. 198–219). San Francisco: Jossey-Bass.

Wallace, S.P., & Villa, V.M. (1999). Caught in hostile cross-fire: Public policy and minority elderly in the United States. In M. Minkler & C.L. Estes (Eds.), *Critical gerontology: Perspectives from political and moral economy* (pp. 237–255). Amityville, NY: Baywood Publishing Company.

Weingarten, K. (1991). The discourses of intimacy: Adding a social constructionist and feminist view. *Family Process, 30,* 285–305.

White, M. (1988, Spring). Saying hullo again: The incorporation of the lost relationship in the resolution of grief. *Dulwich Centre Newsletter.* Reprinted in White, M. (1989). *Selected Papers.* Adelaide, Australia: Dulwich Centre Publications.

White, M. (1991). Deconstruction and therapy. *Dulwich Centre Newsletter, 3,* 21–40.

White, M. (1995). *Re-authoring lives: Interviews and essays.* Adelaide, Australia: Dulwich Centre Publications.

White, M. (1997). *Narratives of therapists' lives.* Adelaide, Australia: Dulwich Centre Publications.

White, M. (1999). Reflecting-team work as definitional ceremony revisited. *Gecko, 2,* 55–82.

White, M. (2000). *Reflections on narrative practice: Essays and interviews.* Adelaide, Australia: Dulwich Centre Publications.

White, M., & Epston, D. (1990). *Narrative means to therapeutic ends.* New York: Norton.

Zimmerman, J.L., & Dickerson, V.C. (1995). Narrative therapy and the work of Michael White. In M. Elkaim (Ed.), *Panorama des thérapies familiales.* Paris: Editions du Seuil.

Zimmerman, J.L., & Dickerson, V.C. (1996). *If problems talked: Narrative therapy in action.* New York: Guilford Press.

12

THE NARRATIVE
SOLUTIONS APPROACH

Bringing Out the Best in People as They Age

Joseph B. Eron and Thomas W. Lund

THE NARRATIVE SOLUTIONS approach developed out of a collaboration between Thomas Lund and Joseph Eron at the Catskill Family Institute (CFI). CFI was founded in 1981 as a private outpatient clinic providing psychological treatment for individuals, families, and couples. At that time, the treatment approach at CFI was modeled after the work done at the Mental Research Institute (MRI) in Palo Alto, California (Watzlawick, Weakland, & Fisch, 1974; Weakland, Fisch, Watzlawick, & Bodin, 1974).

The narrative solutions approach developed within the strength-based principles of the MRI model, offering clear guidelines for conducting conversations that draw on people's resourcefulness to overcome problems. Effective conversations center around who people are when they are at their best and draw attention to their preferred qualities and attributes. In a culture in which becoming older is often seen as a deficiency that must be repaired or covered over, the approach offers another possibility. The narrative solutions approach helps people stay focused on the strengths that have helped them through life and the attributes that come with age—wisdom, know-how, and a wealth of life experience. That older people have lived long lives filled with triumphs and setbacks becomes a resource to be tapped, an advantage in the process of motivating changes.

The work at MRI was an outgrowth of Gregory Bateson's famed research project on families of individuals with schizophrenia and represents one of the early moves toward a constructivist psychotherapeutic position. Paul Watzlawick (1976, 1978, 1984) articulated the constructivist underpinnings of the MRI approach. According to Watzlawick, the meaning people ascribed to events was socially constructed, truth was relative, and reality invented—not discovered.

Constructivist psychotherapists hold basic ideas in common about therapy. They have let go of the idea that therapy is about diagnosing and treating an underlying condition or disorder, and they assume that meaning and action are inextricably interwoven. In other words, constructivists believe that how people construe or view their predicament is intimately connected with what they do about it. At MRI, problems were seen as developing innocently from the mishandling of life situations, often during transitions such as marriage, the birth of a child, a child's leaving home, retirement, divorce, illness, or the death of a loved one. How people viewed their life circumstances and what they did about them determined the course of their problems. Problems were not seen as the result of a person's or the family system's psychopathology.

In practice, MRI became known for its emphasis on *strategic intervention.* MRI practitioners typically assigned behavioral tasks or directives to interrupt problem-maintaining patterns of interaction that often included a paradoxical or illogical bent.

MENTAL RESEARCH INSTITUTE'S APPROACH TO DEPRESSION FOLLOWING AN ILLNESS

The emphasis on strategic intervention is evident in the following case of an older man who became depressed after suffering a stroke (Watzlawick & Coyne, 1980).

William

William, an older man who was depressed after having a stroke, had stopped attending therapy after the first session. The therapist sat down with William's wife and grown children to get more information about William. From the family's description, William prided himself on being the head of the household until the stroke left him unable to accomplish many tasks in which he took pride. Family members, trying hard to be helpful, attempted to cheer him up, encourage him to be more active, and catered to his concerns, but William became more withdrawn and despondent. The therapist, taking into account that the family viewed William as proud and stubborn, reframed his depression as being the last refuge for his pride and self-respect. As part of the course of treatment, the therapist prescribed a series of tasks designed to get family members to act more helpless in his presence. As the family adopted this new approach, they reported a positive change in William's overall mood and activity level.

The reason or rationale for the type of positive change William experienced is not explained to the client or clients but can be understood in the following description of the problem cycle.

In the MRI model, the main unit of assessment and intervention was termed the *problem cycle* (Eron & Lund, 1996; Rohrbaugh & Eron, 1982). The problem cycle, in this case, could be described as follows: The more that family members attempted to help William, the more despondent he became, and the more despondent he became, the more they tried to help. The therapist attempted to break this cycle by persuading family members to act *helpless* rather than *helpful*. Although family members' views were used to promote compliance with the behavioral task, the role that "viewing" played in the evolution and maintenance of the problem and its resolution was largely unaddressed. For example, it was unclear how William's family members regarded him prior to his stroke and how their view of him may have changed following the stroke. Similarly, it was unclear how William viewed his family before and after the stroke. Did he imagine that they now saw him as diminished and incompetent? Did this view affect or shape his depressed behaviors? When family members acted helpless and he became more helpful, did this promote in William a more positive view of self?

FROM THE MENTAL RESEARCH INSTITUTE TO THE CATSKILL FAMILY INSTITUTE

Since the mid-1980s we have studied conversations with individuals, couples, and families who were in distress. Our approach developed as we compared conversations that motivated change with those that did not. We found that we achieved success simply by helping people find new ways of looking at their predicaments. When we altered the key views that were linked to problem-maintaining behavior, people figured out for themselves what to do differently. This approach bypassed the need for behavioral tasks or directives and eliminated the issues of a client's compliance or noncompliance.

As we tracked the development of problems in families, we followed them with the premise of many strategic therapists (Haley, 1980; Weakland, Fisch, Watzlawick, & Boden, 1974). As mentioned previously, strategic therapists postulate that problems often seemed to evolve from the mishandling of ordinary life difficulties. We observed that this occurred frequently at key transition points in an individual's life cycle (e.g., marriage, divorce, birth of a child, separation, illness, children leaving home, death). We found that at these times of transition, not only did people begin to act differently but also their views of self and others became more fluid and unsettled.

We observed that whether a problem developed in the wake of a life transition depended on how a person's views of self and others were affected. In line with the work of Laing, Phillipson, and Lee (1996), three levels of perspective should be considered: 1) a person's self view; 2) a person's view of others; and 3) a person's view of the others' view, or how the person thinks others see him or her. In the case of William, who was depressed after a stroke, the event of this major illness may have challenged his prevailing views of self and others at all three levels. It is likely that William began to see himself differently—as less capable, less independent, and less able to help others. He also may have begun to see his family differently, as more solicitous and more critical of his capabilities. Finally, he may have begun to see his family seeing him differently—to imagine that they regarded him as helpless and incapable of caring for himself.

In general, we found common threads in problem evolution. Contradictions (or *disjunctions,* to borrow Laing's term) across these levels of perspective shaped the development of problems in families. Each individual in the family has a way that he or she wishes to see him- or herself. At unsettling times of transition, problems unfolded as family members came to see their own behavior, themselves, and others seeing them behaving in ways they found discrepant with *preferred* views of self. People often experienced these discrepancies with pain and negative emotion and began to engage in problematic behavior.

Our shift away from the prescriptive practices of strategic family therapy paralleled the growth of the solution-focused and narrative therapies in the late 1980s and 1990s. The solution-focused approaches of Steven de Shazer and Insoo Kim Berg (de Shazer, 1985; de Shazer, Berg, & Lipchik, 1986), and William O'Hanlon and Michele Weiner-Davis (1989) shifted therapists' focus away from talk about problems toward talk of solutions. Solution-focused therapists reoriented family members to see exceptions to the present problem and helped them to imagine the future without the problem. They emphasized people's strengths and competencies, not their deficits and dysfunctions.

> SOLUTION-FOCUSED therapists reoriented family members to see exceptions to the present problem and to imagine the future without the problem. They emphasized people's strengths and competencies, not their deficits and dysfunctions.

Narrative therapists Michael White and David Epston (1990) also spoke about problems in a different way than did their predecessors. They observed that as problems came to dominate people's lives, the stories they told about themselves became negative and problems saturated. *Externalizing conversations* were designed to separate people from problems and to help them marshal their own resources against their problems. Therapists drew people's attention to the broad spectrum of life experiences—times when they did and did not fall under the influence of problems and when they incorporated the past as a potential resource. As people's stories of themselves and their relationships changed, their problems improved.

The narrative solutions approach interweaves elements common to strategic, solution-focused, and narrative therapy that empower people to access the resources needed to resolve their problems efficiently. The approach has been applied to individuals and couples of varying ages and with a variety of presenting problems (Eron & Lund, 1993, 1995, 1996, 1998a, 1998b; Lund & Eron, 1998). Nursing homes, psychiatric hospitals, and residential facilities for youthful criminal offenders have integrated the approach into existing programs. Educators, physicians, clergy, child welfare workers, and helping professionals across a variety of disciplines have also applied it.

PREFERRED VIEW

People have strong preferences about how they would like to behave, how they would like to see themselves, and how they would like others to see them. We refer to these ideas about the self as a person's *preferred view,* a concept we consider the cornerstone of the narrative solutions approach. Preferred view has to do with the following:

- The qualities people want to have, and have noticed, by others. For example, many teenagers wish to think of themselves as capable, competent, cool, independent, and able to manage their own personal business. Many older people often want to see themselves as useful, productive, and helpful to others.

- Preferred attributions that an individual makes about his or her behavior. ("I did that [lost my temper] to show my wife that I am still in control, that she can't boss me around.")

- A person's preferences, hopes, and intentions for his or her life. Preferred view may or may not have anything to do with a person's actual behavior or the effects of that behavior. In other words, a young man may have failed all of his subjects in school, and yet he may have a strong preference to see himself as a hard-working, good student. He may also have a preference for and an intention to go to college, although that likelihood is unrealistic. Similarly, a man may want others to see him as in control, although he has no control over his temper.

The concept of preferred view has appeared in different shapes and forms in the writings of prominent psychologists and family therapists. Traditionally, strategic and structural family therapists promoted the practice of joining with families by understanding and accommodating their values and presenting new ideas in ways that were compatible with their beliefs. Influenced by master strategist Milton Erickson, the MRI group stressed the therapeutic importance of understanding how people want others to see them. In an early summary of their work, Weakland and his colleagues (1974) noted that early in treatment they determined "what approach would appeal most to the particular patient [person]—to observe 'where he lives' and meet this need, whether it is to believe in the magical, to defeat the expert, to be a caretaker [caregiver] of someone, to face a challenge, or whatever" (p. 156). The implication was that the experts should pay attention to how people wish to portray themselves and be seen by others.

The concept of preferred view was implicit in the work of therapist Carl Rogers, whose ideas bear a marked resemblance to narrative concepts about therapy and change. Rogers proposed that people experience distress when there is a gap between their *ideal self* (what we call *preferred view of self*) and *self as perceived.* In describing outcome research on client-centered therapy, Rogers (1961) stated his hypothesis: "It was predicted that during and after therapy, the perceived self would be more positively valued, i.e., would become more congruent with the ideal or valued self" (pp. 234–235). His findings showed a significant increase in congruence between self as perceived and ideal self during therapy. Furthermore, Rogers' therapeutic *unconditional positive regard* was closely akin to what we would call *joining with a person's preferred view.*

Narrative therapists have alluded indirectly to the concept of preferred view in their writings. For example, White and Epston (1990) assumed that people experience problems when the stories of their lives do not sufficiently represent their lived experience. Therapy is geared toward helping people get in touch with *unique outcomes,* which are aspects of lived experiences that fall outside of these dominant, *problem-saturated* stories. These unique outcomes are plotted into an alternative story or narrative. White and Epston often referred to these new stories as "preferred stories" (p. 14), and in working with individuals they help to facilitate performance and circulation of these accounts during the course of therapy. The implication is that it is helpful for people to gain access to stories that are more in line with who it is they wish to be.

In the narrative solutions approach, the concept of preferred view pertains more broadly to an understanding of how problems get started in the first place.

PREFERRED VIEW AND THE SHAPING OF PROBLEMS

Our assumptions about problem evolution are as follows:

1. An event (or events) takes place, often during a time of transition, that is unsettling to people. The event awakens a search for new meaning as people reconsider how they see themselves and how other people see them.

2. In this more charged emotional climate, people may see their own behavior and/or imagine that others see them in ways that clash with their preferred views of self. This perceptual gap is diagrammed in Figure 12.1. People often experience intense, unsettling emotions such as frustration, sadness, and anxiety when they behave in ways that are discrepant with preferred views of self and/or when they think important others see them in ways that conflict with how they wish to be seen. For example, older adults with Alzheimer's disease have a long story of their lives before the onset of illness. They may have strong preferences to be independent and capable, and a sense of self that is not compatible with being disabled and cared for by others. Their desire to preserve a sense of self may become even stronger as that self vanishes with the disease. Actions that are intended to be helpful to people with Alzheimer's disease, such as having their faulty memories corrected,

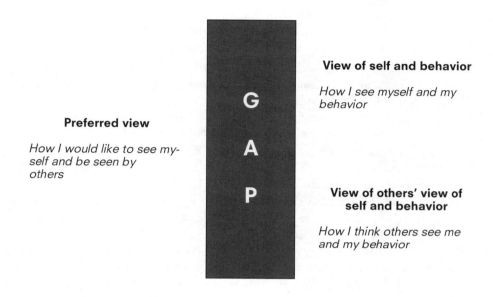

Figure 12.1. Gap diagram depicting the client's mindset. The gap occurs when an individual's preferred view of self is discrepant with his or her actual view of self and behavior and/or how the individual views others viewing his or her self and behavior.

being stopped from wandering, or being bathed or dressed may challenge the older people's preferred views of self and evoke intense emotional reactions such as defiance, agitation, or confusion.

3. Family members and caregivers also may experience a gap between their preferred view, how they see their own behavior, and how they see others seeing them. This experience will affect how they feel and what they do about their situation. For example, the son of a man with Alzheimer's disease may have a long history of seeing his father as strong and caring. Having received considerable support from his father over the years, the son may desire to reciprocate and have his ailing father see him as helpful and caring. Should his efforts to help be met with agitation or defiance, however, the son may feel badly and adjust his problem-solving approach by becoming angry, insistent, and demanding. This approach may aggravate the father's distress and intensify the problem cycle.

4. As this problem cycle churns on, views of self and others become more fixed and actions more restricted. Repetitions of the cycle reinforce negative attributions of self and others and promote more of the same behavior. For example, the person with Alzheimer's disease, seeing himself as helpless through his son's eyes, may become increasingly uncooperative. The son, seeing himself as unhelpful through his father's eyes, may become more demanding or give up and withdraw.

5. As patterns of behavior solidify, family members become more convinced that a problem really exists and usually locate its source or cause in perceived deficiencies of self and others. They lose sight of the problem's transitional and often accidental evolution and have no idea that their own constructions shape its course.

This formulation of *problem evolution* is in line with Bogdan's (1986) notion of *accidentalism* and expands on the basic premise of the MRI model that problems develop innocently from the mishandling of ordinary life difficulties. Even a seemingly trivial event can trigger the onset of a major problem by jostling the pre-existing views of those affected by the event. Steven de Shazer (1985) elucidated a similar theme in describing how problems might evolve out of "damn bad luck." In our view, however, whether a life event or an accident turns into an enduring problem hinges not only on how the event is construed but also on whether these troublesome perceptual gaps emerge in the wake of the event.

HOW THE PROBLEM CYCLE EVOLVES AND DISSOLVES

The therapists of the MRI case analysis viewed the depression of the man who had a stroke as being maintained by the well-intentioned, helpful, and solicitous actions of the family members. These behaviors, however, would only maintain the problem if the man had preferred to see himself as helpful, capable, and self-sufficient prior to the problem's onset.

The concept of preferred view encompasses the broad narrative picture, the full spectrum of an individual's life experience that defines who he or she is, or wants to be. In this sense, history is relevant to understanding the anatomy of a problem-maintaining solution. To explain why helpfulness maintained the stroke victim's depression, certain things would need to be known. For instance, what was this man's dominant role in the family prior to his illness? What were his past triumphs and setbacks? What stories did family members tell that defined his true character—as they see it and as he sees it? In this case, the only clues to the stroke victim's preferred view were references to his stubbornness and pride, which suggested that he would prefer to see himself as someone who gives rather than receives help.

A different prevailing narrative would predict a different reaction to the family's helpfulness. If the man had always seen himself as someone deserving of indulgence and catering, he then might regard helpfulness as his due, as a fitting tribute to his past contributions, and as evidence of his family's love and respect. The net result might then have been a proud self-confirmation rather than a spiraling of depression. Depression spirals when individuals' views of self are out of sync with the way others treat them; in this case, the man viewed the helpfulness of family members as evidence of their disregard for him, as proof that they no longer saw him as he preferred. When the therapist suggested that the family members act helpless, the net result was a lifting of the depression. It could be speculated that the lifting of the man's depression corresponded with the narrowing of the gap between his preferred view and how he viewed others' viewing him. In a sense, the lifting of the depression is like the lifting of the burden of being seen in a distasteful way.

NARRATIVE SOLUTIONS APPROACH: DEPRESSION FOLLOWING ILLNESS

The following example of depression following illness uses the narrative solutions approach.

Al

Al, a 65-year-old man, had recently retired. About 2 years after his retirement, which was going along reasonably well, a trusted family physician diagnosed him as having chronic emphysema. In subsequent meetings with his doctor about his physical symptoms, Al revealed that he was feeling depressed, withdrawn, and "not his old self." He was referred by his physician for treatment of depression brought on by his illness.

When the therapist greeted Al in the waiting room before their first meeting, he noticed first Al's large, powerful hands. Al's hands enveloped him as if to suggest that Al was the one who was supposed to be helping the therapist feel more secure in this relationship. Soon, the therapist learned that Al prided himself in being someone who could work with his hands. Al viewed himself as a real family man, the main breadwinner and primary caregiver of a large family that consisted of his wife, 8 grown children, and 15 grandchildren. Everyone came to Al when they had a problem, when something needed repair, or when someone needed financial advice or assistance. Al's retirement didn't change his position in the family. There was still always something to do, something to fix, someone who needed his help or advice.

After Al developed emphysema, he felt that he was no longer the person he used to be. He sat around all day feeling depressed and useless. Worse, he felt removed from his family, and they noticed this. When the therapist asked Al to help him understand what his family noticed, he told a story about a snowfall that captured his current predicament and illustrated problem evolution.

After a recent snowfall, Al went out to shovel the driveway, an old and familiar job for him. He went at it full tilt, as always. But 5 minutes into the task, he started having difficulty breathing and became quickly frustrated. In disgust, he threw his shovel in the snow, retreated to the house, and collapsed on the couch, where he spent most of the day. His wife and son came around to talk to him, but he didn't have much to say. When the therapist asked what happened to the driveway, Al said that later, without saying a word to him, his son went out and finished the job. A pained look came over Al's face, as if this were a final blow, proof that he was no longer the man he used to be.

Having heard this story, the therapist asked Al what he envisioned for the future when he watched his son finish the snow-shoveling job from his perch on the couch. Al remarked that he pictured himself turning out to be just like his own father. "What would that be like?" The therapist asked. Al said that his father became a different person after he retired from his job. Like Al, his father had been an active, productive, helpful, center-of-the-family person until the time he retired. Soon afterward, however, he turned inward and became reclusive and unproductive. Only 2 years after his retirement, Al's father died suddenly of a heart attack; Al pictured himself following in his father's footsteps. He did not want to be remembered by his children in the last years of his life as he remembered his own father. This idea of the future deeply disturbed him.

The therapist then asked Al how he thought his wife and grown children were viewing him now. Did they notice changes in him similar to the changes he had noticed in his own father after his retirement? Al said that his family regarded him as different, as "not his old self." No one had asked for his help with anything in some time, and everyone seemed to keep his or her distance from him. "How does that feel?" the therapist wondered. "Is it more comfortable to feel removed from your wife and children, or does it feel better to be an active part of their lives?" Al said that it was terrible to feel so separate from his family; that was the worst effect of his recent depression.

At this stage in the conversation, the therapist had enough information to fill out a gap diagram for Al. As you can see from the diagram in Figure 12.2, the onset of emphysema had seriously shaken Al's sense of self. Al experienced a gap between the person he wanted to be (e.g., useful, productive, helpful) and the person he had become under the grip of illness (e.g., depressed, withdrawn). He regarded his own behavior as out of sync with his preferred view, and reminiscent of his father's deterioration following retirement. He felt that family members now saw him as unproductive and no longer useful. Al felt this gap with frustration, sadness, and intense hurt, and these emotions fueled more of the same despondent behavior.

RECALLING PREFERRED STORIES   Having mapped the gap from Al's point of view, the therapist shifted the focus to what life was like in the family before Al's illness and depression. What were things like when Al felt more active, useful, and involved with his family? It was hoped that this inquiry would help Al to recall his positive qualities and attributes and get in touch with the person he wished to be. Al described a

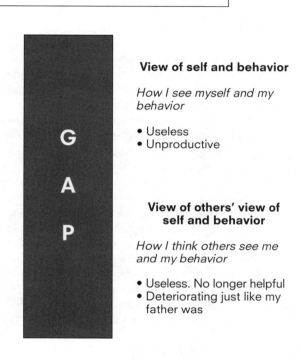

Client's mindset
(Al)

Preferred view

How I would like to see my-self and be seen by others

• Helpful
• Useful
• Productive
• Caregiver to family

View of self and behavior

How I see myself and my behavior

• Useless
• Unproductive

View of others' view of self and behavior

How I think others see me and my behavior

• Useless. No longer helpful
• Deteriorating just like my father was

Emotions: Sadness, frustration
Behavior: Withdrawn, depressed

Figure 12.2. A gap diagram for Al.

life filled with acts of helpfulness and close family involvement. One key story that emerged from this inquiry involved Al's daughter, who had significant mental retardation and lived with the family until the age of 25. He said that one of the most difficult decisions that he and his wife ever had to make was to place their daughter in a residential facility. They realized that they couldn't provide the care she needed anymore, and they supported each other through this difficult period of separation. Ultimately, the decision worked out well for everyone involved. The reason that this was a key story was that it highlighted an important issue relevant to the successful management of Al's illness. This story from Al's past showed how he had once been capable of recognizing limits and knew how to initiate a helpful conversation with his wife to support these limits.

After hearing the story about Al's daughter, the therapist asked Al whether there were other occasions in the past when limits needed to be set and he took charge of the situation. Al responded by talking about his problem with alcohol many years before. At one point, when Al got word from his family physician that his excessive drinking was affecting his health, he decided to stop. He did this on his own, without seeking professional help. When Al announced his intentions of sobriety to his family, they were pleased and supported his efforts at self-control. Thus, Al revealed himself to be a disciplined and determined person who could set realistic limits, make important and difficult decisions, and direct others about how he wanted them to be supportive.

These stories from the past offered clues to the solution. They revealed strengths and positive resources that could be used to change the present situation. Having elicited these *key stories of mastery,* success in setting limits, and directing the support of others, the therapist posed a *mystery question.* Mystery questions invite individuals to explain the gap that exists between the person he or she wants to be and how he or she has been acting. Responses to these questions often provide clues to how problems evolve, which in turn provide clues to solutions. The therapist's question was this: How was it that a man who had managed so many difficult things in his life, known how to set realistic limits, and taken charge of his family would find himself in a position where he no longer felt in charge? This question piqued Al's curiosity. The therapist suggested meeting with some members of his family to pursue how they actually viewed the current situation, and to see if they, too, could be helpful in unraveling this mystery. Al supported this idea.

After only one session with Al's wife and two of his sons, it became clear that they were floundering. Al's illness, they said, had turned their beloved father and husband into someone they didn't know. They had no idea what to make of his illness. They had no facts; no direction; and no sense of what Al still could do, what they should do, and so forth. What Al regarded as loved ones viewing him as useless had actually grown out of their own sense of helplessness. His family members preferred to view themselves as caring and helpful. When Al's family saw Al acting despondent and withdrawn, they tried to lift his spirits by encouraging him to cheer up. When this didn't work, they became even more confused about what to do.

Family members viewed Al viewing them as being unhelpful, which propelled more of the same solicitous behavior. As they began completing tasks for Al, such as shoveling the driveway, Al became more convinced that the people he cared about viewed him as helpless and he grew even more depressed. The more despondent and withdrawn Al acted, the more solicitous his family members became, and the more delicately they approached him.

In the next session with Al, the therapist used verbatim quotes from his conversation with family members to emphasize their bewilderment. The therapist mentioned that family members felt they were "floundering" and that they had no clue about what Al was capable of doing. The therapist described how family members actually viewed Al since his retirement, noting how pleased they were with his positive adjustment to this transition and how active he had remained. He mentioned what Al's wife said about her memories of her father-in-law. She, too, recalled his rapid deterioration after retirement, but she felt strongly that Al was not his father and would not follow his example. Al's pattern of behavior following retirement convinced her that—unlike his father—he would stay active and connected with family members. The therapist also shared with Al the sadness that Al's family members expressed about his recent emotional withdrawal; how they didn't seem to know quite how to approach him or how to ask for his help anymore; how much they wanted him back in the family again. The therapist shared his impression that family members were wallowing in confusion at a time when they most needed Al's guidance.

This conversation with Al about the intentions, preferences, and needs of his family helped him to alter the negative attributions that emerged in the wake of retirement and illness. Al began to view family members as preferring to have him be his old self and regarding him as still being capable and helpful to them. This reconstruction of current events, supported by preferred recollections from the past, inspired swift action toward a solution. Al immediately came up with the idea that it was time to sit down with his doctor and find out what he could or could not do. He entered this meeting from an empowered position, equipped with detailed questions. After finding out that he could still do many things but at a more moderate pace, he sat his family down and explained the facts of his illness to them. When Al started to approach tasks at a more comfortable pace and completed them, his despondency lifted. He later mentioned that he joined a self-help group for emphysema sufferers, and, true to his old form, he assumed a leadership role. He even seemed to be breathing easier.

The problem resolved when Al began to see others seeing him in ways more compatible with his preferred view. As he took charge of his illness and acted more like his old self, family members backed off and resumed interacting with him in familiar ways. Family members began to see Al seeing them in ways that promoted their own preferences. They now knew better how to be helpful and felt more confident that they could once again ask Al for help without upsetting him or aggravating his illness. Now that they could count on Al to counsel them about his limits, their sense of burden lessened.

Although Al had become depressed after developing emphysema, he had a long history of life without depression. The therapist used this extended history to reacquaint Al with his preferences and restore in his mind who he once was and still is in the eyes of others. Al's emphysema did not go away . . . the limits on Al's physical self did not go away . . . yet Al was able to reclaim his sense of self—his preferred self—and maintain this mindset through this difficult life transition. Al soon realized that he could set realistic limits and that his family still needed him. Al altered the worrisome idea that he was following in the path of his father. Al changed his image of the future. Al's depression quickly resolved as he reconstructed present symptoms in the context of past-life experiences.

BRIEF THERAPY

Brief therapy can incorporate the breadth of the life cycle and still be brief. The narrative solutions approach allows therapists to identify strengths and resources over an expanse of time. Therapists needn't restrict their focus to here-and-now problems and solutions in order to achieve rapid change. Therapists can help people develop a cohesive storyline that explains how current problems fit into the tapestry of their lives. Not only do individuals leave therapy with symptoms improved or eliminated but they also depart with a blueprint for how to manage life's future challenges.

People certainly view the loss of a loved one, illness, and the onset of physical limitations as stressful—perhaps even traumatic—life events that may create negative emotions and unhappiness. Yet, if people view themselves as acting in line with their *preferred attributes and qualities,* and see important others seeing them in ways that line up with their preferred view, they seem more able to manage these stressors. "Normal" aging, a process in which individuals at some point do not look particularly young, when their memories may not be what they once were, and when they experience more physical limitations, does not have to adversely affect individuals' emotional well-being. Like Al, many older people can find creative ways to remain useful to others, even when this involves educating them about their own limitations and how they want to be treated.

BRIDGING THE GAP

Gap diagrams (see Figures 12.1 and 12.2) provide a guide to helpful conversations. Note that in talking with Al and his family, the therapist spent a lot of time exploring positive attributes to be added to the left side of the diagram. The therapist and Al explored occasions in the past and present when Al acted in line with the person he wanted to be. The therapist attempted to instill hope in Al's vision for the future. The therapist asked these questions:

- Were there times in the past when you felt useful, helpful, and productive?
- Are there occasions in the present when you feel at your best?
- What will be different when you get back to being you?
- How will you be acting in the future without the problem?

Through this inquiry, positive attributes such as leadership, helpfulness, connectedness, and the ability to set realistic limits revealed themselves. Al was invited to notice these attributes. From this vantage point, the therapist then shifted the focus to the right side of the diagram. It's as if Al and the therapist stood together on the left side of the diagram (noticing Al's preferred view) and gazed over at the right side (beyond the perceptual gap) with a sense of mystery or curiosity about how this could come about. The therapist explored this mystery with questions such as "How is it that someone who had always been a guide and leader to family members would be acting listless and withdrawn?" The therapist then asked Al about the effects of his behavior on himself and others:

- How was it for you when you acted depressed and disconnected from your family?
- How did you feel family members viewed you?
- What did they make of these changes?
- What would they like?

After meeting with family members, the therapist filled in the perceptual gap with useful information. Family members described how they actually saw the current situation, how they regarded Al in the past, and what they wanted to see in the future. This information was then shared with Al, which allowed him to reconsider how his family members thought of him.

As Al began to rethink his life in preferred view terms, he gained confidence to remedy the gap. He came up with creative solutions that fit with his preferred view, such as sitting down and discussing his illness with his physician, informing his family about what he learned, and letting them know how he would like to be treated. As the perceptual gap closed between the person Al wanted to be, how he saw his own behavior, and how he saw others seeing him, his symptoms rapidly improved.

SUMMARY

To summarize, helpful conversations are designed to cultivate a new mindset that motivates change. The new mindset involves people

- Being keenly aware of their actual preferences, hopes, and intentions
- Experiencing a perceptual gap between their preferred view, their view of their own behavior, and their view of how others see them
- Feeling capable of acting in line with their preferred view, that they can remedy or bridge this perceived gap

The therapist also maintains a general mindset or stance in motivating change, which involves

- Being interested in, curious about, or "not knowing" about the person
- Not assuming the person's likes or dislikes
- Not assuming who the person is or wants to be based on cultural or gender biases
- Focusing on what's *strong* in the person, not on what's *wrong* in the person
- Talking about the problem as separate from the person so it becomes a mystery or curiosity that commands an explanation, not a truth that represents who people really are

USING THE NARRATIVE SOLUTIONS
APPROACH WITH PSYCHIATRIC SYMPTOMS

The following case illustrates the application of the narrative solutions approach in treating an older man diagnosed with extreme psychiatric symptoms.

Don

Don was 55 years old when he was first hospitalized for depression. At the age of 65, he was admitted for the seventh time to a psychiatric inpatient facility. He had received numerous shock treatments, a variety of psychotropic medications, and different psychotherapies but felt that nothing had helped. His symptoms had included violent head shaking movements, which he felt were out of his control. Don was told that his symptoms were psychologically based, but he did not accept this diagnosis. He believed that his head movements were neurological despite the fact that tests proved negative.

Don was seen as a difficult client. He did not take his medication reliably. He did not go along with many of the regimens prescribed by the treatment team, such as group activities, occupational therapy, and counseling. He often refused to take showers, grumbled about morning wake ups, and arrived late for activities and meals.

The clinical director of the inpatient facility where Don was staying felt that the narrative solutions approach was worth trying with Don. Don's behavior was making life difficult for the treatment team and was particularly challenging to staff in positions of authority. The psychiatrists were frustrated with Don because he defied their recommendations and challenged their expertise, and the clinical director was constantly receiving complaints about him. Line staff had mixed experiences with Don. Some of the staff felt they could reach him and had little difficulty motivating him to participate in activities. Other staff members said he was driving them crazy; one line staff member commented, in jest, that he might benefit from the medication Don refused.

Before talking with Don, the therapist was shown a videotape of him sitting alone on a couch by a window in one of the day treatment rooms. The scene portrayed Don at his worst. He sat with his face expressionless, his head suddenly making strange sideways movements as he tried desperately to hold it in place. Don did not look like a man who was once a highly paid executive with an insurance company.

The therapist's aim was to conduct an initial interview with Don that would provide a blueprint for helpful conversations for the entire treatment team. Some staff members at the facility were asked to review the videotape of the interview and to fill out the gap diagram. On the left side of the diagram they were asked to jot down the qualities and attributes that fit with Don's preferred view. On the right side of the diagram, they noted how Don saw his own behavior and symptoms and how he felt others regarded him. The staff quickly recognized that there was a major gap. This assessment would offer clues on addressing a variety of issues affecting the staff, for example, how to do the following:

- Talk with Don about his head shaking symptoms
- Talk with Don about medication and promote compliance
- Plan activities that might engage Don's interest and participation
- Develop an aftercare plan that might suit Don's preferences
- Engage the line staff, counselors, and supervisors in a coordinated approach to helpful conversations
- Involve family members (e.g., Don's spouse) as a resource in motivating change

The following conversation began with an assessment of the "gap" for Don.

Therapist:	I understand Dr. Martin [the clinical director] talked with you about us having this conversation today. He hoped it might be helpful.
Don:	He said you're the expert. You wrote a book that everyone's reading here. I'm sorry I haven't had a chance to read it yet. I hope you can help, but I think I'm a hopeless case.
Therapist:	Don, I was curious about how you wound up at this hospital. Was it your idea to come here?
Don:	Not really. My wife thought this might be the place. I've been to a lot of other institutions before this one. She hoped they might cure me [sounds sarcastic].
Therapist:	Your wife's name is?
Don:	Julia.
Therapist:	How did you feel about Julia's idea?
Don:	I didn't like it. I hate these places.
Therapist:	But you came anyway. Julia must be very important to you. She felt it was a good idea and you cooperated, despite hating these places.
Don:	[Looks upset] My wife's been through a lot with me [head starts to shake].
Therapist:	Why did Julia think it was a good idea to come here?
Don:	I've put her though a lot. She feels I'm very sick and that maybe these people will have the answer. I am very sick.
Therapist:	What are your thoughts on how you wound up in this place and the other places you mentioned?
Don:	I don't know. The first time I was depressed. Then they said I was crazy—schizophrenic. I've had every diagnosis you can imagine.
Therapist:	What do you think?
Don:	I think it's neurological, but the doctors can't figure it out.
Therapist:	What did your wife think happened to you, Don? How does she feel you wound up here?
Don:	[Head movements are strong; then, as they slow down a little, Don speaks sadly.] She's disappointed with me. We used to have a great life.

Therapist: Can you tell me about that life? When were things at their best?

The therapist did not begin with a discussion of Don's diagnosis, condition, or symptoms. Instead, he expressed curiosity about what Don thought about being at this facility: Was it his idea to come to an inpatient facility or someone else's? If someone else's idea, what does he think of it? The therapist related to Don as an independent thinker and author of his own life script. If the discussion had begun around Don's psychiatric condition or out-of-control symptoms, it would have appealed to Don at his worst and to the negative ways that he feels many important others have regarded him over the past 10 years. Such a discussion would have been likely to invoke defensiveness, passivity, and perhaps even a display of symptoms.

The discussion of Don's ideas about being in an inpatient facility oriented the interview around preferred view and the gap. Don said that being in an inpatient facility did not suit him; it violated his preferred sense of self. Don mentioned that his wife, Julia, wanted him to go to the hospital and he went along with her preference. When describing how Julia viewed him, Don said, "she's been through a lot with me," and his head began to shake.

The emergence of symptoms at this point in the interview suggested that he experienced a gap between the person he became in the eyes of his wife (e.g., sick, helpless, needing hospitalization), and the person he became through his own eyes (e.g., "I'm very sick."). When the discussion shifted back to Don's point of view about this place and other similar institutions, his head shaking subsided. By consulting Don's opinion and respecting his know-how, Don was more likely to see the therapist seeing him as capable and competent. As the perceptual gap narrowed, Don acted more competent and in control; as the gap widened, he became symptomatic.

At the close of this segment, the therapist asked Don about his wife's opinion of how he wound up at this place. Don stopped talking and his head shaking symptoms intensified. Not wanting to linger with Don in the perceptual gap, the therapist shifted the focus to Don at his best, inviting him to recall his life with Julia before the problem began.

Shifting the focus to the pre-problem past had several advantages. Don told stories of his life that contrasted with his current circumstances and offered clues to preferred strengths and attributes. This process of noticing strengths and attributes helped to build an alliance between therapist and client, minimized resistance, and opened possibilities for change. Don's attention was drawn to others in his life who noticed these positive attributes. For example, was there a time when Julia saw him as competent and in control of his life? What was that like for him? What was that like for her?

Through Don's own narrative, the therapists received clues as to what went awry. How did Don go from being at his best to being at his worst? What transitional life events or circumstances underscored this transformation? When Don spoke about his life before the 10 years of hospitalizations, he perked up. His head did not shake and he did not seem conscious of controlling his head movements. He spoke of his life as an executive for a large insurance firm, his success as a salesman, and his accumulation of material wealth. Although proud of his achievements, his story had another side. He'd refer sarcastically to his ability to "sell things to people they didn't need," and refer with disdain to the "three-martini" lunches that were part of his life routine.

What mattered most to Don during this time was how well he and Julia got along. They traveled a lot, ate at fine restaurants, and bought a beach house. Julia admired Don's talents and looked up to him. Don had helped bring her into the company, and she had moved up the ladder. She now relished her own executive position and enjoyed the corporate lifestyle.

When Don was asked how he and Julia met, he filled in other important pieces of his life story. They met as teenagers, both coming from what Don called "dysfunctional" families. Don's family was poor. His mother was an alcoholic and his father worked several jobs and wasn't around much. Julia grew up in a family where both parents drank. Julia looked to Don for guidance. He was 4 years older. Don liked being seen as helpful, a leader, and someone whom Julia admired.

The therapist expressed curiosity with the theme of alcoholism that appeared in Don's life story—the three-martini lunches, the corporate life style, his mother's drinking, and his wife's background. He learned that Don had become sober during the 10 years of repeated hospitalizations. It was a fact that seemed discrepant with a life of nervous breakdowns and out-of-control symptoms, and this contradiction piqued the therapist's curiosity.

Don was then asked a mystery question. How was it that he had made a decision to take control of his life by seeking sobriety at a time when things seemed out of control (e.g., being hospitalized, being treated for depression)? The discussion with Don about drinking and sobriety went as follows:

Therapist:	What led you to make a decision to stop drinking at a time when you were feeling pretty bad?
Don:	It was just common sense, I guess. I didn't like the effects anymore. Drinking didn't taste good. It didn't feel good anymore.
Therapist:	But what was your motivation?
Don:	As I said, it was just common sense.
Therapist:	Decisions like those require self-control, determination. Don't they?
Don:	Drinking no longer had a pleasurable effect. It wasn't working anymore.
Therapist:	I'm curious, Don. Why, at that particular time in your life, did you make this choice? You said this was after your first hospitalization and you gave up something that was part of your lifestyle—the three-martini lunches and all that. Were you trying to take a stand?
Don:	After I got out of the hospital, I went back to work. I was dysfunctional. I showed up at 11:00. I stayed on the wagon—no

caffeine, no alcohol—but I felt terrible. I recognized that if
alcohol was my problem I should have felt better.

Therapist: But you persisted with sobriety despite not feeling better.
Why?

Don: I don't know. I knew I had to change my lifestyle.

Several preferred qualities and attributes revealed themselves through this conversation about sobriety: common sense, determination, persistence, and self-
control. The therapist helped Don notice these qualities, and as he saw the therapist viewing him as in control and as an initiator of important life changes, his
head movements ceased. The therapist expressed particular interest in the transformation Don underwent at this time in his life. He appeared to be questioning
his old lifestyle, which involved seeking material success, impressing people in
authority, and drinking heavily. Although he seemed determined to do something different with his life, his efforts were not being rewarded. He lost motivation to go to work. His ambition waned. He later said that he went to Alcoholics Anonymous meetings but did not share this important part of his life with
Julia. Julia continued to live the corporate life, work hard, and move up the
ladder. Don seemed to be on a different path, but it was not something he talked
about with people close to him. This preference to live a sober, less materialistic,
and perhaps more spiritual life seemed submerged. Looking at himself through
the eyes of his wife, supervisor, and co-workers, Don appeared as a disappointment, a failure—not a man on a spiritual mission.

The therapist asked Don more about his travels with his wife to see if this
valued aspect of their life together fit within this new, preferred lifestyle.

Don: That fall after my first hospitalization, Julia and I went to the
Middle East. It was fantastic. The cross section of civilizations
and religions inspired me. [As Don talked about his trip, he
suddenly shifted the conversation to the therapist.] You're
Jewish, aren't you?

Therapist: Yes.

Don: Surely you've been to Jerusalem. What did you think?

Therapist: Actually, Don, I've never been.

Don: [Incredulous] You're Jewish and you've never been to Jerusalem!

Therapist: I'm afraid so, Don.

Don: It's important to do these things in your life. I don't think you
can live a full life until you've been to that part of the world.
This is where all the major religions of the world meet. If you're
a spiritual person, and I sense you are, then you must go.

Don was now asking the therapist mystery questions and helping him to notice
gaps in his life narrative. "How is it that someone who's interested in me and my
inner aspirations and who also appears to be a spiritual person would not have

visited this important part of the world? As Don "turned therapist," he grew animated, energetic, and anything but depressed. The therapist thanked him for his insights as their conversation drew to a close.

Two weeks after meeting with Don, the therapist talked with Julia to pursue her ideas about how the problem evolved and what she would like to see for their future. Although the therapist's preference was to meet with Julia alone, Don did not like that idea. Given Don's desire to be in control and his concern about how his wife regarded him, his wish to sit in on the meeting was not surprising. Thus, Don sat in the corner of the room while the therapist talked with Julia, respecting the therapist's preference to talk with her individually by not interrupting. Every time Julia expressed her frustration with Don and his symptoms and the misery of their lives over the past 10 years, Don's head shook violently. When Julia described Don at his best, his symptoms subsided.

The most interesting piece of information came toward the end of the interview. Julia corroborated Don's account that he was at his best during the time between his first and second hospitalizations. It was then that Don sought sobriety and attended AA. It was then that the couple traveled to Israel and Don maintained a leisurely work schedule. Julia mentioned that Don's boss was a bit frustrated with Don's semi-retirement schedule. He appealed to him to increase his hours and do more work-related travel and sales; Julia said that Don agreed. Two weeks later, however, he was in the hospital again, having suffered a second "nervous breakdown," setting in motion a pattern that would continue for 10 years. The interview concluded as follows:

Therapist: [Looking over at Don with puzzlement] I get the impression from you both that Don was content working fewer hours and traveling. In fact, you both seemed to feel that Don was at his best during this time. Did I get that right?

Julia: Yes.

Therapist: Is that like Don to do what his boss wanted, rather than what *he* wanted?

Julia: That's Don all right. [Don looks at the floor; his head is not shaking but he appears sad, forlorn.]

Therapist: [To Julia and Don] That's interesting. I'll be talking with the staff about my conversations with you both. Don helped me see that I need to get in touch with my spirituality and go to Jerusalem. One thing I'll be encouraging people to do here is return the favor and help Don figure out what he would like for his life. You've been very helpful in giving us some clues, Julia. Thank you.

CLUES TO SOLUTIONS   Based on this initial interview with Don and Julia, the therapist filled out the gap diagram with the entire staff (see Figure 12.3). This diagram offered practical clues for how staff might talk with Don to motivate change. Recommendations to the staff were as follows:

- Consult Don's expertise about the effectiveness of medication. Ask him what medications have been helpful for him. What medications have not been helpful? What does he think about taking medication? What are his preferences?

  [Don prefers to be seen as competent and in control. Taking a prescriptive, directive stance about what is best for Don medically, then suggesting that he is noncompliant, challenges his preferred view and invites resistance. Asking Don's opinion about what works for him confirms his preferred view, minimizes resistance, and helps to determine what medications have actually been useful.]

- Talk further with Don about his thoughts regarding lifestyle changes, sobriety, and his emerging spirituality. These preferences appear to be submerged. Don has not spoken to those close to him or staff about what he would like for his life. The primary focus of conversation had been on his symptoms and what staff could do about them. It is hoped that as Don is helped to notice his own preferences, he'll be more likely to talk with others about what he would like for his life.

- Do *not* talk with Don and his wife about his head shaking symptoms or his progress (or lack of progress) in controlling them. These conversations challenge Don's preferred view as a competent, in-control person. Don and Julia's lives have become immersed in symptom talk, which has blocked discussion of preferences and possibilities.

- Consult Julia's expertise about how the problem evolved. Don sees Julia as the most important person in his life. They helped each other grow up and leave dysfunctional backgrounds. At one time, Don saw himself as helpful to Julia; now he sees himself as a miserable disappointment. In talking with Julia, it became clear that her construction of how the problem evolved corroborated Don's account and offered clues about how to talk with Don about his *unspoken preferences.*

- Design activities on the treatment unit that appeal to Don's talents and abilities. Don was at his best when he functioned as an executive leader. Because he was older and had more life experiences than most of his fellow residents, he may feel more comfortable as a group discussion leader, advisor, and confidant. Don prefers to be seen as helpful to others and this attribute may be put to good use on the treatment unit.

- Use the gap diagram to determine which conversations with line staff are helpful. Staff members described varying results in working with Don; some found him to be compliant; others, defiant. By mapping these conversations, we may find that those staff members who are effective with Don appeal to his preferred view, whereas the other members who are not effective do not. This may help staff to become more aware of their conversational approach and coordinate their efforts to bring out the best in Don.

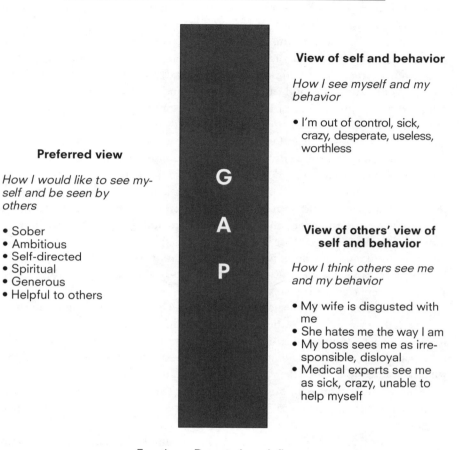

**Client's mindset
(Don)**

**G
A
P**

View of self and behavior

How I see myself and my behavior

- I'm out of control, sick, crazy, desperate, useless, worthless

Preferred view

How I would like to see myself and be seen by others

- Sober
- Ambitious
- Self-directed
- Spiritual
- Generous
- Helpful to others

View of others' view of self and behavior

How I think others see me and my behavior

- My wife is disgusted with me
- She hates me the way I am
- My boss sees me as irresponsible, disloyal
- Medical experts see me as sick, crazy, unable to help myself

Emotions: Depression, defiance
Behavior: Head shaking, refusal to cooperate

Figure 12.3. A gap diagram for Don.

NEW CONVERSATIONS, NEW POSSIBILITIES   Randall, one of the staff members who had been most effective with Don, began talking with him more about Don's hopes and aspirations. Don confided in Randall about his disaffection with the corporate lifestyle, his desire to change his life and help others, and his concern about whether Julia would approve of these changes in him. Filling out the gap diagram, it became clear that Don saw Randall as a regular guy who talked with him as a regular person. Randall did not express interest in Don's symptoms and how they interfered with waking up in the morning and attending activities. Randall's approach was to tell Don to "get off his butt and get moving," that he was needed; that people were waiting for him. Counseling staff began to see the wisdom of talking with Don about his life and tapping into his knowledge about that life rather than monitoring his symptoms. Counseling sessions became focused on Don's wish to be helpful to others, past stories of this attribute, and a future focus on putting this attribute to use.

Staff members also became creative in designing activities that suited Don. Jenny, an activities coordinator, insisted that Don play the piano and lead sing-alongs during the winter holiday party. Afterward, Don delivered an emotional speech about connection and caring for others and what the holidays meant to him, and he recognized Randall, Jenny, and the staff for their kindness and kinship. The activities staff encouraged Don to lead discussion groups focused on philosophy and spirituality. Don and Randall began chatting about what he might do when he left the facility, focusing on retirement, travel, volunteer work, and creative ways to use his leadership skills to help others.

The clinical director and counselors sought Don's expertise about medication, what had worked and what hadn't. They asked Don what medications might help him gain access to inner potential as opposed to dulling his senses and blotting it out. Don acknowledged that he experienced anxiety and that the anti-anxiety medications in moderate doses helped him to feel more competent and in control. Don began taking this medication reliably, stopped second-guessing the psychiatrists, and reported positive results.

Within a month after the interview with Don and Julia, his symptoms dramatically improved. The head shaking gradually subsided and eventually stopped, once he stopped looking at his symptoms as a statement of who he was. He began paying less attention to whether his head shook and more attention to what he wanted to do with the rest of his life. Don made it clear that he wanted to leave his job and devote his time to volunteer work and travel. He discussed these plans with Julia, who was pleased with his progress and accepting of his change in lifestyle.

In 6 weeks, Don returned home and maintained regular contact with Randall during the first year following his discharge. Randall let the therapist and staff know that Don remained symptom free and was enjoying his retirement and being helpful to others. He and Julia resumed traveling together. After 10 years of living in institutional care, Don has not been readmitted to an inpatient facility.

NARRATIVE SOLUTIONS
APPROACH TO SUCCESSFUL AGING

Don's story has interesting implications for how to talk with older people and how to help them be at their best. For 10 years, conversations with Don focused entirely on what was wrong with him as he and the people around him lost touch with what was *strong* with him. He became a person with mental disabilities through his own eyes and the eyes of others. Little attention was paid to Don's struggle to negotiate important life transitions and find new meaning after many years of hard work and material success. In fact, Don lost sight of his own hopes and aspirations and of his intention to keep growing and moving forward in his later years. He lost touch with who he was. Memories of a past filled with triumphs and setbacks, resilience and resourcefulness, had faded from view.

Don's story is not unique. Many older people encounter caregivers who, with the best of intentions, focus on their symptoms, on whether they are taking their medication, and on how they are coping in the present. The richness of their former lives is lost in symptom-focused or problem-saturated discussions. As people grow older they may lose their physical capabilities and lose people they love, but what they have is a lifetime of experience with themselves and others and often a well-developed sense of who they are. An individual's maintenance of his or her sense of preferred self during loss, infirmity, withering memory, and the vicissitudes of aging is essential to his or her emotional well-being and to staying useful.

Another important implication of Don's triumph was the power of having a *solution team* around him. Don changed as conversations converged around his preferred view. A chorus of others reminded him daily of his better self, inviting him to act in line with that person and challenging him when he did not. People sought Don's opinion, his viewpoint, and his expertise about a variety of matters from medication to spirituality. As Don grew more confident, he was able to speak up with his wife, friends, and colleagues about how he wanted to conduct his future. They supported his vision.

This concept of coordinating helpful conversations around people in institutional environments has important implications for successful aging. When older people move into nursing homes or group residences, family members may be consulted (as Julia was) about the person's strengths and attributes, preserving a link to their past lives. These preferred qualities and attributes could then be noticed by staff and incorporated into conversations and activities in the new residence, preserving connection at a time of upheaval. Successful aging is not only about maintaining physical health, of which we have no guarantee. It is also about maintaining a keen sense of who we are as time shortens and our physical selves diminish. Preferred view conversations bridge the gap between past, present, and future, allowing individuals to live their later years with hope and possibility.

REFERENCES

de Shazer, S. (1985). *Keys to solutions in brief therapy.* New York: Norton.

de Shazer, S., Berg, I.K., Lipchik, E., Nunnally, E., Molnar, A., Gingerich, W., & Weiner-Davis, M. (1986). Brief therapy: Focused solution development. *Family Process, 25,* 207–221.

Eron, J.B., & Lund, T.W. (1993). How problems evolve and dissolve: Integrating narrative and strategic concepts. *Family Process, 32,* 291–309.

Eron, J.B., & Lund, T.W. (1995, November/December). The overresponsibility trap: Helping "co-dependents" create a new life story. *Family Therapy Networker.*

Eron, J.B., & Lund, T.W. (1996). *Narrative solutions in brief therapy.* New York: Guilford Press.

Eron, J.B. & Lund, T.W. (1998a). Narrative solutions couples therapy. In F.M. Dattilio (Ed.), *Integrating cases in couples and family therapy* (pp. 311–400). New York: Guilford Press.

Eron, J.B., & Lund, T.W. (1998b). Narrative solutions in brief couples therapy. In J. Donovan (Ed.), *Short-term couples therapy.* New York: Guilford Press.

Haley, J. (1980). *Leaving home: The therapy of disturbed young people.* New York: McGraw-Hill.

Laing, R.D., Phillipson, H., & Lee, A.R. (1996). *Interpersonal perceptions: A theory and method of research.* London: Tavistock.

Lund, T.W., & Eron, J.B. (1998). The narrative solutions approach for retelling children's stories: Using preferred views to construct useful conversations. In M.F. Hoyt (Ed.), *The handbook of constructive therapy* (pp. 358–378). San Francisco: Jossey-Bass.

O'Hanlon, W.H., & Weiner-Davis, M. (1989). *In search of solutions: A new direction in psychotherapy.* New York: Norton.

Rogers, C.R. (1961). *On becoming a person: A therapist's view of psychotherapy.* Boston: Houghton Mifflin.

Rohrbaugh, M., & Eron, J.B. (1982). The strategic systems therapies. In L.E. Abt & R.I. Stuart (Eds.), *The newer therapies: A workbook* (pp. 248–266). New York: Van Nostrand Reinhold.

Watzlawick, P. (1976). *How real is real?* New York: Random House.

Watzlawick, P. (1978). *The language of change.* New York: Basic Books.

Watzlawick, P. (Ed.). (1984). *The invented reality.* New York: Norton.

Watzlawick, P., & Coyne, J.C. (1980). Depression following stroke: Brief problem-focused family treatment. *Family Process, 19,* 13–18.

Watzlawick, P., Weakland, J., & Fisch, R. (1974). *Change: Principles of problem formation and problem resolution.* New York: Norton

Weakland, J.H., Fisch, R., Watzlawick, P., & Bodin, A.M. (1974). Brief therapy: Focused problem resolution. *Family Process, 13,* 141–168.

White, M., & Epston, D. (1990). *Narrative means to therapeutic ends.* New York: Norton.

13

STRENGTHS-BASED APPROACHES TO TRAUMA IN THE AGING

An Albanian Kosovar Experience

Jack Saul

with Shquipe Ukshini, Afrim Blyta, and Shukrie Statovci

CLINICIANS WHO WORK WITH OLDER ADULTS understand the importance of considering the impact of stressful life events on an individual's lifespan development and psychological well-being. Research and clinical knowledge from experts in the trauma field provide those people who work with older adults with useful insights and creative, therapeutic approaches for aiding older adults who may suffer from traumatic sequelae—somatic pain, depression, anxiety, posttraumatic stress disorder, or other severe stress reactions. An awareness that an older person's emotional difficulty may relate to stressful life events can be crucial in helping him or her to recover from past as well as present traumatic experiences.

People exhibit a tremendous range of responses to stressful life events. Some people manage to cope very well, whereas others may live a life of continuous struggle and re-victimization. What are the resources on which older people draw to endure painful memories? How do they survive tragedy and then narrate their lives in ways that promote positive adaptation? What are the protective

This chapter was written with the assistance of members of the Kosovar Family Professional Education Collaborative. The authors would especially like to thank Ferid Agani, M.D., Stevan Weine, M.D., Judith Landau, MB, ChB, DPM, and the other members of the collaborative team.

mechanisms and sources of resilience that prevent people from being severely affected by traumatic events? How can helpers facilitate the internal and external resources that enable older people to continue to strive for, and achieve, fulfilling lives? This chapter examines various interventions that focus on an individual's capacity for resilience and his or her unique strengths to promote healing.

Engaging older adult trauma survivors in conversations that seek solutions to their real-life problems can help restore their dignity and hope for the future. When professionals initiating these solution-oriented conversations invite important members of family and community to take part, new resources become available and the social isolation that is often a consequence of the secrecy and shame associated with the trauma lessens. Many of the strengths that enable people to cope with massive loss and trauma are embedded in a community's collective memory, culture, and religions. When drawing on these resources, the community is able to tap the symbols, rituals, and maps that have traditionally enabled it to navigate through very difficult life events and transitions. The solution-oriented discourses that enable individuals, families, and communities to manage crises and transitions and promote recovery from traumatic events are often a part of a culture's repertoire of healing mechanisms.

SUPPORTING STRENGTHS AND RESILIENCE IN SURVIVORS OF TRAUMA: A SOLUTION-FOCUSED APPROACH

The solution-focused approach emphasizes an individual's strengths or a family's strengths, rather than the problem or an explanation of its pathology. It is a pragmatic and a common-sense approach developed as a therapeutic intervention by Berg (1992); de Shazer (1985); Erickson, O'Hanlon, and Bertolino (1998); Furman and Ahola (1992); and others. Unlike traditional psychotherapy approaches that aim to decrease dysfunctional patterns in order to create room for functional behavior, this approach devotes time and attention to the functional aspects of clients' lives in order to expand and foster helpful behavior. By focusing on an individual's strengths and solutions, his or her problems are not denied but rather are set in an atmosphere in which the individual can examine problems from a perspective of enhanced dignity and a sense of agency. This approach encourages an individual to take advantage of his or her unique resources and opportunities. These conversations support people's competencies by highlighting aspects of their lives that are going well.

> BY FOCUSING ON AN individual's strengths and solutions, his or her problems are not denied but rather are set in an atmosphere in which the individual can examine problems from a perspective of enhanced dignity and a sense of agency.

Many of the prevailing approaches in the trauma field privilege the disclosure or reconstruction of the traumatic experience in the context of an empathic relationship as crucial to the process of healing. A strengths-based approach highlights and enhances the resources that enable survivors of trauma to reclaim

the interests, capabilities, activities, and relationships that are disrupted or diminished in response to highly stressful life events. Judith Herman (1992) described one of the most popular frameworks for understanding recovery from
trauma in her book, *Trauma and Recovery*. She sees the process of recovery as com-
prising three stages:

1. Safety
2. Remembrance mourning
3. Reconnection

Although these stages may not follow a straightforward, linear progression, they
are helpful in organizing the major themes in treatment. An individual revisits
these themes repeatedly in an almost spiraling way in the process of recovery.
From this perspective, a person may view recovery from trauma as a gradual progression from unpredictable danger to reliable safety, from dissociated trauma to
acknowledged memory, and from stigmatized isolation to restored social connection and a sense of future. Within this framework, the therapeutic relationship supports the shoring up of internal strengths that enable the survivor eventually to cope with and integrate painful and destabilizing memories.

The strengths-based approach offers some helpful perspectives on the process of re-narrating or ascribing meaning to traumatic experience. One of the assumptions of this approach is that there are many narrative possibilities for reconstructing the past, and that these possibilities are shaped by *conversational
contexts*. If a therapist asks a client questions about past experiences in the context
of a conversation about the strengths that enabled that person to survive an ordeal, the client will more likely feel a greater sense of control and less of a sense
of victimization as he or she describes these past experiences. This conversational
context can inspire optimism and greater confidence in exploring solutions.

The way a person relates to memories of past events and makes them a part
of his or her identity and history is crucial to the process of healing from trauma.
Conversations that situate painful experiences within a vision of a future that includes solutions add an important dimension to approaches in the trauma field
that emphasize disclosure as the primary mode of healing. When a therapist helps
an older trauma survivor to strengthen his or her resilience, to build a foundation
for a new life, to establish connections with new sources of social support, and to
reconnect with important people in his or her life, this may also help the individual regain a sense of agency in relation to past injury. In other words, when people
are able to weave new sources of continuity and connectedness into their lives, they
are better able to resist the disturbing discontinuities they have had to endure resulting from violence, tragic loss, or displacement from home, country, or culture.

COLLABORATION, CREATIVE IMAGINATION, AND HOPE

Ben Furman, a Finnish psychiatrist and self-proclaimed incurable optimist, proposed collaboration, creativity, and hope as important ingredients in a solution-
focused approach (Furman & Ahola, 1992). The solution-focused approach is

TO ENSURE THE greatest success in the exploration of solutions, people need to work together in an open, nonsecretive exchange that respects the resources and areas of expertise of all of those involved.

based first on the principle of collaboration. To ensure the greatest success in the exploration of solutions, people need to work together in an open, nonsecretive exchange that respects the resources and areas of expertise of all of those involved. Rather than the role of expert, the therapist takes on the role of moderator and/or facilitator, making sure that those individuals who are involved in the solution-seeking conversation each have a voice and can share responsibility in constructing and carrying out the steps toward the solution. In this collaboration it is very important that the therapist creates an empowering context for change.

In the late 1990s I was in India interviewing Tibetan nuns who had been tortured in Tibet by Chinese authorities. These 16 nuns lived in a convent, unaware of each other's experiences of imprisonment and abuse. The nurse at the convent was concerned that many of them were suffering from severe stress reaction; they were experiencing symptoms such as concentration difficulties, nightmares, and somatic pains. The nurse sought help from our team to bring the group together for mutual support. Rather than focusing on their experiences of torture and abuse, we all agreed to have a conversation about what had been helpful to them so far in coping with their refugee experiences in India. We also agreed to ask the nuns for advice that could be helpful for Tibetan refugees living in the United States. This respectful context enabled them to speak in a supportive way about their strengths and coping mechanisms as well as about the problems that they face as a consequence of their mistreatment and exile. The collaborative spirit of our approach enabled members of the group to make new connections and reduce the alienation many of them had felt in not being able to fully participate in the educational program of the convent. It also allowed them to engage in collective recall of prison experiences and to make connections between the past abuse and their present difficulties. (Jack Saul)

Another important aspect of collaborative work with trauma survivors is the therapist's capacity to elicit the client's expression of current needs and problems that they consider their greatest priorities. Too often, therapists—anxious about working with people who have suffered horrible tragedies—quickly impose their own ideas about what will be helpful for their client before patiently listening and understanding the person's stated hierarchy of needs. It is often very difficult to predict what someone who has experienced trauma will identify as his or her most pressing concerns, especially if the survivor comes from a culture or generation that may have very different conceptions of self, suffering, healing, honor, and privacy.

It is important to note that those who have endured severely stressful and dehumanizing ordeals may also have very different needs for acknowledgment of their suffering. Because traumatic events often leave a person ashamed and doubtful of his or her own reality, the act of affirming the person's experience can be a crucial prerequisite for engaging in conversations that are more directly focused on finding solutions. To do so, it is important for the therapist to recognize some of the common challenges faced by older adult trauma survivors:

- Overcoming social isolation
- Giving oneself permission to get access to available resources
- Modulating intense affect
- Dealing with intrusive thoughts and memories, overwhelming fears and anxiety, and intra-familial conflict
- Finding meaning after one's world has been shattered

While being aware of these challenges, it is important for the therapist to be sensitive to those efforts or areas of felt competency that the older adult has already employed in his or her recovery thus far. By joining with an individual or family to focus on the basis of competence, the collaborating therapist can more easily assess the problems that can realistically be solved as well as the clients' readiness to take steps toward change.

The solution-focused therapist is careful not to undermine the clients' competence or self-determination by offering his or her own ideas. The therapist, acting in a collaborative role, can be helpful by proposing possible solutions. He or she will have to negotiate the fine line between being a resource for change and overshadowing others on the collaborative team by asserting his or her position of power and/or authority.

A person's imagination fuels his or her creative problem-solving abilities. Donald Winnicott (1980), in *Playing and Reality,* proposed that through imaginative acts people give meaning to their lives. A creative imagination is one of the most important resources for people who struggle with traumatic experiences. In the process of externalizing painful memories, older adults change their relationship with the experiences from one of passivity to one of action. At the same time, they create the possibility to speak about these experiences with others. Externalizing the stories about difficult experiences and representing them, either literally or symbolically, reduces their destructive capacity.

> In a village of Kosovo, bodies had been removed from mass graves to hide evidence of war crimes. An aging Muslim woman was unable to find the body of her son, who had been killed in a massacre. The woman's religious beliefs dictated that funerals could not be held without remains. Because her family could not locate the son's remains, his funeral had to be postponed. The woman was in a great deal of pain because there was no grave for her to visit and no way for her to express her need to care for her son's body. She spoke about how she turned to prayer in order to cope with this pain. When the therapist asked how prayer had been helpful to her, she responded that when she prayed, she asked God to grow flowers around her son's grave in paradise. She imagined herself taking care of the flowers. She said that her prayers were like water that enabled the flowers to stay alive and grow. In her imagination she had created a place where she could symbolically overcome her frustrated desire to visit her son's grave site.

THOSE SURVIVORS WHO carry a sense of shame or guilt often feel undeserving of a promising future. The exploration of sources of hope is often a crucial step in promoting the process of healing from trauma and massive loss.

Perhaps the most important ingredient in aiding people who have experienced traumatic events in their recent lives is the restoration of hope. For people who have endured tragic loss(es) or dehumanizing ordeals, their previous notions of the future may no longer be possible. Those survivors who carry a sense of shame or guilt often feel undeserving of a promising future. The exploration of sources of hope is often a crucial step in promoting the process of healing from trauma and massive loss.

SOLUTION-FOCUSED INTERVENTIONS

For many survivors of traumatic events, the past is always present, and there is no future. Thus, some of the most useful solution-focused interventions for survivors of trauma are those that help them reclaim their experience of themselves in time—highlighting existing strengths and progress in the present, facilitating positive views of the future, and turning the past into a resource rather than a liability.

An important intervention is the recognition and facilitation of the person's existing strengths and resources, referred to in solution-focused literature as *exceptions.* The basis for exceptions is the notion that people can select or choose to focus on those experiences seen as signs of progress already taking place rather than on those experiences seen as signs of inadequacy. Thus, conversations with an individual or a family can highlight what is already perceived as going well, expand on existing competencies, and promote further progress in solving problems.

When a therapist conducts solution-oriented conversations, he or she invites people to entertain positive views of the future. These future visions or projections facilitate effective coping skills with present dilemmas and help people recognize the signs of change that are already underway; this creates a sense of hope.

The therapist asks individuals to choose or imagine a time, such as in a day, in a week, or in 2 weeks, when they can imagine themselves in a place when things are going better for them. This helps to facilitate conversations about positive futures. Then the therapist sets the scene in the future and asks individuals or families to have a conversation about how aspects of their lives have improved. After that, the people are engaged in a conversation as if the future were present.

The following is the opening of one type of conversation that can reconnect people with resources and generate an exploration of possibilities. A therapist may say, "Imagine that in 3 months from now we meet each other in a park and I say, 'Hi, I heard that things are going much better for you.'" The person may respond, "Yes, I started to leave my apartment for the first time since the accident and I met with some old friends." Then the therapist may say, "That's great. I remember when it had been very difficult for you to leave your apartment. What was it that enabled you to overcome some of your fears enough so that you could leave your apartment and visit with friends?"

Shifting to a conversation that takes place in the future can enable people to gain access to their imaginations and begin to identify the most important problems they need to solve, the steps they already know they need to take, and the resources they already have in their lives that will help them to take those steps. People cannot often imagine solutions to their problems when they approach them from a present perspective and look forward to the future, but they may be able to imagine solutions when they look backward from a future perspective to the present. This change in perspective is not always possible, especially for those who have suffered massive or tragic loss and who may feel guilt for having survived loved ones. Instead, the therapist may ask: "What would your mother have said she wanted for you today or in your future if she were still alive?" or "What hopes do you have for the future of your children, and how do you see yourself contributing to improving their chances for a better future?" Loyalty to the dead or to future generations can be an important resource in creating hope. Within these conversations, therapists begin where hope exists and expand on it.

By co-creating visions of the future with individuals and families, therapists may reveal the outline of a map for their recovery. Questions that lead individuals to thinking about how life may look in the future if and when they are able to put the ordeal behind them and begin to rebuild new lives helps survivors begin to imagine the steps along the way to a positive future. It can also help them map out the resources on which they can draw at different points along the way. A therapist can ask trauma survivors such questions as, "How did your haunting memories become less frightening?" or, "What did you find along your way that enabled you to deal with your rage at the abuser?" Asking such questions in an imaginary trip to the future may enable a person to generate ideas for reclaiming his or her life from the effects of the trauma.

The extent to which survivors relate to their past as resources or liabilities can determine the extent to which they will suffer from traumatic stress symptoms in the years following traumatic events. Many survivors benefit from having conversations in which they retell the stories of past ordeals as opportunities for learning, growth, or transformation. For instance, therapists may engage them in conversations about what they may say to their children or grandchildren in the future about how they were able to cope with their ordeal or, they may discuss the strengths that emerged in themselves and others that enabled them to move beyond the ordeal and build a better life for themselves. This is referred to as *turning the past into a resource rather than a liability.*

Clinical studies of individuals who have been traumatized show that the subjective meaning that the individual gives to his or her traumatic experiences will have a bearing on the degree of traumatic symptoms he or she will suffer. The more an individual can place these past events within a larger or more meaningful context (e.g., historical, political, spiritual) and the less he or she places them in an individual or exclusively personal context, the less the individual will experience traumatic stress symptoms.

A person's culture and religion provide many frameworks for interpreting past tragedy. The karmic philosophy of Tibetan Buddhists, for example, helps them to accept their fate and promotes an optimism and capacity to warmly connect with others. Rather than dwelling on their rage or vengefulness, they engage in spiritual practices aimed at developing compassion for their perpetrators, who, in their cosmic scheme of their religion, will suffer the most because of their actions. Many survivors from non-Western cultures are supported by their culture in the acceptance of their suffering as fate and in seeing past ordeals as opportunities for growth and learning.

One of the effects of trauma is that when people avoid looking at the past, they also avoid connecting with good memories and resources. It is particularly important for them to be able to reconnect to the memories of love and care they experienced before tragedy. One way of reconnecting with positive emotions experienced in the past is through the written word. One African refugee, cut off from his family and unable to contact them, wrote letters to his family anyway. The process of writing enabled him to feel emotionally connected, to have conversations with his family members, and to reminisce about the past he shared with them.

Evoking the spirit of the dead, the missing, or those separated from each another through exile is a powerful resource in recovery and serves many functions for the survivor. It helps the survivor emotionally reconnect to important loved ones and thus to the positive memories of those relationships from before and even during the traumatic period. The process of regeneration for survivors who have endured extreme trauma and loss involves reconnecting with past memories of love and comfort, wisdom and triumph. In cases of torture or violence, the intentional breaking down of the person creates a radical discontinuity in the external and internal life of survivors. Thus, a sense of continuity must be gradually reestablished.

STRENGTHS-BASED WORK WITH ALBANIAN KOSOVAR SURVIVORS OF ETHNIC CLEANSING

In May 2000, a collaborative team effort with American and Albanian Kosovar mental health professionals was initiated to address the enormous psychosocial and mental health needs of the Albanian Kosovar population following the end of the war in 1999. The project was called the Kosovar Family Professional Education Collaborative (KFPEC) and was co-sponsored by the University of Illinois at Chicago, The University of Chicago, the American Family Therapy Academy, the International Trauma Studies Program at New York University, and the University of Prishtina. The Albanian Kosovar team, based in the Department of Psychiatry and Neurology at the University of Prishtina Medical School, decided to develop a strengths-based mental health orientation in their hospital and emerging community mental health system. They decided to draw on existing resources in the Albanian Kosovar people to promote recovery after the period of oppression and war, as well as to address other public mental health concerns.

BRIEF HISTORY In the aftermath of the war in Kosovo in 1999, the Albanian Kosovar society faced having to build a mental health system while contending with widespread experience of loss, violence, and geographical displacement. The Serbian authorities had permitted very few formal services in the previous 10 years, and most mental health and social services for Albanian Kosovars were provided by a parallel system of professionals and paraprofessionals who worked underground, usually without pay. A few mental health practitioners including myself had been able to continue their education and provide services at the University Hospital in Prishtina. This small group of psychiatrists, psychologists, and nurses took on the responsibility of building a mental health system and providing services to a large number of families in need. During the war, most of the Albanian Kosovar mental health professionals had fled the country. Many had lived in refugee camps and had faced serious danger and lost family members and friends.

After the war, Albanian Kosovar mental health professionals who had stayed initiated the development of mobile teams. These teams went to some of the villages to work with families that had suffered major loss during the massacres perpetrated on hundreds of villages in Kosovo. Reports estimate that more than ten thousand murders of Albanian Kosovars occurred during this time.

The American and Albanian Kosovar group visited one of the small villages where it had been working with a number of families. In this small agricultural village of 2,000 people, approximately 30 miles southwest of the capital, Prishtina, Albanian and Serbian Kosovars had lived together for decades. One evening in May 1999, Serbian military forces entered the village. They sent a group of Serbians from the village to identify the male Albanian leaders there. The next day, Serbian forces entered the village, took men from the houses, and shot them, often in front of their families. One group of villagers managed briefly to escape but were later caught and slaughtered. The violence lasted throughout the day. Bodies were buried in mass graves just outside the village.

Days later the Serbian forces returned to the village, and, in an attempt to remove the evidence of their atrocities, dug up the corpses, placed them on trucks, and departed the area. On a hill above the village, half of the graves of the 58 massacred people were empty and likely to remain that way. For many families, their grief associated with losing many family members at one time (some as many as five), was compounded by not having their family members' bodies available for a proper funeral according to Muslim tradition.

As one consequence of the deaths of the younger and stronger men of the family, the elders—often older adult women—had to take an active role in leading their extended families of widows and children. The Kosovar mental health professionals who had begun to work with these families took an approach that explored their sources of strength and resilience. During this initial phase of work with families, the Kosovar professionals were very interested in conducting solution-focused conversations.

We initially felt some cautiousness about using an approach that makes optimism a priority in an environment that had recently experienced such an overwhelming tragedy. We began to discuss how a person could conduct solution-focused conversations in light of Albanian Kosovar values, based on its ideas about optimism, hope, collaboration, progress, attitudes toward the future, loyalty to family members who may be dead or alive, and dignity. We decided that conversations would include speaking about past ordeals of trauma, guilt and shame, and rage and revenge. Furthermore, we believed that it was important to look at how to conduct these conversations in the context of the particular rules, constraints, and communication strengths of the Albanian Kosovar family. Particular attention needed to be given to the use of language:

- What were the concepts and words that were more likely to promote constructive action?
- When and how could a person encourage the use of creative imagination, respectful playfulness, and humor as resources?
- How could cultural practices, rituals, symbols, metaphors, myths, and stories offer, enhance, and legitimize solutions?

REAWAKENING HOPE

One way of thinking about strengths-based and solution-focused conversations in the Kosovar context was described by Dr. Shukrie Statovci, who had naturally begun to engage her clients in such discourses:

In my experience, the family usually knows how to cope with adversity. When I have not known how I could be most helpful, I have come to realize that I could always seek the answers or solutions from the families with whom I was working. The first step in conducting solution-focused conversations with families is finding their sources of strength. And this first has to do with knowing where to link and connect with the family. In my experience with Kosovar families, I have found children to be one of the most important sources of strength. Whenever we try to find some solution for the future, children are always in the picture. Everyone is focused on children. This was true in my own life experience.

During the war in Kosovo, as the NATO bombing was going on, I had the misfortune of being in Blasé—an area that was referred to as "no man's land." There, together with my people, I experienced some of the most severe conditions of the war. Blasé is an area between Macedonia and Kosovo, where during the war some 50,000 people were gathered and not permitted to leave the region for more than 7 days. It was a very inhuman situation—there were many women and children having to endure an extreme shortage of food and water. People did not know where their family members were.

After 3 days, my mother, two brothers, and I were able to get to a bus—but we did not know where the bus was going. The place where we waited for the bus was very dangerous, because the Macedonian police subjected us to violence. I was near my mother, and, in the moment she said, "I would like to go back to the place where we were before."

I was surprised by her wish, because suddenly I found myself between two roads—one road led in the direction of hope where the buses were and the other led back to the nightmare of the camps. I asked her, "Why do you want to go back to those conditions where you could easily die from disease?"

She said, "Over here, if the police start to beat you then I don't need my life anymore. Because of you, I am here. In the other situation I would be in my home and killed by the Serbs. I prefer to go back together to these nylon-tent camps and die all together by diseases than to stay here and see you killed by the Macedonian police."

I was surprised by her answer but did not have a chance at that time to think about what she had said. Later, when I returned to Kosovo and was working with families, I saw that the children were the source of strength, and then I understood my mother's response.

As I listened to families during the war, I understood why the mother of one remaining child could live and cope with all the problems she faced. The child provides the solution to cope with the problem; this is connected with the systems of belief that exist in the family. Although she believed that God had taken her husband, she also believed that God had given her a gift by sparing her child. Usually, the family understands that even though there was evil done to the family, there was also a gift given that was linked to the loss but helped in coping with the loss. Through a child, an image of the future links with the past.

One example of the strength of this connection was when I met a man who, as a child, had witnessed the killing of his uncle during a massacre. As a child he had been very close to his uncle. He had severe post-traumatic stress disorder (PTSD) symptoms and was admitted to the hospital. Gradually his symptoms improved, and one day he came to me and said, "My memories start to pale, but what I cannot cope with is that I was in a very close relationship with my uncle, and I don't know how to go forward without him."

I asked him, "When you and your uncle were together, did you have any sort of conversation about the future?"

He stood up and said, "My uncle's wish was that I would be educated. He liked very much that I would become someone whom he would be proud of."

Then I asked him, "Would you like to accomplish his wish to continue with your education, or what do you want to do?"

He answered, "I never thought about it before, but I think that this is a good idea."

Connections can be made between the future and the past. Everyone makes plans for the future—life can bring obstacles in realizing these plans, but people may use these plans or visions of the future to cope with the crisis situations in their present lives. (Shukrie Statovci, Ph.D.)

Zepa

Zepa, a 70-year-old Albanian Kosovar woman, suffered the murder of five family members during a massacre that took place in her small village in 1979. She and other family members listened to the gunshots as her 75-year-old husband, two grown sons, and two teenage grandsons were murdered in the yard of their home. Only Zepa's 21-year-old son returned to the family from his studies in Germany in the aftermath. Zepa's family also included a daughter with schizophrenia, two widowed daughters-in-law, and nine grandchildren.

Following the massacre in which the senior men of the family were killed, Zepa now had to assume the role of the patriarch for her extended family, becoming the person responsible for communicating with the outside world and ensuring that the women and children were protected and provided for.

In response to her new responsibilities, Zepa explained, "I never thought of being head of the family; it is very hard for me, but there is no choice." In the initial period following the deaths of her family members, Zepa's grief, expressed in depression and avoidance and difficulties in functioning, had a tremendous effect on the rest of the family. Initially, she had struggled to find a way to provide guidance to the wives of her murdered sons and to continue to have a place of importance in the family. Her impatience with her grandchildren's dependency on her resulted in a positive change in the family's behavior. The matriarch's irritation and withdrawal from the daughters-in-law led them to perform their roles as mothers more effectively; they cared for their own children and disciplined them more effectively. The more Zepa withdrew from her family, the more the children felt secure and cared for by their own mothers.

In September 1999, the team started working with Zepa's family. The sister with schizophrenia had de-compensated, and other family members were struggling to cope as they grieved in silence—unable to speak with each other about their losses. Meetings with the family, arranged by a nurse in the village, enabled the members of the team to help each family member to talk about his or her grief and to clarify each individual's role in relation to one another. Zepa and her daughters-in-law found new ways to work together around raising the nine children whose fathers were killed.

The clinical team worked to help the family recover a future focus by asking questions that enabled the children to remember their fathers and what they would have wanted for them in the future. This allowed the family to shift their focus to their hopes. The team asked the family members what the father would say if he had a chance to say some final words. These kinds of questions invited the family to refocus on the children—and the future. The family was encouraged to remember the hopes and goals of the dead and to join in these hopes by renewing their sense of purpose and commitment to caring for the children.

As she felt empowered to recommit to the future, Zepa experienced a subsiding of her symptoms. She was able to remember the hopes of her sons and to focus on the children. The family's recovery involved reconnecting with hopes for the future and addressing the values from the past that created meaning in the face of fear, anguish, anger, and revenge. Zepa was inspired to renew her role of grandmother, to recognize her daughters-in-law more fully, and to support and encourage them in caring for their children. (Afrim Blyta, M.D.)

An Albanian Experience: Avni

Avni was an 83-year-old Albanian man. His wife, brother, and two sons were murdered and their bodies burned during the war. The first time I met Avni, he expressed that he felt unneeded. When I reminded him of the Albanian saying, "A house without an aging, old man is like a house without a basement [foundation]," he responded, "I don't know, I am not sure, is there anyone else who thinks like you?" He gave me a very strange look as if he were trying to understand whether I truly meant what I was saying. Then he smiled and said, "My life experience is very, very long. I have too much experience."

I responded, "I would like to hear about your experience, but do your grandchildren know about it?"

He said, "No, they are young. In the school they are teaching about other things."

When I asked him whether he would be willing to share his life experience with his children in attendance, he accepted. Avni and I began to visit the family weekly for 3 months, followed by visits on major holidays—Ramazan and Bayran. During his visits with his family, he spoke about the family's history and about his 80 years of life experience. When he realized that the children were carefully listening to what he said, he had special, warm feelings.

Avni spoke about important people in the family, and for the first time told his family the reason why they had moved to their village. He talked about how his family was known by others for its humanity and honesty. He was able to speak proudly to his grandchildren about their fathers (his sons), who were murdered in the recent war. He spoke about how they were calm and educated men who went bravely as heroes to their deaths at the hands of the Serbs. He also spoke about how the family would continue to cultivate these values in the new generation. He was able to promote good relations among the cousins, speaking to them and encouraging the children to let God punish the Serbs who were responsible for the atrocities. Through his weekly discussions, Avni was able to help restore the relationships within his family.

The intervention facilitated openness in communication in the family. Avni established good communication with the wife of his dead brother; she joined him in recalling the family's past in a way that they had neither had time nor opportunity to do before. The two older adults spoke about how their lives had never been easy, and how they now needed to learn from the previous generations ways to deal with the difficult situations they still faced.

The family meetings helped Avni and his sister-in-law temper the pain of their enormous losses. When Avni went to take his cows to graze, he began to take a grandchild with him each time and would tell the child stories as they walked together. Avni resumed praying along with other religious practices he had ceased after the war. He was also very happy that one of his sons, who had taken over as authority for the family, would discuss problems with him before making important decisions for the family—a sign of tremendous respect for his place within the family. (Shquipe Ukshini, Fac. Psych)

Fetije

Fetije, a 64-year-old woman, lost her husband and three sons during the war. The first time I met her, she was standing at the door of the family compound with some young women, holding the hand of her 6-year-old grandson. I asked them whether they would like to speak about their experience during the war and their current life. One woman thanked me for the offer and seemed happy that I was there and interested in speaking with them. She said, "I have a lot to speak about, but I would prefer you speak with my daughters-in-law, because they are younger and need you more than I do." They all agreed to meet.

Although their homes were burned during the war, they were able to rebuild their houses through the help of one son who had had been living in Switzerland and who had been able to borrow the necessary money. Fetije spoke for the first time about her experience during the war. While her husband and sons were fighting for their country, she took care of the home and family and provided them food. She said that the day she found her husband and her sons murdered was the most difficult day of her life. She spoke about how she had their pictures on the wall. "The pictures don't speak, but I speak with each of them every day. When I speak with them, I feel like I am giving them my word that I will do my best to raise their children and to rebuild their houses. I will take care of the families together because I do not want to fulfill the Serbs' desire to see us destroyed. Their pictures will be like a light to remind me of my duties and of my meaning in life. I tell them, 'You did not give up, and I am not going to give up.'"

Fetije spoke about how she had given her word to her dead husband and sons that she would rebuild their houses and families. She also encouraged her family members to speak with the son who was alive, because he was feeling a tremendous amount of guilt for not being in Kosovo during the war to help and to fight together with his family. Much of the work with this family focused on seeing how they could find some happiness in a difficult situation.

Fetije worked very hard to make her son feel that he was important to the family and to their future and that his work and the help he was providing the extended family was equal to the fighting of his father and brothers. She also spoke with her grandchildren about how she herself had grown up with her uncle and aunt because soldiers murdered her parents during World War II—and that it was now a family tradition to raise and take care of children who had lost their parents. I asked her if her grandchildren were not with her if she would feel like a tree without branches. She answered, "Yes, but it is exactly here that I have the branches, and with the help of my son, we are able to hold the grandchildren and to help my daughters-in law." (Shquipe Ukshini, Fac. Psych)

The team of Albanian Kosovar mental health professionals worked with families as a whole to promote the recovery of the elder survivors of war and massacre. This approach is based on the Albanian Kosovar society's tremendous amount of respect given to older people. The mental health professionals observed that, at this time in the history of their society, the wisdom and life experience of older people could play an important role for the new generation in helping them bridge the past with the future. Their experience of having coped with World War II and its aftermath was important in helping the new generation deal with their situation following the war in Kosovo. The healing of older people is linked to the healing of the family and the society as a whole. Their presence as a moral force in providing an example of strength and survival enabled the structure of the family to be preserved. Therapists working with these families were able to concentrate on the ethics of the relationships in the families. In these case examples, the Albanian Kosovar therapists recognized the importance of reframing the traumas the family members had experienced as opportunities to help the new generation deal with the traumas in their lives and to look toward the future.

BUILDING RESILIENCE IN THE COMMUNITY

The most effective starting points in promoting community resilience following massive psychosocial trauma are often around finding solutions to real life problems. In Kosovo, Will Mathews, of the International Federation for Red Cross and Red Crescent, described a village where most of the families had lost husbands and sons in a massacre during the war. Eighteen families came together to first solve the problem of getting their fields plowed. This concrete action not only provided a forum for people to come together to discuss community issues, but also it mobilized the group by giving them a sense of accomplishment and renewed competence. One man who had lost his wife and two children during the war had been sitting in his house unable to walk. Mr. Mathews and his colleagues asked whether they could carry him outside so that he could see his garden. This small act began to give the man back his identity, and he soon began walking again and working on his garden. Sometimes solving a small problem can be an important step in helping those who have suffered severe trauma and loss, to restore hope and the confidence to cope with current dilemmas.

A NOTE ON SELF-CARE

The effectiveness of a therapist or other helping professionals in providing aid to trauma survivors depends on the professionals' capacity to recognize the emotional impact of such work and to take care of him- or herself. Trauma is contagious and can produce similar bodily, emotional, and behavioral responses in the therapist. In severe cases, work with trauma survivors may lead to traumatic stress symptoms, depression, and anxiety in the helper. Psychic numbing may prevent the therapist from having access to his or her own emotional resources and intuitive capacities that can be helpful for his or her clients. It has been found that work with trauma survivors is greatly benefited when the therapist is able derive the ongoing support of a group with whom he or she can regularly speak about the clinical work as well as the emotional impact that the work has on the members of the group. It is important that the group support the members in developing strategies for self-care, such as breaks, relaxation exercises, recreation, and enjoyment.

> TRAUMA IS CONTAGIOUS and can produce similar bodily, emotional, and behavioral responses in the therapist. In severe cases, work with trauma survivors may lead to traumatic stress symptoms, depression, and anxiety in the helper.

SUMMARY

A strengths-based, solution-focused approach has the following advantages when working with trauma survivors.

- It enables the therapist to join with an individual or family based on competence.
- It is based on the priority of needs as established by the client—highlighting the problems that are most important to solve.
- It involves assessing which problems can realistically be changed—as well as the clients' readiness to change.
- It enables the therapist to map progress toward the problem's solution as well as elicits the clients' ideas about the steps toward the solution.
- It identifies the resources and people that may be available to help clients solve their problems.
- It may enable clients to turn the past into an asset rather than a liability, by helping them reconnect with the positive resources that remain despite tragedy.
- It promotes overcoming the obstacles to utilizing these resources.
- It gives credit to those who have already been helpful and supports the sharing of credit in the future.
- It can help bridge the life disruptions of massive trauma by linking the positive memories and resources of the past with a hopeful image of the future.

REFERENCES

Bell-Gadsby, C., & Siegenberg, A. (1996). *Reclaiming herstory: Ericksonian solution-focused therapy for sexual abuse.* Philadelphia: Brunner/Mazel.

Berg, I.K., & Miller, S.D. (1992). *Working with the problem drinker: A solution-focused approach.* New York: Norton.

de Shazer, S. (1985). *Keys to solution in brief therapy.* New York: Norton.

Furman, B., & Ahola, T. (1992). *Solution talk: Hosting therapeutic conversations.* New York: Norton.

Herman, J.L. (1992). *Trauma and recovery.* New York: Basic Books.

O'Hanlon, B., & Bertolino, B. (1998). *Even from a broken web: Brief, respectful solution-oriented therapy for sexual abuse and trauma.* New York: John Wiley & Sons.

Perel, E., & Saul, J. (1989). A family therapy approach to Holocaust survivor families. In P. Marcus & A. Rosenberg (Eds.), *Healing their wounds: Psychotherapy with Holocaust survivors and their families.* New York: Praeger.

Saul, J. (2000, Winter). Mapping trauma: A multi-systemic approach. *Psychosocial Notebook.* International Organization for Migration.

Winnicott, D.W. (1980). *Playing and reality.* London: Penguin Books.

14

CARING FOR PEOPLE WITH ALZHEIMER'S DISEASE AND RELATED DEMENTIAS

Strengths-Based Approaches

Judah L. Ronch

AS A GROWING NUMBER OF PEOPLE with Alzheimer's disease (AD) and related dementias enter the United States health care system, particularly the long-term care health care system, interest among professionals has moved away from the medical model of care toward *person-centered* care. Primary caregivers—family and paid staff—are learning to improvise a path of care while cures to AD and related dementias are sought because the system's previous exclusive reliance on the acute care medical model is not proving effective.

As innovation and improvisation took hold among care providers and produced informal consensus and communities of practice, a sense emerged that despite the relentless progression of AD, staff and caregivers were indeed able to help the person with AD by using "whatever [their] ingenuity and hearts suggest"

I wish to thank Drs. Eron and Lund for their discussions over these many years that allowed me to use their constructs and theory in refining my earlier work on the experience of the "self" in AD. I am in debt to Jean Marks for her always astute and expert comments, for her editing of earlier versions of this manuscript, and for help with the references. She often understood the essence of what I wanted to say and helped me clarify the message. Despite this expert help, I am solely responsible for any errors in this chapter.

BEST PRACTICES AND creative programs developed, usually by nursing home and day center paid caregivers, who believed that there had to be a better way to give care than by responding to "problem behaviors" when they occurred.

(Luria, 1985). The literature and professional conferences continued to showcase "best practices" and creative programs that grew from intuitive hunches, adaptations of interventions successful with other populations (e.g., individuals with developmental disabilities), and other ground-breaking thinking. Best practices and creative programs developed, usually by nursing home and day center paid caregivers, who believed that there had to be a better way to give care than by responding to "problem behaviors" when they occurred. Ultimately, the ways of the paid caregiver joined with the innovations thought up by family caregivers.

Family caregivers improvised and became creative on their own to meet the multiple, cascading needs of relatives for whom they cared; they shared their newfound solutions in support groups and Alzheimer's Association newsletters. Because there were few acceptable alternatives, however, people with AD, along with the family members they cared about, were held hostage by a hateful disease characterized by one caregiver as "a maniac" (Roach, 1985). Through support groups and professional channels, an inventory of innovative approaches began to evolve out of family caregivers' and paid caregivers' trial-and-error experiences. A caregiving *wisdom* arose and became popular among paid and family caregivers because it provided a valuable tool kit of practical, commonsense approaches that were more effective than anything modern medicine offered at that time.

The effectiveness of these improvised innovations was difficult to study under strict controlled conditions because controlled studies are confounded by definitional, ethical, and measurement problems (Holmes, Ory, & Teresi, 1994). Uniformity was lacking in treatment approaches, making direct comparisons elusive. This lack of empirical, behavioral research initially led to the use of studies of outcome measurement in which stories of the person with the disease were not subordinated to statistical analysis. This led to a greater breadth of understanding among all caregivers about how the people with the disease responded to various interventions and care practices. To achieve a fuller appreciation of the path to person-centered dementia care and to highlight the positive developments in care for people with AD on which to build future care paradigms, it is important to look at the historical milestones leading up to the current approaches in dementia care.

HISTORICAL PERSPECTIVE OF STRENGTHS-BASED CARE AND ALZHEIMER'S DISEASE

When helping an individual contend with AD, using the person's residual strengths is now the norm because of important changes that have taken place in how society views people with AD and how people with AD view themselves.

This shift toward "person-centered care" (Kitwood, 1997) has resulted in a new way of looking at and talking about AD and its effects that goes beyond thinking of AD as being only a neurological condition.

The impetus for a new care model to help individuals with AD and provide support for care providers arose out of a fortunate confluence of scientific, demographic, and sociopolitical changes during the 20th century. Shaped by advances in how scientific phenomena and people's behavior were understood, these innovative models were the lens though which the behaviors of people with AD were given new meaning. The productive interweaving of scientific advances and optimistic views of what human beings are capable of doing to help themselves continued to evolve and gather momentum at the dawn of the 21st century. With the clarity of hindsight, eight milestones may be identified that combined to generate and energize this movement:

1. Dr. Alois Alzheimer's pioneering work
2. Research that debunked the myth of senility and established the biological, psychological, and social bases of cognitive impairment in aging adults
3. The practice of educating family caregivers about AD and making them the focus of professional intervention, even while the idea persisted that there was nothing that could be done for the person with the disease
4. Patients' rights movement
5. Dynamic view of behavior of AD patients
6. Establishment and growth of the Alzheimer's Association and its affiliated branches around the world
7. Medicines approved for treating AD
8. Strengths-based models of mental health interventions

Each milestone had a pivotal effect on a care paradigm—and the whole had a greater impact than the sum of the parts in promoting person-centered care for people with AD.

THE WORK OF DR. ALOIS ALZHEIMER

Amid the promise of an ultimate cure generated by the biomedical research on AD being conducted as this book was being published, it may be easy to forget Frau Auguste D., the first person to be diagnosed with an Alzheimer's-like condition that now bears Dr. Alzheimer's name. Fifty-one-year-old Frau Auguste D. had been wandering the city of Frankfurt, Germany, screaming in the streets, and causing her socially prominent husband and her family great embarrassment. She accused her husband of infidelity and her doctors of rape (Pierce, 2000).

Dr. Alzheimer believed her to be suffering from "presenile dementia," a condition known for many centuries and believed to be associated with atrophy of the brain. After she died, Alzheimer performed an analysis of tissue taken from Frau Auguste's brain. He found that she had a profusion of thickened neourofibrils, or *tangles,* arranged in bundles within the cells and neuritic plaques in the intra-cellular spaces. These remain the unique pathological signs of the disease. Alzheimer's classic papers, published in 1906 and 1907, proposed that Frau Auguste D. had not been a victim of presenile dementia (presumably vascular in origin) as he had first thought, but rather that she had been a victim of a specific, unique neurodegenerative condition now called Alzheimer's disease.

Dementia senilis, senility (a term that is now considered anachronistic), was a common diagnosis for older adults whose behaviors included wandering and acting suspicious, confused, and verbally disruptive. Though its clinical presentation was remarkably similar to Frau Auguste D.'s, dementia senilis was believed to be the result of reduced cerebral blood flow secondary to normal arterial narrowing or hardening of the arteries as people aged. No one thought at that time, or for many years thereafter, that Frau Auguste D. and the many older adults who were considered senile could be suffering from the same disease.

DEBUNKING THE MYTH OF SENILITY

Based on the groundbreaking work of doctors Blessed, Tomlinson, and Roth (1968) in England, and the research of Katzman (1976), Terry, (1963), and their colleagues (Katzman & Karasu, 1975; Katzman, Terry, & Bick, 1978) in the United States, researchers were able to demonstrate that older people who became forgetful, lost their social and language skills, and had diminishing related cognitive functioning were not suffering from inevitable senility but had specific neural damage in their brains that was visible under the microscope during autopsy. They found that in the majority of individuals with these symptoms who were examined, the neural damage was the same type (i.e., neuritic plaques and tangles) described by Alzheimer in his studies of brain tissue from Frau Auguste D. and other patients with similar clinical pictures who died before age 65. Furthermore, the majority of older people who had no equivalent behavior difficulties (i.e., were not forgetful or functionally limited by memory impairment) did not manifest the same profusion of plaques and tangles in their brains as did those with cognitive, functional, and behavioral problems. The realization that a majority of older people who experienced cognitive impairment were suffering from the same disease as Frau Auguste D. (or some other identifiable organic pathology) was a significant breakthrough in how scientists and practitioners began to view cognitive impairment and dementia (i.e., as a result of illnesses, not merely normal aging) (see Torack, 1983, for a thorough review).

ALZHEIMER'S: THE FAMILY DISEASE

Clinicians traditionally were taught to diagnose the patient's condition and to treat the family of the person with AD. This approach reflected sensitivity to the family's stresses and caregiving burdens but excluded any direct intervention with the person with AD. The family's experience was the focus of the therapeutic intervention; the lack of specific medical intervention to treat the disease itself had made the effect of the dementia on the patient a secondary clinical consideration. Inevitably, sympathetic conversations with the family took place, mostly about placing the person with AD in a long-term care facility (typically in a psychiatric facility or nursing home). Such discussions—and the family's reactions likely based on feelings of guilt and shame—took place without the person with AD being present, or worse, if he or she was present, they were conducted as if the individual was not there.

With the initial breakthroughs in research and practice, Nancy Mace and Peter Rabins, M.D., in their classic book *The Thirty-Six Hour Day* (1981), were able to comfort and empower with knowledge those families caring for individuals with AD. Most important, Mace and Rabins provided families with something they seemed to want most desperately—a way to be caring as well as the primary caregiver (i.e., to keep the AD relative home with the family). Mace and Rabins taught the family about the nature of AD, the underlying bases of the behavioral changes they witnessed, how to be helpful to the patient and other family members when extraordinary behaviors occurred, how to prevent extraordinary behaviors, and how to understand the impact of the disease's manifestations on the emotional and social life of the whole family.

During this same period, public psychiatric facilities downsized and/or focused on patients who were younger and acutely ill, and nursing homes became reluctant to admit people with challenging behavior or AD if there were other, less–problem-prone candidates awaiting admission. Families had limited choices of satisfactory institutional alternatives, and assisted living, day care, and trained home care aides were not available.

The phenomenal response to *The Thirty-Six Hour Day* (now in its fourth edition) demonstrated that family members desperately needed and would embrace a compendium of tools and wisdom that helped many of them follow their preferred way of caring for a person with AD at home for as long as possible. The *Thirty-Six Hour Day* was also one of the first available resources that professional caregivers, especially those in nursing homes, could turn to for in-depth, psychosocially based explanations of the problematic behaviors (e.g., wandering, aggressiveness) that were typical of residents with AD. Mace and Rabins' book explained problem behaviors using motivational models that went beyond the strictly biological explanations of behaviors that were the standard of the time. By demonstrating the differences in behaviors, Mace and Rabins provided caregivers with strategies to prevent these behaviors from occurring by understanding each resident's emotional status and response to the demands of the environment. These insights helped nursing home staff develop special programs and interventions for residents with AD that engaged the residents' interests and reframed their problem behaviors as signs of poor person–environment fit, thus encouraging care providers to modify the environment as the most direct way to reduce the problem behaviors.

PATIENTS' RIGHTS MOVEMENT

The rise of the patients' rights movement in the United States changed the way society viewed people with chronic physical or mental illnesses and the way people with AD viewed themselves. The reports that patients with cancer, heart disease, and other illnesses who became active participants in their treatment had better survival rates and significant increases in longevity (Cousins, 1974, 1989) suggested that patients who were actively engaged in combating their illness did better than those who passively received treatment from others. Recent research findings (Salovey, Rothman, Detweiler, & Steward, 2000; Taylor, Kemeny, Reed, Bower, & Greenwald, 2000) increasingly supported the value of an active model of engaging the disease as a significant and concrete way for people to escape the additional problems arising from the passive experience of their illness. This active model entailed individuals becoming empowered and doing something positive by participating in their care. The presence of a disease does not negate or disallow the patient's intact abilities from being factors the patient can mobilize to contribute to his or her recovery.

As people with physical disabilities had asserted the primacy of who they were as people, those with cognitive disabilities began to speak out on their own behalf and increase society's awareness of the talents, strengths, aptitudes, and the capabilities they had that they could put to use alongside professional intervention to promote their own well-being.

The patients' rights movement illustrated the possibility of reframing society's view of a clinical population previously characterized primarily by diagnoses and disabilities. The movement helped practitioners to focus their care toward enhancing an individual's capabilities without, for example, unearthing the ontogenetic roots of all mental health problems or requiring a cure for all the patient's problems. In other words, for the person who had a physical or mental illness, the patients right's movement portrayed the message, "Just because part of me is not in optimal condition, all of me isn't sick," as well as the message, "We are able to be help ourselves by using what is strong to fix what is wrong." Society had consigned people with disabilities to the wrong side of the "hypermobile" and "hypercoping" worlds of the "well" against their will, much as society presumed that people with AD had left the "hypercognitive world of the intellectually intact" (Post, 1995) once the diagnosis was made.

Society's view of what it means to have an illness had changed. An illness could no longer only be seen as something that defined a person (e.g., hemophiliac, schizophrenic). Having a diagnosis did not make him or her fundamentally different from his or her contemporaries. An alternate view had emerged that proposed that an illness was not something that redefined an individual if he or she did not allow it. The patient's constellation of attributes, strengths, and other coping mechanisms that predated the illness were not forfeited when a serious mental or physical illness occurred. Just as people in society without an illness are expected to be independent and strong on their own behalf (and in whom passivity would be frowned on), this view advocated that people with an illness could be expected to use whatever abilities they had at their disposal to promote a better quality of life while, and possibly after, being ill.

The change from seeing the individual as a passive victim to seeing the individual as being an active participant in the experience of the illness allowed his or her feelings about being ill to occupy a central and even decisive role in informing care and treatment choices. The individual's feelings about the illness, degree of resilience, coping style, available strengths (e.g., humor, faith, tenacity, survival skills, self-control) came to be seen as assets that the patient brought to a new role as a teammate of health professionals, relatives, friends, and other caregivers. One later and very creative manifestation of this development was the rise of therapy groups and organized advocacy activities that involve people in the early stages of AD (see Chapter 15 for examples).

> THE CHANGE FROM seeing the individual as a passive victim to seeing the individual as being an active participant in the experience of the illness allowed his or her feelings about being ill to occupy a central and even decisive role in informing care and treatment choices.

Although a total cure or increased survival rate was not always achieved for all illnesses, new ways of helping people cope with illnesses were emerging. These collaborative strategies and the positive impact they had on people's health allowed the person who was ill to be viewed as the source of unique and critical information—the effect that their experience of the illness had on their symptoms, goals, prognosis, and outcome.

BEHAVIOR AND THE INDIVIDUAL WITH ALZHEIMER'S DISEASE

Dr. Alvin Goldfarb—a gifted clinician, dedicated teacher, and one of the pioneers of geriatric psychiatry—reminded clinicians that the dynamic unconscious, first described by Freud, did not cease to play its usual role in determining a person's behavior after the onset of a dementing disorder (Goldfarb, 1961, 1969, 1974). Goldfarb predated the patients' rights movement by many years. By analyzing the behavior of older people and those with AD through the lens of Freud's dynamic psychiatry, he advised clinicians to look for the evidence of normal psychological processes and their use of available defenses against anxiety when considering each patient's attempts or behaviors—successful or not—to adapt to his or her unique experience, including memory loss. He explained that the disturbed behavior of someone with AD was understandable if the basic tenets of dynamic psychiatry were applied (i.e., that behavior remains motivated by unconscious defenses against anxiety and is not random, accidental, or wholly a result of the disease). By reminding clinicians of the influence of the normal intrapsychic mechanisms in each patient with neurological disease, Goldfarb told them that *Alzheimer's disease* was not the generic answer to all questions about why people with AD behaved as they did. Goldfarb's analysis contained the understanding that the disease *had* the person, and not vice versa.

A related perspective on neurological diseases gained a wider audience through the popular writings of Dr. Oliver Sacks (1985). His many books have personalized a variety of diseases by virtue of his gifted ability to tell the stories of an assortment of people with neurological maladies that do not lose the person *in* the illness. He, too, has encouraged clinicians to attend to the experience of the person with the illness when deciding on treatment strategies, including the gifts, quirks, and all the rest that makes that person human.

THE ALZHEIMER'S ASSOCIATION

The creation and growth of the Alzheimer's Association (see Fox, 1989) and, in particular, its network of affiliated local chapters brought the voices of the people with AD, their families, and friends to the center of public, political, and scientific discourses about AD. As a strong advocacy, educational, and consciousness-raising organization, the Association brought AD out of the shadows and reduced the feelings of shame and isolation felt by so many people with AD and their relatives. The Association has raised public awareness about the disease's devastating impact through public events, caregiver training, and support activities and has sponsored scientific research to find a cure; and public profile of the disease continues to grow as family members of celebrities and well-known individuals are affected by AD. The overall impact of the Alzheimer's Association is probably best appreciated in the way that the public recognizes AD as a disease and the fact that people with AD are not as likely to be written off as senile.

MEDICATIONS FOR AD

Although there is no cure for AD, available medicines demonstrate the ability to slow down the relentless progression of cognitive and functional deterioration in some individuals who are in early and middle phases of the disease. The drugs, and those under development, may help to forestall the financial and psychological cost of institutional placement for some people with AD. In essence, medicines may offer a way to slow down the clock so that families may have a longer period of time during which they may experience and enjoy the intact cognitive functions of the person with AD. The positive effects of these medications is not lost on people with the disease, who have responded with evident relief and pleasure to their therapeutic effects. Although very new to the market and far from what is really needed to turn the disease around, these drugs offer a chance to forestall (but not halt) the effects of the disease as medical science zeros in on better therapies.

STRENGTHS-BASED PSYCHOTHERAPIES

The development of modern, strengths-based psychotherapeutic approaches, such as those found in this volume, have added a pivotal dimension to AD care. These approaches utilize the strengths of the individual to achieve change without first having to impose a pathologizing frame to establish the agenda of therapy. Thus, they don't require the unequal relationship in which the view of the professional dominates when conceptualizing the problem and its possible solutions. In this sense, strengths-based approaches create the basis of "I–Thou" (Buber, 1970) relationships in which each party is an equal of the other and personhood is preserved in both, even if formal psychotherapy is not used as an intervention. In AD, the strengths-based approach (Cohen, Kennedy, & Eisdorfer, 1984) may be combined with an understanding of the perspective of the person with the illness (Cotrell & Schulz, 1993; Ronch, 1996) to establish a collaborative, nonimposing relationship to deal with AD in an active way.

STRENGTHS-BASED APPROACHES AND PROBLEM BEHAVIOR IN AD   One advantage of the strengths-based approach to helping people with AD is that it opens up myriad opportunities to intervene in a psychosocial domain, in which traditional therapies, especially pharmacotherapy, have been less than dramatic in their impact (Cohen, 1997; Maletta, 1992). Although new medications target the neurochemical mechanisms implicated in AD, they have been less successful than "low tech–high touch," interpersonal approaches in altering the impact of dementia on the person's psychosocial functioning in a significant way (Cohen, 1997).

Cognitive-behavioral intervention (Teri & Gallagher-Thompson, 1991), person-centered care cultures (Kitwood, 1997), environmental refitting and normalization (Fagan, Williams, & Burger, 1997), and individualized music selections (Gerdner, 2000) all have been reported to have had a positive impact on the supposedly unmodifiable difficult behaviors assumed to be intrinsic to the disease and primarily caused by associated brain damage. These findings support a paradigm shift from *illness-centered* to person-centered views of behavioral phenomena in AD. As a result, a door is open for clinicians to recast the stereotypes regarding the possible psychosocial origins and treatment of the behavioral symptoms of AD.

The ultimate goal of person-centered care is to improve the quality of life of the person with AD and the lives of those people who care for them in paid and unpaid capacities. Shifting from an illness-centered, biomedical model of disease to a person-centered, biopsychosocial model permits caregivers to go from passive observers of chronicity (Kleinman, 1988) to active caregivers in maintaining an individual's sense of self. This change of view has two interrelated benefits. First, it allows the caregiver to engage the person rather than the illness when trying to bring relief, thus targeting what is potentially alterable (i.e., the behavioral repertoire of the person, rather than the immutable illness). In this approach, a hopeful mindset is created and chronic helplessness and caregiver burnout are avoided; helplessness and burnout being the inevitable consequences of seeing the disease as only responsive (modestly at best) to medication. Second, people with AD are challenged to engage their own coping strengths in a context of optimism about the results, rather than in an atmosphere of despair and inevitable failure. In Kitwood's (1997) terms, a "malignant social psychology" is replaced with an enabling one that supports personhood and all of the positive behavioral potential that such an approach may evoke. The operative interpersonal dynamic is one of collaborative problem solving as opposed to custodial control.

Kitwood's concept of a positive social psychology promotes care of people with AD based on an ecological, adaptational viewpoint of their behavior. It asks the questions: Why did a particular behavior occur *now*? To which aspects of the internal or external environment is an individual responding? And how is he or she experiencing the world and giving meaning to events based on remaining memory for information and of his or her self? This kind of psychosocial model of motivation posits that an individual's behavior results from trying to fulfill unmet needs (Cohen-Mansfield, 2000) or arises because of excess environmental stress that cannot be ameliorated by previously adaptive responses. The model presumes that all behavior of people with AD does not result only from the direct, organic impact of dementia (Cohen-Mansfield, 2000; Lawler, 1995). Because problem behaviors in people with AD are often caused by multiple factors, a complete assessment of possible physiological (e.g., physical illness, medication [Feinberg, 2000]), environmental (e.g., noise, isolation), and other potential bases of the behavior is essential before a psychosocial approach is warranted as the sole intervention (see Cohen-Mansfield, 2000).

If the person with AD is indeed trying to adapt in order to fulfill unmet needs or is responding to environmental stressors, it would be plausible to believe that he or she would rely on available memory, which, in AD and similar disorders, would be composed largely of what is stored and available in remote memory. The person with AD would logically rely less and less over time on his or her recent memory. This approach to understanding behaviors observed in people with AD allows clinicians and caregivers to look at the person's behavioral repertoire, and especially so-called difficult or problem behavior, as evidence of the person's attempts to cope and adapt successfully. The problem results from a person's failure to engage the appropriate behavior in the present situation because of diminished cognition and a dwindling reserve of memory traces associated with successful solutions to the current problem (a poor fit between context and retrieved memory), not from a desire to create a problem.

This analysis is at odds with the typical interpretation of problem events reflected in the behavioral lens of traditional terms used to categorize them, such as *acting out, infantile, regressive,* or *disruptive.* Terms such as these carry implicit messages of malevolent intent or psychopathological origins of the behavior and create a mindset in caregivers that orients them toward protecting themselves or controlling the behavior by force to prevent an impending catastrophe. Unfortunately, responses tied to these interpretations usually bring about precisely those awful consequences caregivers were hoping to prevent.

The dominating frame of reference in dementia care used to categorize and cope with problem behaviors preserves the viewpoint of the caregiver when attempting to explain and intervene. As long as the behavioral repertoire of the person with AD is seen through the lens of an implicit cultural bias embedded in contemporary caregiving (i.e., that the motivation of the patient's behavior is viewed from the point of view of the caregiver), the behavior will be seen and responded to as problem *creating* rather than problem *solving* in origin. The older adult's behavior and intent are judged on the basis of their impact on the caregiver, not from the viewpoint of the older adult attempting to cope with his or her daily life that has been co-opted by a disease and his or her reaction to it. It is a decidedly unempathetic and defensive view, aggravated by misattribution and misunderstanding about what happens to the person with the disease and where the purpose of behavior originates (Feinberg, 2001).

> TERMS SUCH AS *acting out, infantile, regressive,* or *disruptive* carry implicit messages of malevolent intent or psychopathological origins of the behavior and create a mindset in caregivers that orients them toward protecting themselves or controlling the behavior by force to prevent an impending catastrophe.

PERSON-CENTERED CARE AND THE ROLE OF THE SELF IN THE EXPERIENCE OF THE DISEASE

Approaches to dementia care at the dawning of the 21st century have a postmodernist spirit because the approaches perceive that the biological condition as well as the person's experience with it make up the field for intervention (Morris, 2000). This view is similar to a line of thinking that advocated more humanized care (see Bowker, 1982) that could be achieved by changing the focus of care to the individual with the illness and away from the modernist scientific practice of caring for a class of people through a uniform set of care tasks. The evolving, postmodernist view benefits patients and care providers when the patient, not the dementia, is cared for in an atmosphere rooted in collaborative, interpersonal relationships because illness is "a social state of affairs" (Gadamer, 1993) that involves people, social institutions, cultural practices, and shared meanings (Morris, 2000).

The central and inescapable role of an individual in a caring relationship with someone with AD was addressed in Cohen and Eisdorfer's (1986) characterization of AD as the "loss of self." Molly, a patient of mine, first articulated the essence of this phrase many years ago during our initial interview. She explained her tendency to rummage through closets and drawers of other residents in her nursing facility as an attempt to find herself. At this time she could no longer do things (e.g., read and remember what she'd read) that defined for herself who "the real me, the real Molly was" (Ronch, 1987).

Molly's definition of her experience with AD and how it was a "self-altering" phenomenon, was echoed in Oliver Sacks's classic stories about the vicissitudes of people's lives as they are affected by neurological illness. He observed that "a disease is never a mere loss or excess—there is always a reaction of the affected organism or individual to restore, to replace, to compensate for, and to preserve its identity, however strange the means might be" (Sacks, 1985, p. 4). Feinberg's work (2001) on how brain damage inevitably affects the patient's experience of self, like Sacks's observation, is an important dictum for practitioners to remember while they contemplate the social state of affairs of people with AD. They must incorporate this concept when creating a theory of why a particular behavior has occurred.

Damasio (1994, 1999) and Feinberg (2001) both proposed that an individual's *self*, the core target and potential participant in the collaborative, person-centered care relationship, has an identifiable neurological substrate but no single neuroanatomical locus (site). Though a fuller explanation of their intriguing ideas is beyond the scope of this chapter, their attempts to locate the neurological mechanisms at the root of an individual's self in the structure and function of the brain permits use of the term *self* as more than a vague theoretical construct. It suggests a physical basis for the essence of an individual's experience of AD and a target of therapeutic impact.

Damasio described the neural basis of the self as being built on a continuously growing body of autobiographical data; that is, the self is a "perpetually created neurobiological state" (1994, p. 99). This conceptualization helped to build a self-based, problem-solving view of what happens in people with AD when problem behaviors occur. "In brief," he wrote, "the endless reactivation of updated images about our identity (a combination of the past and of the planned future) constitutes a sizable part of the sense of self as I understand it" (Damasio, 1994, p. 239). People with AD increasingly rely on images from the past that are contained in the remote memory of self and are increasingly unable to plan a future. Thus, it would appear that the portions of autobiographical memory they use to make sense of current events, to recall, as everyone does, "interpretations of past events" (Damasio, 1994) in the context of the present, and to maintain identity in the process increasingly would reflect knowledge of the self from the past. This was, as Molly described in our interview, the goal of her rummaging behavior. The self is not composed of objective or photographic memories of events, says Damasio (1994), but rather is the product of a subjective and creative process of selecting and interpreting personal experiences into an ongoing sense of self (Scheibe, 1989). Attempts at problem solving such as Molly's will make use of responses that are likely to fit with her remaining knowledge of her self, even as her memory of specific events and the ability to recall them vanish. Possible solutions are retrieved because of having been confirmed *in the past* as successful solutions in situations that have sufficient similarity to her current problem. Thus, for Molly and other individuals with AD, meaning is largely determined by the self as embedded in memories of the past that appear to fit the present contextual demands. But, sadly, these old memories of self increasingly do not fit the present.

Feinberg made use of contemporary neurological data to conclude that the self is "the subject of our conscious experience and at the core of our being":

Many different areas of the brain contribute to the preservation of the self, but there is no "material locus of the self" or inner "I" within the brain. The brain creates the self by producing a nested hierarchy of meaning and purpose, where the levels of the self, and the many parts of the brain that contribute to the self, are nested within all other levels of the hierarchy. (2001, p. 149)

We experience ourselves as unified, he concluded, "because our meanings and our actions are unified within the nested self" (p. 149). That suggests that the person with AD engages in the act of maintaining the unified self as the disease progresses and would presumably continue to do so until the areas of the brain necessary to process meaning and purpose are gone. This is what Molly expressed to me, only more simply. Behavior, such as her rummaging, can therefore be viewed as her attempt to maintain her *unified self* in the face of missing some vital personal information she needs to do so successfully.

Feinberg's position that *purpose* exists "only from the inside perspective of the self" suggested that the knowledge of why people with AD do something cannot be located in the brain or known by identifying where the brain is damaged. "The ontology of purpose and action, like meaning, is irreducibly personal" (2001, p. 148). The self is not a *static entity,* according to Damasio (1994) and Feinberg (2001), so it would follow that the self undergoes changes as dementia is experienced. The "margins of the self" are always being transformed, wrote Feinberg, claiming that this process occurs in all of us, whether or not we have brain damage.

These observations allow those who work with people who have AD to put problem behavior into a completely different context and analytical frame, and the behavior of people with AD can now be viewed from a strengths-based perspective. Their behavior may now be interpreted as motivated to preserve their *unified self.* Eron and Lund (1996; see Chapter 12) observed that people have strong preferences with regard to how they would like to behave, to see themselves, and to be seen by others. They referred to this constellation of ideas about self as a person's *preferred view.* These are the ideas about the person's behavioral preferences that best fit how they see themselves and, thus, provide the basis or motivation for preferred explanations about why a person does something. A person's behavior, and how others respond to it, may confirm or contradict his or her preferred view. For example, a person with AD might explain his or her behavior to his or her self and/or others by making reference to the diagnosis: "I lose my way at times because I have AD. Can you tell me where the men's room is?" He or she might explain his behavior by attributing it to some other cause: "I can't find my money; why did you hide it?" The essential point is that having AD might or might not fit a person's preferred view at any time, and is less likely to fit it as the dementia progresses and the images of an individual's self in old or remote memory storage lacks any knowledge of having AD. This lack of knowledge is not denial in the classic sense but rather amnesia for an aspect of autobiography and a missing piece of the self as it is presently known.

When a practitioner attempts to help an individual with memory impairment using interventions predicated on demands that the individual acknowledges his or her memory impairment (i.e., as by accepting the "fact" that they are "forgetful"), the practitioner runs the risk of confronting the individual with input that doesn't fit his or her preferred view. The individual with AD has little or no memory of that aspect of the self he or she currently knows. At times like this, the person with AD is faced with his or her own perceptions that are in conflict with those of helpers who clash with his or her preferred view and is pressured to believe the "truth" of his or her forgetfulness. Though trying to be helpful, the practitioner is actually imposing an aspect of the patient's self that is largely or entirely unknown at that time. The experience can create a gap or *disjunction* that fuels problem cycles, creating negative and unsettling emotions.

Interactions like these that are based on the medical model approach to AD deny the validity of the individual's experience of the illness and introduce an additional burden. That is, the person with AD will experience a negative emotional state (e.g., frustration, sadness, anxiety, dysphoria, resistance, oppositional behavior, anger) and more behavioral difficulties as the gap between his or her preferred view ("I do remember") and the disjunctive view of the caregiver ("You have a memory problem") widens (Eron & Lund, 1996).

STRENGTHS-BASED CARE IS PERSON-CENTERED

Recognizing that people with AD retain adaptive capacities, it is possible to examine how strengths-based care embodies a person-centered approach and how these ideas may be put into practice. One advantage of this particular view of people with AD, and, therefore, of the culture of care best suited to enhancing quality of life, is that relationships with them can now include them as active participants up to the limits imposed by the disease. Their role is no longer subject to the limits imposed by therapeutic treatment models. For example, it has been found that when the person with AD is expected to be passive, as is typical of some traditional care practices, bathing people with AD creates more work for staff and excess disability (reduced optimal level of function created by care practices or medical intervention with the patients). When increased independence is introduced and encouraged, the excess disability may be reversed and people with AD become more autonomous (Rogers et al., 2000).

In essence, person-centered care (Kitwood, 1997) sees the behavior of people with AD as a reflection of the experience of the illness and as a manifestation of the narrative or story of the illness in their lives (Morris, 2000). Commenting on Frank's (1996) *The Wounded Storyteller,* Morris wrote about the essence of what practitioners might consider the essential process of mutual personal change in the caregiving relationship that defines the process of becoming (continual evolution of the self). "Telling the stories of their illness," Morris explained, "constitutes a moral action by which the ill negotiate the reshaping of their own lives. Listening to such stories and responding to them with empathy constitutes for the listener an equally important moral act that also contains a possibility for significant life changes" (Morris, 2000, p. 257). It is largely through their behavior that people with AD tell their stories. By observing, listening, and responding with empathy rather than with judgment and avoiding the temptation of "translating them into biomedical dialects" (Morris, 2000, p. 258), the caregiver avoids becoming merely an attendant to deterioration (Kleinman, 1988). The caregiver is able to be a healer by being a witness, not a judge, as the "margins of the self" (Feinberg, 2001) in both participants transform.

The person-centered approach rewards caregivers with more opportunities to engage their own personal strengths and chances to bring out and support the strengths of people with AD. As Kitwood (1997) observed, caregivers can connect with a person with AD by bringing their own emotions and empathy to the caring relationship. As caregivers do this and depart from the emotional detachment and scientific objectivity demanded by the medical model, they make restitution for the emotional impact of loss of self, a gradually occurring process, which is at the heart of developing dementia. This model addresses the problems of caregiver demoralization and burnout by validating and celebrating the mutual emotional exchange that typically happens in human relationships of any value. Due to the collaborative nature of the psychosocial model, both the practitioner's and the patient's feelings are involved in and enhanced by the process.

DESTROYING THE MYTH

The myth that the person with AD has passed into an existence that is fundamentally different once the diagnosis of AD (Post, 1995) has been made is an additional barrier to person-centered, strengths-based care. This belief encourages practitioners to treat everyone with the same diagnosis as if by applying an unalterable formula, a stance that results in a closed-loop dynamic in which treatment and explanation are mutually reinforcing and self-perpetuating. Post (1995) wrote of the passage out of the "hypercognitive world" of the cognitively intact once a person is diagnosed, in which the explanations of human behavior and the validity of personal choices no longer apply to the person with AD—regardless of the actual nature or severity of an individual's cognitive loss. Though alternate models for understanding the behaviors of a person with AD have received empirical support (Cohen-Mansfield, 2000), biomedical frames still predominate in most approaches to explain the behavioral difficulties in people with AD (Lyman, 1989).

The following pages contain examples that illustrate the person-centered, strengths-based approach. The first vignette reveals how this approach helped a woman with AD and her family to resolve an issue of problem behavior by looking at the experience of the woman with dementia as expressed in her behavior. This demonstrates the role of collaboration in arriving at a solution and how the practitioner can discover information by understanding the experiences of the person with AD and his or her family members. Because the person-centered approach enlists the strengths of an individual, this case's intervention demonstrates how the practitioner builds on the individual's past and successful attempts to solve similar problems in order to learn about the preferred view currently held by the person with AD.

Mary

Mary, age 76, was brought to my office by her very distraught daughter Helen and Helen's husband John. They all appeared angry, frustrated, and ready to explode—though they all tried to be in control and objective about why they had come to see me. As I welcomed them, John presented me with a small package of papers. He told me that the papers were documents for me to sign to attest that Mary was forgetful and lacked the capacity to make a competent decision; the one at issue being to return to her own home that very afternoon. John and Helen had informed Mary that she was unable to take care of herself, and that if she chose to do so, they were not legally liable for the outcome. They believed that Mary was suspicious of them, and she resisted any advice they gave to her about the inadvisability of her return home at this time.

After I recovered from the surprise I experienced on being confronted by this demand, I gently informed the family that I was not prepared to sign any papers attesting to anything about Mary's mental or functional status, nor would I be at any point that day. I further informed John that if it was a legal opinion he wanted or if he wished to avoid legal penalties for the outcome of Mary's decision, he had come to the wrong place. I did ask to see the papers and found that they were a detailed presentation of what had happened with Mary and how she had refused to go along with the family's attempts to ensure her safety. I then asked them to come into my office so we could all talk about the problem.

Helen told me that her mother, Mary, who was a retired nurse, came to live with her and John to continue her recovery from a recent fall and broken forearm, which had resulted in a 2-week hospital stay in Mary's home town 50 miles away. Mary had been found to be forgetful and mildly malnourished on her admission to the hospital and had lost 10 pounds. After her accident, Mary regained sufficient functional ability to dress herself with assistance and to eat—but not to prepare her own meals. But, Helen and her family members worried about Mary's forgetfulness and felt that she couldn't take care of herself even when her arm was fully healed.

Mary smiled and immediately said that her daughter and son-in-law were very caring but overly concerned and that her memory was quite good for someone her age. When I asked her whether she remembered why she had been admitted to the hospital, Mary correctly responded that she had fallen after "passing out, I guess." Helen interjected that Mary's next-door neighbor, who had called the police for help, had found Mary unconscious. Mary said that while she had not been well, she now felt ready to go home and wished to "stop imposing on the children's hospitality." "They have been wonderful to me and that's why I'm in such good shape," she volunteered, "but it's time for me to go home today and get out of their way."

John then added that Mary had spent the last 2 days packing her bags and then unpacking them as she and her children went back and forth about Mary's readiness to return home. "And," John continued, "her bags are now sitting in the entry foyer of our house pending the outcome of our visit with you." I then asked about the papers that I was asked to sign and inquired about the intended readers. John said that Helen's brother, who lived in Oklahoma, didn't understand how bad his mother was and that if Mary insisted on going home before she was ready to, they feared they would be held accountable for any possible injuries Mary might cause to herself or to others as a result of her "impaired" mental status. As they left the room at my request so Mary could be interviewed alone, Helen whispered, "And ask her about the drinking."

I had learned that John and Helen were worried about being viewed by others as irresponsible and uncaring—if not legally liable—in the midst of this troublesome and confusing situation. I could now join with them to deal with the crisis that originated in Mary's stated desire to unburden her children now that they had done such a good job in aiding her recovery. The next step involved learning about Mary and her memory problem.

THE INTERVIEW WITH MARY   I spoke with Mary about her situation and how she felt. When I asked her how her memory was working, she replied, "Fine, I think." I then asked whether she would mind if we tested how good her memory was, especially because people are sometimes unaware of memory problems. She agreed, and the examination revealed that her Mini-Mental Status Examination score (MMSE) (Folstein, Folstein, & McHugh, 1975) was 16 of a possible 30 (moderate memory loss), with particular problems in short-term memory and 5-minute recall items. But what was most interesting was her answer to the question that asked the present year; Mary answered that it was 1942. I inquired about the significance of this date and she said, woefully, that it was when her "baby brother" died in World War II. Her brother's death was a particularly painful loss because their mother had died when Mary was 11 years old and her brother was 3—leaving Mary to raise him. "He was like my own child," she said through tears, "and I miss him like it was yesterday that we got the news that he had died."

After listening to Mary talk about her brother and witnessing her grief, I shared the MMSE findings with her and explained that her type of memory loss was especially difficult to acknowledge and cope with since by its very nature people who had it usually couldn't remember that they had a memory problem. Then, in an attempt to engage an aspect of Mary's preferred view, I asked her whether she had learned about this kind of mental status testing in nursing school. She laughed and answered, "They didn't tell us about anything like that in those days."

Mary's focus on the loss of her brother and the possibility of long-standing, unresolved grief suggested that Mary might have a depressive syndrome (Kennedy, 1995) and, therefore, be sleeping poorly. I asked her if she used any medicines to help with her sleep or to calm her nerves (both insomnia and anxiety are common to older adults with depression and related insomnia). She responded by pulling a huge bottle of an anxiolytic medication out of her purse; it did not have her name on it, in fact, it had no prescription label at all! I asked where she got the medicine, and she replied that her doctor gave it to her while she was in the hospital, to help her sleep. When I expressed doubts that a physician would give a patient a bottle of 500 pills like this, Mary said: "Oh, then maybe I got it from Frances, my next-door neighbor." It was quickly apparent to me that Mary's memory problem was not a simple issue and that the roles played by drug use, poor nutrition, depression, and other causes yet unknown had to be investigated. I proposed to Mary that she meet with me again to investigate these factors as contributing to her memory problem and appealed to her retained professional identity as a nurse, specifying that more assessments were necessary to understand why her memory wasn't functioning optimally. "Well," she said with a smile, "I think that's a good idea but I live too far away to drive back by myself, so I guess I'll have to stay with my daughter until then."

With Mary's permission, I called her primary physician in her presence and informed him about the problem and my assessment of her status, and asked whether the physician was aware of her use of an anxiolytic. He was quite surprised to hear about her use of this drug and he said that he had not prescribed any for her. Because I believed that Mary's mental status might improve if she discontinued using anxiolytics, I arranged for the physician (who agreed with me) to tell her over the telephone to stop taking the pills.

Mary agreed to cease her pill usage when I explained that they might be making her sleep worse. She then cheerily volunteered that she drank a glass of wine most nights to help her sleep when she woke up at 3 A.M. after the pill's effects had worn off. She volunteered: "Maybe I should stop drinking wine at night, too." Mary, who had estimated that this one glass held approximately 6 ounces of wine, announced, "But it's not a problem because it's not like I'm drinking liquor or anything that's not good for you." Mary also agreed to see her primary physician within 2 weeks to receive a thorough physical evaluation.

She informed her family of her decision to stay with them until the next week and her decision to stop using the sleeping pills and wine at night. John and Helen were surprised and slightly confused, but I explained the findings and theorized that Mary's memory problem might be due to or complicated by many factors discovered in the evaluation (depression, alcohol, anxiolytic medication).

THE FOLLOW-UP VISIT   Mary, John, and Helen returned the next week and reported that Mary was sleeping better, was less irritable, and was no longer suspicious. They mentioned that her memory was much better but still a problem. A quick re-evaluation showed that Mary's MMSE score had indeed improved by four points, but that her short-term memory was still impaired enough to warrant concern for her safety and necessitated a more in-depth diagnostic assessment.

The most remarkable change was in everyone's affect. Mary was no longer suspicious in front of her daughter and son-in-law and they, too, had become more relaxed and less fearful. They volunteered that Mary was so much better that they were ready to take her back home, and she remarked that they were taking such good care of her that she was not sure that she wanted to leave. We all agreed that Mary needed a complete medical and functional evaluation to see whether she was able to live safely alone at home and to take care of all of her needs. It was also agreed that Mary would see a social worker and other mental health professionals to assess her emotional status and that she would have a proper diagnostic work-up for dementia. Finally, Mary agreed to become involved with community agencies that could monitor her overall well-being and to maintain contact with her health care providers and her family about her status. The papers I had been asked to sign the previous week were not mentioned.

The problem-centered paradigm of treatment would have involved a therapist confronting Mary about her lack of memory and her poor judgment. The approach would have attempted to get her to accept the need for subordinating her view of the situation to that of her "rational" family members (i.e., with no memory impairment). It would have required Mary to accept information about her self and her memory status about which she was amnesic. In view of her need to defend herself from John and Helen's insistence that she had memory impairments, I saw their accusations as a likely cause of her defensiveness, suspiciousness, and anxiety in her interactions with her family.

According to Eron and Lund (1996), the presence of these emotions (defensiveness, suspiciousness, and anxiety) indicated that the gap between Mary's preferred view and other people's view of her (i.e., John's and Helen's) was widening and perpetuated problematic emotional states that further reduced her ability to be part of the "realistic" solution. All the talk of her problems made her strengths too difficult to derive and created more entrenched defensive behaviors. It fuelled her insistence that her view of herself was correct and that her children were well-meaning but wrong. Likewise, Mary's daughter and son-in-law were dealing with a widening gap between their need to get along with Mary and at the same time to take care of Mary appropriately, and their belief that others would see them as neglectful or ill-informed if they allowed Mary to go home and she got hurt.

Finally, any attempts by me to impose a solution on Mary that agreed with the family members' view of her dilemma would have indicated that the clinician also saw her as having lost her place in the "hypercognitive" world (Post, 1995) and totally unable to make decisions. Signing the papers provided by John or referring them to an attorney to arrange a capacity evaluation could have served to increased the polarity the family members were experiencing. This could have further threatened Mary's ability to realign her view of her self in the situation while maintaining her preferred view. It could have prevented a formation of alliances among Mary, her family, and myself. By aligning with John and Helen and abandoning Mary, I would have been at risk of widening the gap between Mary's preferred view and others' view of her into a chasm (Eron & Lund, 1996) and exacerbating her symptoms so much that she would be unable to use her remaining ability to collaborate on a solution to this crisis.

When aspects of Mary's preferred view were discerned, it was possible for me to align with her wish to be seen as caring, thoughtful, capable, and open to new information to make decisions. It was also possible to engage her preferred view in how she wanted others to see her. Being seen by others as a well-informed nurse helped Mary to agree to an empirical approach (i.e., "let's see what the data say about your condition before we proceed"), and allowed her to stop acting exclusively on her desire to deny her memory problem and spare her children any further caregiving burden by overstaying her welcome. By aligning with many aspects of her preferred view as revealed in the conversation with Mary, I was able to find a basis for collaborating with her based on the view of her self that remained. We were also able to work on actively realigning the margins of the self (Feinberg, 2001) with her remaining functional capacities and personal preferences.

Wilbur

Wilbur was an 82-year-old resident of a long-term care facility who began a habit of waking up at 2 A.M., getting dressed, and heading toward the main entrance. Staff tried to redirect him and get him to go back to bed, but within 5 minutes he would be headed toward the lobby of the building. He was sent by his interdisciplinary care planning team to see the consulting mental health practitioners in the hope that a sleeping medication would be prescribed or that some other psychotropic drug could be tried for this "agitation" and "wandering." When staff confronted Wilbur, he insisted that it was time to get up; he had things to do. Wilbur's son Frank kept close tabs on his father's status and asked that his father not receive any drugs. He had heard about the possible side effects of the drugs that are used to control behavior in patients who have AD; he didn't want his father to develop more problems. Frank asked whether a staff member could sit with his father when he got up and talk with him, but the facility staff was reluctant to "set a precedent" because "then everyone on his unit would get up and want to have attention paid to them." Staff expressed concern to Frank that his father's "wandering made him an elopement risk" and that they might have to discharge him to a more secure setting if medication failed to solve the problem.

In an attempt to understand what was motivating Wilbur's behavior and to achieve a view of his behavior as strengths-based, the clinician suggested that a nurse's aide ask Wilbur why he was getting up and dressing himself at 2 A.M. Wilbur, a retired superintendant of a large apartment building in New York City, responded that he had to await the coal truck that was due to arrive soon (to re-fuel the coal furnaces). When viewed from Wilbur's perspective, his explanation provided a suggested reframing of the behavior from problem creating to problem solving.

To explore Wilbur's explanation, the nurse's aide on duty during the night was told to accompany him to the lobby and see what happened. Everyone was curious to see what Wilbur would do when no coal truck appeared and especially interested to see how he continued problem solving when his memory of the past didn't produce a solution in the present.

The nurse's aide and Wilbur made their way to the front lobby at 2 A.M. and drank coffee together while Wilbur read the newspaper and awaited the truck. After waiting 30 minutes in which he finished his coffee and scanned the newspaper, Wilbur stood up and announced: "I'm going to bed!" When the curious nurse's aide asked him why, he replied, "Those trucks are never on time, and if they think that I'm waiting up for them, they're crazy." Wilbur's son confirmed that this was a typical occurrence during his father's working life, and that when he would return to bed around 3 A.M., he muttered about the unions that made his life miserable by not delivering coal on time.

This pattern was repeated every night for approximately 6 months. One night, however, when Wilbur awoke and was asked by the night nurse if he was going to await the coal truck, he said he wasn't going to wait for it in the lobby that night. "If they want me they can find me," he proclaimed as he went back to his room, without cueing, and went to sleep.

Staff viewed Wilbur as a *problem creator* because their modernist, scientific explanation of his actions didn't allow for any alternate view of his behavior. For them, Wilbur's actions were seen from the perspective of how his behavior negatively influenced them and their well-being. Their fear of liability if he wandered out or their belief that they would be overwhelmed with requests to give all residents individual attention determined their view. The need for staff members to preserve their preferred view of being competent professionals supported their need to protect themselves because they believed there was nothing they could do except restrain or medicate Wilbur. Allowing him to get up and move about, possibly fall, or escape the facility would conflict with the staff's preferred view and widen the gap between how they viewed themselves and how they feared others might view them. If Wilbur came to any harm they might view themselves—or others might view them—as incompetent, a view that is at odds with their preferred view that they are good care providers. Staff provided support for their theory by being able to see only one stereotypical, medical model perspective and they did not allow alternative views as to why Wilbur behaved the way he did. Only when staff went with Wilbur and found out why his behavior made sense to him were they led to respond to Wilbur's behavior in a way that fit his logic.

An alternative approach, one that would allow staff to align their preferred view of themselves, would be for them to recognize Wilbur's behavior as *problem solving*. Staff must identify Wilbur's behaviors as his attempt to use a successful solution, recalled from his unique life story, and apply it to his present situation. Though the behaviors he chose as his solution did not fit the time and place, they were close enough to fit the current context as Wilbur perceived it. Wilbur's best solution about what to do when he awoke at 2 A.M. was to be a responsible building superintendent and do what was required, but he still maintained his customary limitations. Although he was unable to orient himself to time and place, he relied on his remote memory to tap an adaptive response to the present context.

Wilbur's thinking was based on a view of the world that was determined by his experiences only, one that the staff's appeal to current reality (i.e., he was supposed to return to bed) was unable to modify.

Attempts at reality orientation are typically unsuccessful in similar cases with people who have AD; after sufficient cognitive decline, they lack the requisite cognitive function to decenter and adopt the other views of the world. Telling Wilbur that it was not time to get up and that the staff's view of reality was the correct one would only serve to confront him with his memory loss, an aspect of self for which he had no memory. These dueling paradigms are at the heart of many well-intentioned but ineffective interventions in AD care. They are the basis of the gap wideners that, for someone with AD, disconfirm the "self as now known" and fuel negative emotional states (Eron & Lund, 1996) so challenging to family caregivers and paid staff.

> TELLING WILBUR THAT it was not time to get up and that the staff's view of reality was the correct one would only serve to confront him with his memory loss, an aspect of self for which he had no memory.

The staff was eventually able to view Wilbur's behavior as meaningful and, from his point of view, they were able to de-center from their view of his behavior and participate in his story and his solution in a helpful way. Reframing Wilbur's behavior from problem creating to problem solving allowed staff to align with his preferred view and support their own at the same time by displaying their helpful and competent selves. It also evoked aspects of Wilbur's self that limited the problem behavior at each occurrence and ultimately stopped it for good. The staff's comfort with Wilbur's use of solutions, drawn from strengths based in his unique history, increased as he acted according to this familiar nighttime pattern and provided the meaning that made them modify their theory of what motivated Wilbur's behavior, seeing it as problem solving rather than as problem creating.

A STRENGTHS-BASED, PERSON-CENTERED PERSPECTIVE OF MARY AND WILBUR

Each vignette attempted to demonstrate how the contrast in views and consequent interventions arising from them set the traditional analysis of behaviors apart from strengths-based, person-centered approaches. Each revealed how alternatives to the traditional approach provided opportunities for successfully resolving episodes of difficult behavior. The ability to place the origins of behavior in Mary's or Wilbur's desire to use their coping ability (albeit flawed due to the effect of dementia on cognition) provided the platform for collaborative problem solving based in the person's operative theory of self or preferred view. But more critically, it provided a win-win method for the preferred view of both the person with AD and the caregiver (family or paid) to confirm their respective preferred views.

SUMMARY

This chapter demonstrates the validity and value of a strengths-based, person-centered approach to AD and related dementia care. This approach is a complementary, synergistic construct that points the way for an individual to care for his or her *self* while coping with the effects of dementia. Above all, it is the responsibility of those who provide paid and unpaid care—and for the social institutions that represent sanctioned cultures of care and those who oversee them—to ensure that an individual's loss of self is not his or her price of care. Strengths-based, person-centered care is one way to prevent the excess disability that results when care providers focus on the person's illness and fail to "respond to fragile clues of selfhood" (Post, 1995). As Sabat and Harre observed, "as an organizing center, the 'self' is not lost even in much of the end stage of the disease" (1992, p. 460).

The following is a list of principles of high-quality dementia care (Bradley, Ronch, & Pohlmann, 1999) that captures the essence of strengths-based, person-centered ways to help people with AD and other related dementias. It is my hope that the reader will use these ideas to develop his or her own approach to caring for those with AD and related dementias through a creative application of these principles.

PRINCIPLES OF STRENGTHS-BASED CARE FOR PEOPLE WITH AD AND RELATED DEMENTIAS

- People with AD process information despite their cognitive impairments and do not experience their condition passively. They remain actively involved with both the external and internal (e.g., emotions, sensations, comfort) environments.

- Caring for people with AD is more effective and less difficult if their perspective and their "experiences of the illness" (Cotrell & Schulz, 1993) are included when formulating care approaches.

- People with AD, like the rest of us, have a preferred view that constitutes the basic operating assumptions and frames of reference that they use to interpret and give meaning to events in their lives.

- People with AD attempt to act in line with their preferred view as they try to cope with life's daily demands. Their preferred view typically may not include recognition of being cognitively impaired. Quality caring supports the preferred view reflected in coping attempts and tries to guide the person with AD toward successful coping responses that are in line with his or her preferred view.

- People with dementia try to make sense of their experiences so that they feel emotions and try to provide for themselves or seek from others solace when upset, meaning when confused, and self-esteem when dignity is compromised. They must increasingly make use of less recent, more remote historical information about their individual ways of coping in such circumstances; quality care helps provide a bridge to information so that the individual can cope to the best of his or her abilities.

- Problem behavior may be viewed as a sign that the person with AD is cognitively or emotionally overtaxed, is trying to solve a problem, is making sense of his or her experiences with information that is incomplete or "out of date" due to memory loss, and/or is having an unsettling emotional reaction to how he or she feels.

- Person-centered, strengths-based care reinforces self-esteem by providing the cognitive, emotional, and biographical information to enhance the individual's ability to be successful without first having to acknowledge his or her memory loss. Likewise, these behaviors are understood to originate in the mechanisms used by all humanity to cope rather than as signs of mental illness, willful misbehavior, purposeful malevolence, or moral failings.

- AD undermines the preferred view of the person with the disease, their family members, friends, and/or paid caregivers. As the disease progresses, they all experience the universal challenge to their long-held images of personal agency and competency as a result of the devastation of the illness and the corresponding loss of options they might normally use in the face of other illnesses to "fix it."

- Not all behavioral phenomena observed in people with AD are attributable to symptoms of dementia, per se, and thus, those who provide care can help achieve optimal quality of life by mobilizing the personal resources of the person with AD to achieve better adjustment to life with dementia.

- People with AD respond better and use their remaining strengths when they are presented with attractive opportunities to do things that fit their preferred view as adults than if they are faced with demands for mandatory participation in situations built around the illness paradigm in which everything is centered on therapy.

- Person-centered care mobilizes and makes optimum use of the strengths of people with AD and the people with whom they interact.

THE OBJECT OF CARE

The experience of a person with amnesia was characterized as his or her "having lost faith in actuality" (Palmer, 2000). If professionals provide care to people with dementia and other forms of amnesia amid a battle over actuality, they will win the battle and lose the war. The object of such care is the person (with dementia) as she knows him- or herself. The object is not to get the individual to see reality as others do, if only for a moment, before care is given. By doing that, one asks the person to lose faith in his or her own actuality—where the self still exists.

REFERENCES

Alzheimer, A. (1906). Uber einen eigenartigen schweren Krankheitsprozess der Hirnrinde [Remarks about a peculiar, severe disease process of the cortex]. *Neurologisches Centralblatt, 25,* 1134.

Alzheimer, A. (1907). Uber eine eigenartige Erkrankung der Hirnrinde [A peculiar disease of the cortex]. *Allegemeine Zeitschrift fur Psychiatrie, 64,* 146–148.

Blessed, G., Tomlinson, B.E., & Roth, M. (1968). The association between quantitative measures of dementia and senile change in the cerebral grey matter of elderly subjects. *British Journal of Psychiatry, 114,* 797–811.

Bowker, L. (1982). *Humanizing institutions for the aging.* Lexington, MA: Lexington Books.

Bradley, A.M., Ronch, J.L., & Pohlmann, E. (1999). The EDGE project. Retrieved from Dementia Solutions Web site: http://www.dementiasolutions.com.

Buber, M. (1970). *I and thou.* New York: Charles Scribner's Sons.

Cohen, D., Kennedy, G., & Eisdorfer, C. (1984). Phases of change in the patient with Alzheimer's dementia: A conceptual dimension for defining health-care management. *Journal of the American Geriatrics Society, 32*(1), 11–15.

Cohen, D., & Eisdorfer, C. (1986). *The loss of self: A family resource for the care of Alzheimer's disease and related disorders.* New York: Norton.

Cohen, G. (1997). Progress in Alzheimer's disease-pause and perspective. *American Journal of Geriatric Psychiatry, 5,* 185–187.

Cohen-Mansfield, J. (2000). Theoretical frameworks for behavioral problems in dementia. *Alzheimers Care Quarterly, 1*(4), 8–21.

Cotrell, V., & Schulz, R. (1993). The perspective of the patient with Alzheimer's disease: A dimension of dementia research. *The Gerontologist, 37,* 205–211.

Cousins, N. (1974). *Anatomy of an illness as perceived by the patient.* New York: W. W. Norton and Company.

Cousins, N. (1989). *Head first: The biology of hope.* New York: E.P. Dutton.

Damasio, A. (1994). *Descartes' error.* New York: Avon Books.

Damasio, A. (1999). *The feeling of what happens.* New York: Harcourt Brace.

Eron, J., & Lund, T. (1996). *Narrative solutions in brief therapy.* New York: Guilford Press.

Fagan, R., Williams, C., & Burger, S. (1997, October 1). *Meeting of pioneers in nursing home culture change: Final report.* Privately distributed by the authors.

Feinberg, J. (Ed.). (2000). Medication and aging. *Generations, 24,* 4.

Feinberg, T. (2001). *Altered egos: How the brain creates the self.* New York: Oxford University Press.

Folstein, M.E., Folstein, S.E., & McHugh, P.R. (1975). Mini-Mental State: A practical method for grading the cognitive state of patients for the clinician. *Journal of Psychiatric Research, 12,* 189–198.

Fox, P. (1989). From senility to Alzheimer's disease: The rise of the Alzheimer's disease movement. *The Milbank Quarterly, 67*(1), 58–102.

Frank, A.W. (1996). *The wounded storyteller: Body, illness and ethics.* Chicago: University of Chicago Press.

Gadamer, H. (1993). *The enigma of health: The art of healing in a scientific age* (Translated by J. Geiger & N. Walker). Stanford, CA: Stanford University Press.

Gerdner, L. (2000). Effects of individualized versus classical music on the frequency of agitation in elderly persons with Alzheimer's disease. *International Psychogeriatrics, 12*(1), 49–65.

Goldfarb, A. (1961). Current trends in the management of the psychiatrically ill aged. In P.H. Hoch & J. Zubin (Eds.), *Psychopathology of aging* (pp. 248–265). New York: Grune & Stratton.

Goldfarb, A. (1969). The psychodynamics of dependency and the search for aid. In R.A. Kalish (Ed.), *The dependencies of old people* (pp. 1–15). Ann Arbor: Institute of Gerontology, University of Michigan.

Goldfarb, A. (1974). Institutional care of the aged. In E.W. Busse & E. Pfeiffer (Eds.), *Behavior and adaptation in later life* (pp. 264–292). Washington, DC: American Psychiatric Association.

Goldsmith, M. (1996). *Hearing the voice of people with dementia: Opportunities and obstacles.* London, England: Jessica Kingsley Publishers.

Holmes, D., Ory, M., & Teresi, J. (1994). Special dementia care: Research and practice issues. *Alzheimers Disease and Associated Disorders: An International Journal, 8*(Suppl. 1).

Katzman, R. (1976). The prevalence and malignancy of Alzheimers disease. *Archives of Neurology, 33,* 217–218.

Katzman, R., & Karasu, T. (1975). Differential diagnosis of dementia. In W. Fields (Ed.), *Neurological and sensory disorders in the elderly* (pp. 103–134). New York: Intercontinental Medical Book Corp.

Katzman, R., Terry, R., & Bick, K. (1978). *Alzheimer's disease: Senile dementia and related disorders.* New York: Raven Press.

Kennedy, G. (1995). The geriatric syndrome of late-life depression. *Psychiatric Services, 46*(1), 43–48.

Kitwood, T. (1997). *Dementia reconsidered: The person comes first.* Buckingham, England: Open University Press.

Kleinman, A. (1988). *The illness narratives: Suffering, healing and the human condition.* New York: Basic Books.

Lawler, B. (1995). Possible neurological basis for behavioral symptoms. In B. Lawler (Ed.), *Behavioral complications in Alzheimer's disease* (pp. 91–127). Washington, DC: American Psychiatric Press.

Luria, A. (1985). In O. Sacks, *The man who mistook his wife for a hat* (p. 32). New York: Summit Books.

Lyman, K. (1989). Bringing the social back in: A critique of the biomedicalization of dementia. *The Gerontologist, 29,* 597–605.

Mace, N., & Rabins, P. (1981). *The thirty-six hour day.* Baltimore: The Johns Hopkins University Press.

Maletta, G. (1992). Treatment of behavior symptomatology in Alzheimer's disease with emphasis on aggression: Current clinical approaches. *International Psychogeriatrics, 4*(Suppl. 1), 117–130.

Morris, D. (2000). *Illness and culture in the postmodern age.* Berkeley: University of California Press.

Palmer, T. (2000). Dream science. In J. Lethem (Ed.), *The Vintage book of amnesia* (pp. 3–20). New York: Vintage Books.

Pierce, C.P. (2000). *Hard to forget.* New York: Random House.

Post, S. (1995). *The moral challenge of Alzheimers disease.* Baltimore: The Johns Hopkins University Press.

Roach, M. (1985). *Another name for madness.* Boston: Houghton Mifflin.

Rogers, J., Holm, M., Burgio, L., Hso, C., Hardin, J.M., & McDowell, B.J. (2000). Excess disability during morning care in nursing home residents with dementia. *International Psychogeriatrics, 12*(2), 267–282.

Ronch, J. (1987). Specialized Alzheimer units in nursing homes: Pros and cons. *American Journal of Alzheimers Care and Related Disorders and Research, 2,* 10–19.

Ronch, J. (1996). Assessment of quality of life: Preservation of the self. *International Psychogeriatrics, 8,* 267–275.

Ronch, J., & Crispi, E.L. (1997). Opportunities for development via group psychotherapy in the nursing home. *Group, 21*(2), 135–158.

Sacks, O. (1985). *The man who mistook his wife for a hat.* New York: Summit Books.

Salovey, P., Rothman, A., Detweiler, J., & Steward, W. (2000). Emotional states and physical health. *American Psychologist, 55*(1), 110–121.

Scheibe, K. (1989). Memory, identity, history and the understanding of dementia. In L. Thomas (Ed.), *Research on adulthood and aging; The human science approach* (pp. 141–162). Albany: State University of New York Press.

Taylor, S., Kemeny, M., Reed, G., Bower, J., & Greenwald, T. (2000). Psychological resources, positive illusions and health. *American Psychologist, 55*(1), 99–109.

Teresi, J., Lawton, M.P., Ory, M., & Holmes, D. (1994). Measurement issues in chronic care populations: Dementia special care. In D. Holmes, M. Ory, & J. Teresi (Eds.), Special dementia care: Research and practice issues. *Alzheimers Disease and Associated Disorders: An International Journal, 8*(Suppl.1).

Teri, L., & Gallagher-Thompson, D. (1991). Cognitive-behavioral interventions for treatment of depression in Alzheimer's patients. *The Gerontologist, 31,* 413–416.

Terry, R.D. (1963). The fine structure of neurofibrillary tangles in Alzheimer's disease. *Journal of Neuropathology and Experimental Neurology, 22,* 629–634.

Torack, R. (1983). The early history of senile dementia. In B. Reisberg (Ed.), *Alzheimers disease: The standard reference* (pp. 23–28). New York: The Free Press.

ON LEARNING THAT I work with individuals with Alzheimer's disease, people regularly volunteer their suicidal thoughts to me: "As long as my mind is working, I'd like to live a long life. When that starts to go . . . I'm finished. Just put me out of my misery. What's the point?"

15

LESSONS FROM THE LIFELINES WRITING GROUP FOR PEOPLE IN THE EARLY STAGES OF ALZHEIMER'S DISEASE

Forgetting that We Don't Remember

Alan Dienstag

FEW ILLNESSES INSPIRE the kind of dread as that caused by the prospect of Alzheimer's disease—which is understandable. For people in the early stages of the illness who are experiencing impairments but still entirely cognizant of the dissolution that lays ahead, the challenge is to construct a life in the shadow of an advancing darkness: to answer the question, "What is the point?"

Professionals working to improve the lives of people in the early stages of Alzheimer's disease should be able to fashion a meaningful response to this question. The difficulty lies in the fact that despite our best efforts, our attention is continually drawn to the unraveling taking place before us. The individuals' strengths and character, the very core of the person with whom we are interacting, seem to recede.

As we watch our clients lose their memories, powerful feelings surface that have a profound effect on how we think about our work. These feelings can narrow our field of vision in ways that are often insidious and make it difficult to think creatively about possibilities. This was the first among many lessons I learned through my experience with the Lifelines Writing Group.

As someone who has run support groups for people in the early stages of Alzheimer's disease since 1995, I did not think I needed to be convinced that valuable psychological work could be done with people in the early stages of the illness. I saw firsthand that, allowing for modifications in the process, the benefits of supportive group psychotherapy for people with serious medical illnesses could be extended to people in the early stages of Alzheimer's disease. With these groups, individuals were not only supported but also encouraged to grow. I was resolute in encouraging group members to resist being defined by what they could *not* do and inspired by their valiant efforts to find meaning and purpose in their lives. Despite this, my sense of the therapeutic possibilities available for these people now appears to have been limited in some important ways.

In the spring of 1996, I got a call from the director of the local Alzheimer's Association chapter. She told me that a member of a caregiver support group was married to a writer who wanted to speak with someone about using writing as a therapy for people with Alzheimer's disease. She asked if she could give him my name and number. I agreed but was not enthused. I thought that this was not a good idea and would be unlikely to succeed. The activity would be too frustrating, too dependent on an interest in writing, too solitary, and so forth. I was also not excited about having to explain all of this to someone who was surely well intentioned but, in all likelihood, naïve and unrealistic. When I realized that I was going to be speaking with Don DeLillo, a highly acclaimed and renowned author, I was more intrigued but still unconvinced. We discussed the difficulties and, in the course of our discussion, Don said something that sparked my curiosity. He talked about the experience of writing as a more concentrated type of thinking. "Writing is a form of memory," he said.

Writing is a form of memory. The phrase stayed with me for some time. I repeated it to myself and told it to others with whom I worked. I realized that for all of my work with people with memory impairments, I had thought very little about memory. To the extent that I thought about memory at all, it was in fact about the *loss* of memory. It had never really occurred to me to think about other forms of memory and the possibilities inherent in them. It was a writer's insight on the nature of memory that suggested these possibilities, and although I still had only a vague idea of how we might put them to work, I saw the potential and committed to working out an intervention plan with Don.

We agreed that working in a group would reduce some of the pressure on any particular member to perform. We also agreed that the group would be neither a class nor a therapy group per se. Writing would not be taught or critiqued and written self-expression would be valued above all else. Don and I would function as co-leaders, providing support and encouragement as needed. I believed that the writing should be done during the group time and left with us at the end of the session. This took the burden of locating and remembering a notebook every week from the participants and their family members. It also freed the group from the onus and pressure of assignments. Group members would write and read their work to one another and discuss whatever came up in the process.

As with all successful collaborations, ours had many advantages that could not be designed or "worked through." Don, who was shy and reserved by nature, was perfectly content to let me "run" the group. This is not to suggest that his role was less important. Don contributed to the group in a way that was uniquely suited to his identity and expertise; he was critical to its success. If I had run the group by myself, it would have inevitably evolved into writing as *therapy*, but Don's involvement guaranteed that the focus on writing would be maintained. His belief that people need stories to live, and his appreciation of the unique value of writing as a means of expression, elevated the group members' efforts.

In our group, my clinical sensibilities and Don's creative sensibilities intermingled. The group's functioning was more of an intuitive and creative process than existed in other groups I had led. Don had no interest in "teaching" writing, and I was not inclined to run a traditional therapy group as long as he was around. Our primary focus was on making people comfortable and structuring the group so that people would be inspired to write. The fact that I was making no effort to place the work of the group into some kind of traditional psychotherapeutic framework enabled me to see and understand my work with group members in a fresh way.

> THE FACT THAT I WAS making no effort to place the work of the group into some kind of traditional psychotherapeutic framework enabled me to see and understand my work with group members in a fresh way.

Our goal was to stimulate memories and feelings. We began by devising a list of topics, one or two of which we would present at each meeting, which might serve as a point of departure. The original list was made up of the following subjects/titles:

- I remember . . .
- My friend
- An unforgettable person
- The house where I grew up
- Summer memories
- The last time I saw . . .
- The ocean
- What is happening to me
- Birthdays
- My doctor
- A movie
- My mother's voice

- My father's hands
- A photograph
- What other people notice
- A precious object
- The future
- My life now

Group members were free to reject these and choose their own, ask for another suggestion, or not write at all. We followed a strict no-pressure policy. Don came up with the official name of our undertaking: Lifelines: Alzheimer's Narratives. Over time, this changed to The Lifelines Writing Group.

The criteria for inclusion in the group were as follows:

- Confirmed diagnosis of Alzheimer's or related dementia
- Awareness and understanding of the diagnosis
- Sufficient physical stamina to participate in a 90-minute group
- Sufficient cognitive and language abilities to communicate and to form relationships with other group members as well as to understand the rules of the group
- Willingness and ability to write (potential participants were asked to write "a few sentences" about their day or a favorite activity in the screening interview)

Our first efforts at recruitment through announcements in the Alzheimer's Association newsletters and in the local paper were not successful. Very few people called, and those who did were interested in activities for individuals who had not yet been diagnosed with Alzheimer's disease or whose illness was more advanced. Initially, we hoped to reach out beyond the relatively small group of people already being seen in early-stage support groups. It became clear, though, that for many people among the population from which we were recruiting the idea of writing "in public" was intimidating. Consequently, we turned to two support groups in the New York City area and focused our efforts on them. We were able to easily recruit six group members from these two groups and set a date to begin.

Offering the group to people who were already support-group members turned out to have significant advantages. The screening process could be streamlined, and the group members' familiarity with one another helped them to relax. An interesting synergy developed between the two experiences. They were distinct but also complementary. Group members often would continue a discussion that had begun in their support group in our writing group. We used these themes at times to generate subjects for writing. Group members also reported feeling a deepening sense of understanding and connection with their writing colleagues to their support group leaders.

The first topic we presented to the group, and one that we returned to several times, consisted simply of two words followed by ellipses: "I remember . . . ."

Here is what group members wrote in response (spelling and punctuation are verbatim):

- From Ron, a 68-year-old who spoke very little in his support group:

  I remember how nervous I'd been at various times in my life—for no reason at all. I remember how so few of them ever came to fruition.

- From Elizabeth, a 73-year-old retired nurse:

  I remember when I was a little girl sitting under a tree during the eclipse. It got dark and the birds went to bed.

  I remember that I want to make a boke of what I have things that I have had in my life.

  I can remember picking a fig from a tree in Athens. My lover watched me with delight.

- From Charlotte, an 84-year-old:

  I remember the first time I walked with my parents on the bridge that went to Brooklyn. It was hard for me and I fell very often. My father would pick me up and carry me for a while and put me back to walk. It took a little time to learn to walk all the way but I did. I remember as I write this about the cat that lived with us who also like to walk and when he saw us ready to go he was right with us and we loved it.

  I carried a love for walking all through my life, and even now when things go bad I walk and things seem to get better.

  I hope I'll be able to walk as long as I live.

- From Sarita, an 86-year-old retired psychotherapist:

  I remember when Poppa's horse brought him home and Poppa having fallen back in his seat. I heard Mamma's outcry as she rushed out and maybe brother Lou was there or brother Nat—because he was brought in and laid on the bed in the downstairs bedroom. Mamma gathered all us kids together and sent us down to Mrs. Carr's house which was always so clean and neat and we spent the night there.

  The next morning we all returned home and I looked out of the bedroom sitting room window I think I saw a hearse going down the street. But I was really happy because someone had left an orange and it was all mine.

From the outset, I was surprised at the directness and poignancy of the work produced by the group. I shared the writing with the co-leaders of the support group to which many of the writing group members belonged. These co-leaders were struck by the amount of feeling in the work and by the ways that the writing presented new facets or information about people that they had come to know quite well. The writing seemed to open a different door into the lives of these people.

Very quickly, the group settled into a comfortable pattern of working, in which we would meet, talk together about what was on people's minds for a time, and then write and read the work.

INTERESTINGLY, IN THE moments when the group would fall silent and settle into writing, my own memory was often stimulated. I remembered school-mates, childhood friends, and visits with long-forgotten relatives.

Interestingly, in the moments when the group would fall silent and settle into writing, my own memory was often stimulated. I remembered schoolmates, childhood friends, and visits with long-forgotten relatives. The setting very powerfully evoked in me positive recollections of being in a hushed classroom and concentrating on an assignment. I recalled vividly the quiet pleasure of thinking and the comfort of the group quietly thinking together. This was a particular kind of quiet that I had not thought of in many years, and it was the sound I heard when the writing group did its work.

One important aspect of memory and group dynamics that I had overlooked in my work with these people prior to this experience was that many things are transmittable within groups. This includes everything from feelings to coughs. Although I am very familiar with emotional contagion in the group setting, I had never thought of how this might also apply to the mental activity of writing and remembering. We tend to think of these activities as solitary, and often they are, but the effect of group contagion operates here as well. When individuals are around others who are doing a writing and remembering activity, this serves as a powerful inducement to do it themselves.

How does understanding this phenomenon translate into helping people who are forgetting? One answer that emerged from the Lifelines group is that we should surround people who are forgetting with *acts of remembering*. People in the early stages of Alzheimer's disease are in danger of forgetting that they can still remember, as are those of us who work with people with Alzheimer's.

Writing and remembering became the work of the group, then, and once the routine was established and a level of acceptance and security had been reached, group members took to the task with surprisingly little resistance. Often, individuals requested help spelling or finding a word. Occasionally, a group member would laugh or start to cry while writing, and of course some participants became frustrated when words and thoughts that once flowed became tangled and confused or stopped altogether. When gentle encouragement failed to help, I sometimes offered to have a group member dictate his or her thoughts to me or I would just write words that would help the person remember a story to tell us. Stories written or told with great difficulty were almost always worth the effort. A particular example of this was the work of a woman named Charlotte, mentioned previously.

Charlotte

For many years, Charlotte had written a column that appeared in the newsletter of a Jewish women's organization and was especially distressed by the loss of her writing abilities. Charlotte had joined our group with a good deal of apprehension. She had been with us for 1 ½ years (during which her abilities declined steadily) when we asked group members to write something that would be entitled "My Doctor."

Charlotte struggled mightily to write the following in an almost indecipherable script:

My Docter

My life if my life was growing in going to going—

    My mother lost her first darghter when she was one hear and when I was born mother watched me although all the time.

    I reamontay when my brother and I bosh my mother called the Docter and up the six flights and said was very sick My parents worred a lot and the Docter soften his and said do worred she will life for all time.

Charlotte fought despair with every word and gave up repeatedly, trying to read and explain her story to the group. Eventually it became quite clear what she was writing about. Her story was about her mother's fear over losing another child, the impact this had on Charlotte and her brother, and her gratitude to the doctor, whose voice she still remembered softening as he reassured her mother that she was fine and would live for a long time. "I was glad for that voice," she said with a smile. After reading the story she went on to explain that she and her brother did everything they could to conceal any sign of illness from their mother. This piece of information certainly helped me understand her stubborn unwillingness to consult with a doctor at various times over the 2 years that she was in the group. More important, it was a heroic act of recollection and self-expression at a level of emotional connectedness and specificity that was not readily available in other ways.

Charlotte's spontaneous verbal contributions to the group were growing infrequent at this point in her participation; yet here was an essential part of her life story that she was able to reconnect to and to communicate to us through the act of writing.

GROUP SATISFACTION

Through group members' participation and attendance, I realized that they looked forward to our meetings. They expressed surprise at what they remembered and satisfaction that they were part of such a group. The writing seemed not to remind them so much about what they could *not* do, or if it did, this awareness did not predominate. Of course, there were those for whom the frustration was too great, and even among those who participated eagerly, the time came when they could no longer write well enough to continue.

As the group flourished, I began thinking more about the nature of the experience and ways of explaining it. These musings led me to think about my own grandmother who had died shortly before we started the Lifelines group. When she reached a certain age, my grandmother started giving her possessions away. This was imperceptible at first but became obvious over time. It got so that I had to think twice before admiring anything of hers or even glancing too long at something lest I be required to take it with me.

Occasionally I would protest—but it was of no use. Her determination and the obvious pleasure she derived in this giving away were too great. She would say things such as "I want to *see* you enjoy this . . . " or "I want you to have this now." The objects she gave me covered the full range of the old-closet spectrum: a jazzy black suit of my grandfather's that fit me perfectly, cufflinks and studs inlaid with opaque reddish earthen stones, dishes and servers of every description, lamps, sea shell–encrusted salt and pepper shakers with missing shells, and dusty bed sheets deeply yellowed at the creases from being folded for 35 years. What she gave was what she had saved, and this was their value.

As she neared the end of her life, my grandmother seemed to understand that if you can give something away, you don't lose it. This, as it turns out, is as true of memories as it is of objects and is yet another aspect of memory that is often overlooked. Memories are, in a sense, fungible. Writing is a form of memory, and unlike the spoken word, leaves a mark in the physical world. As a form of memory, writing creates possibilities for remembering, for the sharing and safeguarding of memories not provided by talking. The writing group gave memory back to its members. They were transformed in the experience of writing from *people who forget* to *people who remember*. A member of the writing group once said that when the group was together " . . . we forget that we don't remember." This is a statement of cure, not of the biological and cellular disorder, but of the human disorder, the disorder of loss of personhood brought about by Alzheimer's disease.

> THE WRITING GROUP gave memory back to its members. They were transformed in the experience of writing from *people who forget* to *people who remember.*

If the writing gave memory back to the group members, then the reading—the moment at which the entire group would fall silent and listen—returned something equally essential: the power to give. The thought content of people in the later stages of Alzheimer's disease is described in clinical terms as "impoverished." Alzheimer's disease is an illness in which the losses accumulate moment by moment and day by day. Giving reverses the tide and represents a refusal to be defined by loss. Members of the writing group regularly enriched themselves by giving to one another their most precious possessions.

As the writing became more difficult for group members, yet another important transformation took place. We began to re-read the old work and it became clear that in most cases, the members could not recall having written it and would not likely recall what they had written about spontaneously or be able to write about it with the same richness as they had in the past. We took great pleasure in this reading and in the re-discovery of old memories, however. Here was recollection in the literal sense of the word, a reclaiming through writing and reading of lost parts of the self. "I haven't thought about that in 40 years!"— how often we heard these or similar words while running the group, and what a deep sense of accomplishment and satisfaction they inspired in all of us. During these moments of writing and reading, long-lost memories of friends and family, strangers encountered on trips or at crucial moments, once-precious objects, feelings of joy and sorrow, lessons learned, all became threads of the fabric of life that sprang back along with individuals' sense of self.

A FITTING END

After operating continuously for 2 years, the group appeared to have run its course. Illness and cognitive deterioration were taking their toll. It became harder and harder to get the group members to write new material, and when they did, they wrote much less. We thought inviting family and friends to a reading would be a fitting end to our work together and the group members supported the idea wholeheartedly. The group members could not choose which stories to read from among the many they had written and asked me to make the selections. Prior to our final meeting, I collected their stories and bound them in a book with their names inscribed on the front. When we met for the last time as a group, I returned their memories to them and watched as they leafed through the pages smiling, laughing, crying—remembering their "selves" and their stories. At our reading they recollected these memories yet again, and left their stories to be safeguarded by friends and loved ones, beyond the clutches of disease.

SUMMARY

The challenge of putting Don DeLillo's observation about writing and memory to work for people in the early stages of Alzheimer's disease brought to light aspects of memory and the psychology of people experiencing memory loss that I knew about but had failed to put to any therapeutic use. I would summarize the most important of these aspects as follows: Writing is a form of memory. As a form of memory, its characteristics create some unique therapeutic possibilities for people with Alzheimer's disease. Because it presents another way of remembering, it provides an individual with additional experiences of being a remembering person and access to different kinds of memories. Perhaps most important, it returns to those whose memories are failing the opportunity to experience and share the memories they have. In this respect, the writing group transformed a weakness into a strength.

What was true of the writing was also true of the reading. In reading the written work, the insecurity of unprompted verbal recall (a factor that over time tends to discourage talking in this population) was replaced with something that is not only tangible and therefore more secure but also lasting. The group format seemed to extend and intensify these effects as well as to provide therapeutic benefit in more traditional ways. In a remark that beautifully encapsulated the acceptance, recognition, and sense of belonging found in the group, one of our members put it this way: "We may not remember everything, but we remember each other and I'm a part of everyone here."

A patient of mine in the early stages of Alzheimer's disease once said, "I feel like a picture that's fading; every time I look, there is less of me here. I almost don't recognize myself." Watching the group members in their struggle to remember, write, and read their work is a moving experience on many levels. One of these is surely our awareness that the picture is fading along with the sparks of recognition. This awareness lends a poignancy and triumph to the work with which one can identify. In this identification there is also a healing of the breach that separates us from people with Alzheimer's. We all know what fading is like, and we all know that our fate is not so different from theirs. The triumph is temporary; it is of this moment, but it is the triumph of life over death. If we do need stories to live, then these are truly lifelines, acts of writing that are life preserving.

The members of the Lifelines Writing Group have taught us about the power of writing and the nature of memory and memory loss. Their lifelines have also served as a means of closing the psychological distance between the Alzheimer's and non-Alzheimer's world. Perhaps most importantly, they have demonstrated that there is a way to give meaning to the precarious station in life in which they find themselves, and they suggest a path for others in the early stages of Alzheimer's to follow: to live with memories; to give them to others; and to preserve in some form a record of who you are, who you were, and who you wanted to be in this world before it slips away.

16

EXPLORING THE CREATIVE POTENTIAL OF PEOPLE WITH ALZHEIMER'S DISEASE AND RELATED DEMENTIA

Dare to Imagine

Anne Davis Basting

NARRATIVE THERAPIES can be enormously effective with people of all ages who are able to follow a *linear, narrative structure*. Because individuals with Alzheimer's disease and related dementia (ADRD) are unable to conform to the linear aspect of that structure, however, therapists are challenged to expand their understanding of *non-linear narrative*. Non-linear narrative is in the realm of poetry and experimental, artistic expression that has been recognized in the arts in various forms for more than two centuries.

Gene Cohen (2000), author of Chapter 5, described creativity as the process of bringing something new into the world that has value. To truly encourage creative expression, therapists and caregivers must give it enough value so that it is taken seriously. The creative expressions of people with dementia, which, to observers may range from the ridiculous to the sublime, should not merely be categorized as the end products of therapy, but recognized as art that can teach people without cognitive disorders something about the meaning of living with ADRD.

When memory fades and one's grasp on the factual building blocks of one's life loosens, what remains? Is a person still capable of growth and creative expression even when dementia strikes? To answer these questions, I relay the story of the Time*Slips* Project. But first, some background is necessary. My work in creative expression began in 1996, when I experimented with a variety of creative activities with people with ADRD. I worked in a wing of a long-term care center, where the noises of blaring televisions, radios, and alarms and the administering of medication made it exceedingly chaotic and difficult for both clients and staff to concentrate. Despite these interruptions, however, after trying a series of exercises, I found one that worked consistently. Rather than ask clients to reminisce, I asked them to work together to make up a story from their imaginations. Inevitably, clients would share fragments of memories. But the shift in expectation—from asking them to retrieve memories to asking them to create—invited them to enter the story with whatever sound, gesture, or morsel of language they could summon. The storytelling process invited them to share their strengths in symbolic expression.

As a playwright and scholar of avant-garde drama, I had few expectations of linearity in narrative forms; I could follow the strands of their stories into faraway places with multiple names in multiple times. The stories that developed from my work were not about a linear narrative's beginning, middle, rising action, and denouement falling into resolution. They were about opening the rules of narrative so that metaphors and images of the storytellers' fears and desires could find a place for expression; they were about laughing, singing, and hearing the emotional meaning behind garbled words. They were also about staff, volunteers, and family members relaxing their expectations and learning a new language in which they could communicate with individuals with dementia. The group's emphasis in the storytelling circles was on an individual's creativity rather than memory. This wasn't always an easy transition for participants to make: Throughout the study, when facilitators first began working with a group of storytellers to create stories by asking probing questions, the participants usually relied on the default expectation of memory. Even clients in the middle stages of ADRD are often aware that their memories are impaired. When parts of speech are beyond their reach, they smile, gesture, and use kindly *cover phrases* such as "Do you think so?" or "Oh yes; me too" to help them confidently answer all questions. "I don't know," said most storytellers. "I used to know, but I don't know anymore." The facilitators encouraged the transition to creativity by saying something like, "You know what? I don't know either! We can make up whatever we want. We're making up a new story."

Our aim for the evaluation of the storytelling process was twofold: to look for behavioral changes in the storytellers and to look for shifts in attitudes of the student facilitators, staff, and primary family caregivers. I began the research with the assumption that selfhood is relational and that improving the quality of life for people with Alzheimer's disease is contingent on improving their relationships with those people who care for them.

In this chapter, I outline the storytelling method that resulted in the Time*Slips* project and my study of it; analyze the content of the stories; describe interviews with staff, family caregivers, and student participants; and discuss the Time*Slips* outreach program's effectiveness in changing public perception of people with ADRD.

THE STORYTELLING METHOD

The Time*Slips* storytelling method evolved out of a year of experimenting with a variety of exercises in creative dramatics.[1] After espousing the virtues of theatrical performance for older adults in my research on senior theater troupes across the United States, I wanted to see if "playing a new role" could benefit people with ADRD as much as it did older adults without ADRD.

People with dementia have few meaningful social roles available to them. With holes where memories of their children and spouses used to be, people with ADRD often lose even a sense of the most basic roles held by individuals—including partner, parent, sibling, or child. In creating the Time*Slips* method, I set about to establish a social role for people with ADRD—that of storyteller—which would, in turn, provide access to meaningful self-expression.

After running a storytelling circle for 3 months in a long-term care facility, I set up a research study of the storytelling method to test its effectiveness in four adult day centers: two in Milwaukee, Wisconsin, and two in New York City. Although the storytelling method has evolved since the research study began in 1998, I describe here the structure of the initial storytelling circles in these adult day center test sites.

THE STRUCTURE OF THE SESSION

The Time*Slips* storytelling method followed a clear, ritualized structure. At least once a week, a group of people with symptoms consistent with middle-stage Alzheimer's disease gathered in a circle of chairs. My program assistant and I trained undergraduate students from a wide range of disciplines (predominantly in the humanities and arts) to facilitate the storytelling. Throughout this chapter, I refer to students and staff as "facilitators" and the people with ADRD as "storytellers." Students and staff worked together to encourage the storytellers to respond to a picture the students brought in each week.

The storytelling circles began with a "welcome," in which the facilitators introduced the activity and greeted the storytellers. With the exception of the very first session, facilitators would then tell a story that had been created by story-

[1]The research phase of the Time*Slips* Project received support from the Helen Bader Foundation, Inc., the Fan Fox and Leslie Samuels Foundation, The Isaac H. Tuttle Fund, The Brookdale Foundation, the Extendicare Foundation, BlueCross & BlueShield, the University of Wisconsin–Milwaukee, and the Brookdale Center on Aging/Hunter College.

tellers the previous week to prove to the participants that they were indeed capable of creative expression. Next, facilitators handed out an image such as a photograph or illustration to each member of the storytelling circle and asked the group open-ended questions (avoiding "yes" or "no" questions). Facilitators used a wide variety of images, but all of the images shared one characteristic—they appeared staged or fantastical in some way. We avoided images of celebrities or family photographs because we found that storytellers became too fixated on the real story behind the image to freely launch into the realm of the imagination. The images guided facilitators in their choice of questions, which were carefully worded to give the storytellers ownership of the story. Instead of "What is this character's name?" for example, a facilitator asked, "What would you like to call him?" Questions focused on the sensory ("What sounds do you imagine in the background?") and on the world outside the environment depicted in the picture ("Does he have a family?"). One facilitator wrote down all of the responses on a sketchpad large enough for all of the storytellers to see. All responses, including any nonsensical answers, were validated and woven into the fabric of the story.

The free-form storytelling process demanded that facilitators leave behind preconceived notions of what constitutes a *story*. If several storytellers responded with names for a single character, that character had several names. Events often took place in several places at once. Multiple plot turns created a meandering storyline that read more like a chronicle of the storytelling process than a traditional, linear story with a clear beginning, middle, and end, or one that focused on conflict and resolution.

THE FREE-FORM storytelling process demanded that facilitators leave behind preconceived notions of what constitutes a *story*. If several storytellers responded with names for a single character, that character had several names.

Because facilitators reassured the storytellers that they could say anything they wanted to because they were making up a new story, the facilitators often received answers that did not make sense to them. These nonsensical answers were of two kinds. First, some were clearly meant to challenge the facilitators' promise that they would accept any answer. We referred to these as "challenge" answers. In one exchange, for example, a facilitator asked for a name of a character and promised she would accept any answer. A storyteller looked up at her slyly and said "Oh, yeah? ABCDEFG." The facilitator wrote down the response and the name "ABCDEFG" became part of the story. The second type of nonsensical answer was related to symptoms of ADRD. Several storytellers in each group had great difficulty with language, for example. As the storytelling workshops proceeded and they grew to trust the process, these storytellers would often respond by adding fragmented words or sounds. Facilitators repeated these answers back to them and wrote them down as best as they could to capture them.

Facilitators re-read the story when they noticed the storytellers' attention starting to drift. The telling of a single story often lasted up to an hour, but most ran 30 minutes on average. In the final step in the ritual, as a way to acknowledge the risk and energy demanded by a full hour of creative storytelling, facilitators thanked each storyteller for his or her input.

THE OUTREACH PROGRAM

The second goal of the Time*Slips* Project was to share the stories that emerged in the storytelling circles with the public in order to increase awareness of the creative capacity of people with ADRD. We did this in several ways. First, the facilitators and Time*Slips* staff created books of the stories told at each center and presented them to the storytellers and their families in celebrations held at each facility. Second, in both Milwaukee and New York, a team of artists associated with the project created a professional play production (with professional actors) and an art exhibit inspired by the stories told in each city. Each performance of the play was followed by a post-show discussion in which audience members could share their reactions to the stories and ask questions about the disease. Third, we created a website that included stories from all four test sites as well as detailed information about the history and aims of the project.

THE RESEARCH MODEL

We received approval from the Institutional Research Board (IRB) at the University of Wisconsin—Milwaukee and secured consent forms from all participating staff, students, and family caregivers as well as assent forms from all participants with ADRD. My assistant and I interviewed staff, students, and primary family caregivers at the outset of the project, in the middle of the storytelling sessions, and again at the end of the project. We held the interviews in person or over the telephone, depending on the interviewee's preference. The interviews were "open-structure," loosely following our aim to assess their reactions to and observations of the storytelling sessions without leaning on a prefabricated set of questions. The responses that I share here retain the anonymity of the subjects. Gender or other details of the respondents may be changed to protect their identity. In this chapter, I refer to the adult day center test sites as A and B (in Milwaukee), and C and D (in New York).

To test the outreach model, we received approval from the Hunter College IRB. The main aim of this study was to test whether the art exhibit and/or play production generated a change in audience members' perceptions of the creative potential of people with ADRD. To address this, Time*Slips* staff created an evaluation form and inserted them in each play program. A separate evaluation was also available at the art exhibit. All responses were anonymous. Although we held a play and art exhibit in Milwaukee, all responses were anecdotal. This research, therefore, focuses on the New York play and art exhibit.

ANALYSIS OF THE STORIES

All told, the storytelling workshops in all four sites yielded more than 100 stories. Some stories were only partially complete because facilitators tried to squeeze in one more tale before the hour was over. I discerned the stories' main themes and noted their unique qualities, such as the prevalence of humor or nonsensical answers. Although the stories reflected the unique personality and diversity of each storytelling group, several themes emerged in all four groups, including humor and the desires for freedom and human connection. I focus on individual groups first, and then turn to themes that appeared in all four. I mainly refer to portions of stories. A full story appears at the end of this chapter, and others are available on the project's website (www.timeslips.org).

ALTHOUGH THE stories reflected the unique personality and diversity of each story-telling group, several themes emerged in all four groups, including humor and the desires for freedom and human connection.

CENTER A Storytelling workshops in Center A featured a fairly consistent group of up to twelve enthusiastic participants who regularly added songs and even dances to their stories. Of the 17 stories I analyzed, humor was a consistent theme in all of them, and eight of them featured main characters who were happy, confident, and likable. These characters commonly encountered social obstacles, including the negative opinions of people around them. The characters usually overcame these obstacles by remaining true to themselves.

The most common theme was the desire for freedom—to make decisions, to be uninhibited, and to make choices. In "All the Way to Seattle," a woman pilot flies "because it makes her feel free and because her family doesn't pay her enough attention." In another story, "Italians From Ireland Getting Their Independence," the main characters are fighting for their "'[Mil]Waukean independence and they are doing what's right." The story's final line, "They got it right where they want it," asserts the characters' power and freedom. In the story "Look at Those Legs," a woman rides to church on an ostrich only to be ridiculed by her fellow congregants. She overcomes this ridicule "because she is very sophisticated," and leads the church in the song "Amazing Grace."

References to religion and spirituality were also common in this group. In "I'm Glad You're Dead You Dog You," the two main characters are wrestling over a picture of the Virgin Mary "because she symbolizes all that they desire." In "She's Down There Under the Puppy," an elephant named Grandfather is not allowed to enter a church because he might break down the walls. He takes solace in his friendship with a little girl who is not afraid of his size, and together they sit outside the church and listen to the choir sing "Abide with Me."

Another common theme that emerged was the desire for human relationships, both platonic and intimate. Two main characters in one story, two nuns, were in love but couldn't remember with whom. Sexual innuendo and even explicit sexual references were common. In "Tiny Bubbles," the main character lives underwater and is thinking about a woman he left on the shore. "He's thinking a whole lot about that woman," said a storyteller. In "It Goes Toot Toot," John Hibby and Bill Hobby and their wives "all fool around together." These sexual references could make some participants uncomfortable. Rather than edit the story, however, which would run counter to our promise to the storytellers that we would include all of their responses, we simply encouraged more responses.

Several stories from Group A dealt with difficult relationships. Some reflected disagreements between children and their parents. In one story, for example, the children sharply disapproved of their parents' wrestling. Some stories joked about traditional gender relationships; men would commonly take on women's duties, as in "Italians from Ireland," where eight women were fighting for independence while their husbands were washing dishes.

The group at Center A was warm and supportive, comfortable with responding to the facilitators' questions with nonsensical answers. For example, in "Everybody Is Eating Corn," a story of a raucous dinner party at a restaurant, one of the main characters is "allegering all over the horn." Nearly every story at Group A featured a fragmented or nonsensical answer. But taken in the context of the storytelling circle, such answers had clear emotional resonance. When repeating nonsensical answers in the retelling process of the storytelling, facilitators aimed to capture the emotional intent behind the sound or words. "Allegering all over the horn" was, in context, a clear reference to a joyful celebration at the dinner party.

> WHEN REPEATING nonsensical answers in the retelling process of the storytelling, facilitators aimed to capture the emotional intent behind the sound or words.

CENTER B   At Center B in Milwaukee, we worked with a group of storytellers much more mixed in their abilities than the group at Center A. Of the six storytellers at Center B, one storyteller had practically no verbal language at all. Because communication was more difficult for this group of storytellers, the pace of storytelling was slower. Several unique characteristics emerged in the stories created by this group, possibly due to the smaller size and slower pace, but certainly due to the strong personalities of several storytellers. Although none of the 17 stories in Center A included the names of storytellers, in Center B almost half of the 21 stories I analyzed included the name of a storyteller or student facilitator as characters. When asked to name a character, some of the group's less verbal storytellers would point to a fellow group member instead of naming the person directly. This drawing of fellow storytellers into the tale was sometimes a gesture of intimacy, and at other times, a gesture of friendly mocking. Either way, it always drew the group into a deeper engagement with the process. Facilitators called out and emphasized the storyteller's/character's name repeatedly with each retelling, acknowledging the storyteller's presence, creativity, and new role (as character).

Nearly all of the stories at Center B contained challenge answers and answers that sharply redirected what might be the assumed journey of the tale. The stories generated by the Center B participants were less concerned with the direction of the plot and much more focused on word play. "He's a Tuba Player," for example, begins with "He's Tony the trumpet player from Tampa, trying to get a tune."

Tony's wife, whose name is "Music," is "rumored to be dead." In "Thanksgiving Celebration," a story based on an image of a raucous dinner party, storytellers named one couple "Pardon Me I Burped" and "Charles, Who Is No Prince." When the check comes for the dinner party, "they'll sober up!" said one storyteller.

Although this group commonly used their own names as the names of characters, they also tended to separate themselves from the storylines and, in turn, from fellow storytellers. For example, in a story about a pancake-cooking club, one storyteller said, "I wouldn't join that club." In "Waltzing Ladders," when one storyteller said, "Everyone is married and has children so they don't have parties anymore," another countered with, "then I'm never going to get married!" When one storyteller added church music to a story, another countered with "No, that's too holy."

In spite of their penchant for sharp wit, Center B also created some remarkably poignant images in their stories that seem to mirror their own feelings and fantasies. Tony the trumpet player, for example, "should be 42, but he's 99. He's happy, even though he's alone." In "We Want to See Castro," a little girl goes to Cuba with an elephant. "She's gone far away," said one storyteller, "because kids do that." In response to an image of a man hiding his head in his coat, storytellers named the main character "Headless Joe Wonder," and said, "He lives in a room of despair. He takes it as it comes. You think you can't do anything without a head, but headless Joe Wonder can . . . "

CENTERS C AND D   The storytelling groups at both New York City centers fluctuated dramatically in size from week to week. Center C had an average of 10 storytellers; they ranged considerably in verbal skills, with the majority able to put together two or three words. At Center C, the names of storytellers found their way into the tales as they had at Center B. But at Center C, storytellers sometimes competed with one another to add their own names in the stories. In one story about a male painter and his female model, for example, two women storytellers wanted to add their own names to the name of the female model. We included both and hyphenated the character's name. Similarly, in "Mama Bear Does the Cha-Cha," Mama Bear is named after one of the storytellers. The story grew poignant as the storytellers decided that Papa Bear was far away having affairs, but that Mama Bear didn't just sit at home and mope. "Mama Bear and the two cubs are at home, doing the cha-cha." The namesake storyteller, confined to a wheelchair, would lead the group in a dance with her arms with each retelling.

The storytellers at Center C gave few "challenge" answers. Their stories generally featured likable characters and were peppered with humor. The raucous dinner party image was imagined to be "John Gotti's birthday party," where the characters were "eating diet food, because they are all fat!" In a story based on an image of an older couple arm wrestling, storytellers said, "they are falling in love for the first time." Similar to Group A, this group was also patient with non sequiturs that emerged out of illness and acknowledged the contribution of the storyteller who added them with each retelling. For example, one storyteller could not or would not answer more than "I don't know." Facilitators asked if they could add this to the story, and the characters, a group of women accordion players, became the "I Don't Know" band. In another example, when asked if there was music in a story about a man with a pigeon sitting on his head, one storyteller enthusiastically made up a song whose only word was "beep." To great crowd approval, she energetically sang it with each retelling of the story.

Center D's group was very small but always had at least four participants. The group was more physically and emotionally fragile than the others and more linguistically challenged. One member could only add sounds interspersed with occasional shards of words. Another storyteller had a remarkable gift for poetic images, but struggled to stay awake and to tolerate multiple stimuli. Her struggle was evident in her input to the stories; she often tried either to focus or silence the group. "Every person has a story," she said, "there's not a human being that doesn't have a story. But making it mish-mosh is bad. It's like a bomb." In other stories, however, her input served to encourage the group to create powerful images. In a story based on an image of a man sitting in an enormous pile of books, they said "He is accepting responsibility to organize this into something. He is orchestrating an orchestra in his mind." In a tale about a can-can dancer who works with an ostrich, they named her "Holding On, because she's really just holding on." The story ended with Holding On contemplating her career. "She never had children, and she thinks she might have missed something. But she has a complex sense of happiness."

Non sequiturs were much more common at Center D, another small group, than in larger groups where the increased amount of input meant storytellers could edit themselves. In a story based on the image of the older couple wrestling, one storyteller looked perplexed and said, "All I know is Winnie the Pooh." After this response was woven into the story it became a favorite phrase among the storytellers. Similar to the playfulness of the other groups, the Center D storytellers used the process to play with each other and with the staff. Their humor was vivid. In "An Exquisite Woman," a woman pilot flies to Russia where she eats "chicken Kiev in a box." In "A Horse Is a Horse of Course," a handsome cowboy is "any age we want him to be . . . probably 28. And he's attracted to beautiful women like us!"

COMPARING AND CONTRASTING CENTERS

Clear differences and similarities emerged in the four storytelling groups. Led by strong personalities of group members and by the size and nature of the group dynamics, groups at Centers A and C yielded harmonious and playful stories, whereas Center B challenged the process at every step, and Center D's stories were powerful, dreamlike images pierced by sharp wit. As mentioned previously, common themes emerged in all four groups, including the desire for freedom, confidence, and intimate relationships. These desires were also evident in the group dynamics, in which storytellers teased each other (and facilitators) by placing each other in the stories, suddenly changing the direction of the story, or deliberately adding humorous or provocative remarks. In all four groups, storytellers engaged in the process as a method of self-expression, whether they were attempting to contradict the flow of the story or encourage its progress—whether they were challenging facilitators or sharing a poetic image. In all four groups, storytelling provided storytellers a valued social role and rare access to meaning making for people whose language had broken down. Laughter and singing were a prominent part of all four storytelling groups as well, so much so that staff who weren't directly involved with the storytelling tended to gather at the edge of the room to listen to the sessions. Clearly, the storytellers retained the capacity to entertain others and themselves with laughter, humor, and joy.

> IN ALL FOUR GROUPS, storytelling provided storytellers a valued social role and rare access to meaning making for people whose language had broken down.

INTERVIEWS: VOLUNTEERS, STAFF, AND FAMILIES

The storytelling process and the stories that evolved from it show that people with ADRD do have creative potential and can play valuable social roles. The stories themselves can only tell us so much about the effectiveness of the workshops; however, interviews with staff, family caregivers, and students can help us discern whether providing people with ADRD access to a meaningful social role can shift the attitudes of people who care for them.

In Milwaukee, three students participated in the full 18 weeks of workshops, and five of them facilitated storytelling for 9 weeks. In New York, five students facilitated the 9 weeks of sessions. All student facilitators were interviewed in their first week in the program and again at the end. During the project, they kept weekly journals of their feelings about the workshops. Interviews with students were open structure and focused on their perceptions of aging, dementia, and people with dementia.

Students in both Milwaukee and New York City revealed an initial fear or substantial hesitation about working with people with dementia. Several articulated it as worry that they might hurt the storytellers, physically or psychologically. One student who was studying art therapy had considerable knowledge about dementia from gerontology courses but worried about her lack of practical experience working with such a population. Only one student had worked with people with dementia before and was fairly confident in her abilities. She, however, was fearful of revealing her own disability (dyslexia) in the group. The student volunteers had a high incidence of disability themselves. Of the 13 students, three had dyslexia and another student was deaf. I can only speculate that they were especially drawn to a project that encouraged growth among people with cognitive disabilities. But I can freely conclude that throughout the storytelling process, all four remarked that they gained confidence in their own writing and creative abilities.

After revealing an initial fear of working with people with dementia, the student journals and final interviews show that students were surprised at how much they enjoyed the sessions. They described the laughter and emotional connection with the storytellers as "giving meaning to their day" and making them feel as though they were "useful" and "important" in the storytellers' eyes. After several weeks of storytelling, students commonly remarked that the storytellers didn't seem to exhibit what they imagined to be symptoms of Alzheimer's disease. In their final interviews, three students shared their concerns that some of the storytellers were misdiagnosed.

Three students wrote that they felt hurt when the storytellers didn't remember their names from week to week. If certain storytellers did seem to remember the students, they felt particularly accepted. But, two of these students also wrote that if they were not remembered, it gave them as much satisfaction to feel that the storytellers trusted and accepted them in the moment. Two students described their growing understanding that the product, the story itself, was not the focus of the project, including this individual:

> I think that at the beginning I was looking for the product. I was looking for the good story to come out at the end. And it was so hard! We just had to pull and push and it was like nothing was happening. And then it kind of hit me that we were not really there to get this good story. We were there to be with these people and, you know, maybe appreciate them for being individuals. You know it's to *our* advantage that we are there sharing with them their ideas and wisdom and creativity.

The students became very attached to both the process and the storytellers. By the end of the storytelling workshops, they were all able to separate their fears of ADRD from their dissipating fears of the people who were diagnosed as having it. After the initial, cautious couple of weeks, the students' body language, vocal tone, and energy level all grew as they interacted easily with the storytellers.

Interviews that I conducted with staff at the four day centers revealed their surprise at the storytellers' creative abilities. Open structure interviews at the beginning and the end of the process showed that staff grew in their appreciation of the process and observed positive behavioral changes in clients. Center B staff, were not directly involved in the storytelling process but remarked in interviews that they regularly read the stories and noticed positive changes in clients. One staff member noted:

THE STUDENTS became very attached to both the process and the storytellers. By the end of the storytelling workshops, they were all able to separate their fears of ADRD from their dissipating fears of the people who were diagnosed as having it.

> We have a few people who are in the project who are very, very quiet, and I'm very happy to see them coming forward. The first couple of sessions . . . they were very quiet and you really had to pull everything out of them and now I've noticed that as each class has been happening, they are more and more open; they'll talk openly and they're more comfortable. They are so happy after you leave, and honestly, we can really get a lot out of them for the rest of the day.

Staff at Center C were also not involved at the outset of the storytelling work-shops. At first they were grateful for our giving them an hour to invest their attention elsewhere. After the third storytelling session, however, staff were in-creasingly lured by the laughter and singing in our circle. In the final few ses-sions, staff had joined the circle, asking questions and laughing and singing with us. Interviews with the two key staff members at Center C suggest two things: that they were surprised by the quality of the stories and that they gained in-sights into clients they hadn't previously imagined possible. One staff member related:

> What they say, I mean, some of these stories . . . I gave them to [the director of the day center] and she said, "Gee, these guys are smart! And funny!" And the family members, [they] loved it. And I said, "See? That's what we're doing here on Thursdays!"

Staff at Centers A and D were fully involved in the storytelling from the begin-ning. They joined us in the storytelling circles on the first day and continue the storytelling today—a loyalty that is testimony to their belief in the process. Center A went beyond what we had hoped. The Time*Slips* Project presented each center with books of all of the stories, inexpensively duplicated and spiral bound. The staff at Center A took the initiative to put together (and pay for) three-ring binders and plastic page protectors for high-quality duplications of each image and its corresponding story. They invited the families of storytellers to attend a party at which staff presented the beautiful books to each storyteller and thanked them for their contributions. As the storytellers reviewed their efforts with their families, the party became quite moving. One storyteller took my arm and said, "You know what's so great about this? It ain't cheap!" I knew just what he meant. The books the staff created were works of art, giving honor and value to the sto-rytellers' creativity. The Director of Center A, who was actively involved with the storytelling sessions, offered these remarks:

> Being an active participant in this Time*Slips* Project, I have seen the joy that the process has brought to the participants, the comfort that it has brought to families, the satisfaction and empowerment that it has brought to staff in-volved. I am also impressed by the insight and awareness that it has brought to the students, as they grow in their understanding of aging, disease, and [the] development of humanness.

Interviews with family caregivers differed radically between Milwaukee and New York. All but two storytellers in Milwaukee lived with family.[2] The two lived in long-term care programs and attended day centers for added social interaction. In New York, the few storytellers who lived with family commonly had at least part-time, paid attendants to care for them. Perhaps because of differences in the

---

[2]Interviews with family caregivers were open structure telephone interviews, held in the first 3 weeks of the project and again at the end of the storytelling sessions. We also produced a series of arts events inspired by the creative stories, and interviewed families again after they had attended the arts events.

structure of care or because of the gaps in communication with the day centers, only two of the family caregivers we interviewed in New York were aware of the stories. Consequently, they had little input about changes in observed behavior.

Milwaukee families had a much greater awareness of the storytelling process and its impact on the storytellers themselves. Of the 15 family caregivers we interviewed in Milwaukee, the majority had read the stories either in the single sheets we sent home each week or in the books of stories we presented the storytellers at the end of the project. Three family caregivers said they regularly read the book with their loved one with ADRD. Two said they duplicated the books and sent them to other members of the family as a way for them to understand and connect with the storyteller. One told us the storyteller had become possessive of the book and hid it from her, calling it "his work." Four family caregivers told us that they believed the storytelling made clear changes in their loved one's behavior; for example, the individual initiated more conversation, exhibited less confusion, and expressed an increased sense of enjoyment in life. Caregivers face tremendous challenges caring for someone with ADRD, not the least of which is the adjustment to the change in roles the couples play. I find the fact that family caregivers could find meaning and affirmation in the stories and the storytelling process in the face of these challenges a testament to the power of creative self-expression.

EDUCATIONAL OUTREACH:
CHANGING PUBLIC PERCEPTION

In Milwaukee and New York, the Time*Slips* Project sponsored art exhibits and staged professional play productions inspired by the stories and characters created in the storytelling workshops. Our aim was to improve audience members' perceptions about the creative potential of people with ADRD.[3] In Milwaukee, we collected anecdotal responses to the exhibit and play, but in New York City we created a more official analysis of the educational outreach model. Analysis of the New York data suggests that it is indeed possible to positively affect public perception of people with dementia.

The New York Time*Slips* play was produced at an intimate (99 seats), downtown (off-off Broadway) theater known for innovative performances. We selected theater as a genre because the physical presence of the actor on stage can create a sense of empathy with another human being in a way that film can not, and because people with dementia exist in a fragile world that, like live performance, disappears after the moment has passed. Our hope was to capitalize on the intimacy of the space, the power of the present moment, and the potential for empathy to engender a sense of empathy for people with dementia.

The play is set in an adult day center, where a small group of people gathers in a creative storytelling circle. Weaving communal stories, they free them-

---

[3]The average age of audience members was 42. Fifty-eight percent had experience with dementia, either personal or professional, and 37% of audience members came from an arts background, while 21% came from health care fields.

selves from their private struggles with Alzheimer's disease to create a wondrous world inhabited by fantastical characters that take on a life of their own. A can-can dancer conceals the long legs of an ostrich beneath her skirts, a singing cowboy serenades his devoted horse with song, a determined swimmer battles the Hudson River to break a world record, and a bookworm struggles to liberate himself from a mountain of books. Through the storytelling process, these fragmented personalities band together to help each other complete their journeys even as memory fails their authors.

> THROUGH THE STORY-telling process, these fragmented personalities band together to help each other complete their journeys even as memory fails their authors.

We inserted evaluation forms in each play program in New York and allowed time after the show and before a post-show discussion for audience members to complete the forms. We received 539 responses over the course of 20 performances in 3 weeks. We asked a series of general questions to ascertain audience members' ages, occupations, and their experience with dementia. We also asked a series of questions directly about the play, including a request for a description of the play's theme. The most common response (34%) was "self-expression," or "expression of an inner-life." Next, we asked people if, *before* viewing the play, they thought people with dementia could express themselves creatively, with 1 being *not at all,* and 10 being *quite well.* The average response was 6.3, which fell in the range of the area that we described on the form as *somewhat.* In the next question, we asked if, *after* viewing the play, they thought people with dementia could express themselves creatively. The average response was 8.2. We analyzed the *before* and *after* responses according to differences in age, experience, occupation, and the date of the performance. Age did have an impact on people's responses, but the impact was barely significant. We found that younger audience members were slightly more optimistic in terms of recognizing the creative potential of people with dementia. Each age group's rating went up approximately two points from before to after, but younger audience members had given a higher initial score, indicating that they already had higher expectations when it came to the creative abilities of people with ADRD.

Those with experience with dementia (personal or professional) were more positive than were people without experience with dementia in their initial views of the potential of people with dementia to express themselves creatively, yet the attitudes of those without experience changed overall more than did those with experience. The differences, however, were weak, and the play had a significant impact on every group.

THE ART EXHIBIT

The art exhibit in New York City featured two-dimensional silhouettes of characters, some as large as 12 feet tall, from the stories that emerged in storytelling workshops. The story itself was handwritten on the figure, so viewers could read it in its entirety. Evaluation cards were displayed prominently in the exhibit, but in spite of high attendance, only a smattering of people completed cards and dropped them in the evaluation box. The results were similar to what we found in the play. Of those who responded, approximately half had had experience with people with ADRD, yet all showed positive change in their perception of the creative ability of people with ADRD. The small number of evaluations makes it difficult to generalize the results or to compare them with the results of the play evaluation cards.

SUMMARY

Creative storytelling supplies a social role, one with value that allows for the integration of past and present and that acknowledges the strengths and potential of the present lives of people with ADRD. It offers storytellers an avenue for self-expression that frees them from the demands of memory and rational language that they can no longer master. Creative storytelling can reorient the expectations of professional caregivers to recognize new and untapped strengths of their clients including capacities for humor, creative imagination, and social skills. It offers staff an enjoyable activity that can also help them develop *their* creative potential. It offers student volunteers an opportunity to separate their fears of Alzheimer's disease and aging from the people with whom they associate them and can be a first step toward encouraging young people to consider working or volunteering with older adults. Where broken communication skills fracture relationships with family caregivers and their extended families, creative storytelling can provide a way for individuals to forge new relationships through poetic and openly symbolic expression.

Perhaps because most people assume that people with Alzheimer's disease have no meaningful present, caregivers tend to encourage them to remember the past and underestimate their remaining strengths. Although I believe reminiscence work can be very effective and fulfilling for people wrestling with early stages of ADRD, it can lead to frustration and even shame among people in middle stages, whose ability to gain access to and control language and memory can be severely impaired. As caregivers, shifting our focus from memory to creativity can open channels of communication with people with ADRD and offer both client and caregiver potential for growth and the exercising of strengths. Sharing the creative products of people with dementia in a respectful way can be very effective in raising public awareness about the creative capacity of people with dementia. This two-pronged approach, changing the mindset and actions of caregivers directly and assuaging public fear of the people who have ADRD, is a certain step toward the culture change so needed to help these individuals and those who care for them to have fulfilling lives.

REFERENCE

Cohen, G. (2000). *The creative age: Awakening human potential in the second half of life.* New York: HarperCollins.

AFTERWORD

When Judah L. Ronch and Joseph A. Goldfield asked that I write an Afterword for *Mental Wellness in Aging: Strengths-Based Approaches*, author Allan Gurganus's (1999) short story "He's at the Office" immediately came to mind. In the story, a son narrates his father's descent into dementia and describes the family's puzzlement, frustration, and ultimate solution to problem behaviors. In the exposition, we read that the father was a bit of a free spirit before World War II but strictly business afterward. His life was the office, and he refused to retire until forced to do so by dementia. At home and unattended, the father invariably headed for the office. When held back he refused to dress, to shave, and to eat. He was aggressive at times.

Then the son had an idea. If his father was so determined to go to the office, the spare bedroom could be converted and outfitted with office furniture, invoices, telephone, folders, and pencils. Sure enough, just showing the father the mock office, even though it was in the man's own home, triggered the desired response. He immediately became oriented to the environment and settled in to the task at hand. At the home office he could be left unsupervised for hours. He never "quit" until time for dinner, never wandered from the room. When his wife returned one day and checked the office, he was dead in his chair with his face buried on the desk. Even in death he was "at the office." But his last days had been filled with peace for all concerned. The story is as touching as it is satisfying, with an elegant solution and a dignified ending—no medications, no caregiver counseling, no adult day center, no home health aides—just the strength of family ingenuity and the patient's lasting identity.

The artful solution Gurganus devised is inspiring, but more is required for most of the patients and families who care for an older adult. We have entered the era of evidence-based health care, which promises a new empiricism borne of clinical science rather than practitioner art. Intervention based on the reliability of aggregate patient samples is but one step toward better outcomes for individuals. And this is where playing to the individual's strengths is the wise course taken by skilled therapists.

The message is not that problems can be simply wished away or that old age will be full of health and independence for all of us. Neither does this volume argue that diagnosis is trivial or that we can avoid the reductionism necessary to sort through the mass of biomedical and psychosocial patient data. Rather, a new perspective on old age has emerged that contrasts seniors' potential against their vulnerabilities rather than the other way around; where one places the emphasis is critical.

For example, although there are no healthy centenarians, an increasing number of people entering their eleventh decade remain independent (Anderson-Ranberg, Schroll, & Jeune, 2001). The novelty of the finding is not the ill health of centenarians but, rather, their enduring autonomy. And it is autonomy—and the extent to which the person's strengths will allow it—that most matters to older adults. I have also seen a similar phenomenon in my older patients' efforts to master events following the terror in New York of the September 11, 2001, attacks on the World Trade Center. These older adults have lived through war before and know they will get through this one as well. They are in the habit of mastery. The basic neuroscience supporting their faith is well understood. Mental health professionals know the neural circuitry that causes the frozen stance and autonomic discharge of an acute stress response. They also know that simply taking action, nearly any action, activates the off-switch that turns paralysis into a temporary problem rather than an enduring posttraumatic stress disorder (Ledoux & Gorman, 2001). What is so curious about the findings is not that some older adults have developed or will develop a disorder following the events of September 11 but, rather, that so many have prevailed or will prevail intact.

This is not just accentuating the positive. In the aftermath of the terrorist attacks of September 11, it became important for mental health professionals to emphasize the normal, adaptive aspect of being shaken by the terrible events. It was important not to pathologize what was otherwise the inner strength that traumatized persons use to heal. Not that the healing is easy or effortless. Rowe and Kahn (1998) argued that seniors who have aged successfully have had to work at it to do so. In their sense, "working at it" means being engaged physically, intellectually, and socially. When an individual practices active mastery, rather than assuming a defensive posture toward getting old, it preserves the person's autonomy. This is, of course, academic language for the adage "use it or lose it," but the point is that more seniors are "using it" than ever before.

In geriatrics and gerontology it is time to focus on mastery rather than on mere coping. This is crucial for the seniors we work with, but also it is critical to attracting students and trainees to the field. *Mental Wellness in Aging: Strengths-Based Approaches* argues that in order to maintain health as well as to repair symptoms, strengths should be emphasized. Emphasizing what older Americans can do rather than what they cannot do also lightens the bureaucratized, heavily regulated environment of long-term care by placing greater weight on personal options and well-being to balance the imperatives of disease detection and treatment. This is the point of Judah Ronch's chapter on nursing home care (Chapter 8), which continues to be a difficult policy area for both the public and practitioners. The problem is best expressed as paradox: Although nursing homes are regulated to provide hospital-like services, they are also mandated to achieve a home-like atmosphere.

In summary, the strengths-based approach advocated by Judah L. Ronch, Joseph A. Goldfield, and their associates in this book provides 1) the individualized perspective necessary to fully implement evidence-based care, 2) a more accurate portrait of seniors as people as well as patients, 3) an incentive to attract more students and trainees to the field, and 4) a mediating force for the sometimes contradictory values of the biomedical and psychosocial models of care. The health professionals who have authored *Mental Wellness and Aging* have set the stage for seniors to seize the initiative. Through political and social action, seniors will make their needs and preferences and their contributions known. Regarding strength, seniors have much to teach if we have the good judgment to learn (Kennedy, 2000).

Gary J. Kennedy, M.D.
The University Hospital for the
Albert Einstein College of Medicine
Bronx, New York

REFERENCES

Anderson-Ranberg, K., Schroll, M., & Jeune, B. (2001). There are no healthy centenarians. *Journal of the American Geriatrics Society, 49*, 900–909.

Gurganus, A. (1999, February). He's at the office. *The New Yorker.*

Kennedy, G.J. (1999). *Geriatric mental health care: A treatment guide for health Professionals.* New York: Guilford Press.

Ledoux, J.E., & Gorman, J. (2001) A call to action: Overcoming anxiety through active coping. *American Journal of Psychiatry, 158*, 1953–1955.

Rowe, J.W., & Kahn, R.L. (1998). *Successful aging.* New York: Pantheon.

INDEX

Page numbers followed by "*f*" indicate figures; those followed by "*t*" indicate tables.